Science and Engineering Applications Discussed in
Excel for Scientists and Engineers (continued)

UNIVERSITY BOOKSTORE
TEXTBOOK DEPARTMENT
UNIV. OF WIS.–EAU CLAIRE 54701

_____   9-2-9

(Signature)   (Date)

_____

Sold by UNIVERSITY BOOKSTORE
TEXTBOOK DEPARTMENT
University of Wisconsin–Eau Claire
Eau Claire,   54701

Retail _____

Discount $ _____   Init. _____

-IMPORTANT-

1. **ALL RENTAL TEXTBOOKS MUST BE RETURNED BY LAST**
   DAY OF FINALS EACH SEMESTER. The late fine, per book,
   will be $1.00 beginning the first day after the last final exam,
   through the next full week following exams. After that "grace
   period" the fine per book will be increased to $5.00.

2. You are responsible for the books you check out. If a book is
   lost, you must pay for it before a new copy will be issued. No
   student may check out two copies of the same text.

3. Signing your books is recommended to prevent theft and so if
   the book is lost and returned we can locate its owner.

4. I agree to the terms of the UW-Eau Claire Payment Plan.

5. I understand that if the books are not returned by the due
   date, I will be required to purchase the textbooks.

GAYLORD MG

EXCEL

FOR SCIENTISTS AND ENGINEERS

Second Edition

EXCEL

FOR SCIENTISTS AND ENGINEERS

Second Edition

William J. Orvis

SYBEX®

SAN FRANCISCO • PARIS • DÜSSELDORF • SOEST

Acquisitions Manager: Kristine Plachy
Developmental Editor: Richard Mills
Editor: Julia Kelly
Project Editor: Brenda Frink
Technical Editor: Kurt Hampe
Book Designer: Suzanne Albertson
Assistant Book Design Director: Heather Lewis
Desktop Publisher: jc graphics
Production Coordinator: Kimberley Askew-Qasem
Indexer: Nancy Guenther
Cover Designer: Design Site
Cover Photographer: David Bishop

Screen reproductions produced with Collage Complete.
Collage Complete is a trademark of Inner Media Inc.

SYBEX is a registered trademark of SYBEX Inc.
IMSL and Visual Numerics are registered US trademarks of Visual Numerics, Inc.

TRADEMARKS: SYBEX has attempted throughout this book to distinguish proprietary trademarks from descriptive terms by following the capitalization style used by the manufacturer.

Every effort has been made to supply complete and accurate information. However, SYBEX assumes no responsibility for its use, nor for any infringement of the intellectual property rights of third parties which would result from such use.

Library of Congress Card Number: 95-71900
ISBN: 0-7821-1761-9

Manufactured in the United States of America
10 9 8 7 6 5 4 3

For Pat and Wib.
Your dedication, perseverance,
and honesty show in the
character of your children.
I know, I married one.

CONTENTS AT A GLANCE

TABLE OF CONTENTS

PREFACE

A few years ago, I wrote *1-2-3 for Scientists and Engineers*, extolling the ease with which numerical analysis could be done using the Lotus 1-2-3 spreadsheet program. The book was about Lotus 1-2-3 because that was what most scientists and engineers had access to. However, the readers of that book might be surprised to learn that many of the book's examples were developed on the Macintosh, using the then new spreadsheet program from Microsoft known as Excel. Excel has grown since then, and is an extremely powerful numerical analysis environment, operating on both the Windows and Macintosh platforms.

A few years later, I produced an Excel version of *1-2-3 for Scientists and Engineers*. Excel has changed considerably since that time, with the biggest change being the addition of Visual Basic for Applications as the primary macro language. Of importance to scientists and engineers is the addition of a large number of science and engineering functions to the tool set. Hence this new version of Excel for Scientists and Engineers contains all the new tools and methods through version 7 of Excel, though the methods are applicable to most of the versions. Users of version 5 of Excel will have no problem using this book (there is no version 6) nor will Macintosh users. I hope you enjoy this book, as you watch what used to be arcane numerical methods become transparent when implemented on a worksheet.

Numerical analysis is usually done using traditional programming languages such as Fortran or C. You insert the input data into a program, and the program performs some numerical magic on it and spits back the result. Using these programs, you see only the beginning and the end of a calculation and miss out on the middle. With a worksheet implementation of a numerical analysis method, you see the whole problem. When doing iterative solutions to differential equations, you get to watch the values at every node in the problem converge (or not) to the answer. Being able to see the solutions converge makes the method much more understandable, and with understanding comes new innovation and growth.

The push to write the revision to this book and to add more examples and problems was long and hard, and I want to thank Richard Mills for finally letting me do it, Prof. Charles Finn at Northeastern University for pushing both Richard and I to do the revision, Julia Kelly and Kurt Hampe for finding and fixing all my mistakes, and all the others at SYBEX who made this book possible. And most especially, I want to thank B.J., Skye, Sierra, and Shane for staying out of my hair so I could get this done, and Julie for keeping them out.

I hope you have fun with this book—I know I did.

INTRODUCTION

The numerical calculations performed by scientists and engineers range from the simple to the complex. The simple task of calculating the value of a function is an everyday occurrence. Complex tasks, such as numerically integrating a differential equation, often consume many weeks of concentrated effort. Thus, any tool that facilitates numerical calculations increases a scientist's or engineer's productivity. Excel is one such tool. It offers facilities for numerical calculations, graphics, and programmability in a single, easy-to-use package.

In the past, the slide rule was the primary tool for performing numerical calculations, and graph paper was the usual data-display device. With the advent of the hand calculator, the slide rule was quickly retired to a place of nostalgic reverence (most likely the bottom of a drawer); however, the graph paper still remained.

Those of us who had access to mainframe computers could use them for our calculations and data display. These mainframe computers had tremendous computing power, and many had impressive graphics output devices. But usually, we had to hire a computer scientist (or a high school student), or learn a computer language such as FORTRAN or ALGOL, to program them and to make the high-powered graphics work.

Microcomputers put a lot of computing power on the desktops of scientists and engineers, and the BASIC computer language included with most microcomputers provided a good environment for most numerical calculations. Many desktop computers had plotters and, with a little work, could produce good-quality graphics output. These computers still had to be programmed, however, to generate and plot numbers.

Even with personal computers available, most scientists and engineers still generated their numbers with an engineering calculation sheet. An engineering calculation sheet is a piece of lined paper, much like binder paper, that also has vertical lines spaced approximately every inch or so. You put successive calculations in alternate columns until the final column contains the result. For example, if you want to calculate the function $y = 2x^2 + 3x$ for a list of x values, you place the x values in the first column, calculate $2x^2$ in the second column, calculate $3x$ in the third column, and place the sum of columns 2 and 3—the final result—in column 4.

Interestingly, these engineering calculation sheets bore a remarkable resemblance to the spreadsheets that business students used when I was in school (they must have stolen the idea from the engineers). You might occasionally have a beer or two with a business student, but you never involved yourself in their studies, so little was made of these similarities. Much of this indifference was because we used sines, cosines, and exponentials, whereas they used only addition, subtraction, multiplication, division, and percentages (they got really good with percentages: percent interest, percent penalty, percent royalty, and so on).

Many years ago, the business spreadsheet was automated with the microcomputer program VisiCalc. Some of us in science and engineering immediately saw the potential of this program as an engineering tool, especially since it could calculate scientific functions such as sines, cosines, and exponentials. Since then, spreadsheet programs have grown tremendously in power and versatility.

Microsoft Excel is currently one of the most powerful spreadsheet programs. It runs on both the PC under Windows or NT and on the Macintosh. Excel is well suited for science and engineering calculations, because it includes a high-powered worksheet coupled with graphics, BASIC programmability, database functions, and database access capabilities. Combine this with the current crop of high-powered desktop workstations, and you have a significant amount of computational power at your disposal.

Scope of This Book

In this book, you will learn how to tap Excel's power to solve your science and engineering problems. You will learn not only how to calculate and plot simple equations but how to perform curve fitting; calculate statistics, numerical derivatives, and integrals; access external databases; and solve systems of equations and one- and two-dimensional differential equations. This book also explains how to create graphics and how to use the built-in Visual Basic for Applications programming language to extend the capabilities of the Excel worksheets.

Windows and Macintosh Versions of Excel

This book applies to both the Macintosh and Windows versions of Excel. Worksheet files can be freely transferred between these versions of Excel. The differences in their usage are minimal. The images in this book are from Excel 7 for Windows 95, so Macintosh users will see a difference in some of the screens; however, the contents of the windows are the same. The implementation and worksheet methods (the location and contents of cells) employed in both the Windows and Macintosh versions of Excel are the same. Users of Excel (versions 5 and later, on both the Macintosh and Windows platforms) should have no problems implementing these methods.

The differences between the Windows and Macintosh versions of Excel are mentioned when they affect the work at hand. The main differences are in the special keystrokes required to activate some functions. The Macintosh keyboard has a Command key, which is lacking on the PC. Thus, keystrokes that employ the Command (Cmd) key on the Macintosh are mapped onto the Control (Ctrl), Alt, and Shift keys on the PC. For example, the keystroke for the Calculate Now function is Ctrl+= on the PC and Cmd+= on the Macintosh, and the keystroke for the Store As Array function is Ctrl+Shift+Enter on the PC and Cmd+Enter on the Macintosh.

Older Versions of Excel

This new edition of *Excel for Scientists and Engineers* was developed with Microsoft Excel versions 5 and 7 running under Windows 95. Excel versions 5 and 7 are nearly identical in capabilities. Excel 5 is a 16-bit version and runs under Windows 3.1 or Windows 95, while Excel 7 is a 32-bit version that runs under Windows 95. Excel 5 also runs on the Macintosh. Readers with earlier versions of Excel will have no problem with most of the examples. The biggest differences between versions 5.0 and 7.0 and the earlier versions of Excel are in the change to Visual Basic for Applications as the macro language, the data-entry area, and in the availability of advanced functions. The techniques used in this book, however, do not significantly rely on the advanced functions, but rather on worksheet methods, and the methods are applicable to most versions of Excel or any other advanced spreadsheet programs.

Real Examples

This book was written by a practicing scientist and engineer for other practicing scientists and engineers. It is based on real uses of a spreadsheet as an engineering tool. Many of the problems were developed as part of my work or are adaptations of problems that I solved using other techniques before I realized the full potential of spreadsheets. In many cases, you will be solving real problems rather than simplified textbook problems. A few of the problems are somewhat longer than you normally find in a textbook. In those few cases, I have included abbreviated versions of the problems that still illustrate the relevant techniques.

Because this book is based on my own work in the science and engineering fields, many of the problems are electronics and solid-state physics problems, with some astronomy thrown in for fun. I apologize to practitioners in other branches of science and engineering for not including problems in their areas of expertise, but the problems are used only to illustrate the calculation methods. It is the methods, not the problems, that are important. You can apply these methods to any branch of science and engineering.

This book does not teach science and engineering; it teaches the practical application of numerical methods to science and engineering problems. I do not discuss much of the theoretical background or mathematical justification for most of the numerical techniques described here, but concentrate on how to apply them using a spreadsheet. If you are interested in background material, a number of good numerical methods books are available to sate your curiosity. I primarily depend on Curtis F. Gerald's book, *Applied Numerical Analysis*, and William H. Press's book, *Numerical Recipes*, for most of the numerical methods I use. The FORTRAN version of *Numerical Recipes* is particularly useful, because FORTRAN is not that different from BASIC, making conversion of a mathematical algorithm to the Visual Basic language relatively easy. Other books and references related to the examples are listed at the end of each chapter.

Examples on Disk

If you do not want to type all of the examples but still want to be able to run them, the disk included with this book contains the working examples developed in each chapter and solutions to the Review Problems at the end of each chapter. Note that the disk does not contain the solutions to the exercises. The examples are archived in Excel 7 format, which is equivalent to Excel 5 format. The disk is a Windows format disk, and Macintosh users will have to use Apple File Exchange, PC Exchange, or a similar tool to copy the files to a Macintosh disk. See Appendix B for more information.

User Background

To use this book, you must have a background in science, engineering, or mathematics. Although the book is intended for the practicing scientist or engineer, a college student in one of these disciplines should have no trouble understanding the problems and solutions and using them to enhance his or her studies. In fact, the spreadsheet versions of the numerical methods applied in this book are much more intuitive than the same methods applied with Fortran or C, which makes the spreadsheet an excellent learning tool.

You should also know how to use your computer and the basics of working with Excel. If you do not know how to turn on a computer, put this book down, get a good tutorial, and play with the computer for a while. When you feel comfortable with the computer (when you can delete a file without cringing), then continue with this book.

If you do not know how to start up Excel, move around a worksheet, insert data in cells, save a file, and load an old file, study the tutorials and manuals that came with the software. You should also skim through the *online function reference* to get a feel for the types of functions available in Excel. Once you understand the basics, you can continue with the problems in this book.

This book starts slowly to give you time to become comfortable with Excel. Readers who are more familiar with Excel may want to skip the first, simple example and begin with the second. From there, the worksheets quickly become increasingly complex but, I hope, not difficult to understand.

Hardware Requirements

If you don't have the right hardware, Excel either won't run or won't be completely functional. The Windows version of Excel requires a machine capable of running Windows 3.0, which is a minimum of an IBM AT-class machine (80286 processor) with 2 megabytes of system memory and an EGA or better monitor. Of course, more memory and a more powerful processor (80386, 80486, or Pentium) will increase the speed and functionality of Excel.

Excel will run on any Macintosh computer with System 6.02 or later, including the 128K, if you have increased its memory to 1 megabyte or more. Again, Excel works much better with more memory and with a more powerful processor.

The examples in this book were originally developed on a Today, 386SX-20 computer, with 4 megabytes of random-access memory (RAM) and never enough hard-disk space. The system was running DOS 5.0 and Windows 3.1. The examples were also run on a Macintosh SE computer with 4 megabytes of RAM and even less hard-disk space. For the current edition, the examples were revised on a Today 486DX2-80, with 16 MG of RAM and still not enough disk space. The examples all run considerably faster on the new hardware. If you intend to run Windows 95, a 486-class system is a minimum if you expect good response times from the software.

Conventions Used in This Book

Many of the illustrations in this book do not show the whole worksheet, because some of the problems would fill pages. In most cases, I place the important results in the upper-left corner of the worksheet and show only that corner in the illustrations.

Excel is not case-sensitive, so functions, variable names, and formulas can be typed in uppercase or lowercase letters. In the problem descriptions, the spreadsheet functions are in uppercase, because that is how they appear in the spreadsheet, and the variables and defined names are in the case in which they were defined. You can use either uppercase or lowercase letters for your entries, and Excel will change them as appropriate.

In the descriptions of the examples, what you are expected to type is in **bold face**, while characters typed by the program are not.

In the margins of this book, you will often see images of toolbar buttons. A button pictured in the margin, such as the one shown here, is the toolbar button described in the adjacent paragraph. The one shown here happens to start the ChartWizard tool. If more than one button is shown, the buttons are displayed in the same order that they are listed in the paragraph.

This book also contains Notes, Warnings, Shortcuts, and Sidebars, offset from the main text of the chapter. These sections contain information that does not fit with the text of the chapter, but that serves to amplify or explain some of the concepts described there.

A Road to Understanding

Now that the preliminaries are out of the way, it's time to get at the worksheet and start solving problems. In the next few chapters, you will see numerical methods come to life on a spreadsheet. You will also start to understand things that you never fully understood before. Good luck, and please enjoy your trek into the world of numerical analysis on a worksheet.

Release Notes for Excel 97

All of the worksheets, macros, and methods introduced in this book for Excel 5 and 7 are fully applicable to Excel 97. All of the examples on the included disk will run in Excel 97. The biggest differences you will see are in the layout of some of the menus and in the addition of the Visual Basic Editor. In Excel 5 and 7, modules appear in the workbook along with the worksheets and are accessed by clicking on a tab (the same way that you access a worksheet). In Excel 97, all modules are accessed using the Visual Basic Editor, which runs as a separate application from Excel even though it opens the same files that Excel has open.

When using the steps to create the examples in this book, watch for steps that require you to create a new module or to open and edit an existing one. To create a new Visual Basic module in Excel 5 or 7, use the Insert ➤ Macro ➤ Module command as indicated in the steps. If you are using Excel 97, substitute the Tools ➤ Macro ➤ Macros command to open the Macros dialog box and then create a new module by typing its name and clicking Create. Whenever the steps for an example say to switch to a macro sheet by clicking on the macro's tab, you must switch to the Visual Basic Editor and select the sheet there instead. In all, you should have no trouble finding and using the few commands that have changed.

CHAPTER
ONE

Using Excel in Science and Engineering Applications

- Numeric precision and range in Excel

- Basic cell and range references

- Excel's operators

- Excel's mathematical functions

- Excel's science and engineering functions

Microsoft Excel was developed to compete in the lucrative business software market, so you may wonder if the program is suitable for science and engineering calculations. Can a business program perform the types of calculations that are required in science and engineering? Are the precision and range of the numbers suitable for engineering calculations? Are all the standard science and engineering mathematical functions available? Can you construct useful algorithms?

As you will see, not only does Excel have precision and accuracy comparable to large computer systems, it also has more mathematical capabilities and functions than many high-level computer languages, and it is programmable in a high-level language.

Evaluating Excel's Numeric Precision and Range

Probably the most important question is whether Excel's numeric precision and range are sufficient for science and engineering calculations. Numeric precision is usually not important for simple calculations. You can calculate many science and engineering problems using a slide rule which has, at best, only three places of accuracy. On the other hand, many numerical algorithms are quite sensitive to numeric precision. Any algorithm that uses iteration is likely to be sensitive to numeric precision, because errors in the calculation grow with each iteration and can overwhelm the calculation if the numbers aren't sufficiently precise. Algorithms that solve problems in nonlinear dynamics are especially sensitive to numeric precision, because the solutions involve iteration and the formulas are extremely nonlinear.

Celestial mechanics calculations also require an extreme number of digits of precision. In celestial mechanics, objects are often integrated for many thousands of orbits about their primary (sun or planet), and the cumulative round-off error can put the object on the wrong side of that primary if the precision is too small.

Table 1.1 lists Excel's precision and range limits.

TABLE 1.1: Excel's Numeric Precision and Range

Precision	Range
15 digits	$\pm 1.798 \times 10^{+308}$

Numeric Precision

Excel's numeric precision meets or exceeds that of several established computational tools used in science and engineering. Excel maintains an internal numeric precision of 15 digits. In comparison, a typical scientific calculator displays 10 digits and probably stores one or two more digits internally to reduce round-off error; a VAX minicomputer maintains only 7 digits in single-precision, floating-point numbers, and 15 in double-precision; and a CRAY 1 supercomputer has 15 digits of precision in single-precision, floating-point numbers.

Excel maintains the 15 digits internally, but rounds the number for the screen display according to the format of the cell in which the number appears; however, you can store the rounded numbers as they appear on the screen rather than the full 15 digits: select the Tools ➤ Options command (the Options command on the Tools menu,) then select the Calculation tab and check the Precision As Displayed checkbox. Reducing the precision is useful when you are working with monetary amounts and do not want to have fractional cents, but it is not usually desirable for science and engineering calculations and it will not be used in the examples in this book. Also, using reduced precision actually slows down spreadsheet recalculation slightly.

Numeric Range

Numeric range generally determines the sensitivity of the spreadsheet to overflow and underflow errors. Excel stores numbers between $-1.798 \times 10^{+308}$ and $1.798 \times 10^{+308}$, which provides a numeric range of $\pm 10^{+308}$. In comparison, a typical hand calculator handles a range of $10^{\pm 99}$; a VAX minicomputer has a range of $10^{\pm 38}$ in single-precision and $10^{\pm 308}$ in double-precision; and a CRAY 1 supercomputer has a range of $10^{\pm 2500}$. Although the largest number Excel can store is $1.798 \times 10^{+308}$, the largest number that you can type in is about $9.999 \times 10^{+307}$. If you type in a larger value, Excel treats it as a string.

Most scientific and engineering results have reasonably sized numbers, roughly in the range of 10^{-40} to 10^{+40} (reasonable for scientists and engineers, that is). But when these numbers are used in an equation, the intermediate results are often quite large. If the size of an intermediate result exceeds the range of the computer, the calculation overflows and returns an error. For example, consider this simple expression from quantum mechanics:

$$\frac{2m}{\hbar^2}$$

where $\hbar$ is Planck's constant divided by 2π (1.0546×10^{-34} J–s) and m is the electron rest mass (9.11×10^{-31} kg). The result of this calculation is $1.64 \times 10^{+38}$, which is also a reasonably sized number. But the intermediate result of squaring and inverting Planck's constant has a value of $8.99 \times 10^{+67}$, which is 29 orders of magnitude larger than the final result. Taking the cube of the inverse of Planck's constant easily overflows a hand calculator, and it is far beyond the capability of single-precision numbers on a VAX.

Numeric overflow usually indicates an error in the problem setup. If that is not the case, an overflow of an intermediate value can often be corrected by reordering the formula or by splitting it into two formulas to limit the size of the intermediate values. You would set up the equation above to first divide the electron mass by Planck's constant, and then divide that result by Planck's constant again. The final result would be the same, but the intermediate value would not be so large.

With a range of $10^{\pm308}$, Excel is not likely to have problems with numeric overflow. If you do manage to overflow a number, Excel stores the error value #NUM! to mark that cell and any cell that depends on it as bad. If a number underflows (because it is less than 2.225×10^{-308}) Excel stores the value as zero. If that underflow is in the denominator of a fraction, Excel returns #DIV/0!, again to mark any cell that depends on this value as bad.

Error Numbers

In addition to the standard real numbers, Excel treats seven error values as if they were numbers:

#DIV/0!	Division by zero.
#NAME?	A variable name in a formula has not been defined.
#N/A	No value is available.
#NULL!	A result does not exist, or is an invalid intersection of two areas.

#NUM!	Numeric overflow, underflow, or incorrect use of a number, such as SQRT(−1).
#REF!	Invalid cell reference; the cell is not on the worksheet.
#VALUE!	Invalid argument type, such as text where a number is required.

When one of these error values is used in a formula, the formula's result also has that error value. Thus, the error values propagate throughout a worksheet, marking any values that depend on them as bad. This propagation of error values ensures that you don't use a number calculated from bad data.

TIP If you want to use error values to test error-recovery formulas on a worksheet, you can type these values directly into a cell on the worksheet.

A Brief Review of Cells and Cell References

The cells in an Excel worksheet can hold text, numbers, dates, times, or formulas. Excel looks at what you type and converts the cell contents as appropriate. If a cell contains a number, Excel stores it as a numeric value, and you can use it for calculations. If a cell contains a mixture of text and numbers, Excel stores it as text. If the contents of a cell begin with an equal sign (=), Excel stores it as a formula. If a cell's contents look like one of Excel's date or time formats, Excel stores it as a serial date number. A serial date number is the date in days since 1/1/1900 (or 1/1/1904 if the 1904 checkbox is checked on the Tools ➤ Options, Calculation tab dialog box), with the time expressed as fractions of a day.

Every cell in Excel has two properties associated with it: *contents* and *value*. The content is what you type into a cell, and the value is what is visible on the screen. Cell formatting does not affect the value of a cell, although it does change how the value appears on the screen. For text and numbers, the content and the value are the same. For formulas, the content is the formula you typed in, and the value is the result of evaluating that formula.

Cell References

Range or Reference Type	Example
Row	Number
Column	Letter
Relative reference	B5
Absolute reference	$B$5
Mixed reference	$B5 or B$5
External reference	'D:\STATS\CARS.XLS'!B5
Range reference	B5:F7

You insert the value of a different cell into a formula by using a *cell reference*. A cell reference consists of a letter-number pair, where the letter corresponds to the column that contains the referenced cell and the number corresponds to the row that contains the referenced cell. For example, C5 corresponds to the value in the cell at column C and row 5 shown below on the left. This is known as the A1 style of cell reference. You can also reference cells as a row-and-column pair, as in R5C3 shown below on the right, which refers to the same cell as C5. This is called the R1C1 style of cell reference.

	A	B	C	D
1				
2				
3				
4				
5			Cell C5	
6				
7				
8				

In the A1 style, the columns are lettered.

	1	2	3	4
1				
2				
3				
4				
5			Cell R5C3	
6				
7				
8				

In the R1C1 style, the columns are numbered.

To set or change cell reference style, choose the Tools ➤ Options command, then click the General tab. Click the A1 or R1C1 option button in the Reference Style box. If you create a worksheet using one style and then change the reference style, all your references are converted to the other style.

External Cell References

If you are referencing a cell that is on a different worksheet (not the worksheet in which you are typing a formula), you must include the worksheet name so that Excel knows where to look for the cell. This is known as an *external reference*. The worksheet containing the external reference does not need to be open for you to access the contents of one of its cells. To create an external reference, type the worksheet name, followed by an exclamation point, followed by the cell reference. If the worksheet is not in the default directory, include the path to it as well.

For example, if you want to reference cell H7 on the CARS.XLS worksheet in the default directory, use this reference:

`CARS.XLS!H7`

To reference cell H7 in the CARS.XLS worksheet in the D:\STATS directory, which is not the default directory, use this form:

`'D:\STATS\CARS.XLS'!H7`

The single quotation marks are required for a reference that is not a valid Excel name, such as one that includes a directory path.

TIP The simplest way to ensure that you are correctly addressing a cell, especially a cell in another worksheet, is to have Excel insert the reference for you. Open the worksheet that contains the cell to be referenced, then switch back to your original worksheet and start typing your formula. When you reach the point where you want to insert the cell reference, switch to the worksheet that contains the cell you want to reference, and click on that cell with the mouse. Excel writes the correct cell reference in your formula.

Range References

You can reference a group of cells as a *range*. A range of cells is a rectangular region on the worksheet. All the cells within the rectangle are included in the range (there are no holes). You specify a range with the cell references of the cells in the upper-left and lower-right corners of the rectangular region, separated by a colon. For example, H4:J6 specifies all the cells within the rectangle that has H4 in the upper-left corner and J6 in the lower-right corner (H4, H5, H6, I4, I5, I6, J4, J5, and J6). A range reference can be as small as a single cell (H2:H2). It can also be a single row (J2:M2) or column (L4:L7).

SHORTCUT

Range references can be quickly created with the mouse. When you reach the point in a formula where you want to insert the reference, click on the cell in one corner of the reference you want to select and drag diagonally to the opposite corner. The range reference is inserted into your formula. This method also works for most dialog boxes that require a cell or range reference.

You can combine multiple ranges in a single cell reference by separating them with commas. For example, the four selected cell ranges in the graphic above can be referenced as H2:H2,H4:J6,J2:M2,L4:L7. All the cells in the selected regions are contained in the reference (H2, H4, H5, H6, I4, I5, I6, J4, J5, J6, J2, K2, L2, M2, L4, L5, L6, and L7).

If you use a space instead of a comma to separate two ranges, the resulting reference is to the intersection of those two regions instead of to the union. For example, in the following graphic, B3:D4 D2:E6 is a range reference to cells D3 and D4 only, because they are the only cells that are contained in both rectangular regions.

TIP

To select a multi-area region with the mouse, select the first region, hold down Ctrl (Cmd on the Mac,) and select subsequent regions.

Relative and Absolute References

Cell references are either *relative, absolute,* or *mixed.* Relative cell references point to cells relative to the cell where the reference is typed. Absolute cell references always point to a specific cell. Mixed references have a relative row and absolute column reference or an absolute row and relative column.

Relative Cell References

All of the cell references mentioned so far are *relative* cell references. Relative cell references are defined in relation to the cell that contains the typed reference.

For example, suppose that the formula in cell G5 contains the cell reference E3. The E3 does not actually refer to the contents of the cell in column E and row 3, but points to the cell that is two columns left and two rows up from cell G5, which just happens to be E3. This distinction becomes apparent when you copy cells. If you copy the contents of cell G5 into cell I8, the cell reference changes to G6, which is two columns to the left and two columns above cell I8.

In the R1C1 reference style, you enclose the row and column number in square brackets, which changes them into row and column offsets. The origin of this cell-reference system is the upper-left corner of the worksheet, so positive directions are down and to the right. For example, R[–2]C[2] is a relative cell reference to the cell two rows up and two columns right from the cell that contains the reference.

Relative cell references are extremely handy when you want to apply a formula to a list of values. Instead of typing the formula for each value in the list, you write a formula using relative cell references and copy that formula down the list of values. For example, if you want to calculate a formula for 50 different values in one column of a worksheet, it would be a tedious job to type the same formula 50 times. Instead, you type the formula once into a column adjacent to the data, and then copy the formula into the 49 cells below the first cell. Excel adjusts all the relative cell references so that each reference points to the appropriate data value. You will see how this works as you develop some worksheets in later chapters.

Absolute Cell References

An absolute cell reference does not change when you copy a formula. It always points to a specific cell, no matter where it is on the worksheet. To make a cell reference absolute, precede the row and column coordinates with a dollar sign. For example, $G$5 is an absolute reference to cell G5.

The R1C1 cell reference style is absolute unless you use the brackets to make the reference relative. For example, R5C7 refers to the specific cell at the intersection of row 5 and column 7.

Absolute cell references are useful for pointing to the coefficients in a formula that you are going to copy into multiple cells. A good formula-writing strategy is to specify the independent variables in a formula by using relative cell references that point to adjacent cells, but make the coefficients of the formula absolute cell references. Then, when you copy the formula down a column, the relative cell references change to reference adjacent cells, but the absolute references always point to the coefficients and are not adjusted. This way, you need only one set of coefficients on your worksheet. No matter where you copy the formula, it still refers to the appropriate coefficients. You can then change the value of a single coefficient to see what happens, and all copies of the formula show the result of that change.

Mixed Cell References

A mixed cell reference contains an absolute reference to only the column or row coordinate and a relative reference to the other coordinate. To create a mixed reference, place a dollar sign before the coordinate that you want to be absolute.

For example, the reference $G5 fixes the column, but the row coordinate is relative and will change if the referencing cell is copied to a different row. G$5 is just the opposite, with the row coordinate absolute and the column coordinate relative.

In the R1C1 style, R1C[4] is an absolute reference to row 1 and a relative reference to the column that is four columns right of the column containing this reference.

Range and Cell Names

You can name a range or cell and then use the name instead of a cell reference in formulas and commands. To name a single cell or apply a single name to a range of cells, select the cell or range, then on the Insert menu, select the Name ➤ Define command. Type the cell or range name in the dialog box and click OK. The cell or range is now named and that name can be used in a formula.

To name a list of cells in a row or column, type the names in an adjacent row or column, then select the cells to be named and the adjacent cells containing the names. On the Insert menu, select the Name ➤ Create command, select the location of the names and click OK. All the cells are named using the names typed in the adjacent cells.

SHORTCUT To name a single cell or cell range, select the cell or range, type the name into the name box on the left side of the formula bar and press Enter. Be sure you press Enter or the name won't be registered.

When Excel evaluates a formula that contains names, it replaces each name with its definition, and then calculates the result. Named ranges are absolute references, so they do not change when you copy cells that contain them.

Using a name is efficient when you reference the same cell or range many times. Names also make your formulas more understandable. For example, if cell C5 contains a mass value, you could name it Mass. Formulas that reference this cell will contain the word Mass, which is much more descriptive than C5.

When you type a range name into a formula that requires a single value, Excel uses only a single cell in that range. The cell used depends on the relative locations of the cell containing the reference and the range being referenced. If the reference is to a column of cells to the right or left of the cell containing the reference, the cell used is the one on the same row as the cell with the reference. Likewise, if the reference is to a row that is above or below the cell containing the reference, the cell used is the one that is in the same column as the cell containing the reference. If you have more than one row or column in the reference in the same row or column as the referencing cell, you get the #VALUE! error. You will also get the #VALUE error if none of the cells in the reference is in the same row or column as the referencing cell.

> **WARNING**
> If you use a range name in a function that can take multiple arguments (such as the AND( ) function), the whole named range is used in the function, not just the single value in the same row or column as the formula. This can give unexpected results if you are not careful.

Actually, you can use the Insert ➤ Name ➤ Define command to name just about any value, including numbers or text that are not contained in any cell. Treat the list of named ranges and values as simple replacement table, where the value of a name is inserted into a formula before the formula is evaluated. The Insert ➤ Name ➤ Define command is also used to edit or delete names and references. Select any cell, then select the Insert ➤ Name ➤ Define command. In the Define Name dialog box, select an existing name from the Names In Workbook list, then look at the name's value in the Refers To box.

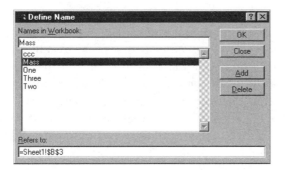

Copying versus Moving Cell References

As explained earlier, when you *copy* a formula from one cell into another cell, the absolute cell references do not change, but the relative cell references change according to where the formula is copied. In the illustration below, a formula was typed into cell B3 and then copied down into cells B4:B6. Note how the relative references to cells in column A change in each formula and the absolute references to cell B2 do not change.

	A	B	C	
1				
2		3		
3	1	=$B$2*A3		
4	2	=$B$2*A4		
5	3	=$B$2*A5		
6	4	=$B$2*A6		
7				
8				

SHORTCUT

The Copy and Paste commands are used to copy a formula into other cells. If the cells to be pasted into are adjacent to the cell that is copied from, select the cell to be copied along with the cells to be copied into, choose the Edit ➤ Fill command and select the direction to fill (Up, Down, Left, Right) from the submenu. An even quicker shortcut is to use the *fill handle* (the small black square on the lower-right corner of a selected cell or range). Select the cell to copy, then click on the fill handle and drag to the end of the range you want to fill. The contents of the first cell are copied to the whole selected range.

When you *move* the contents of a cell, Excel assumes that you are changing only the layout of your worksheet and do not want to change the mathematical logic. To that end, cell references in the moved cells that point to cells outside the moved cells do not change; they still point to the same cells after the move. Any cells that refer to the moved cells are adjusted so that they point to new cells that have the same contents as the cells that they pointed to originally. A move operation should not change any of the results of your formulas, unless you delete data by moving cells on top of it. If cell B3 in the graphic above is moved to cell C7, the result is shown in the illustration below. Nothing has changed in the formula.

	A	B	C	
1				
2		3		
3	1			
4	2	=$B$2*A4		
5	3	=$B$2*A5		
6	4	=$B$2*A6		
7			=$B$2*A3	
8				

SHORTCUT Cells are moved using the Edit ➤ Cut and Edit ➤ Paste commands. You can also move a cell by selecting the cell, then clicking down on the border and dragging the cell to a new location.

Using Operators in Calculations

Operators are the basic building blocks of mathematical formulas. Their action determines how numbers (or text strings) are combined to produce numeric results. Excel provides three types of operators: mathematical, text, and logical. The single text operator is concatenation (&), which is used to join two text strings together into a single string of text. Table 1.2 lists all the operators available in Excel.

Mathematical Operators

The mathematical operators consist of the standard set you would expect to find in any high-level computer language or scientific calculator.

The unary operators are percent and negation. The percent operator divides the number to its left by 100 (/100). If the number with the percent operator is the only value in a cell, the cell's format is also changed to percent. Excel does not provide a positive unary operator; a positive value is assumed if a unary operator is not present. In fact, if you insert a + in front of a value or formula, Excel removes it (except when it is in the exponent of a number in scientific notation).

The mathematical operators are addition, subtraction, multiplication, division, and exponentiation. These operators work as you would expect them to.

Logical Operators

The logical operators (called comparison operators in the manual) are used to compare two numerical values or strings. The result of the operation is the value True or the value False. When you use logical results in mathematical formulas, True has the value 1, and False has the value 0.

When Excel compares strings with the logical operators, it ignores the case (uppercase or lowercase) of the characters; however, you can use Excel's EXACT function to compare strings considering their case.

Operator Precedence

The precedence of the operators determines the order in which a formula is evaluated. Table 1.2 lists the precedence along with each operator. In any calculation, the operators listed with a precedence of 1 are executed first, then the operators shown with a precedence of 2, and so on. If there are two operations of equal precedence in a formula, they are evaluated from right to left.

If you are unsure how a formula will be evaluated, use parentheses to force the formula to be evaluated in the correct order. Parentheses always override the operator precedence shown in Table 1.2.

TABLE 1.2: Excel Operators and Order of Precedence

Operator	Description	Precedence in Calculations
	Unary Operators	
–	Negation (operates on the value to its right)	1
%	Percent (operates on the value to its left)	2
	Mathematical Operators	
^	Exponentiation	3
*	Multiplication	4
/	Division	4
+	Addition	5
–	Subtraction	5
	Text Operator	
&	Concatenation	6
	Logical Operators	
=	Equal to	7
<	Less than	7
>	Greater than	7
<=	Less than or equal to	7
>=	Greater than or equal to	7
< >	Not equal to	7

WARNING

The precedence of operators in a formula on the worksheet is slightly different from that used in Visual Basic for Applications (described in Chapter 4). On the worksheet, negation is performed before exponentiation, while the opposite is true in Visual Basic for Applications. For example, on the worksheet, –1^2 returns 1, while in Visual Basic for Applications the same formula returns –1, and must be written as (–1)^2 to give the expected result.

Using Worksheet Functions

An important consideration when planning to use Excel for science and engineering calculations is the availability of frequently used mathematical functions. Without these functions, relatively simple calculations can become quite tedious. For example, have you ever tried to calculate the sine of an angle using a business calculator whose most complicated function is a square root? It can be done, but it is tiresome and prone to error.

Excel provides 10 different types of worksheet functions: math/trigonometry, engineering, logical, text, statistical, date/time, database/list management, financial, informational, and lookup/reference. In addition, you will find a large number of add-in functions for use in creating computer programs in Excel (Visual Basic for Applications programming will be covered in Chapter 4). If the internal functions, add-in functions and Visual Basic for Applications programs aren't sufficient for your purposes, you can create your own functions in a compiled language, such as C or FORTRAN, and call them from within Excel (see Appendix D for information on declaring and using external functions.)

The functions that are of special interest to scientists and engineers are described here. For a complete discussion of all the functions and operators and their syntax, refer to Excel's online help.

Entering Functions

Excel functions are used in much the same manner as functions in most computer languages. To use a function in a formula, type the function name, a left parenthesis, some arguments separated by commas, and a right parenthesis. Arguments of functions can be numbers, strings, cell references, or other functions (with nesting up to seven levels deep). If the argument of a function is not within the range accepted by that function, the function returns the error value #NUM!. If the argument is not the correct type for a particular function, the function returns the error value #VALUE!.

TIP To insert a function directly into a formula, use the Function Wizard. Start typing a formula, and when you reach the point where you want to insert the function, click the Function Wizard button on the toolbar. The Function Wizard dialog box appears with a list of functions. Select the function you want, then click Finish to insert the function and its arguments into your formula. Or, click Next to display a second dialog box to help you type the arguments.

In this book, the function names appear in uppercase letters. You can type the function names in either uppercase or lowercase; Excel does not distinguish between the two cases.

Array Functions

A normal function returns a single value; however, some of Excel's functions return an array of values. For example, the MINVERSE (*matrix*) function calculates the inverse of a matrix, and returns a matrix of values of the same order (height and width) as the argument matrix.

An array function must be entered into a range of cells that is large enough to contain all the elements of the array. For example, if you are using the MINVERSE function to invert a three-by-three array, the result is also a three-by-three array, so you must insert the function into a three-by-three range of cells.

To insert an array function into a range of cells, select the cells and then type the array function and its arguments into the upper-left cell of the range. Then hold down the Ctrl and Shift keys, and press Enter (Cmd+Enter on the Macintosh) or click on the check mark in the formula bar (the check mark appears after you begin typing). The array function, surrounded by curly braces ({}), is placed in every cell in the range. You don't type the curly braces; Excel inserts them to mark the entry as an array function.

Actually, any formula can be applied to an array of values in the same manner. For example, this formula calculates the sum of squares of a set of values and returns a single value:

```
=SUM((A7:A15–$B$1)^2)
```

If you type this formula and then press the Ctrl and Shift keys while you press Enter (or click on the check mark), Excel first subtracts the value in cell B1 from all the values in cells A7 through A15, squares the differences, and then sums them. If you enter this formula without holding the Ctrl and Shift keys down, Excel uses only one of the values in the range of cells from A7 through A15 (the one in the same row as the cell that contains the formula).

You can get very creative with array functions, calculating complex summations in a single cell. Be careful though, they can be difficult to validate or debug. For example, the following formula when entered as an array function calculates the standard deviation of the contents of A1:A10.

```
=SQRT((SUM((A1:A10-AVERAGE(A1:A10))^2))/(COUNT(A1:A10)-1))
```

Mathematical Functions

The mathematical functions take numerical data as arguments, transform that data in some way, and produce a numerical value as a result. The mathematical functions are of four general types: basic mathematics, logarithmic, trigonometric, and matrix. Table 1.3 lists Excel's mathematical functions.

TABLE 1.3: Excel's Mathematical Functions

Function	Returns
Basic Mathematical Functions	
ABS( )	The absolute value.
CEILING( )	Round up to the next integer that is a multiple of the specified significance.
COMBIN( )	The number of combinations that can be made from a given number of objects.
COUNTBLANK( )	Count the number of blank cells in a range.
COUNTIF( )	Count the number of cells that match a criteria.
EVEN( )	Round up to the next even integer.
FACT( )	The factorial.
FLOOR( )	Round down to the next integer that is a multiple of significance.
GCD( )*	The greatest common divisor of a list of numbers.
LCM( )*	The least common multiple of a list of numbers.
INT( )	The integer part of a number.
MOD( )	The modulus (remainder of two numbers).

TABLE 1.3: Excel's Mathematical Functions (continued)

Function	Returns
MROUND( )*	Round a number to the nearest multiple of significance.
MULTINOMIAL( )*	The multinomial of a list of numbers.
ODD( )	Round a number up to the nearest odd integer.
POWER( )	Raise a number to a power.
PRODUCT( )	The product of the numbers in the list.
QUOTIENT( )	Integer division of one number by another number.
RAND( )	A random number between 0 and 1.
RANDBETWEEN( )*	A random number between the limits of the lower and upper numbers.
ROMAN( )	Convert a decimal number to a roman numeral.
ROUND( )*	Round a number to the specified number of digits.
ROUNDDOWN( )	Round a number towards 0 to the next integer.
ROUNDUP( )	Round a number away from 0 to the next integer.
SERIESSUM( )*	Sum a power series.
SIGN( )	The value 1 with the sign of a number.
SQRT( )	The square root of a number.
SQRTP( )*	The square root of &p times a number.
SUBTOTAL( )	A subtotal of a list or database.
SUM( )	Add the numbers in a list.
SUMIF( )	Sum values that match a criteria.
SUMPRODUCT( )	The sum of the products of matrix elements.
SUMSQ( )	The sum of the squares of a list of numbers.
SUMX2MY2( )	The sum of the difference of the squares of the elements in two matrices.
SUMX2PY2( )	The sum of the sum of the squares of the elements in two matrices.
SUMXMY2( )	The sum of the squares of the differences of the values in two matrices.
TRUNC( )	Truncate a number to the specified number of digits.

Logarithmic Functions

Function	Returns
EXP( )	Exponential of a number (power of **e**).
EXP(1)	The value **e** (2.7182818284590).
LN( )	Natural logarithm of a number (base **e**).
LOG( )	Logarithm of a number with the specified base.
LOG10( )	Common logarithm of a number (base 10).

TABLE 1.3:   Excel's Mathematical Functions (continued)

Function	Returns
Trigonometric Functions	
COS( )	Cosine of a number.
SIN( )	Sine of a number.
TAN( )	Tangent of a number.
Inverse Trigonometric Functions	
ACOS( )	Arccosine of a number.
ASIN( )	Arcsine of a number.
ATAN( )	Arctangent of a number (from $-\pi$ to $+\pi/2$).
ATAN2( )	Arctangent of two numbers (from $-\pi$ to $+\pi$).
Hyperbolic Functions	
COSH( )	Hyperbolic cosine of a number.
SINH( )	Hyperbolic sine of a number.
TANH( )	Hyperbolic tangent of a number.
Inverse Hyperbolic Functions	
ACOSH( )	Inverse hyperbolic cosine of a number.
ASINH( )	Hyperbolic sine of a number.
ATANH( )	Inverse hyperbolic tangent of a number.
PI( )*	The value π (3.1415926535898).
Angular Conversion Functions	
DEGREES( )	Convert an angle in radians to degrees.
RADIANS( )	Convert an angle in degrees to radians.
Matrix Functions	
MDETERM( )	Determinant of a matrix.
MINVERSE( )	The inverse of a matrix.
MMULT( )	The multiple of two matrices.
See also TRANSPOSE( ) in Table 1.14	
*These functions are part of the Analysis Toolpack Add-In.	

Basic Mathematical Functions

The basic mathematical functions perform common calculations. For example, ABS(x) returns the absolute value of x.

The CEILING(x,sig), EVEN(x), FLOOR(x,sig), INT(x), MROUND(x,sig), ROUND(x,sig), ROUNDDOWN(x,sig), ROUNDUP(x,sig), ODD(x), and TRUNC(x,sig) functions convert x to an integer, each using different logic to perform the conversion. The argument sig is the significance, which is the value whose multiple you want to round to. Table 1.4 shows examples of the results of using some of these functions.

The function SIGN(x) returns the value 1.0, with the same sign as x, or 0 if x is 0. The function MOD($x1$,$x2$) returns the modulus or remainder of the quotient $x1/x2$. It is

TABLE 1.4: Rounding and Truncating Numbers

x	n	CEIL-ING (x,n)	EVEN (x)	FLOOR (x,n)	INT (x)	MROUND (x,n)	ROUND (x,n)	TRUNC (x,n)	ROUND-DOWN (x,n)	ROUND-UP (x,n)
1.5263	0	0	2	#DIV/0!	1	0	2	1	1	2
−1.5263	0	0	−2	#DIV/0!	−2	0	−2	−1	−1	−2
2.48554	0	0	4	#DIV/0!	2	0	2	2	2	3
2.61756	0	0	4	#DIV/0!	2	0	3	2	2	3
−2.48554	0	0	−4	#DIV/0!	−3	0	−2	−2	−2	−3
−2.61765	0	0	−4	#DIV/0!	−3	0	−3	−2	−2	−3
1.5263	2	2	2	0	1	2	1.53	1.52	1.52	1.53
−1.5263	−2	−2	−2	0	−2	−2	0	0	0	−100
132.4855	2	134	134	132	132	132	132.49	132.48	132.48	133.49
642.6176	2	644	644	642	642	642	642.62	642.61	642.61	643.62
−132.486	−2	−134	−134	−132	−133	−132	−100	−100	−100	−200
−642.618	−2	−644	−644	−642	−643	−642	−600	−600	−600	−700
1.5263	0.01	1.53	2	1.52	1	1.53	2	1	1	2
−1.5263	−0.01	−1.53	−2	−1.52	−2	−1.53	−2	−1	−1	−2
2.48554	0.01	2.49	4	2.48	2	2.49	2	2	2	3
2.61756	0.01	2.62	4	2.61	2	2.62	3	2	2	3
−2.48554	−0.01	−2.49	−4	−2.48	−3	−2.49	−2	−2	−2	−3
−2.61765	−0.01	−2.62	−4	−2.61	−3	−2.62	−3	−2	−2	−3

most commonly used to map a large angle $(x1>2\pi)$ back onto the unit circle $(0<x1<2\pi)$, as in this example:

```
MOD(2.703×PI(),2×PI())= .703π
```

The MOD function is also often used as part of a logical formula to determine when a value is an even multiple of some other value, as in this formula:

```
(MOD(X,10)=0)=TRUE for X=... ,-10, 0, 10, 20,...
```

The SQRT(x) function returns the value of the square root of x. SQRTPI(x) returns the square root of $x\pi$.

The functions SUM(*list*), PRODUCT(*list*), QUOTIENT(*x1,x2*), SERIESSUM (*x,n,m,coefs*), SUMPRODUCT(*matrix1,matrix2*), SUMSQ(*list*), SUMX2MY2 (*matrix1,matrix2*), SUMX2PY2(*matrix1,matrix2*), and SUMXMY2(*matrix1,matrix2*) perform different summations of lists of terms. The RAND( ) and RAND-BETWEEN(*lower,upper*) functions both return random numbers.

The function COMBIN(*n,chosen*) calculates the number of ways *chosen* objects can be combined from a pool of n objects. The FACT(n) and FACTDOUBLE(n) functions calculate the factorial of a number ($n!=1\times2\times3\times...n$) and the double factorial of a number ($n!!$). The GCD and LCM functions calculate the greatest common divisor and the least common multiple of a list of numbers.

Logarithmic Functions

The logarithmic functions calculate the natural and common logarithms of a number. LN(x) and EXP(x) calculate the natural logarithm of x, and the exponential of x (e^x) respectively. Theoretically, the value of x in the exponential function can take on any value; however, a value of x greater than about 709 causes numeric overflow, and the function returns the value #NUM!.

EXP(1) returns the base **e** of the natural logarithm (2.71828182845904). LOG10(x) returns the common logarithm (base 10) of x. LOG(x,b) returns the logarithm of x to any base b.

Trigonometric Functions

The trigonometric functions SIN(x), COS(x), and TAN(x) return the sine, cosine, and tangent, respectively, of the angle x. The angle x must be in radians, so convert an angle in degrees to one in radians using the RADIANS( ) function or multiplying by $\pi/180$. For example, if y is in degrees, this is the formula for the sine of y:

```
SIN(RADIANS(Y)) = SIN(Y×PI()/180)
```

To reverse the process and convert an angle in radians to degrees, use the DEGREES( ) function or multiply by $180/\pi$. For example, this is the formula to get the arcsin in degrees of z:

```
DEGREES(ASIN(Z)) = ASIN(Z)×180/PI()
```

Precision of the Trigonometric Functions Near Zero

Because of Excel's numeric precision, the sine or cosine of π, 2π, ..., or the cosine of $\pi/2$, $3\pi/2$, ..., are not exactly zero; therefore, you must be careful not to write equations that depend on the results of these functions being exactly zero, as in the following:

```
SIN(PI())=1.22x10⁻¹⁶
SIN(2*PI())=−2.45x10⁻¹⁶
COS(PI()/2)=6.12x10⁻¹⁷
TAN(2*PI())=−2.45x10⁻¹⁶
```

In most cases these values are close enough to zero, but they can cause problems in some formulas.

The trigonometric functions for calculating the secant, cosecant, and cotangent are not available in Excel. However, you can use other Excel functions to obtain the results:

- To calculate the secant of the angle x, SEC(x), use the formula

  ```
  1/COS(x)
  ```

- To calculate the cosecant of the angle x, CSC(x), use the formula

  ```
  1/SIN(x)
  ```

- To calculate the cotangent of the angle x, COT(x), use the formula

```
1/TAN(x)
```

Inverse Trigonometric Functions

The inverse trigonometric functions ASIN(x) and ACOS(x) return the arcsine and arccosine, respectively, in radians of x. Since the arctangent is multivalued, Excel provides two different versions of that function. The first version, ATAN(x), does not have enough information to be able to determine which quadrant the result should be in, so it returns a value in the range of $-\pi/2$ to $+\pi/2$. The second version, ATAN2(x,y), has sufficient information to determine the correct quadrant, so it returns a value in the range of $-\pi$ to $+\pi$. The function PI returns the value of π (3.141592653589879).

You can calculate the inverse trigonometric functions that are not supplied with Excel as follows:

- To calculate the arcsecant of x for $x > 0$, ASEC(x), use the formula

```
ATAN(SQRT(x^2-1))
```

- To calculate the arcsecant of x for $x < 0$, ASEC(x), use the formula

```
ATAN(SQRT(x^2-1))-PI()
```

- To calculate the arccosecant of x for $x > 0$, ACSC(x), use the formula

```
ATAN(1/SQRT(x^2-1))
```

- To calculate the arccosecant of x for $x < 0$, ACSC(x), use the formula

```
ATAN(1/SQRT(x^2-1))-PI()
```

- To calculate the arccotangent of x, ACOT(x), use the formula

```
PI()/2-ATAN(x)
```

Hyperbolic Functions

Excel provides the three hyperbolic functions SINH(x), COSH(x), and TANH(x). These functions calculate the hyperbolic sine, cosine, and tangent of x, respectively. The rest of the hyperbolic functions can be calculated from the existing functions, as follows:

- To calculate the hyperbolic secant of x, SECH(x), use the formula

`1/COSH(x)`

- To calculate the hyperbolic cosecant of x, CSCH(x), use the formula

`1/SINH(x)`

- To calculate the hyperbolic cotangent of x, COTH(x), use the formula

`1/TANH(x)`

Inverse Hyperbolic Functions

The inverse hyperbolic functions in Excel are ASINH, ACOSH, and ATANH. These functions calculate the inverse hyperbolic sine, cosine, and tangent, respectively. The other inverse hyperbolic functions can be calculated as follows:

- To calculate the inverse hyperbolic secant of x (dual-valued), ASECH(x), use the formula

`LN((1±SQRT(1−x^2))/x)`

- To calculate the inverse hyperbolic cosecant of x (dual-valued), ACSCH(x), use the formula

`LN((1±SQRT(1+x^2))/x)`

- To calculate the inverse hyperbolic cotangent of x, ACOTH(x), use the formula

`0.5×LN((x+1)/(x−1))`

Matrix Functions

Four matrix functions are supplied with Excel. Three are part of the mathematical functions: MDETERM(*matrix*), MINVERSE(*matrix*), and MMULT(*matrix1,matrix2*). One is part of the table and vector lookup functions: TRANSPOSE(*array*). The MDETERM function calculates the determinant of a matrix. MINVERSE calculates the inverse of a matrix. MMULT calculates the matrix product of two matrices. The primary use for the matrix functions is for solving matrix equations, particularly those that result from solving systems of linear equations.

MINVERSE and MMULT are array functions: they return an array of values rather than a single value. While entering these functions, you must hold down the Ctrl and Shift keys (Cmd+Enter on the Macintosh) to insert them into an array of cells instead of just one cell, as explained in Array Functions earlier in the chapter.

The TRANSPOSE function performs the matrix transpose operation on its argument. That is, it exchanges the rows and columns. This function is useful for changing horizontal vectors into vertical vectors and vice versa.

Engineering Functions

Excel's engineering functions include the following types:

- Bessel functions
- Base conversion functions
- Angular conversion functions
- Error functions
- Numeric comparison functions
- Complex arithmetic functions

NOTE Complex numbers are stored as strings in the form $x + yj$, where x is the real part and y is the imaginary part.

Table 1.5 lists Excel's engineering functions. More complete descriptions are in Appendix C.

Logical Functions

The logical functions are those that return or manipulate the logical values True or False. In addition, many of the informational functions in Table 1.13 (the Isxxx( ) functions) also return logical values as the result of a test. Table 1.6 lists Excel's logical functions.

The logical values True and False are equivalent to the numerical values 1 and 0, respectively. That is, for all values of x True $\times x = x$ and False $\times x = 0$. Functions that expect a logical argument interpret all nonzero values as True and the value zero as False.

TABLE 1.5: Excel's Engineering Functions

Function	Returns
Bessel Functions	
BESSELJ( )*	Bessel function $J_n(x)$.
BESSELI( )*	Modified Bessel function $I_n(x)$.
BESSELK( )*	Modified Bessel function $K_n(x)$.
BESSELY( )*	Weber's Bessel function $Y_n(x)$.
Base Conversion Functions	
BIN2DEC( )*	Convert a binary number to a decimal number.
BIN2HEX( )*	Convert a binary number to a hexadecimal string.
BIN2OCT( )*	Convert a binary number to an octal string.
CONVERT( )*	Convert a number from one measurement system to another.
DEC2BIN( )*	Convert a decimal integer to a binary string.
DEC2HEX( )*	Convert a decimal integer to a hexadecimal string.
DEC2OCT( )*	Convert a decimal integer to an octal string.
FACTDOUBLE( )*	The double factorial.
HEX2BIN( )*	Convert a hexadecimal number to a binary string.
HEX2DEC( )*	Convert a hexadecimal number to a decimal number.
HEX2OCT( )*	Convert a hexadecimal number to an octal string.
OCT2BIN( )*	Convert an octal number to a binary string.
OCT2DEC( )*	Convert an octal number to a decimal number.
OCT2HEX( )*	Convert an octal number to a hexadecimal string.
Error Functions	
ERF( )*	Error function.
ERFC( )*	Complementary error function.
Numeric Comparison Functions	
DELTA( )*	Delta function; returns 1 if both numbers are the same or 0 if they are different.
GESTEP( )*	Step function; returns 1 if the number is greater than the step or 0 if the number is less than or equal to the step.

TABLE 1.5: Excel's Engineering Functions (continued)

Function	Returns
Complex Arithmetic Functions	
COMPLEX( )*	Convert the two coefficients into a complex number in a string "$x + yj$".
IMABS( )*	The absolute value of a complex number in a string.
IMAGINARY( )*	The imaginary coefficient y of a complex number in a string.
IMARGUMENT( )*	The angle, in radians, in the complex plane of a complex number in a string.
IMCONJUGATE( )*	The complex conjugate of a complex number in a string.
IMCOS( )*	The cosine of a complex number in a string.
IMDIV( )*	Quotient of two complex numbers in strings.
IMEXP( )*	Exponential of a complex number in a string.
IMLN( )*	Natural logarithm of a complex number in a string.
IMLOG2( )*	Base 2 logarithm of a complex number in a string.
IMLOG10( )*	Common logarithm (base 10) of a complex number in a string.
IMPOWER( )*	Complex number in a string raised to an integer power.
IMPRODUCT( )*	Product of two complex numbers stored in strings.
IMREAL( )*	Real coefficient of a complex number in a string.
IMSIN( )*	Sine of a complex number in a string.
IMSQRT( )*	Square root of a complex number in a string.
IMSUB( )*	Difference of two complex numbers stored in strings.
IMSUM( )*	Sum of two or more complex numbers stored in strings.

*These functions are part of the Analysis Toolpack Add-In.

The IF(*logical,x,y*) function tests logical values, but it does not necessarily return a logical result. If the value of *logical*, which may be a logical formula, is True or nonzero, the function returns the value x. If *logical* is False or zero, the function returns the value y.

A common use of the IF function is to watch for invalid numeric calculations (such as dividing by zero) and select an alternate calculation. When x or y are formulas, they are evaluated only if they are needed. For example, to calculate the value of $SIN(x)/x$ for all values of x, use the following formula:

```
IF(x=0,1,SIN(x)/x)
```

TABLE 1.6: Excel's Logical Functions

Function	Returns
Logical Value Functions	
TRUE( )	TRUE or 1
FALSE( )	FALSE or 0
Logical Test Functions	
IF( )	Select one of two values depending on a logical value.
Boolean (Operators) Functions	
AND( )	Logical AND of logical values.
NOT( )	Return TRUE if the argument is FALSE or FALSE if the argument is TRUE.
OR( )	Logical OR of logical values.

If x is equal to 0, the function returns the correct value, 1; otherwise, it calculates and returns the value of $SIN(x)/x$. If you do not use the IF function, you will get the error value #DIV/0! when x equaled zero, even though $SIN(0)/0$ is equal to 1.

Included with the logical functions are the three Boolean operators, $AND(A,B)$, $OR(A,B)$, and $NOT(A,B)$. They combine logical values according to the rules of Boolean algebra to produce a logical result. The Boolean operators are usually used as binary operators, but Excel supplies them as functions.

A complete set of Boolean operators or functions should also contain XOR (exclusive OR), EQV (logical equivalence), and IMP (logical implies). You can create these functions by combining the three available functions, as follows:

- For the XOR function, use the formula

  `=OR(AND(A,NOT(B)),AND(B,NOT(A)))`

- For the EQV function, use the formula

  `=OR(AND(NOT(A),NOT(B)),AND(A,B))`

- For the IMP function, use the formula

  `=OR(NOT(OR(A,B)),B)`

TABLE 1.7: Truth Table for Boolean Functions

A	B	AND(A,B)	OR(A,B)	NOT(A)	XOR(A,B)	EQV(A,B)	IMP(A,B)
T	T	T	T	F	F	T	T
T	F	F	T	F	T	F	F
F	T	F	T	T	T	F	T
F	F	F	F	T	F	T	T

Table 1.7 is a truth table for the six Boolean operators.

Text Functions

A string is an ordered sequence of text characters, such as a word or sentence. The text functions manipulate or create strings. Table 1.8 lists Excel's string functions.

The functions DOLLAR(*number,digits*) and FIXED(*number,digits,no-commas*) both round the value *number* to *digits* decimal places, and then convert it into a string of characters. If the *no-commas* argument is true, FIXED does not insert commas in the

TABLE 1.8: Excel's Text Functions

Function	Returns
	Numeric-Text Conversion Functions
DOLLAR( )	A number as text in currency format.
FIXED( )	A number as text, rounded the specified number of digits.
T( )	Convert the value to text.
TEXT( )	A number as a string using a specified string format.
VALUE( )	The value of a string representation of a number contained in the text.
	Text Manipulation Functions
CLEAN( )	Remove nonprintable characters from text.
CONCATENATE( )	Combine two or more strings together.
FIND( )	Locate a substring (case-sensitive).
LEFT( )	Extract characters from the left.

TABLE 1.8: Excel's Text Functions (continued)

Function	Returns
LEN( )	The number of characters in a string.
LOWER( )	Convert text to lowercase.
MID( )	Extract a substring.
PROPER( )	Capitalize the first letter of each word in a string.
REPLACE( )	Replace a substring.
RIGHT( )	Extract characters from the right.
SEARCH( )	Locate a substring (not case-sensitive).
SUBSTITUTE( )	Replace multiple substrings.
TRIM( )	Remove leading and trailing spaces.
UPPER( )	Convert text to uppercase.
String Creation Functions	
CHAR( )	The character specified by the ASCII code.
CODE( )	The ASCII code of a character.
REPT( )	Repeat a string.
String Comparison Function	
EXACT( )	Case-sensitive string comparison.

resulting string. The difference between them is that DOLLAR produces a number in currency format. As with the ROUND function, negative values of *digits* are rounded to the left of the decimal.

The function LEN(*text*) determines the length of the text string *text*. The functions MID(*text,start,number*), LEFT(*text,number*), and RIGHT(*text,number*) extract characters from within a string or from the ends. Characters are numbered with the first character as 1, the second as 2, and so on. The SUBSTITUTE(*text,old,new,num*) and REPLACE(*text,start,num,new*) functions replace substrings within a string. The SEARCH(*text1,text2,start*) and FIND(*text1,text2,start*) functions locate a substring within a string. The SEARCH function's search is not case sensitive; the FIND function's search is case sensitive.

Date and Time Functions

The date and time functions perform calculations and transformations of dates, times, and combinations of dates and times. Excel performs these calculations by converting the dates into a *serial date number*. A serial date number is the number of days since January 1, 1900 (or 1904 in Excel for Mac). All dates, whether entered by hand or returned by a formula, are stored in terms of these serial date numbers. To see the actual date that a number represents, format the cell containing it as a date.

A time value is also stored as a serial date number. Excel calculates times as the fractional part of a day, with midnight being time 0, noon being time 0.5, and so on. All times are stored as this fraction. To display the time associated with a fractional time number, format the cell as time.

Since dates and times are both expressed in days, you can combine them simply by adding them. To find the difference between any two dates and times, subtract one date-time number from the other. The result is in days and fractional days.

Table 1.9 lists Excel's date and time functions. The NOW and TODAY functions return the current date and time, or the current date as a serial date number.

Date Functions

The function DATE(*year,month,day*) converts the specified date into a serial date number. Use this function to create a date-time number from the year, month, and day.

The DATEVALUE(*text*) function converts the text representation of a date into a serial date number. Excel will also convert these two strings to serial date-time numbers when they are enclosed in quotation marks:

- "*month/day/year*", where *month*, *day* and *year* are numbers.
- "*day-month-year*", where *day* and *year* are numbers and *month* is the spelled out name or abbreviation of the name of the month.

You can use the DATEVALUE function or text string, as appropriate for your situation.

The functions YEAR(*number*), MONTH(*number*), and DAY(*number*) return the numeric value of the year, month of the year, and day of the month of the date specified by *number*. These three functions perform the inverse of the DATE function.

TABLE 1.9: Excel's Date and Time Functions

Function	Returns
	Current Date Functions
NOW( )	The serial date number of the current date and time.
TODAY( )	The serial date number for today's date.
	Date Functions
DATE( )	Serial date number for the year, month, and day.
DATEVALUE( )	Convert a date in text format to a serial date number.
DAY( )	The day of the month corresponding to the serial date number.
DAYS360( )	The number of days between two dates assuming a 360-day year.
EDATE( )*	The serial date number for the day that is the specified months before or after the specified date.
EOMONTH( )*	The serial date number for the last day of the month that is the specified months before or after the specified date.
MONTH( )	The month of the year corresponding to the serial date number.
NETWORKDAYS( )*	The number of workdays between two dates.
WEEKDAY( )	The day of the week corresponding to the serial date number. Sunday is 1 and Saturday is 7.
WEEKNUM( )*	The week number in the current year of a date.
WORKDAY( )*	The date a certain number of workdays in the future.
YEAR( )	The year corresponding to the serial date number.
YEARFRAC( )*	The fraction of a year the difference between two dates represents.
	Time Functions
HOUR( )	The hour of the day corresponding to the serial date number.
MINUTE( )	The minute of the hour corresponding to the serial date number.
SECOND( )	The second of the minute corresponding to the serial date number.
TIME( )	The serial date number for the hour, minute, and second.
TIMEVALUE( )	Convert a time in text format to a serial date number.

* These functions are part of the Analysis Toolpack Add-In.

The function WEEKDAY(*number*) returns a numeric value for the day of the week of the date specified with *number*. For this function, Sunday is 1 and Saturday is 7.

Time Functions

The time functions are similar to the date functions, except that they deal with the time of day rather than the date. The function TIME(*hour,minute,second*) returns the specified time as the decimal fraction of a day. Note that the arguments must be integers. Any fractional parts of these arguments are ignored. Thus, the smallest time that you can manipulate with these functions is the second.

The TIMEVALUE(*text*) function converts a time stored in a string into a serial date number. You could also use either of these strings, enclosed in quotation marks:

- "*hour:minute:second*", for 24-hour time, where *hour*, *minute*, and *second* are integers.

- "*hour:minute:second* PM", for 12-hour time, where *hour*, *minute*, and *second* are integers.

The functions HOUR(*number*), MINUTE(*number*), and SECOND(*number*) are the inverse of the TIME function. They return the hour, minute, and second corresponding to the time stored as *number*. Excel rounds all numbers to the nearest second.

Statistical Functions

The statistical functions are generally applied to sets of numbers, and they return statistical values. The statistical values not only include sums and deviations, but also some simple linear and exponential curve fitting. Several of the functions return an array as a result. Table 1.10 lists Excel's statistical functions.

Basic Statistics

The functions AVERAGE(*numlist*), and COUNT(*numlist*) operate on lists of values and return the average, and number of values in *numlist*, respectively. The functions MIN(*numlist*) and MAX(*numlist*) simply locate and return the minimum or maximum value in *numlist*. Cells containing blank, text, or logical values are ignored.

TABLE 1.10: Excel's Statistical Functions

Function	Returns
	Basic Statistics Functions
AVERAGE( )	The average of a list of values.
COUNT( )	The number of values in a list.
COUNTA( )	The number of nonblank cells in a list.
DEVSQ( )	Sum of squares of the deviations of the values in a list from their mean.
GEOMEAN( )	Geometric mean of the values in a list.
HARMEAN( )	Harmonic mean of the numbers in a list.
MAX( )	The maximum value in a list.
MEDIAN( )	Middle value in a list after it is ranked from high to low.
MIN( )	The minimum value in a list.
STDEV( )	The standard deviation of the values in a list.
STDEVP( )	The standard deviation of the values in a list, assuming it is the entire population.
VAR( )	Variance of the numbers in a list.
VARP( )	Variance of the numbers in a list, assuming it is the entire population.
	Advanced Statistics Functions
AVEDEV( )	Average deviation of the points in a list from their mean.
CORREL( )	Correlation coefficient between two lists.
CONFIDENCE( )	Population confidence interval.
COVAR( )	Covariance between two lists.
FISHER( )	Fisher transformation of a number.
FISHERINV( )	Inverse of the Fisher transformation of a number.
FREQUENCY( )	Frequency distribution of the values in a list.
KURT( )	Kurtosis of the values in a list.
LARGE( )	The kth largest value in a list.
MODE( )	The most common value in a list.
PEARSON( )	Pearson product moment correlation coefficient of two arrays.
PERCENTILE( )	Value from the kth percentile in a list.
PERCENTRANK( )	Percentage rank of the number in a list.
PERMUT( )	Number of permutations for objects chosen at a time from a specified number of objects.
PROB( )	Probability that the values in a list are between the lower and upper numbers.

TABLE 1.10: Excel's Statistical Functions (continued)

Function	Returns
QUARTILE( )	Quartile limits from a list.
RANK( )	The rank of a number in a list.
SMALL( )	The kth smallest value in a list.
STANDARDIZE( )	Normalizes a number with the mean and standard deviation.
TRIMMEAN( )	Mean of a list with specified percent points removed from the ends of the distribution.

Curve-Fitting Functions

Function	Returns
FORECAST( )	Extrapolates a value with a linear fit.
GROWTH( )	Extrapolates a value with an exponential fit.
INTERCEPT( )	The y-intercept of the linear-regression line.
LINEST( )	The slope and y-offset of a linear curve fit.
LOGEST( )	The parameters of an exponential curve fit.
RSQ( )	The goodness of the fit; r^2 value for a linear-regression line.
SLOPE( )	Slope of a linear-regression line.
STEYX( )	Standard error of the predicted y value for each x in a linear-regression line.
TREND( )	A list of predicted values from a linear curve fit.

Distribution Functions

Function	Returns
BETADIST( )	Cumulative beta probability density function.
BETAINV( )	Inverse of the cumulative beta probability density function.
BINOMDIST( )	Individual term in the binomial distribution.
CHIDIST( )	One-tailed probability of the Chi-squared (χ^2) distribution.
CHIINV( )	Inverse of the Chi-squared distribution.
EXPONDIST( )	Exponential distribution.
FDIST( )	F probability distribution.
FINV( )	Inverse of the F probability distribution.
GAMMADIST( )	Gamma distribution.
GAMMAINV( )	Inverse of the gamma cumulative distribution
GAMMALN( )	Natural logarithm of the gamma function.
HYPGEOMDIST( )	Hypergeometric distribution.
LOGINV( )	Inverse of the lognormal distribution.
LOGNORMDIST( )	Lognormal distribution.

TABLE 1.10: Excel's Statistical Functions (continued)

Function	Returns
NEGBINOMDIST( )	Negative binomial distribution.
NORMDIST( )	Normal cumulative distribution.
NORMINV( )	Inverse of the normal cumulative distribution.
NORMSDIST( )	Standard normal cumulative distribution.
NORMSINV( )	Inverse of the standard normal cumulative distribution
POISSON( )	Poisson probability distribution.
SKEW( )	Skewness of the distribution represented by the numbers in the list.
TDIST( )	Student's t-distribution.
TINV( )	Inverse of the Student's t-distribution.
WEIBULL( )	Weibull distribution.
	Significance Test Functions
CHITEST( )	Chi-squared test for the independence of two distributions.
CRITBINOM( )	Smallest value for which the cumulative binomial distribution is less than or equal to the criterion value.
FTEST( )	F-test on two distributions.
TTEST( )	Student's t-test for the significance of a coefficient.
ZTEST( )	Z-test, two-tailed P-value.

In addition to the average, the geometric mean is calculated with GEOMEAN(*numlist*), and the harmonic mean is calculated with HARMEAN(*numlist*). The median value in a distribution is returned by MEDIAN(*numlist*).

STDEV(*numlist*) calculates the sample standard deviation of the values in *numlist*. That is, it gives the best estimate of the standard deviation of a population, given the sample *numlist*. This value is computed using the following equation:

$$\sqrt{\frac{\sum_{i=1}^{N}\left(x_i - \bar{x}\right)^2}{N-1}}$$

where x is the average of the *n* values x_i.

If *numlist* is the whole population rather than a sample of the population, use STDEVP, which is computed using this equation:

$$\sqrt{\frac{\sum_{i=1}^{N}\left(x_i - \bar{x}\right)^2}{N}}$$

The variance function VAR(*numlist*) is just the square of the standard deviation. Thus, it gives the sample variance of a population. To get the population variance when *numlist* is equal to the whole population, use the VARP(*numlist*) function, which is the square root of the population standard deviation.

Advanced Statistical Functions

Excel's statistics functions include many of the more advanced functions for testing relationships between lists of numbers. For example, the CORREL(*numlist1,numlist2*) function calculates the correlation between two lists of numbers, and the COVAR(*numlist1,numlist2*) function returns the covariance.

Some of the advanced statistics functions work with ranked lists of values. For example, the LARGE(*numlist,k*) and SMALL(*numlist,k*) functions select values from the top and bottom of the list, respectively. The PERCENTRANK(*numlist,num,sig*) function gives the ranking of a new value.

Curve-Fitting Functions

Excel provides two types of curve fitting: linear and exponential. The functions, LINEST(*yarray,xarray*), TREND(*yarray,xarray,xlist*), and FORECAST(*x,yarray,xarray*) calculate a linear least-squares curve fit to the *x,y* data in *xarray* and *yarray*.

The LINEST function returns a two-element horizontal array containing the slope (*m*) and *y*-intercept (*b*) of the line: $y = mx + b$. The TREND and FORECAST functions return the estimated *y* values obtained by inserting the *x* values in *xlist* (or *xarray* if *xlist* is not supplied) into the equation of the line. The TREND function returns an array of *y* values; FORECAST returns only one value. In both functions, if *xarray* is not supplied, it is assumed to be equal to the list of values: 1, 2, 3,…. As with other functions that return arrays of values, you must hold down the Ctrl and

Shift keys when entering them to place the function into a list of output cells rather than a single cell.

Exponential curve fits are calculated with the functions LOGEST(*yarray,xarray*) and GROWTH(*yarray,xarray,xlist*). These two functions operate in the same manner as the linear curve fitting functions, except that they calculate the fit to the exponential growth curve rather than to a linear curve: $y = bm^x$.

The growth curve coefficients are calculated by taking the natural logarithm of the *yarray* data, applying the LINEST function, and then taking the exponential of the results after getting the coefficients *m* and *b*:

```
EXP(LINEST(LN(yarray),xarray))
```

This formula must be inserted into two cells as an array function. It gives the same result as the GROWTH function.

However, if the range of values in *yarray* is large (with orders of magnitude between the largest and smallest values), the curve fit will be skewed. The smaller values will have more weight (be more closely fitted) than the larger values. This is because the fit is to the logarithm of the *y* data rather than to the data itself.

The least-squares method minimizes the residual error (the difference between the data and the curve fit). In this case, the formula minimizes the difference in the logarithms of the *y* data rather than the *y* data itself. Since the logarithm is a nonlinear function, the residual error will be larger for larger values of the *y* data. On the other hand, the percent error will be roughly constant for all values of the *y* data.

Distribution and Significance Test Functions

Excel's distribution functions produce values for most of the common distributions used for testing the significance of values, as well as for predicting the lifetime or failure rate of products. The distributions include binomial (BINOMDIST), Chi-squared (CHIDIST), F (FDIST), gamma (GAMMADIST), hypergeometric (HYPGEOMDIST), normal (NORMSDIST), Poisson (POISSON), T (TDIST), and Weibull (WEIBULL).

Along with the distribution functions are functions for significance tests based on the Chi-squared, F, T, and Z distributions. These tests check the significance of values, the regression coefficients, and the dependence or independence of different distributions of values.

Database Functions

The calculations of the database functions are the same as those of the basic statistical functions; however, the database functions are applied to values selected from a database using selection criteria. A *database* is a rectangular area of cells on a worksheet. Each row in the database is a *record*, and each column is a *field*.

Table 1.11 lists Excel's database functions. These functions all take the same three

TABLE 1.11: Excel's Database Functions

Function	Returns
DAVERAGE( )	The average of the values in a field for records that match criteria.
DCOUNT( )	The number of records in a database that match criteria.
DCOUNTA( )	The number of records in a database that match criteria and contain values in a field, ignoring blanks.
DGET( )	Extract a single record that matches criteria.
DMAX( )	The maximum of the values in a field for records that match criteria.
DMIN( )	The minimum of the values in a field for records that match criteria.
DPRODUCT( )	Multiply the values in records that match criteria.
DSTDEV( )	The sample standard deviation of the values in a field for records that match criteria.
DSTDEVP( )	The population standard deviation of the values in a field for records that match criteria.
DSUM( )	The sum of the values in a field for records that match criteria.
DVAR( )	The sample variance of the values in a field for records that match criteria.

arguments: the database name, the field name or the column number of the field to act on, and the criteria. Only records that match the criteria are processed by the database functions. Working with Excel databases will be discussed in Chapter 5.

In addition to accessing a database on a worksheet, Excel can access an external database using the JET database engine. Most popular database formats can be queried.

Financial Functions

The financial functions are useful for keeping track of your investments or calculating the cost of refinancing your mortgage. A good book on accounting or management theory will explain the uses of the financial functions. Excel's financial functions are listed in Table 1.12.

You can refer to a book about accounting for more information about the calculations of the financial functions.

TABLE 1.12: Excel's Financial Functions

Function	Returns
Annuity Functions	
CUMIPMT( )	Cumulative interest paid between the specified starting and ending periods.
CUMPRINC( )	Cumulative principal paid between the specified ending and starting periods.
FV( )	Future value of an annuity.
FVSCHEDULE( )	Future value of an annuity after a scheduled series of interest rates.
IPMT( )	The interest payment for an investment for a given period.
NPER( )	Number of periods of an annuity.
PMT( )	Payment of an annuity.
PPMT( )	Principal paid in a specific payment.
PV( )	Present value of an annuity.
RATE( )	Interest rate returned of an annuity.
Investment Functions	
ACCRINT( )	Accrued interest for a security that pays periodically.
AMORDEGRC( )	Prorated linear depreciation of an asset for a period.
AMORLINC( )	Prorated linear depreciation of an asset for a period.
ACCRINTM( )	Accrued interest for a security that pays at maturity.
COUPDAYBS( )	Days from the beginning of the coupon period to the settlement date.
COUPDAYS( )	Days in the coupon period that contains the settlement date.
COUPDAYSNC( )	Days from the settlement date to the next coupon date.
COUPNCD( )	Next coupon date after the settlement date.
COUPNUM( )	Number of coupons payable between the settlement date and maturity date.
COUPPCD( )	Coupon date before the settlement date.

TABLE 1.12: Excel's Financial Functions (continued)

Function	Returns
DISC( )	Discount rate for a security.
DURATION( )	Macauley duration for a security with periodic interest payments and an assumed par value of $100.
EFFECT( )	Effective annual interest rate.
INTRATE( )	Interest rate for a fully invested security.
MDURATION( )	Modified Macauley duration for a security with an assumed par value of $100.
NOMINAL( )	Nominal annual interest rate.
ODDFPRICE( )	Price per $100 face value of a security with a short or long first period.
ODDFYIELD( )	Yield of a security with a short or long first period.
ODDLPRICE( )	Price per $100 face value of a security with a short or long last period.
ODDLYIELD( )	Yield of a security with a short or long last period.
PRICE( )	Price per $100 face value of a security that pays periodic interest.
PRICEDISC( )	Price per $100 face value of a discounted security.
PRICEMAT( )	Price per $100 face value of a security that pays interest at maturity.
RECEIVED( )	Amount received at maturity for a fully invested security.
TBILLEQ( )	Bond-equivalent yield for a Treasury bill.
TBILLPRICE( )	Price per $100 face value for a Treasury bill.
TBILLYIELD( )	Yield for a Treasury bill.
YIELD( )	Yield on a security that pays periodic interest.
YIELDDISC( )	Annual yield for a discounted security.
YIELDMAT( )	Annual yield of a security that pays interest at maturity.

Depreciation Functions

DB( )	Declining-balance depreciation for an asset using a fixed rate.
DDB( )	Double-declining-balance depreciation for an asset.
SLN( )	Straight-line depreciation for an asset.
SYD( )	Sum-of-years'-digits depreciation for an asset.
VDB( )	Variable-declining-balance depreciation for an asset.

Other Business Functions

DOLLARDE( )	Converts a dollar price expressed as a fraction into a dollar price expressed as a decimal number (for example, 1-1/8 to 1.125).

TABLE 1.12: Excel's Financial Functions (continued)

Function	Returns
DOLLARFR( )	Converts a dollar price expressed as a decimal number into a dollar price expressed as a fraction (for example, 1.125 to 1⅛ dollar).
IRR( )	Internal rate of return for the payments.
MIRR( )	Modified internal rate of return for the payments.
NPV( )	Net present value of the values.
XIRR( )	Internal rate of return for cash flows on the specified dates.
XNPV( )	Net present value of the cash flows on the specified dates.

Information Functions

You can use the information functions in combination with the logical functions to examine the contents of a cell, to check its type, or to get its location or reference. Excel's information functions are listed in Table 1.13.

The function TYPE(*value*) returns the type of *value*: 1 for a number, 2 for text, 4 for a logical value, 16 for an error value, and 64 for an array. You can use the TYPE function to ensure that values are of the correct type before performing operations with them.

The other logical test functions—ISBLANK, ISERR, ISERROR, and so on—test the content of values for specific types. They return True if the value is the specified type and False if it is not.

Lookup and Reference Functions

The lookup and reference functions allow you to manipulate or examine areas on the worksheet. These functions are listed in Table 1.14.

Table and Vector Lookup Functions

The CHOOSE(*index,value1,value2,…*) function uses the value *index* to pick a value from the list *value1,value2,…*. If *index* is 1, *value1* is returned, if *index* is 2, *value2* is returned, and so forth. If *index* is less than 1 or larger than the number of values, the function returns #VALUE!.

TABLE 1.13: Excel's Information Functions

Function	Returns
CELL( )	Gets information about the contents, formatting, or location of a cell.
ERROR.TYPE( )	An error number that corresponds to the type of error value the error is.
INFO( )	Gets information about the operating environment.
ISBLANK( )	TRUE if the argument is a reference to a blank cell.
ISERR( )	TRUE if the argument is any error value but #N/A.
ISERROR( )	TRUE if the argument is one of the error values (#N/A, #REF!, #DIV/0!, #NUM!, #VALUE!, #NAME?, or #NULL!).
ISEVEN( )*	TRUE if the argument is an even number.
ISLOGICAL( )	TRUE if the argument is a logical value.
ISNA( )	TRUE if the argument is the error value #N/A.
ISNONTEXT( )	TRUE if the argument is not text string.
ISNUMBER( )	TRUE if the argument is a number.
ISODD( )*	TRUE if the argument is an odd number.
ISREF( )	TRUE if the argument is a cell reference.
ISTEXT( )	TRUE if the argument is a text string.
N( )	Converts values to numbers.
NA( )	Returns the error value #N/A.
TYPE( )	Gets information about the type of number stored in the value.

*These functions are part of the Analysis Toolpack Add-In.

The table lookup functions are HLOOKUP, VLOOKUP, and LOOKUP. Use them to search a tabular function or data table for particular values. If range_lookup is True or missing, HLOOKUP(*value,array,index,range_lookup*) and VLOOKUP(*value,array, index,range_lookup*) search the first row or column of *array* for the greatest value that is less than or equal to *value*. They then move down that column or row by *index* cells and return the value there. *Value* can be a numeric value, text string, or logical value. HLOOKUP looks from left to right, so the values in the first row of *array* must be in ascending order. VLOOKUP searches from the top down, so the values in the first column of *array* must be in ascending order as you move down the column. Ascending order is numbers first, then text, then logical false values, then logical true values. If *range_lookup* is False, the values can be in any order and

TABLE 1.14: Excel's Lookup and Reference Functions

Function	Returns
	Table and Vector Lookup Functions
CHOOSE( )	Selects a value from a set of values, based on an index value.
HLOOKUP( )	Looks up a value in a horizontal array.
INDEX( )	Selects a value in the specified row, column, and area.
LOOKUP( )	Locates a value in an array.
MATCH( )	Locates the position of a value in a vector.
TRANSPOSE( )	The matrix transpose of an array.
VLOOKUP( )	Looks up a value in a vertical array.
	Reference Characteristics
ADDRESS( )	The reference as text to the cell at the intersection of a specified row and column.
AREAS( )	The number of areas in a cell reference.
COLUMN( )	A vector of column numbers, one for each column in a cell reference.
COLUMNS( )	The number of columns in an array.
INDIRECT( )	The contents of a reference to a reference.
OFFSET( )	A reference that is offset from a cell.
ROW( )	A vector of row numbers, one for each row in a reference.
ROWS( )	The number of rows in a reference.

these functions only return a value if they find an exact match, otherwise they return #N/A.

If *range_lookup* is true or missing, the LOOKUP (*value,vector1,vector2,range_lookup*) function scans *vector1* for the largest value that is less than or equal to *value* and returns the corresponding value from *vector2*. As with VLOOKUP and HLOOKUP, the values in *vector1* must be in ascending order unless *range_lookup* is False; then the values can be in any order and LOOKUP only returns a value if it finds an exact match (otherwise it returns #N/A).

Another version of the LOOKUP function is included to make Excel compatible with Microsoft Multiplan. The LOOKUP(*value,array*) function searches the first row or column of *array* for the greatest value that is less than or equal to *value* and returns the corresponding value in the last row or column of *array*. It looks in the longest side of *array*. If *array* has more columns than rows, its first row will be searched. If *array* has more rows than columns, the first column will be searched. If the array is square, it is searched along its first column.

The MATCH(*value,vector,type*) function is similar to the LOOKUP function, except that it returns the index number of the looked-up value. The argument *type* determines how *value* is compared to the values in *vector* to determine a match. If *type* is 1, the largest value that is less than or equal to *value* is located. If *type* is –1, the smallest value that is greater than or equal to *value* is located. If *type* is 0, the value that is equal to *value* is located. Use 0 for *type* to search text strings for matching strings. Locate a string that contains a specific substring by using the wildcard characters × and ?. The function matches only the first occurrence of the string or substring, not any later occurrences.

One of the more useful lookup functions is INDEX(*ref,row,column*), which returns the value at the intersection of *row* and *column* of *ref*. Use it to select values in an array according to the row and column indices. If *ref* contains multiple areas, add a fourth argument *area*, to determine which area of *ref* to use. If *ref* is a simple vector, only one index is needed. The indices are all base one, so the first row is number 1, the second column is number 2, and so on. If the requested row or column number is negative, the function returns #VALUE!. If the requested row or column number is too large, INDEX returns #N/A.

Reference Characteristics Functions

The AREAS(*ref*) function returns the number of areas in the cell reference *ref*. An area is a continuous rectangular region on the worksheet

The functions COLUMN(*ref*), COLUMNS(*array*), ROW(*ref*), and ROWS(*array*) return information about the rows and columns in a cell reference. COLUMN returns a vector containing the column references for each column in *ref*. ROW returns a vector containing the row references for each row in *ref*. COLUMNS and ROWS return the number of columns or rows in *array*.

Visual Basic for Applications Functions

The Visual Basic for Applications programming language is built into Excel. Using that language, you can create almost any numerical function and make it available to a cell on an Excel worksheet. Visual Basic for Applications is discussed in Chapter 4.

Add-In Functions and Tools

Note that more functions and tools are available as add-ins, which must be attached to Excel before they can be used. To attach an add-in, use the Tools ➤ Add-Ins command to access the Add-In Manager, shown below. Check the add-in file you want and choose OK. After you attach the add-in files, you can use the attached functions and tools. Of primary interest to scientists and engineers is the Analysis Toolpack, which contains all the Engineering functions plus some of the functions in the other tables listed here, and adds several statistical tools to Excel.

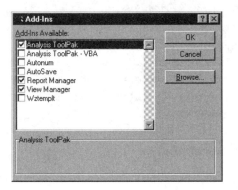

External Functions

In addition to internal functions and functions coded in macro sheets, Excel can access subroutines stored in external Dynamic Link Libraries (DLLs). It can also pass values to and from other programs by using Dynamic Data Exchange (DDE), Visual Basic for Applications, and Object Linking and Embedding (OLE). Using these features, you can create a custom function in another program and then access it from within Excel.

TABLE 1.15: Excel's Analysis Toolpack Add-In Programs

Program	Description
Anova: Single Factor	Single-factor analysis of variance.
Anova: Two factor with replication.	Two-factor analysis of variance with replication.
Anova: Two-factor without replication.	Two-factor analysis of variance without replication.
Correlation	Calculate correlation coefficients.
Covariance	Calculate the covariance.
Descriptive statistics	Multiple statistics about a sample.
Exponential smoothing	Forecasting with error analysis.
F-test two-sample for variances	Two-sample F-test.
Fourier analysis	Fourier transform analysis.
Histogram	Calculate the data for a histogram chart.
Moving average	Moving average of a sample.
Random number generator	Generate random numbers from selected distributions.
Rank and percentile	Table of ranking of a data set.
Regression	Multiple linear regression.
Sampling	Sample a data set.
T-test paired two-sample for means	Two-Sample student's t-test for means.
T-test, two-sample assuming equal variances	Two-sample Student's t-test for equal variances.
T-test, two-sample assuming unequal variances	Two-sample Student's t-test for equal variances.
Z-test , two-sample for Means	Two-sample Z-test for means and known variances.

To use an external function, Declare it in a Visual Basic for Applications module, or use the CALL(*file,function,type,args*) function. *File* is the DLL file name, *function* is the name of the function in the DLL file, *type* is the data type of the returned value, and *args* are the arguments to be passed to the function.

NOTE On the Macintosh, you access the contents of a CODE resource to access a function in an external procedure.

You need to know how the external function operates in order to call and use it. Generally, you must test the values you plan to pass to ensure that they are valid and of the correct type. If you use bad arguments, you may hang the program in the external library and crash your system. The advantage of external functions is that they operate much faster than functions implemented with Visual Basic for Applications.

Solver

The Solver program is a tool that uses the method of steepest descents to locate the roots of a formula. By carefully crafting your formulas, you can use Solver to solve them.

Summary

This chapter briefly examined the usability of Excel as the calculational engine for solving scientific and engineering problems. As you have seen, Excel is well-equipped to handle calculations in science, engineering, mathematics, and statistics. Its numeric precision and range compare well with the other computational engines for scientific and engineering calculations.

In addition to raw computational capability, a program for performing scientific and engineering calculations must have a minimum set of built-in functions to speed the setup of a technical calculation. Excel has all the standard mathematical functions available in high-level computer languages, plus many more that are usually found only in expensive engineering subroutine libraries. Refer to Excel's on-line help for more information about the functions and their arguments.

TIP

If you are unsure how a function works, experiment with it on the worksheet by trying different values as arguments to see the result. Better yet, experiment with the functions even if you *do* think you know how they work, because the documentation may be wrong. As in science and engineering, the final proof is in the experiment.

For More Information

Mathematical Formulas

S. M. Selby, *CRC Standard Math Tables*, (Cleveland, OH: The Chemical Rubber Co., 1970).

Statistical Formulas

C. Lipson and N. J. Sheth, *Statistical Design and Analysis of Engineering Experiments* (New York: McGraw-Hill, 1973).

R. M. Bethea, B. S. Duran, and T. L. Boullion, *Statistical Methods for Scientists and Engineers* (New York: Marcel Dekker, 1975).

Review Problems

1. Cell G5, which contains a reference to cell H2, is copied to cell J7.

   a. How is the reference adjusted when cell G5 is copied to another location?

   b. How should the reference to cell H2 be written so that it will not be adjusted when it is copied?

   c. How should the reference to cell H2 be written so that the row number will be adjusted but the column letter will not?

   d. How should the reference to cell H2 be written so that the column letter will be adjusted but the row number will not?

   e. How is the reference adjusted if you move the contents of the cell instead of copying the cell?

2. With what character must a formula begin?

3. If cell G5 contains a formula with a reference to cell H2, and you copy it to cell B25, to what cell will the reference in the copy point?

4. To what cells does the cell range B4:C8 refer?

5. If A1 = True, and B1 = False, what are the results of the following formulas?

```
=AND(OR(AND(A1,A1),A1),B1)
=OR(AND(A1,A1),AND(A1,B1))
```

6. Write a string formula that combines the strings "My name is" and "Bill".

7. Write a formula that calculates the common logarithm (base 10) of the value in cell A7.

8. Write a formula that calculates the secant of 10 degrees.

9. Write two different formulas that both add the contents of cells B1, B2, B3, B4, and B5.

10. If cell A1 contains the string "Excel for Scientists and Engineers":

   a. Write a formula that extracts the string "Excel" from cell A1.

   b. Write a formula that extracts the string "Engineers" from cell A1.

   c. Write a formula that extracts the string "Scientists" from cell A1.

   d. Write a formula that replaces the string "Scientists" with the string "Dogs" and the string "Engineers" with the string "Horses".

Exercises

1. Cell R34 contains the formula:

```
=P34*3+$R$7*N34
```

   a. If the cell is copied and pasted into cell F40, how does the formula change?

   b. If the cell is cut and pasted into cell F40, how does the formula change?

2. Cell D3 contains the formula:

```
=4*$C3+3*B$2
```

   a. If the cell is copied down into cells D4:D6, what is the formula in each of those cells?

   b. If the cell is copied right into cells E3:G3, what is the formula in each of those cells?

   c. If the cell is copied into cell G6, what formula does cell G6 contain?

3. If I have a formula in cell B3 and I want to copy it into cells B4:B15, how do I do that using the mouse?

4. Write an Excel formula to calculate the tangent of 37 degrees.

5. Write an Excel formula to calculate the arcsecant in radians of 8.5.

6. Cells A1:A4 have the following contents:

    A1: "Excel"

    A2: " for "

    A3: "Scientists"

    A4: "Engineers"

    Write a cell formula that evaluates to the title of this book, using the values in cells A1:A4.

7. Write a formula for calculating the standard deviation for a range of cells containing blanks. Ignore cells containing blanks. Compare that to the result calculated with the STDEV( )function.

8. Describe two ways to name a single cell. Describe how to name all the cells in a group when the names for the cells are to their left.

9. Write a formula for the following equation:

    $$Ax^2 + By^2$$

    Write the formula so that it can be copied into a rectangular region with the x values across the top of the region, the y values down the left side of the region, and the two coefficients A and B in two cells outside the region. Write the formula so that it can be copied anywhere in the region and always refers to the correct cells, creating a table for the values of x and y along the edges.

10. What happens if a date is typed as a string into a formula? For example, what is the result of the following formula?

    ="1/1/95" + 5

    What is the result if the cell containing this formula is formatted as a date?

CHAPTER

TWO

2

Engineering Tables

- Using Excel's controls

- Calculating single values

- Calculating lists of values

- Calculating tables using copied formulas

- Calculating tables using the Table command

- Creating function calculators

The first chapter described Excel's potential to be an exceptional engineering tool. This chapter will start putting that potential to work. You will start by calculating the values of simple analytical equations, and continue with more complicated engineering tables. As you develop each example, you will slowly expand your repertoire of modeling methods to use more of the power and functionality of Excel.

As scientists and engineers, we must frequently take an analytical equation, put numbers into it, and calculate the result. This task is not difficult, and calculators do it well. You don't need to resort to an expensive worksheet to calculate the value of a single equation. For most equations, a hand calculator can complete this task long before your computer even finishes booting. But if you want to use the same equation with many sets of numbers, and create a table of calculated results, a calculator starts looking a lot less attractive. A worksheet, on the other hand, is designed for problems of this type, and will perform faster, more easily, and more accurately.

Using Excel's Controls

To start a new problem, begin with a blank worksheet in a new workbook. Start Excel, or if you have been experimenting, close the current workbook by choosing File ➤ Close or by clicking the Close box in the upper-right corner of the workbook window. If the window is maximized, click the Close box on the right side of the menu bar (on the Macintosh, click on the window's close box). If there is something in the workbook that you want to keep, save it with the Save command on the File menu before you close its window. To open a new workbook, choose File ➤ New, choose Workbook, and choose OK. Your screen should now look like Figure 2.1.

Along the top of the screen just below the title bar is the menu bar, and just below that is the Standard toolbar. Each of the buttons on the toolbar executes a different command, as if it were selected from a menu or dialog box. The Standard toolbar, shown in Figure 2.2, contains buttons for opening and closing workbooks, cut, copy, paste and undo commands, buttons to start the wizards and to control the magnification of the visible worksheet (shown is the Excel 5 toolbar; in Excel for Windows 95, the Text Box button is replaced by the Map button). To see what a tool does, place the mouse pointer on it; a pop-up label describes its function. In addition, a longer description appears in the status bar along the bottom of the screen (just above the Windows 95 taskbar). To execute an attached command, simply

Workbooks and Worksheets

Users of earlier versions of Excel will notice the emphasis on workbooks instead of worksheets. In versions of Excel prior to version 5, the primary object and file was the worksheet. Workbooks were available, but you had to create them separately and then insert worksheets into them. Starting with version 5, the workbook became the primary object. A workbook opens initially with 16 blank worksheets attached to it, which are selected with the sheet tabs along the bottom of the window. Saving a workbook saves all the attached worksheets together in a single file.

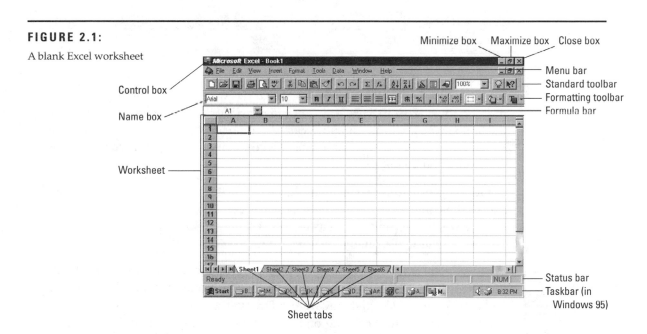

FIGURE 2.1:

A blank Excel worksheet

click its button on the toolbar. Below the Standard toolbar is the Formatting toolbar. The Formatting toolbar contains buttons for setting the appearance of text and numbers on the screen.

There are 13 different toolbars built into Excel (shown in Figure 2.3). Most of the toolbars are tied to a particular sheet type and are automatically displayed when

FIGURE 2.2:

Excel's built-in toolbars

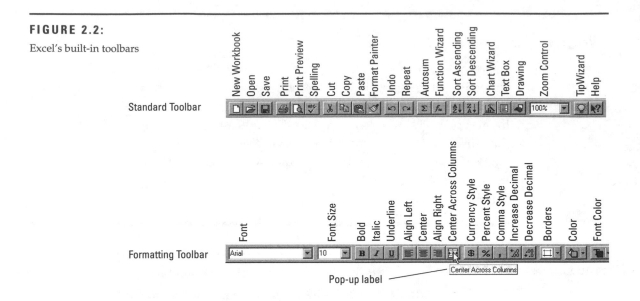

the sheet is active. For example, the Visual Basic toolbar is usually visible when a module sheet is the active sheet. You can override this behavior and display any of the toolbars at any time using the View ➤ Toolbars command. In addition, you can create custom toolbars that use existing commands or commands you create for yourself using Visual Basic for Applications.

Below the Formatting toolbar in Figure 2.1 is the formula bar. The formula bar shows the contents of the currently selected cell (the *active* cell), and is where you type or edit values and formulas in cells. Whatever you type in the formula bar is inserted in the active cell on the worksheet.

While you are editing a formula in the formula bar, three buttons appear to the left of the formula. The button with an *x* in it is an undo button, which returns the contents of the cell to what they were before you started editing. The second button has a checkmark in it; clicking on the checkmark button accepts the changes you made and stores the contents of the formula bar in the active cell. Clicking on the checkmark button is the same as pressing the Enter key on the keyboard. The third button is a function wizard button. The Function Wizard lists all the available functions and their arguments, and inserts the function into your formula when you choose Finish.

FIGURE 2.3:

Excel's built-in toolbars

Standard ——
Formatting ——
Query & Pivot ——
Drawing ——
TipWizard ——
Forms ——
Visual Basic ——
Workgroup ——
Auditing ——
Microsoft ——
Chart ——
Stop Recording ——
Full Screen ——

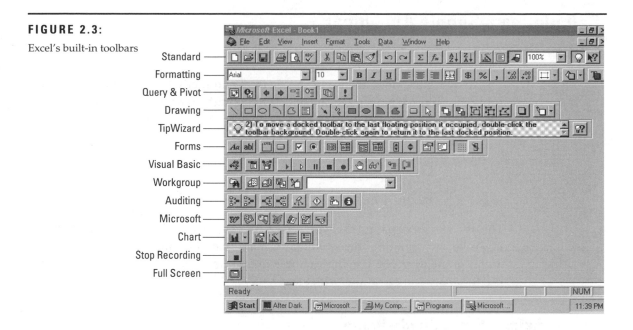

On the far left side of the formula bar is the Name box. The Name box contains the name of the current selection. If the selection is not named, the Name box contains the cell reference of the current selection. You can use the Name box to name the current selection: select a cell or cells, type a name into the Name box and press Enter.

WARNING

If you don't press Enter after typing a name in the Name box, but instead click on some other cell, the name is lost.

SHORTCUT

To quickly locate a named cell or cell range, choose the name from the drop down list in the Name box. The cells with the chosen name will be selected.

Calculating a Simple Analytical Equation

The temperature dependence of the thermal conductivity of silicon for temperatures between 200 and 700 K can be described with an analytical equation:

$$K(T) = \frac{K_0}{(T - T_0)}$$

where $K_0 = 350W/cm$, and $T_0 = 68$ K.

This is a simple equation that you can calculate quickly with your hand calculator; however, recalculating the equation for many temperatures takes a lot more time and is prone to errors. Use this example to examine the methods of calculating values for analytical equations with Excel.

Calculating a Single Value

First calculate a single value: the thermal conductivity at room temperature.

1. Start with a blank worksheet.

2. Make cell B5 the active cell, by clicking on it with the mouse or by using the arrow keys.

3. Type =350/(300–68)

	A	B	C	D
1				
2				
3				
4				
5		=350/(300-68)		
6				
7				
8				
9				

4. Press Enter.

	A	B	C	D
1				
2				
3				
4				
5		1.508621		
6				
7				
8				
9				

As soon as you press Enter, the number 1.508621 appears in cell B5. This is the result of letting T be 300 K (room temperature) in the thermal-conductivity equation. You can check it with your calculator (or a slide rule, if you have one).

Using Cell References in Formulas

You can insert other temperatures into this formula by selecting cell B5 and editing the value of the temperature in the formula bar. When you press Enter, Excel recalculates the formula using the new value. This method of changing the temperature is a bit cumbersome, though. To make it easier to change the value, move the temperature from the formula to an adjacent cell and then reference that cell in the formula.

> **TIP**
> If you click the checkmark box on the formula bar instead of pressing Enter, the active cell does not move down to the next cell.

1. Select cell B5.

2. Change the 300 in the formula to the cell reference **A5** and press Enter. The formula in cell B5 should now be

   =350/(A5−68)

3. Select cell A5.

4. Type **300** and press Enter.

	A	B	C	D
1				
2				
3				
4				
5	300	1.508621		
6				
7				
8				
9				

SHORTCUT To quickly insert a cell reference for the 300 in cell B5, select the 300 and click on cell A5. The reference to cell A5 is inserted into the formula.

Cell B5 again has the value 1.508621. Changing the temperature in the formula is now simple; whatever temperature you enter into cell A5 is used by the formula in cell B5, and the formula is recalculated. Using cell references instead of values in formulas is much easier than editing the formula every time you want to change values. This formula structure is the basis for building engineering tables with Excel.

Calculating a List of Values

Suppose you want to calculate the thermal-conductivity equation for a list of different temperatures. You could enter the list of temperature values one at a time in cell A5 and then write down the results of each calculation, but working with lists of data is what a spreadsheet does best.

Now use Excel to calculate the thermal conductivity every 50 degrees between 200 and 700 K. First you need to create the list of temperatures to be inserted in the formula.

1. Select cell A5.

2. Type **200** and press Enter.

3. Select cell A6, type **250** and press Enter.

Instead of typing the remaining values, use the fill handle (the small black box in the lower right corner of the active selection) to fill the cells with evenly spaced values.

4. Select cells A5 and A6 by placing the mouse pointer on cell A5 and holding down the left mouse button while dragging down to cell A6, then release the mouse button.

	A	B	C	D
1				
2				
3				
4				
5	200	2.651515		
6	250			
7				
8				
9				
10				
11				
12				
13				
14				
15				
16				

5. Select the fill handle, drag it down to cell A15, and release the mouse button.

Excel senses the difference between cells A5 and A6, and repeats that difference down the selected cells. The cells are filled with a range of numbers from 200 to 700 in steps of 50. Now copy the formula in cell B5 down into the cells adjacent to the temperature data.

	A	B	C	D
1				
2				
3				
4				
5	200	2.651515		
6	250			
7	300			
8	350			
9	400			
10	450			
11	500			
12	550			
13	600			
14	650			
15	700			
16				

6. Select cell B5 and drag its fill handle down to cell B15.

	A	B	C	D
1				
2				
3				
4				
5	200	2.651515		
6	250	1.923077		
7	300	1.508621		
8	350	1.241135		
9	400	1.054217		
10	450	0.91623		
11	500	0.810185		
12	550	0.726141		
13	600	0.657895		
14	650	0.601375		
15	700	0.553797		
16				

Excel copied the formula from cell B5 into the range of cells B5:B15 and then evaluated each formula. If you look at the contents of cells B5 through B15, you see that the relative cell reference that you used for the temperature was adjusted so that it always points to the cell immediately to the left of the cell containing the formula.

Extracting the Coefficients

Now suppose you want to change the coefficients in the formula to see what happens to the thermal conductivity. You could change the values in cell B5 and then copy the new formula into the rest of the cells (copying into a cell that already has data causes the old data to be replaced by the new data); however, this becomes cumbersome if you want to try several different values for the coefficients. A better way is to take the coefficients out of the formula and replace them with absolute cell references.

SHORTCUT To quickly change the 350 in the formula into an absolute cell reference, select the 350 and then click on cell B2 to insert the cell reference into the formula. Then, press the F4 key to change B2 into an absolute cell reference ($B$2). Pressing the F4 key while the insertion point is touching a cell reference cycles the cell reference through all four possible reference types repeatedly.

1. In cell B5, type =$B$2/(A5–$B$3) and press Enter.
2. In cell B2, type 350 and press Enter.

3. In cell B3, type **68** and press Enter.

You made the cell references for the coefficients absolute so that you can copy the formula into cells B6 through B15. The absolute cell references for the coefficients are not adjusted in the copies; they always point to the coefficients in cells B2 and B3.

4. Select cell B5 and drag the fill handle down to cell B15.

The worksheet should now look like Figure 2.4. You can insert other values of K_0 and T_0 by changing the contents of cells B2 and B3. Your change will be applied to all the formulas in cells B5 through B15.

Dressing Up the Worksheet

To anyone but us, the worksheet shown in Figure 2.4 is meaningless, and even we will not know what it is all about in a month or two. You need to add some titles and labels so that anyone (including us) will know what is being calculated.

By now, you know that you must press the Enter key, press one of the arrow keys, or click the checkmark box on the formula bar to enter a value into a cell or to complete a command. From now on, the instructions will indicate the Enter key-presses only when they are not obvious.

Enter Labels   Begin by entering informational labels.

1. In cell A1, enter the title: **Thermal Conductivity of Silicon**

FIGURE 2.4:

Calculating the thermal-conductivity equation for a list of data with modifiable coefficients

	A	B	C	D
1				
2		350		
3		68		
4				
5	200	2.661616		
6	250	1.923077		
7	300	1.508621		
8	350	1.241135		
9	400	1.054217		
10	450	0.91623		
11	500	0.810185		
12	550	0.726141		
13	600	0.657895		
14	650	0.601375		
15	700	0.553797		
16				

2. In cell A2, enter **K0**

3. In cell A3, enter **T0**

	A	B	C	D
1	Thermal Conductivity of Silicon			
2	K0	350		
3	T0	68		
4				
5		200	2.651515	

Align the Labels   You need to right-align the labels in cells A2 and A3. The commands for formatting cells, such as setting the font, size, and color, are on the Format Cells dialog box, accessed with the Format ➤ Cells menu command. Most of the more common formatting commands are also available on the Formatting toolbar (see Figure 2.2).

1. Select cells A2 and A3.

2. Click on the Align Right button on the Formatting toolbar. Alternatively, choose Format ➤ Cells, click the Alignment tab, select the Right option, and then click OK.

	A	B	C	D
1	Thermal Conductivity of Silicon			
2	K0	350		
3	T0	68		
4				
5		200	2.651515	

Center the Headings   Put centered headings on the two columns of data.

1. In cell A4, enter **T (K)**

NOTE   A new feature in Excel for Windows 95 is AutoComplete, which makes data entry easier by completing your entries for you based on previous entries in the same column. In this case, when you type the **T**, AutoComplete fills in a **0** (which you entered earlier). Just ignore the AutoComplete entry and continue typing. If AutoComplete begins to annoy you, you can turn it off (choose Tools ➤ Options, click the Edit tab, and clear the Enable AutoComplete For Cell Values checkbox).

2. In cell B4, enter **K (W/cm–K)**

3. Select cells A4 and B4.

4. Click on the Center button in the Formatting toolbar.

	A	B	C	D
1	Thermal Conductivity of Silicon			
2	K0	350		
3	T0	68		
4	T (K)	K (W/cm-K)		
5	200	2.651515		

Widen the Columns and Reduce Decimal Places   The label in cell B4 does not fit within the cell, and the numbers in column B are displayed with far too many decimal places. Widen the column to make the title fit and format the numbers to have fewer decimal places.

1. Move the mouse pointer to the vertical line that separates the B and C column headings. The pointer changes to a vertical line with two opposing horizontal arrows.

	A	B	C	D
1	Thermal Conductivity of Silicon			
2	K0	350		
3	T0	68		
4	T (K)	K (W/cm-K)		
5	200	2.651515		

2. Hold down the left mouse button and drag the right edge of the column B heading to the right about a half-inch, then release the mouse button. While you are dragging the column, its width shows on the left side of the formula bar. Repeat the dragging procedure until you can see the whole label.

	A	B	C	D
1	Thermal Conductivity of Silicon			
2	K0	350		
3	T0	68		
4	T (K)	K (W/cm-K)		
5	200	2.65151515		

3. Select cells B5:B15, then choose the Format ➤ Cells command and click the Number tab.

4. Select the Number Category with two decimal places, and choose OK.

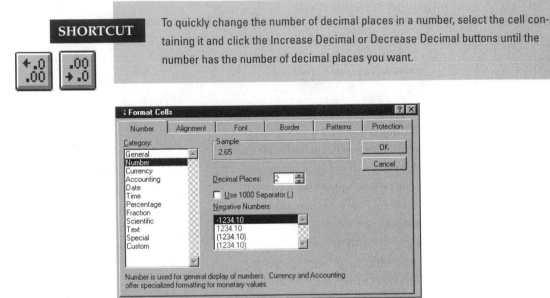

Add Borders and Turn Off Gridlines   Next add some cell borders and remove the worksheet gridlines to make the table more readable.

1. Select cells A4 and B4.

	A	B	C	D
1	Thermal Conductivity of Silicon			
2	K0	350		
3	T0	68		
4	T (K)	K (W/cm-K)		
5	200	2.65		

2. Click on the down arrow next to the Borders button on the Formatting toolbar, and select the outline border from the palette.

3. Select cells A5:B15, then click the Borders button. Because the outline border is the currently selected border, it is displayed on the Borders button face.

4. Select cells B4:B15, then click the Borders button.

5. Hide the worksheet gridlines by choosing Tools ➤ Options; click the View tab, uncheck the Gridlines checkbox, and click OK.

The completed worksheet for the
simple thermal-conductivity
equation

	A	B	C	D
1	Thermal Conductivity of Silicon			
2	K0	350		
3	T0	68		
4	T (K)	K (W/cm-K)		
5	200	2.65		
6	250	1.92		
7	300	1.51		
8	350	1.24		
9	400	1.05		
10	450	0.92		
11	500	0.81		
12	550	0.73		
13	600	0.66		
14	650	0.60		
15	700	0.55		
16				

Your completed worksheet should look like Figure 2.5. All the data cells are labeled
and boxed to make the meaning of the table clear to anyone who might use it. You
could also have included the formula as a label (enter the formula with a single
quote before the equal sign), so that a user could see exactly what is being calculated without having to look at the contents of the cells containing the formulas. At
this point, if you want to keep the worksheet, you should save it by choosing File
➤ Save, or by clicking the Save button on the Standard toolbar.

Figure 2.6 shows the contents of all the cells in the worksheet. To see the worksheet's formulas instead of their results, choose Tools ➤ Options, click the View tab,
check the Formulas checkbox, and click OK.

The contents of the cells in the
Thermal Conductivity worksheet

	A	B	C	D
1	Thermal Conductivity			
2		K0 350		
3		T0 68		
4	T (K)	K (W/cm-K)		
5	200	=$B$2/(A5-$B$3)		
6	250	=$B$2/(A6-$B$3)		
7	300	=$B$2/(A7-$B$3)		
8	350	=$B$2/(A8-$B$3)		
9	400	=$B$2/(A9-$B$3)		
10	450	=$B$2/(A10-$B$3)		
11	500	=$B$2/(A11-$B$3)		
12	550	=$B$2/(A12-$B$3)		
13	600	=$B$2/(A13-$B$3)		
14	650	=$B$2/(A14-$B$3)		
15	700	=$B$2/(A15-$B$3)		
16				

SHORTCUT   To quickly switch between formulas and values, press Ctrl+ ` (the grave accent mark above the Tab key).

Creating Tables with Copied Formulas

In the previous section, you created an engineering table of values of the thermal conductivity of silicon. Creating tables of values like this is probably the second most common numerical task of a scientist or engineer (the first is calculating individual values of a function with a calculator). There are two ways to create tables in Excel: by copying the formulas or with the Data ➤ Table command. You used the former method for the thermal-conductivity equation, and it is probably the most versatile way to create tables of values on a worksheet. The following sections describe several engineering tables generated in this manner. Using the Data ➤ Table command is discussed later in this chapter.

Setting Up Single-Input Tables

First set up a single input table. A single input table is created with one or more formulas that each take a single input value and return a single result.

Precession of the North Celestial Pole

In astronomy, two common frames of reference are used for locating the positions of celestial objects: the equatorial system and the ecliptic system. The celestial reference systems are illustrated in Figure 2.7.

The *equatorial system* is based on the orientation and rotation axis of Earth. Imagine a world globe with latitude and longitude lines on it, but no continents, with the same orientation as Earth. If you expand the size of that globe to infinity, you have the celestial sphere, overlaid with the equatorial reference system.

The plane of Earth's equator is also the plane of the reference system's equator and is known as the celestial equator. If you extend the axes of rotation of Earth through the North Pole and South Pole and out to the celestial sphere, they form the

FIGURE 2.7:

Orientation of the equatorial and ecliptic coordinate systems and the motion of the equatorial system due to precession of Earth's rotational axis

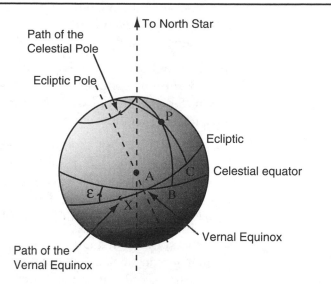

celestial poles. The north celestial pole is near the North Star, which has been used for navigation for centuries.

Specification of the location of a star (point P in Figure 2.7) in the equatorial system is much the same as latitude and longitude on Earth's surface. Similar to latitude, the declination of a celestial object is the angular measurement of that object's position north or south of the celestial equator (the angle from B to P in Figure 2.7). The equator is at 0 degrees, and the north and south celestial poles are at 90 degrees north or south declination.

The second coordinate is similar to the longitude, and it is known as the right ascension. An object's right ascension is measured in hours, minutes, and seconds from the vernal equinox (point A, in the constellation Aries, in Figure 2.7), eastward to the meridian passing through the star (the angle from A to B in Figure 2.7). The meridian is a line from the celestial equator to the celestial pole, much like a longitude line on Earth's surface.

The *ecliptic system* of measurement is similar to the equatorial system, but it is based on the plane of Earth's orbit around the sun rather than the plane of Earth's equator. If Earth's orbit is expanded to the celestial sphere, it forms a great circle known as the ecliptic. Ninety degrees above or below the ecliptic are the ecliptic poles. Measurement is in ecliptic longitude and ecliptic latitude (angles A to C and

C to P, respectively, in Figure 2.7). This measurement system is also similar to latitude and longitude on Earth's surface, but it is oriented to the ecliptic rather that the equator.

The great circles that are the ecliptic and the celestial equators intersect at the vernal and autumnal equinoxes at an angle of about 23 degrees. This is the well-known 23-degree tilt of Earth with respect to the plane of its orbit, and it is known as the obliquity of the ecliptic.

The equatorial system is useful for Earth-based observational astronomy, and the ecliptic system is useful for sun-based celestial mechanics calculations. Both systems are equally relevant, being related by a simple 23-degree rotation of coordinate systems. Unfortunately, nature is not so simple. The relationship between these two systems is not static but variable.

The action of the sun and the moon cause the rotation of Earth to wobble, like a spinning top does when you give it a little push on one side. This wobble is known as precession, and causes the North Pole, and hence the north celestial pole, to move in a small circle with a radius of 23° degrees about the north ecliptic pole. While the plane of the ecliptic does not change, the location of the vernal equinox, which is the origin of the right ascension and the ecliptic longitude, does.

The action of the planets causes precession in the ecliptic, which makes the ecliptic pole move as well. Now, if you are not an astronomer, you might think that these are really atrocious coordinate systems, wobbling around the universe as they do. But the period of this movement is about 26,000 years, which makes the movement tolerable. The following two equations calculate the annual change in the ecliptic longitude (X) and the value of the obliquity of the ecliptic (ε)

$$X = 50.2564'' + 0.00222''t$$
$$\varepsilon = 23^0 27' 8.26'' - 0.4684''t$$

where t is the number of years since 1900. While these changes will not cause large changes in a star's coordinates, they must be accounted for by any Earth-based observatories that are fixed to this wobbly planet's coordinate system.

Now create a table of the annual change in the ecliptic longitude and the obliquity of the ecliptic, for every ten years between 1900 and 2000.

Set Up the Worksheet   Begin by setting column widths and entering labels. You don't normally set the column widths before entering data, but doing so makes it easier to see the development of this example.

1. Start with a new workbook, or a new worksheet in the existing workbook, and name the worksheet **fig. 2.8** (double-click the sheet tab, type the name in the Rename Sheet dialog box, and click OK).

2. Change the widths of columns A through P according to the following list:

Column	Width	Column	Width	Column	Width
A	3	G	1	M	7
B	5	H	7	N	2
C	8.43	I	1	O	8.43
D	9.57	J	5.43	P	4.57
E	3	K	2		
F	3	L	1		

3. In cell A1, enter **Precession of the North Pole**

4. In cell C3, enter **Annual Precession**

5. In cell C4, enter **in Longitude**

6. In cell E3, enter **Obliquity of the**

7. In cell E4, enter **Ecliptic**

8. In cell B4, enter **Date** and right-align it.

9. In cell J3, enter **Annual Precession in Longitude**

10. In cell J6, enter **Obliquity of the Ecliptic**

11. In cell M9, enter **For t in years after 1900**

Enter Equations   You are writing the equations as text so that anyone reading the worksheet can tell what is being calculated; however, the coefficients of the equations in the text representations are the actual values that the worksheet formulas will reference.

1. In cell J4, enter **X=** (don't type any spaces)

2. In cell M4, enter **50.2564**

3. In cell N4, enter "+ (don't type any spaces)

4. In cell O4, enter **0.000222**

5. In cell P4, enter "*t (don't type any spaces)

Your next cell entry includes a degree symbol (°), which is part of the DOS extended character set. On most computers, you access these characters by holding down the Alt key while typing the ASCII code number (248 in this case) on the numeric keypad. In Windows 95, you can also insert the degree symbol by using the Character Map (click the Start button, point to Programs, point to Accessories, click Character Map; double-click the ° character, click Copy, then press Ctrl+V to paste the symbol in the cell).

6. In cell J7, enter **e=23°** (don't type any spaces)

7. In cell K7, enter **27**

In cell L7, enter two single quotation marks. Excel uses the first one as an alignment symbol (to be compatible with Lotus 1-2-3). The second one is the abbreviation for minutes, to go with the value in cell K7.

8. In cell L7, enter '' (two single quotes)

9. In cell M7, enter **8.26**

10. In cell N7, enter " (double quote)

11. In cell O7, enter **–0.4684**

12. In cell P7, enter "*t (don't type any spaces, double quote)

Enter Values   Next enter the values of the dates to be calculated.

1. In cell B5, enter **1900**

2. In cell B6, enter **1910**

3. Select cells B5:B6.

4. Using the mouse, drag the fill handle down to cell B15 and release it.

The values 1900 through 2000, in steps of 10, should now fill those cells. Excel used the arithmetic relationship you established in the first two cells to fill the rest of the range.

Enter Precession and Obliquity Formulas   Now enter the formula for the annual precession in longitude.

1. In cell C5, enter =$M$4+$O$4*(B5–1900)

2. In cell D5, enter " (double quote)

Your next entries are the formula for the obliquity of the ecliptic. The value of the number of degrees does not change over this short amount of time, so simply enter the value instead of calculating it.

3. In cell E5, enter 23°

The number of minutes does change, so you need to calculate the number of seconds, divide it by 60, and take the integer part to get the number of minutes.

4. In cell F5, enter =($K$7)+INT(($M$7+$O$7*(B5–1900)/60))

5. In cell G5, enter " (two single quotes).

Now calculate the number of seconds and then use the MOD function to map the total number of seconds back onto the range 0 to 60, since seconds in excess of 60 have already been carried over into the minutes column.

6. In cell H5, enter =MOD($M$7+$O$7*(B5 1900)+60,60)

7. In cell I5, enter " (double quote)

You need to copy all these cells down into the rest of the table. Select the top row of the range and use the fill handle to fill the rest.

8. Select cells C5:I5.

9. Grab the fill handle in the lower-right corner of the selection, drag it down to cell I15, and release it. The formulas and values are copied down into the rest of the table.

Format the Worksheet   Give the cells a numeric format with four decimal places, add boxes around the tables, and turn off the gridlines.

1. Select cells H5:H15, press and hold down the Ctrl key, and select cells C5:C15.

> **NOTE**
>
> When applying the same formatting to multiple non-adjacent cells, select them as a multi-area group by holding the Ctrl key down when clicking on the cells and then format the group. Another way is to select and format one cell, select a second cell or group of cells and choose the Edit ➤ Repeat Formatting command (Ctrl+Y).

2. Choose Format ➤ Cells and click the Number tab; select the Number category, set 4 decimal places, and choose OK.

3. Select cells C5:I15, then press and hold down Ctrl to select ranges B3:B15, B3:I4, and J3:P9.

4. Click on the Borders button on the Formatting toolbar, and click the outline button on the palette. All the selected ranges will be outlined simultaneously.

5. Select ranges C3:D4 and E3:I4 (use the Ctrl key to select noncontiguous ranges).

6. Select the Center Across Columns button on the Formatting toolbar.

7. Choose the Tools ➤ Options command, select the View tab, clear the Gridlines check box in the dialog box, and click OK.

8. Use the Save button to save the workbook.

Your worksheet should now look like Figure 2.8.

FIGURE 2.8:

The tables for annual precession of the celestial longitude and the obliquity of the ecliptic between the years 1900 and 2000

	Annual Precession in Longitude		Obliquity of the Ecliptic					Annual Precession in Longitude		
Date								$X = 50.2564 + 0.000222$ "*t		
1900	50.2564 "		23°	35 '	8.2600 "					
1910	50.2586 "		23°	35 '	3.5760 "			Obliquity of the Ecliptic		
1920	50.2608 "		23°	35 '	58.8920 "			$e=23°$ 27 ' 8.26 " -0.4684 "*t		
1930	50.2631 "		23°	35 '	54.2080 "					
1940	50.2653 "		23°	34 '	49.5240 "			For t in years after 1900		
1950	50.2675 "		23°	34 '	44.8400 "					
1960	50.2697 "		23°	34 '	40.1560 "					
1970	50.2719 "		23°	34 '	35.4720 "					
1980	50.2742 "		23°	34 '	30.7880 "					
1990	50.2764 "		23°	34 '	26.1040 "					
2000	50.2786 "		23°	34 '	21.4200 "					

Precession of the North Pole

Temperature Dependence of the Intrinsic Carrier Density

The intrinsic carrier density of silicon is the density of electrons or holes in intrinsic silicon at equilibrium. It is an important parameter for the modeling of silicon solid-state devices. Intrinsic silicon is defined as silicon where the electron density equals the hole density at equilibrium. This situation is satisfied in extremely pure silicon at room temperature, or in less pure silicon at higher temperatures. Holes are places in the electronic structure of silicon where an electron could be but is not. A hole is treated as if it were an electron with a positive charge.

The intrinsic carrier density (n_i) is defined with the following equation:

$$n_i = \left(4 M_c \left(\frac{2\pi m_0 k}{h^2} \right)^3 \right)^{1/2} \left(\frac{m_e^* m_h^*}{m_0} \right)^{3/4} T^{3/2} e^{-E_g/2kT}$$

The coefficients have the following values:

Coeff	Value	Description
M_c	6	The number of equivalent electron valleys in silicon
m_0	0.91095×10^{-30} kg	Electron rest mass
k	1.38066×10^{-23} J/kg	Boltzmann's constant
h	6.62618×10^{-34} J-s	Planck's constant
m_e^*	$0.33\, m_0$	Electron effective mass
m_h^*	$0.56\, m_0$	Hole effective mass

E_g is the value of the energy gap in silicon. The following equation has been fit to the experimental data for the energy gap versus temperature:

$$E_g = \left(EG0 - \frac{EG1 \cdot T^2}{T + EG2} \right) q$$

where EG_0 is 1.17 eV, EG_1 is 4.73×10^{-4} eV/K, EG_2 is 636 K, and q is 1.60219×10^{-19} coulombs (the electron charge).

You could algebraically insert the equation for the energy gap into the equation for the intrinsic carrier density—this would give you a single complicated equation for the intrinsic carrier density. But it is simpler, and just as valid, to calculate the value of the energy gap separately and then insert that value into the equation for the intrinsic carrier density.

The intrinsic carrier density equation has numerous constants that precede the temperature coefficients. Calculating these constants every time you use the equation is a needless waste of computational effort, which will slow down the worksheet calculation. To make the worksheet more efficient, combine all the constants into a single value, and then reference that value whenever you write a formula for the equation. You should also name the constants to make the formulas to make them more readable.

Create a table for calculating the intrinsic carrier density of silicon.

Enter Values   Begin to create the new table by entering values.

1. Start with a new worksheet, and name the worksheet **fig. 2.9**.

2. Format and enter the following values into the indicated cells:

Cell	Contents	Formatting
A1	**Intrinsic Carrier Density in Silicon**	
A3	**EG0=**	Align Right
A4	**EG1=**	Align Right
A5	**EG2=**	Align Right
A7	**Cons=**	
B3	**1.17**	
B4	**4.73E-4**	
B5	**636**	

Now calculate the coefficient of the intrinsic carrier density equation and change the units from $1/(m^3\text{-}K)$ to $1/(cm^3\text{-}K)$.

3. In cell B7, enter the following formula:

=SQRT(4*6*(2*PI( )*0.91095E–30*1.38066E–23/(6.62618E-34)^2)^3)*(0.33*0.56)^(.75)*1.0E–6

At this point, you could calculate this formula, and then replace the formula with its value, but leaving the formula makes it easier for someone else (or you at some later date) to determine what it is that you are calculating.

> **TIP**
>
> To replace a formula or part of a formula with its value, select the cell and click in the formula bar. Select the part of the formula you want to evaluate and press Ctrl+= (Cmd+= on the Macintosh). Click on the check mark or press Enter to replace the formula with the value, or click on the **X** box or press the Esc key to restore the original formula. You can use this technique when you need to see the current value, not the formula, or when you are debugging your worksheet and need to see the value of part of a formula.

Name Cells and Ranges   Next, name the cells so that you can use the names in the formulas. You can use the Insert ➤ Name ➤ Define or the Insert ➤ Name ➤ Create commands to name the cells. The Insert ➤ Name ➤ Create command uses the entries in adjacent cells to name a group of cells. The Insert ➤ Name ➤ Define command names single cells and ranges. When Excel evaluates a formula, it replaces any names you have defined with their values before calculating the result of the formula.

1. Select cells A3:B7 and choose the Insert ➤ Name ➤ Create command.

2. In the Create Names dialog box, make sure the Left Column checkbox is checked, and choose OK.

The Insert ➤ Name ➤ Define command can also be used to name a value. In the Define Name dialog box, type the value in the Refers To box, the Name in the Names In Workbook box, and click Add. For example, you could define the name h-bar to refer to the number 1.0546E–34 (Planck's constant divided by 2p).

The selected cells in column B now have the names of the entries in the left column (column A), but without the equal signs. You can see which names have been defined on a worksheet using the Define Name dialog box (choose the Insert ➤ Name ➤ Define command). If you select a name, you'll see its definition in the Refers To box at the bottom of the dialog box. To see the name of a specific cell, select it, and its name (if one has been assigned) appears on the left side of formula bar in the Name box.

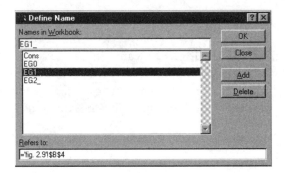

In the Define Name dialog box, you can see that cells B4 and B5 are named EG1_ and EG2_ instead of EG1 and EG2. Excel added the underscore because EG1 is a valid cell reference (column EG, row 1), and cannot be used as a name. If you use names such as A1 and C7 for variables in algebraic equations, they must also include underscores or some other symbol so they won't be cell references. If you don't like the underscore, you can rename the cells.

Enter Labels and Temperature Values   Next enter the labels to make the table understandable.

1. Enter the following values into the indicated cells, and then format the cells. To create the superscript in cell F3, select the –3 and then choose the Format ➤ Cells command. Click the Font tab and check the superscript check box.

Cell	Contents	Formatting
D3	T(K)	Center Align
E3	Eg (eV)	Center Align
F3	ni (cm^{-3})	Center Align

Now enter the range of temperatures to use in the formulas.

2. In cell D4, enter **300** and in cell D5 enter **350**.

3. Select cells D4:D5, grab the fill handle in the lower-right corner of the selection, drag it down to cell D14, and release it.

Enter Formulas   Next enter the energy-gap equation. When you are typing a formula that includes a name, you can either type the name or use the Insert ➤ Name ➤ Paste command and select a defined name from the Paste Name dialog box.

> **TIP**   You can enter a formula containing a name that you have not defined yet, and define the name later. The formula will evaluate to the value #NAME? until you define all the names used in the formula.

1. In cell E4, enter =EG0–EG1_*D4^2/(D4+EG2_)

Now enter the formula for the intrinsic carrier density, using the values of the temperature and the energy gap.

2. In cell F4, enter the following formula:

=Cons*(SQRT(D4)^3)*EXP(–E4*1.60219E-19/(2*1.38066E-23*D4))

Finally, copy the formulas down into the rest of the table.

3. Select cells E4:F4, grab the fill handle, drag it down to cell F14 and release it.

Format Cells   Format the numeric results, and draw some boxes to make the table more readable.

1. Set the formatting of the indicated cells using the Format ➤ Cells command.

Cells	Formatting
E4:E14	Numeric, 2 decimal places
F4:F14	Scientific, 2 decimal places

2. Draw borders around the table (as shown in figure 2.9) using the Borders button on the Formatting toolbar. Remove the worksheet gridlines by choosing the Tools ➤ Options command; select the View tab and clear the Gridlines check box.

3. Save the workbook.

Your completed worksheet should look like Figure 2.9.

FIGURE 2.9:

The Intrinsic Carrier Density in Silicon engineering table

	A	B	C	D	E	F	G	H	I
1	Intrinsic Carrier Density in Silicon								
2									
3	EG0=	1.17		T(K)	Eg (eV)	ni (cm^{-3})			
4	EG1=	4.73E-04		300	1.12	6.21E+09			
5	EG2=	636		350	1.11	2.18E+11			
6				400	1.10	3.28E+12			
7	Cons=	3.33E+15		450	1.08	2.79E+13			
8				500	1.07	1.58E+14			
9				550	1.05	6.70E+14			
10				600	1.03	2.26E+15			
11				650	1.01	6.44E+15			
12				700	1.00	1.60E+16			
13				750	0.98	3.54E+16			
14				800	0.96	7.18E+16			
15									
16									

fig. 2.5 / fig. 2.6 / fig. 2.8 \ **fig. 2.9** / fig. 2.10 / fig. 2.1

Hyperbolic Functions

As explained in Chapter 1, you can calculate the hyperbolic functions that Excel does not provide with equations that use the available hyperbolic and logarithmic functions. In the following example, you'll use those equations to calculate the values of the hyperbolic functions for several different arguments. You will also calculate the inverse hyperbolic functions to see if they return the original argument.

The arc hyperbolic secant and arc hyperbolic cosecant are both double-valued, so calculate both values for these functions.

1. Start with a new worksheet, and name it **fig. 2.10**

2. Enter the following values into the indicated cells:

Cell	Contents	Cell	Contents	Cell	Contents
A1	**Hyperbolic Functions**	A10	**0**	B2	**Sech(x)**
A2	**x**	A11	**0.1**	C2	**ASech+**
A3	**−5**	A12	**0.5**	D2	**ASech−**
A4	**−4**	A13	**1**	E2	**Csch(x)**
A5	**−3**	A14	**2**	F2	**ACsch+**
A6	**−2**	A15	**3**	G2	**ACsch−**
A7	**−1**	A16	**4**	H2	**Ctanh(x)**
A8	**−0.5**	A17	**5**	I2	**ACtanh**
A9	**−0.1**				

3. Select cells A3:A17 and name the range x (use the Insert ➤ Name ➤ Define command).

4. Enter the following values into the indicated cells:

Cell	Contents
B3	=1/COSH(x)
C3	=LN((1+SQRT(1−B3^2))/B3)
D3	=LN((1−SQRT(1−B3^2))/B3)
E3	=1/SINH(x)
F3	=LN((1+SQRT(1+E3^2))/E3)
G3	=LN((1−SQRT(1+E3^2))/E3)
H3	=1/TANH(x)
I3	=0.5*LN((H3+1)/(H3−1))

5. Select cells B3:I3, and drag the fill handle down to cell I17 to copy the formulas into the rest of the table.

6. Outline the table as shown in Figure 2.10.

7. Turn off the gridlines with the Tools ➤ Options command, View tab.

8. Save the workbook.

Your worksheet should now look like Figure 2.10. Even though the range A3:A17 is named x, the formulas that use x always get the value from the cell that is in the same row as the formula.

FIGURE 2.10:

The table for calculating hyperbolic and inverse hyperbolic functions

	A	B	C	D	E	F	G	H	I
1	Hyperbolic Functions								
2	x	Sech(x)	ASech+	ASech-	Csch(x)	ACsch+	Acsch-	Ctanh(x)	ACtanh
3	-5	0.013475	5	-5	-0.01348	#NUM!	-5	-1.00009	-5
4	-4	0.036619	4	-4	-0.03664	#NUM!	-4	-1.00067	-4
5	-3	0.099328	3	-3	-0.09982	#NUM!	-3	-1.00497	-3
6	-2	0.265802	2	-2	-0.27572	#NUM!	-2	-1.03731	-2
7	-1	0.648054	1	-1	-0.85092	#NUM!	-1	-1.31304	-1
8	-0.5	0.886819	0.5	-0.5	-1.91903	#NUM!	-0.5	-2.16395	-0.5
9	-0.1	0.995021	0.1	-0.1	-9.98335	#NUM!	-0.1	-10.0333	-0.1
10	0	1	0	0	#DIV/0!	#DIV/0!	#DIV/0!	#DIV/0!	#DIV/0!
11	0.1	0.995021	0.1	-0.1	9.983353	0.1	#NUM!	10.03331	0.1
12	0.5	0.886819	0.5	-0.5	1.919035	0.5	#NUM!	2.163953	0.5
13	1	0.648054	1	-1	0.850918	1	#NUM!	1.313035	1
14	2	0.265802	2	-2	0.275721	2	#NUM!	1.037315	2
15	3	0.099328	3	-3	0.099822	3	#NUM!	1.00497	3
16	4	0.036619	4	-4	0.036644	4	#NUM!	1.000671	4
17	5	0.013475	5	-5	0.013477	5	#NUM!	1.000091	5
18									

fig. 2.5 / fig. 2.6 / fig. 2.8 / fig. 2.9 \ **fig. 2.10** / fig. 2.11

Many cells contain error values, which result from functions that are undefined for the arguments used. The Csch and Ctanh functions have poles at 0, which means that their values go to ±∞, making the function undefined. The ACsch and ACtanh functions depend on the values of Csch and Ctanh, so they show the error values as well. The ACsch function is also double-branched, with one formula that is valid only for negative arguments and one that is valid only for positive arguments.

WARNING

When you use these double-valued functions, be sure to use the correct formula, or they may return the wrong value. As you can see, some of the formulas return the negative of the correct value.

TIP

You could use an IF function here to test the value of the argument of ASech or ACsch and select the correct formula depending on its value. For example:

ACsch =IF(x>0,LN((1+SQRT(1+E3^2))/E3),LN((1−SQRT(1+E3^2))/E3))

Creating Two-Input Tables

The previous examples each have one independent variable (the input) and one or more dependent variables (the output, or result of the equation). Some equations, however, require two or more input variables, which must be handled separately. You can handle equations with two input variables in either of two ways:

- Put the input variables in parallel columns.
- Use a rectangular format with one variable in a column on the left side, the other in a row along the top, and the calculated formula in the center.

The next two examples demonstrate both methods.

Van der Waals Equation of State

The ideal gas law shows the relationship between pressure (p), volume (V), and temperature (T) of an ideal gas. The law is expressed as $pV = \mu RT$, where μ is the number of moles of gas and R is the universal gas constant. To develop this equation, the volume of the individual gas molecules and the range of the intermolecular forces were ignored. The equation works well for low-density gases, but it becomes less and less accurate as the gas density increases. In a real gas, molecules have a definite volume, and the intermolecular forces are not localized to the volume of the molecules.

In an attempt to better model the behavior of a real gas, J. D. van der Waals modified the ideal gas law to account for these facts. His modified equation of state takes the following form:

$$\left(p + \frac{a}{v^2} \right)(v - b) = RT$$

where v is the volume per mole (V/mole), and a and b are constants, derived from experiments. For carbon dioxide gas, the constants have these values:

a 3.59 l^2–atm/mole^2

b 0.0427 l/mole

Create a Parallel Column Two-Input Table

This equation has three variables, any one of which could be solved in terms of the other two. In the following example, calculate the pressure for different values of the volume and temperature.

1. Start with a new worksheet and name it **fig. 2.11**

2. Set the width of column A to 5 characters (drag the edge of the column header).

3. In cell A1, enter **Van der Waals Equation of State**

4. Enter the following values and format the cells as indicated.

Cell	Contents	Formatting
A3	**a=**	Align Right
B3	**3.59**	
C3	**l^{2}atm/mole^2**	Align Left
A4	**b=**	Align Right
B4	**0.0427**	
C4	**l/mole**	Align Left
E1	**T(K)**	Align Left
F1	**v(l/mole)**	Align Left
G1	**P(atm)**	Align Left
E2	**264**	
F2	**0.05**	Number, 2 decimals
F3	**0.1**	Number, 2 decimals

5. Select cells A3:B4 and choose Insert ➤ Name ➤ Create. In the Create Names dialog box, make sure Left Column is checked, and click OK.

6. Select cell E2, then drag the fill handle down to cell E9 to copy the contents of E2 into cells E3:E9.

7. Select cells F2:F3, then drag the fill handle down to F9.

Now enter the van der Waals equation, solved for the pressure. Convert the universal gas constant from J/mole-K to l–atm/mole–K with the factor 101.3.

8. In cell G2, enter the following formula and set the format to Number with one decimal place:

   =(8.3143/101.3)*E2/(F2–b)–a/(F2^2)

9. Copy the contents of cell G2 into cells G3:G9.

10. In cell E10, enter **304** and copy it into cells E11:E17.

Next you want to copy the data series in column F and the formulas in column G down into the range F10:G17. Do this with copy and paste commands instead of typing it all again.

SHORTCUT A shortcut for the Copy and Paste commands on the Edit menu is to select the cells, hold down the Ctrl key (Cmd key on the Macintosh), and drag the selection to where the copy is to appear. (Dragging a selection without holding down the Ctrl key moves the selection.)

11. Select cells F2:G9.

12. Place the mouse pointer on the edge of the selection (but not on the fill handle), hold down the Ctrl key, and drag the selection by its edge down into the range F10:G17.

13. In cell E18, enter **344** and then copy that value into cells E19:E25.

14. Copy cells F10:G17 into cells F18:G25.

15. Outline the cell ranges as shown in Figure 2.11.

16. Turn off the worksheet gridlines.

17. Save the workbook.

The table for Van der Waals equation of state

To be able to see more of the table, choose the View ➤ Full Screen command. Your worksheet should now look like Figure 2.11. The table works well for this number of variable values, but it could get quite long and difficult to understand if you input many values. A more efficient way to set up two-input tables is to have one variable in a column and the second variable in a row, as demonstrated in the next example.

Absolute Magnitude of a Star

In astronomy, the apparent brightness of a star is measured in magnitudes. This system of measurement was first used by Hipparchus, an early Middle Eastern astronomer. He called the brightest stars in the sky first magnitude and the dimmest visible ones sixth magnitude. Differences in magnitude were based on a person's ability to discern a difference in brightness between two stars. That is, if you could just barely discern a difference in brightness between two stars, they differed by one magnitude. Since that time, the magnitude scale has been formalized, mathematically, for more precise measurement of a star's brightness. Currently, a difference in magnitude of 5 is equal to a measured 100 times increase in brightness. This leads to a simple formula for the relative magnitude of any two stars based on their measurable difference in brightness:

$$\left(m_2 - m_1\right) = \frac{1}{0.4}\mathrm{Log}\left(\frac{b_1}{b_2}\right)$$

where m_1 and m_2 are the magnitudes of the two stars and b_1 and b_2 are the brightnesses of the two stars. With at least one star as a standard, the magnitude of any other star can be calculated from its brightness relative to the standard.

The magnitude of objects visible from Earth range from –26.7 for the sun to +23 for the dimmest object discernible in the 200-inch Hale telescope, or possibly dimmer for some of the new multiple-mirror telescopes. Two of the brightest stars are Sirius at a magnitude of –1.58 and Vega with a magnitude of +0.14. After astronomers agreed on a zero point for the magnitude system, they found that some stars were brighter. This is why the magnitudes of the sun and some of the brighter stars are negative.

The brightness of a star as we see it from Earth's surface is its *apparent magnitude*, which is dependent on the actual brightness of a star and the distance of the star from Earth. Apparent magnitude does not tell us a lot about a star's characteristics, nor does it allow us to make meaningful comparisons between stars. To remedy this, astronomers have defined the *absolute magnitude* as the magnitude that a star would have if it were 10 parsecs (192 trillion miles) from Earth. Using absolute magnitudes, the brightness of different stars can be compared. The relationship between apparent magnitude and absolute magnitude is expressed as $M = m + 5 - 5\mathrm{Log}(r)$, where M is the absolute magnitude, m is the apparent magnitude, and r is the distance to the star in parsecs.

In 1913, Hertzsprung in Germany and Russell in the United States compared the absolute magnitude with the spectral class (essentially the color) of stars and came up with a nearly linear relationship. The now classic Hertzsprung-Russell diagram allows astronomers to determine the absolute magnitude of a star from its spectral class (color). Knowing the absolute magnitude and the apparent magnitude, you can use the equation above to calculate the distance to a star.

In the following example, create a table of distances based on the absolute and relative magnitudes of a star. First, solve the absolute magnitude equation for the distance:

$$r = 10^{\left(\frac{5+m-M}{5}\right)}$$

Create a Rectangular Format Two-Input Table

You'll create a two-input table with apparent magnitude on the left, absolute magnitude on the top, and distance in the body.

1. Uncheck the View ➤ Full Screen command if it is still checked (or click the Full Screen button).

2. Start with a new worksheet and name it **fig. 2.12**

3. Set the width of column A to 8.57 and column B to 3.

4. Enter the following values into the indicated cells.

Cell	Contents
A1	**Distance to a star based on its absolute and apparent magnitude**
B2	**Distance in parsecs (1 parsec = 3.26 light years)**
G3	**Absolute Magnitude**
A9	**Apparent**
A10	**Magnitude**

5. In cell C4, enter **–5** and in cell D4, enter **–3**. Select cells C4 and D4, then drag the fill handle to M4 (to fill C4:M4 with the set of integers from –5 to 15 in steps of 2).

6. In cell B5, enter **–5** and in cell B6 enter **–3**. Select cells B5 and B6, then drag the fill handle to B18 (to fill B5:B18 with the set of integers from –5 to 21 in steps of 2).

7. In cell C5, enter the following formula and format the cell as Scientific with 1 decimal place.

   =10^((5+$B5–C$4)/5)

   You are using mixed cell references to keep the arguments pointing to the correct row or column when the cells are copied into the rectangular body of the table.

8. Select cell C5 and drag the fill handle to cell C18. Select the fill handle again and drag it to M18 to fill cells C5:M18 with the formula in C5 (the fill handle only works in one direction at a time, so you have to drag it twice).

9. Outline the cells as shown in Figure 2.12.

10. Turn off the worksheet gridlines.

11. Save the workbook.

On the Standard toolbar, click the down arrow on the Zoom Control button and choose 75 percent. Your worksheet should now look like Figure 2.12.

FIGURE 2.12:

The table for calculating distance to a star based on its absolute and relative magnitudes

Distance to a star based on its absolute and apparent magnitudes
Distance in parsecs (1 parsec = 3.26 lightyears)

Absolute Magnitude

		-5	-3	-1	1	3	5	7	9	11	13	15
	-5	1.0E+01	4.0E+00	1.6E+00	6.3E-01	2.5E-01	1.0E-01	4.0E-02	1.6E-02	6.3E-03	2.5E-03	1.0E-03
	-3	2.5E+01	1.0E+01	4.0E+00	1.6E+00	6.3E-01	2.5E-01	1.0E-01	4.0E-02	1.6E-02	6.3E-03	2.5E-03
	-1	6.3E+01	2.5E+01	1.0E+01	4.0E+00	1.6E+00	6.3E-01	2.5E-01	1.0E-01	4.0E-02	1.6E-02	6.3E-03
	1	1.6E+02	6.3E+01	2.5E+01	1.0E+01	4.0E+00	1.6E+00	6.3E-01	2.5E-01	1.0E-01	4.0E-02	1.6E-02
Apparent	3	4.0E+02	1.6E+02	6.3E+01	2.5E+01	1.0E+01	4.0E+00	1.6E+00	6.3E-01	2.5E-01	1.0E-01	4.0E-02
Magnitude	5	1.0E+03	4.0E+02	1.6E+02	6.3E+01	2.5E+01	1.0E+01	4.0E+00	1.6E+00	6.3E-01	2.5E-01	1.0E-01
	7	2.5E+03	1.0E+03	4.0E+02	1.6E+02	6.3E+01	2.5E+01	1.0E+01	4.0E+00	1.6E+00	6.3E-01	2.5E-01
	9	6.3E+03	2.5E+03	1.0E+03	4.0E+02	1.6E+02	6.3E+01	2.5E+01	1.0E+01	4.0E+00	1.6E+00	6.3E-01
	11	1.6E+04	6.3E+03	2.5E+03	1.0E+03	4.0E+02	1.6E+02	6.3E+01	2.5E+01	1.0E+01	4.0E+00	1.6E+00
	13	4.0E+04	1.6E+04	6.3E+03	2.5E+03	1.0E+03	4.0E+02	1.6E+02	6.3E+01	2.5E+01	1.0E+01	4.0E+00
	15	1.0E+05	4.0E+04	1.6E+04	6.3E+03	2.5E+03	1.0E+03	4.0E+02	1.6E+02	6.3E+01	2.5E+01	1.0E+01
	17	2.5E+05	1.0E+05	4.0E+04	1.6E+04	6.3E+03	2.5E+03	1.0E+03	4.0E+02	1.6E+02	6.3E+01	2.5E+01
	19	6.3E+05	2.5E+05	1.0E+05	4.0E+04	1.6E+04	6.3E+03	2.5E+03	1.0E+03	4.0E+02	1.6E+02	6.3E+01
	21	1.6E+06	6.3E+05	2.5E+05	1.0E+05	4.0E+04	1.6E+04	6.3E+03	2.5E+03	1.0E+03	4.0E+02	1.6E+02

fig. 2.10 / fig. 2.11 / fig. 2.12 / fig. 2.13 / Sheet10 / Sh

Setting Up Multiple-Input, Multiple-Column Tables

Many functions have more than one or two input values. You cannot create tables of these functions in the simple rectangular format used in the previous example. Instead, you can put a different variable in alternate columns, with the function in the last column, as for the Van der Waals equation (Figure 2.11). Another way to handle multiple inputs is to place one of the variables in a row and the others in alternate columns, which would tend to compact the table somewhat. How you set up a particular table depends on what you are calculating and how you want to view the results.

Electron Mobility in Silicon

The next example calculates the electron mobility in silicon versus electric field, doping density, and temperature. The formula requires three input values to calculate the one output value. Set up the table as three columns of independent variables: two columns of intermediate values, and one column for the calculated result.

The mobility equation was developed for use in a large-scale computer model that calculates the effects of high-power electrical transients in semiconductor devices. It consists of curve fits of mobility versus electric field, doping density, and temperature. It is expressed as follows:

$$\mu_0 = \frac{\mu_{max} - \mu_{min}}{1 + (N/N_r)^\alpha} + \mu_{min}$$

$$E_c = \frac{2.319 V_m}{(1 + 0.8 \exp(T/600)) \mu_0 (T/T_0)^\delta}$$

$$\mu = \frac{\mu_0 (T/T_0)^{-\delta}}{(1 + (E/E_c)^\beta)^{1/\beta}}$$

The coefficients have the following values:

μ_{max}	0.1330 m^2/V-s	α	0.72
μ_{min}	0.0065 m^2/V-s	β	2
N_r	8.5x10^{22} m^{-3}	δ	2.42
V_m	1.1x10^5 m/s	T_0	300 K

where N is the net positive doping density (that is, the donor density minus the acceptor density) in inverse cubic meters, T is the temperature in Kelvin, E is the electric field in volts per meter, and μ is the electron mobility in meters squared per volt-second.

Set Up the Table   The formula is in three parts, which you could combine into a single formula; however, it is much simpler to assemble the table in columns and then calculate each part of the formula in a separate column.

1. Start with a new worksheet and name it **fig. 2.13**

2. Set the width of columns A through F to 10.

3. Enter the following values and format the cells as indicated. The μ is part of the extended character set and is created by holding down the Alt key while typing 230 on the keypad, or pasting it from the Character Map application.

Cell	Contents	Formatting
A1	**Electron Mobility in Silicon**	
A3	μmax	**Align Right**
A4	μmin	**Align Right**
A6	**Doping**	**Center Align**
A7	**Density**	**Center Align**
A8	(m^{-3})	**Center Align**
B3	0.133	
B4	0.0065	
B6	Temp.	**Center Align**
B8	(K)	**Center Align**
C2	Nr	**Align Right**
C3	Vm	**Align Right**
D2	8.5E22	
D3	1.1E5	
D4	300	
D6	μ0	**Center Align**
D8	$(m^2/V{-}s)$	
E2	alpha	**Align Right**
E3	beta	**Align Right**
Cell	Contents	Formatting
E4	**delta**	Align Right
E6	Ec	Center Align
E8	(V/m)	Center Align

F2	0.72	
F3	2	
F4	2.42	
F6	μ	Center Align
F8	$(m^2/V-s)$	Center

4. Select cell B4, choose Insert ➤ Name ➤ Define, and name this cell **umin**

> **NOTE**
>
> The name μmin is not a valid Excel variable name, so use the define name command and insert a u for the μ.

5. Name cell B3 **umax**

6. Select C2:D4, choose Insert ➤ Name ➤ Create, check Left Column, and click OK. Do the same with cells E2:F4.

Enter Data in the Table   Now that the table is set up, you can put some data in the range.

1. In cell A9, enter **1.0E19**, and then copy it into A10:A16.

2. In cell B9, enter **300**, and then copy it into B10:B12.

3. In cell B13, enter **600**, and then copy it into B14:B16.

4. Enter **1E4** in cell C9, **1E5** in cell C10, **1E6** in cell C11, and **1E7** in cell C12.

5. Copy cells C9:C12 into cells C13:C16.

6. In cell D9 enter the following formula:

   =(umax–umin)/(1+(A9/Nr)^alpha)+umin

   Then copy it into D10:D16.

7. In cell E9, enter the following formula:

   =2.319*Vm/((1+0.8*EXP(B9/600))*D9*(B9/T0)^delta)

   Then copy it into E10:E16.

8. In cell F9, enter the following formula:

   =(D9*(B9/T0)^delta)/(1+(C9/E9)^beta)^(1/beta)

   Then copy it into F10:F16.
9. Format cells A9:A16 and C9:C16 as Scientific with 0 decimals.
10. Format cells D9:F16 as Scientific with 3 decimals.
11. Copy cells A9:F16 to cells A17:F24.
12. In cell A17, enter **1.0E21** and copy it into A18:A24.
13. Outline the cells as shown in Figure 2.13.
14. Turn off the worksheet gridlines.

FIGURE 2.13:

The table for calculating electron mobility in silicon

	A	B	C	D	E	F
1	Electron Mobility in Silicon					
2			Nr	8.50E+22	alpha	0.72
3	µmax	0.133	Vm	1.10E+05	beta	2
4	µmin	0.0065	T0	300	delta	2.42
5						
6	Doping	Temp.	Electric	µ0	Ec	µ
7	Density		Field			
8	(m^{-3})	(K)	(V/m)	(m^2/V-s)	(V/m)	(m^2/V-s)
9	1.E+19	300	1.E+04	1.328E-01	8.282E+05	1.328E-01
10	1.E+19	300	1.E+05	1.328E-01	8.282E+05	1.319E-01
11	1.E+19	300	1.E+06	1.328E-01	8.282E+05	8.472E-02
12	1.E+19	300	1.E+07	1.328E-01	8.282E+05	1.096E-02
13	1.E+19	600	1.E+04	1.328E-01	1.130E+05	7.000E-01
14	1.E+19	600	1.E+05	1.328E-01	1.130E+05	5.324E-01
15	1.E+19	600	1.E+06	1.328E-01	1.130E+05	7.984E-02
16	1.E+19	600	1.E+07	1.328E-01	1.130E+05	8.035E-03

fig. 2.9 / fig. 2.10 / fig. 2.11 / fig. 2.12 / fig. 2.13 / fig.

	A	B	C	D	E	F
1	Electron Mobility in Silicon					
2			Nr	8.50E+22	alpha	0.72
3	µmax	0.133	Vm	1.10E+05	beta	2
4	µmin	0.0065	T0	300	delta	2.42
5						
6	Doping	Temp.	Electric	µ0	Ec	µ
7	Density		Field			
8	(m^{-3})	(K)	(V/m)	(m^2/V-s)	(V/m)	(m^2/V-s)
17	1.E+21	300	1.E+04	1.280E-01	8.591E+05	1.280E-01
18	1.E+21	300	1.E+05	1.280E-01	8.591E+05	1.272E-01
19	1.E+21	300	1.E+06	1.280E-01	8.591E+05	8.344E-02
20	1.E+21	300	1.E+07	1.280E-01	8.591E+05	1.096E-02
21	1.E+21	600	1.E+04	1.280E-01	1.173E+05	6.828E-01
22	1.E+21	600	1.E+05	1.280E-01	1.173E+05	5.214E-01
23	1.E+21	600	1.E+06	1.280E-01	1.173E+05	7.981E-02
24	1.E+21	600	1.E+07	1.280E-01	1.173E+05	8.035E-03

fig. 2.9 / fig. 2.10 / fig. 2.11 / fig. 2.12 / fig. 2.13 / fig.

Freeze the Titles   Now lock the rows containing the titles so you can scroll the data but still see the titles. This is accomplished by selecting the row below the titles and choosing the Window ➤ Freeze Panes command. All rows above the selected row are locked in place and scrolling the vertical scroll bar only changes the contents of the rows below the locked rows. You can do the same to one or more columns of labels on the left, or some rows along the top and the left.

1. Select row 9 by clicking on the header for row 9 on the left side of the screen.

2. Freeze the area above the selected row by choosing the Window ➤ Freeze Panes command.

3. Save the workbook.

Your worksheet should now look like Figure 2.13. Because you split the window and froze the titles, you can click above or below the thumb on the scroll bar (the thumb is the rectangular slider that you slide up and down on the scroll bar to change the contents of the screen) to switch between the two blocks of the table. You could add more blocks for different doping densities, and they will also scroll under the labels fixed at the top. To unfreeze the labels, choose the Window ➤ Unfreeze Panes command.

Using the Data ➤ Table Command to Create Tables

Excel's Data ➤ Table command allows you to produce one- and two-input tables from a single copy of a formula, instead of copying the formula into every cell. Additionally, with the single-input table command, you can create a table for several single-input formulas, placed in adjacent columns. With the two-input table command, you can calculate only a single, two-input table for a single formula.

Using the Data ➤ Table command has several advantages over copying formulas. Because you need only one copy of a formula, you have less to enter, and you can quickly alter a formula and see the results in the table. Another advantage is that the table does not need to be recalculated every time you make a change to the worksheet. You can use the Tools ➤ Options command, click the Calculation tab and set recalculation to automatic for all cells except those that are part of a data table by clicking the Automatic Except Tables option button. Then your tables are recalculated only when you press the F9 key.

A disadvantage of using the Data ➤ Table command is that you cannot have special formulas for different parts of the table. For example, you cannot use the Data ➤ Table command to create a table that contains a different formula for the areas where the arguments are zero. You can put logic in the formula to make the selection, but not by inserting a different formula in different parts of the table. Another difficulty is using multiple functions to calculate the value of a formula. In general, you calculate a single formula, not a series such as was used in the last example.

Whether or not you use the Data ➤ Table command is largely a matter of preference. The time required to set up tables using copied formulas or the command is about the same, so there is no advantage there. The speed with which the table is calculated is also about the same for both methods. If you frequently change individual formulas or groups of formulas to better handle a part of the range of the input variable, you will need to use copied formulas since this cannot be done with the Table command. You will probably prefer to use copied formulas if the formulas you calculate are usually not available as a single formula, but as a set of formulas that each calculate an intermediate value leading to the final result. Although you could probably do all the algebra to make these into single formulas, you would be doing extra work, and the equations would quickly become unwieldy.

The Data ➤ Table Command's Single-Input Table

To create a single-input table with the Data ➤ Table command, you must first set up the worksheet, following this general procedure:

- Put the list of input values in the column immediately to the left of the body of the data table.

- Select a convenient cell outside the table to use as the input cell. Use this cell in all your formulas for the input variable.

- Put the formula to be evaluated in a cell that is one row above the body of the table, in the same column as the table. You can calculate several single-input tables at the same time, as long as they use the same set of input data. Just put the formulas in adjacent columns.

- Select the range containing the input values and the formulas.

> To use multiple formulas to calculate a single result, set up the table as for a single formula, but place the intermediate formulas outside of the table. The restrictions are that the final result must be in the cell at the top of the table and that the formulas refer only to themselves and the input cell.

After setting up the worksheet, you can select the Table command on the Data menu. In the Table dialog box, specify the input cell. Excel then calculates the table by inserting the input values into the input cell, calculating the formula, and listing the results in the column below the formula and in the same row as the input value. You can also create a horizontal table, with the input data in the top row and the formula on the left side. Transpose the setup described here for vertical tables.

Stress and Deflection in a Cantilever Beam

Calculating stress and strain in beams is a common requirement in mechanical and civil engineering. In most cases, standard beams can be modeled with a set of simple analytical equations. You can find lists of these equations for different beams and methods of support in a number of handbooks.

Stress (S) in a cantilever beam with a single-point load, illustrated in Figure 2.14, can be calculated at any point x with the following equation:

$$S = \frac{W}{Z}(l - x) \quad (\text{for } x < l)$$

where W is the applied load, l is the location of the load, and Z is the section modulus of the beam. The deflection (y) of the beam is calculated with the equations:

$$y = \frac{Wx^2}{6EI}(3l - x) \qquad (\text{for } x \leq l)$$

$$y = \frac{Wl^2}{6EI}(3x - l) \qquad (\text{for } x \geq l)$$

where E is the modulus of elasticity and I is the moment of inertia.

FIGURE 2.14:

Cantilever beam with a single-point load

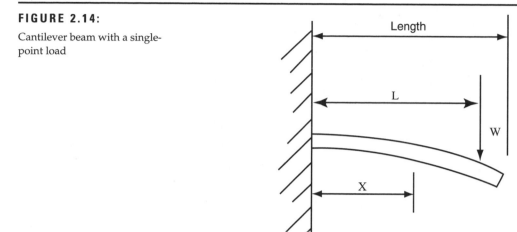

Suppose you have a 12-foot cantilever beam with a 15,000-pound load located 2 feet from the end. You want to calculate the stress in the beam and the deflection at every point. The beam is a type W 12 × 53 beam, an I-beam that is 12 inches deep and has a weight of 53 pounds per foot. A beam of this type has a section modulus (Z) of 70.7 in³, a moment of inertia (I) of 426 in⁴, and a modulus of elasticity (E) of 2.9×10^7 psi.

Create an engineering table that shows the stress and deflection of the cantilever beam every foot along its length. Actually, this table is two engineering tables applied to the same set of input data with the Table command. The first table is the stress calculation, and the second is the deflection calculation.

1. Start with a new worksheet, and name it **fig. 2.15**

2. Set the widths of columns A through G as follows:

   A: 9   C: 9   E: 3   G: 9
   B: 4   D: 9   F: 19   H: 5

3. Enter and format the following values as indicated:

Cell	Contents	Formatting	Cell	Contents
A1	**Cantilever Beam**		F9	**Moment of Inertia**
A6	**^^input^^**	Center Align	F10	**Modulus of Elasticity**

Cell	Contents	Formatting	Cell	Contents
A7	cell	Center Align	G3	144
A10	Distance	Center Align	G4	120
A11	from Wall	Center Align	G5	15000
A12	(in)	Center Align	G7	W 12 x 53
C3	Stress	Center Align	G8	70.7
C4	(psi)	Center Align	G9	426
D3	Deflection	Center Align	G10	2.9e7
D4	(in)	Center Align	H3	in
F3	Length of Beam		H4	in
F4	Location of Load		H5	lbs
F5	Weight of Load		H8	in^3
F7	Beam Designation		H9	in^4
F8	Section Modulus		H10	psi

Mark the input cell to emphasize its location and to prevent you from typing anything into it at a later date. It is not necessary to do this if you intend to protect the cells in your tables with the Tools ➤ Protect Document command.

4. Select cell A5 and use the Format ➤ Cells command, Patterns tab and select a light gray pattern.

5. Name cells as follows:

G4	L
G5	W
G8	Z
G9	I
G10	E

Enter the input data for the calculation. You want to calculate the stress and deflection every 12 inches along the beam.

6. In cell B6, enter 0, and in cell B7, enter 12; select cells B6 and B7, then drag the fill handle to cell B18.

This problem uses two stress and two deflection equations: one each for x between the wall and the location of the weight, and the other for x beyond the location of the weight. Use the logical IF statement to select the correct equations for the input range.

7. In cell C5, enter the following formula:

=IF(A5<L,(W/Z)*(L–A5),0)

8. In cell D5, enter this formula:

=IF(A5<L,(W*A5^2)*(3*L–A5)/(6*E*I),(W*A5^2)*(3*A5–L)/(6*E*I))

The table is now set up for execution of the Data ➤ Table command. The range of the table includes the column of input values and the formulas, but not the input cell.

9. Select cells B5:D18 and choose Data ➤ Table.

10. In the Table dialog box, place the cursor in the Column Input Cell text box, then click on cell A5 to insert its reference in the dialog box as the input cell. Click OK to create the table.

11. Format cells C5:C18 as Numeric, 0 decimals.

12. Format cells D5:D18 as Numeric, 4 decimals.

13. Outline the table as shown in Figure 2.15.

14. Turn off the worksheet gridlines.

As a final step, hide the values calculated by the formulas at the top of the columns.

15. Select cells C5:D5, then choose Format ➤ Cells and click the Number tab. Select the Custom category, and in the Type box or Code box (depending on your version of Excel), type ;;; as the format code, then click OK. This custom format hides the cell values. Alternatively, if you are planning to protect the worksheet, you can hide a cell's contents by setting the Hidden attribute in the Format Cells dialog box, Protection tab. When you protect the sheet with the Tools ➤ Protect Document command, the contents of cells with the Hidden attribute set cannot be seen.

16. Save the worksheet.

Your worksheet should now look like Figure 2.15. If you look at any of the formulas in the body of the table, you will see that they are all array formulas (the formulas are surrounded by curly brackets). While these values can be used in other formulas, you cannot change the value of any single cell in the table independently of the rest of the table.

FIGURE 2.15:

Single-input table for calculating the stress and deflection in a cantilever beam

Cantilever Beam

		Stress (psi)	Deflection (in)
^^input^^ cell	0	25460	0.0000
	12	22914	0.0101
	24	20368	0.0392
	36	17822	0.0850
Distance from Wall (in)	48	15276	0.1455
	60	12730	0.2186
	72	10184	0.3021
	84	7638	0.3941
	96	5092	0.4924
	108	2546	0.5948
	120	0	0.6994
	132	0	0.9732
	144	0	1.3092

Length of Beam	144	in
Location of Load	120	in
Weight of Load	15000	lbs
Beam Designation	W 12 x 53	
Section Modulus	70.7	in^3
Moment of Inertia	426	in^4
Modulus of Elasticity	2.90E+07	psi

fig. 2.10 fig. 2.11 fig. 2.12 fig. 2.13 fig. 2.15

The Data ➤ Table Command's Two-Input Table

You create a two-input table with the Table command in much the same manner as a single-input table. Put the values of the first variable in the column immediately to the left of the body of the table. Place the second variable in the row immediately above the body of the table, and insert the formula at the intersection of the row and column containing the input data. Define two input cells outside the table area and reference them in the Table dialog box.

Linear Variable Differential Transformer

As part of this nation's nuclear safety program, laboratories conduct tests to stress nuclear reactors and reactor components to failure in order to determine the nominal failure levels. As fuel rods are heated and cooled, their length changes. Rod length also changes drastically when a fuel rod breaks, which often happens in the destructive tests. A linear variable differential transformer (LVDT) is used to measure the change in length.

An LVDT consists of two identical secondary coils of wire spaced symmetrically about a primary coil. The secondary coils are wired in a series-opposed circuit. When the primary coil is excited with an AC source, the magnetic field is coupled to the secondary coils through a movable core. If the core is centered in the device, the coupling to each of the secondary coils is identical. Since they are wired in a series-opposed configuration, the resultant voltage is zero. If the movable core is displaced in either direction, a differential voltage is produced. The series-opposed configuration also helps to reduce thermal-and radiation-induced noise.

The LVDTs are calibrated at several different temperatures, and then linear curve fits are performed on the voltage-versus-displacement data. Then you can fit the coefficients of the curve fit to a linear function of the temperature to get the temperature sensitivity. Combining these curve fits results in this calibration equation:

$$x = a_0 + a_1 V + a_2 (T - 608) + a_3 V(T - 608)$$

where x is the fuel-rod elongation in millimeters, V is the transducer voltage, and T is the transducer temperature in Kelvins. For a particular device, the coefficients are as follows:

a_0 0.3347 mm

a_1 10.6592 mm/V

a_2 -2.19701×10^{-3} mm/K

a_3 -6.32662×10^{-4} mm/K-V

Use these values to create a table of fuel-rod elongation versus transducer voltage and temperature.

1. Start with a new worksheet, and name it **fig. 2.16**

2. Change the widths of columns A through G as follows:

Column	Width	Column	Width
A	13	E	9
B	7	F	9
C	10	G	9
D	9		

3. Enter and format the following values as indicated:

Cell	Contents	Formatting
A1	LVDT Calibration Table	
A3	Fuel rod elongation	
A4	in millimeters	
A8	^Column Input	Center Align
A10	^Row Input	Center Align
A12	Transducer	Center Align
A13	Voltage	Center Align
A14	(V)	Center Align
C2	Coefficients	
D1	a0	Center Align
D2	0.3347	
E1	a1	Center Align
E2	10.6592	
F1	a2	Center Align
F2	−0.00219701	
G1	a3	Center Align
G2	−0.000632662	
C4	Transducer Temperature (K)	
C5	300	
D5	400	
E5	500	
F5	600	

Now mark the input cells to clarify how the table works. Use the Format Cells command, Patterns tab and select a light gray color to shade the cells.

4. Select cell A7, choose the Format ➤ Cells command, Patterns tab, select a light gray color and click OK. Do the same for cell A9.

In the left column of the table, enter the values for the first input.

5. In cell B6, enter **1.2**, and in cell B7, enter **1.0**; select cells B6:B7, and drag the fill handle to B18.

The final setup task is to enter the two-input function in the table at the intersection of the row and column containing the input values. Remember, the formula must reference both of the two input cells.

6. In cell B5, enter the following formula:

=D2+E2*A7+F2*(A9–608)+G2*(A9–608)*A7

Now use the Data ➤ Table command to create the table, then format the table. Hide the contents of the cell containing the formula so that it does not detract from the rest of the table (use the custom format code ;;;).

7. Select cells B5:F18 and choose Data ➤ Table. In the Table dialog box, click in the Row Input Cell box, then click on cell A9 to insert the row input cell reference. Click in the Column Input Cell box, and then click on cell A7 to insert the column input cell reference.

8. Format cells B6:B18 as Number, 1 decimal place.

9. Format cells C6:F18 as Number, 2 decimal places.

10. Format cell B5 as Custom ;;; to hide it.

11. Outline the table as shown in Figure 2.16.

	A	B	C	D	E	F	G	H
1	LVDT Calibration Table			a0	a1	a2	a3	
2			Coefficients	0.3347	10.6592	-0.002197	-0.000633	
3	Fuel rod elongation							
4	in millimeters		Transducer Temperature (K)					
5				300	400	500	600	
6		1.2	13.80	13.58	13.36	13.14		
7		1.0	11.67	11.45	11.23	11.01		
8	^Column Input	0.8	9.54	9.32	9.10	8.88		
9		0.6	7.41	7.19	6.97	6.75		
10	^Row Input	0.4	5.28	5.06	4.84	4.62		
11		0.2	3.14	2.92	2.70	2.48		
12	Transducer	0.0	1.01	0.79	0.57	0.35		
13	Voltage	-0.2	-1.12	-1.34	-1.56	-1.78		
14	(V)	-0.4	-3.25	-3.47	-3.69	-3.91		
15		-0.6	-5.38	-5.60	-5.82	-6.04		
16		-0.8	-7.52	-7.74	-7.96	-8.18		
17		-1.0	-9.65	-9.87	-10.09	-10.31		
18		-1.2	-11.78	-12.00	-12.22	-12.44		
19								
20								

fig. 2.11 / fig. 2.12 / fig. 2.13 / fig. 2.15 / fig. 2.16 / fi

12. Turn off the worksheet gridlines.

13. Save the worksheet.

Your worksheet should now look like Figure 2.16. You could now change one of the values in an input row or column, or change the table formula. Excel will automatically recalculate the table, unless you have set the Update option to Automatic Except Tables or to Manual on the Tools ➤ Options, Calculation tab. To update a table that is not automatically recalculated, press the F9 key.

If you want to add rows to the bottom or columns to the right of the table, you must select the data and choose the Data ➤ Table command again to include them in the table. If you want to insert rows or columns within the body of a table, you must first select and clear the body of the table (not the input values or the formula), then insert the new rows, select the new table, and choose the Data ➤ Table command again.

Creating and Using Function Calculators

Function calculators are special worksheet templates that work like a specialized hand calculator. You insert one or more numbers and other numbers are calculated from them. Generally a function calculator does not calculate tables of numbers for a single function but instead calculates single values.

A function calculator contains an input area where the user enters the input values and an output area where the results appear. You can also protect parts of the worksheet so that users can enter values only in the input area and not in other areas of the worksheet.

Creating a Simple Function Calculator

A function calculator need not be complex. In this first example, you'll create a function calculator that has a single input value and a single output value, and is calculated with a single simple formula.

Julian Day Calculator

One of the principle tasks of astronomers is recording the dates and times of events, measurements, and sightings. Although the dates can be in conventional days, months, and years, the irregularity of months and years makes calculations difficult. If you need to know the difference in time between two different events, you must take into account the lengths of the years (how many were regular years and how many were leap years) and the lengths of the months between the events.

Astronomers do not want to spend time calculating the lengths of months and years when there is a clear night sky and the seeing (the amount of twinkle in starlight) is good (less is good); therefore, they use a system of time measurement known as the Julian Day, proposed by Joseph Scalinger in 1582. The Julian Day calendar consists of consecutively numbered days, starting with January 1, 4713 BC. (I don't have any idea why he chose this particular date, but it is well before any accurately recorded history.) To find the difference in time between two events, you simply subtract their Julian Days.

Time of day is also incorporated into the Julian Day calendar as decimal fractions of a day. As you might expect, since astronomers generally work at night, Julian Days run noon to noon instead of midnight to midnight. Therefore, midnight between December 31, 1979, and January 1, 1980, is Julian Day 2,444,239.5.

Julian Days work well with Excel's date and time functions, which store dates and times in much the same way. The difference is that Excel starts numbering days on January 1, 1900, and uses the more traditional midnight to midnight definition to get the time of day. The conversion between Excel's date system and Julian Days is accomplished by simply adding the offset for a known date and time.

WARNING To be compatible with Lotus 1-2-3, Excel counts a day for 2/29/1900, even though that day does not exist. If you restrict yourself to dates after 3/1/1900, you will not have this problem. Also, the Macintosh uses the 1/1/1903 as the starting date, so be careful when transferring programs from one platform to another.

In the following example, create a simple function calculator that converts a standard date into a Julian Day.

1. Start with a new worksheet, and name it **fig. 2.17**

2. Set the width of column A to 12, B to 15, and D to 11.

3. Enter and format the following values as indicated:

Cell	Contents	Formatting
A1	**Julian Day Calculator**	
A3	**Input the date and time in one of Excel's date and time formats.**	
A4	**The date must be between 3/1/1900 and 12/31/2078**	
A7	**Date:**	Align Right
C7	**Time:**	Align Right
A9:	**Julian Day:**	Align Right
A11	**Julian days go from noon to noon rather than midnight to midnight.**	
A12	**Time of day is specified as fractions of a day.**	
A1	**The Julian day calendar starts at noon on Jan. 1, 4713 BC.**	

The Julian Day for 1/1/80 in the afternoon is JD 2,444,240. Use this date to synchronize the Julian Day calendar with Excel's date and time functions. You don't need to apply the DATEVALUE( ) function to the contents of cell B7 or TIMEVALUE( ) to D7, because Excel automatically converts dates and times that are entered as text into serial date numbers.

4. In cell B9, enter the following formula:

    =B7+D7–DATEVALUE("1/1/80")+2444239.5

5. Outline cells B7, D7, and B9.

6. Format cells B7 and D7 as Text.

7. Format cell B9 as Number with two decimal places, and with Use 1000 Separator (,) checked.

The text in cells A11:A13 looks a bit ragged. You can use the Edit ➤ Fill ➤ Justify command to form a compact paragraph. The text to be justified must be in a single column. The range you select determines the width of the text when it is justified.

8. Select A11:D15 and choose Edit ➤ Fill ➤ Justify.

9. Turn off the worksheet gridlines.

Finally, protect this worksheet so that other users cannot ruin your work. You want to protect all cells except the ones in which the user enters the date and time to be converted to a Julian Day. Use the Format ➤ Cells command, Protection tab to mark cells as *not* protected, then the Tools ➤ Protection ➤ Protect Sheet command to protect the worksheet. If a user tries to change a protected part of the worksheet, Excel beeps and displays a dialog box explaining that the cell cannot be changed. Another option here is to use a password to protect the document. If you use a password, the user cannot unprotect the document and make changes. If you check the Hidden checkbox on the Format Cells dialog box, Protection tab as well, the user won't be able to see your formulas either.

10. Select cell B7, choose Format ➤ Cells, Protection tab, then clear the Locked checkbox and click OK. Do the same for cell D7.

11. Choose Tools ➤ Protection ➤ Protect Sheet. In the Protect Sheet dialog box, the Contents checkbox should be checked. Click OK.

12. Save the workbook.

Now enter a date into cell B7 and a time into D7 using Excel's date and time formats; the Julian Day appears in cell B9. For example, if you enter January 19, 1997, in B7 and 1600 in D7, the worksheet would look like Figure 2.17.

FIGURE 2.17:

A Julian Day function calculator

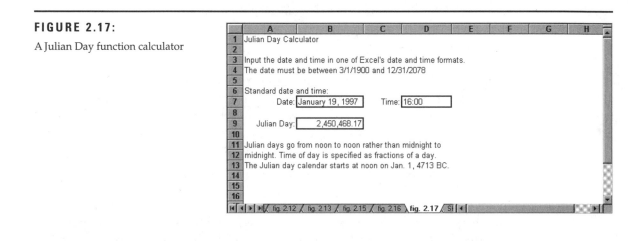

CAUTION

If you get the error value #VALUE! instead of a Julian Day, you probably have not used a date or time format that Excel understands. Check what you have entered into the date and time cells.

Setting Up a More Complex Function Calculator

A function calculator does not need to be as simple as that shown in Figure 2.17, but can contain many inputs and outputs. A complex function calculator is created in much the same way as a simple calculator; input cells are unprotected, and output cells contain formulas that calculate values from the inputs. A good use for complex calculators is engineering analysis and optimization. Often, when designing a new system or device, the calculated optimum values for some parameters are not practical. For example, having smaller tires on the left side of a car makes it corner better when making left turns. This smaller size may be optimum, but is certainly not practical for anything but a race car on a circular track. If you can't use the optimum values, you must make tradeoffs between slightly less than optimum values to get a mix of values that is both practical and that gives acceptable performance. A complex function calculator is a useful vehicle for examining the results of different tradeoffs.

Thermoelectric Cooler

A thermoelectric cooler is a solid-state heat pump. It is a semiconductor device that uses electrons to carry heat from one side of the device to the other. When you apply a voltage to a thermoelectric cooler, one side gets hot and the other side gets cold, the opposite of a thermocouple. In fact, if you drive a thermoelectric cooler with heat on one side and cold on the other, it generates an electric current. If you reverse the current through the thermoelectric cooler, the opposite sides of the device are heated and cooled.

Thermoelectric coolers have been used for many years to cool small volumes in restricted spaces, such as a single integrated circuit in the middle of a large circuit board. More recently, they have been used to heat or cool a food chest, so that you can have hot food and cold beer at a picnic.

In the next example, you'll create a complicated function calculator to analyze a thermoelectric cooler. The calculator will calculate all the relevant design and operational parameters for the problem.

The input parameters for a thermoelectric cooler consist of material parameters and device parameters. The material parameters are the Seebeck coefficient (α), the resistivity (ρ), and the figure of merit (Z), for the n-type and p-type semiconductor materials that make up the two legs of the cooler. Here are the material parameters for two semiconductor materials commonly used in thermoelectric coolers:

Parameter	n-type	p-type
Composition	75% Bi_2Te_3 25% Bi_2Se_3	25% Bi_2Te_3 75% Sb_2Te_3
Seebeck coefficient (α)	-1.65×10^{-4}	2.10×10^{-4} V/K

Parameter	n-type	p-type
Resistivity (ρ)	1.05×10^{-3}	9.8×10^{-4} ohm-cm
Figure of merit (Z)	2.0×10^{-3}	3.5×10^{-3} $(K)^{-1}$

The thermal conductivities (λ) of the materials are calculated using this equation:

$$\lambda = \frac{\alpha^2}{\rho Z}$$

The junction Seebeck coefficient is calculated by this equation:

$$\alpha = |\alpha_n| + |\alpha_p|$$

The device parameters start with the ratios of the areas to the lengths of the n- and p-legs of the thermoelectric cooler: γ_n and γ_p. These are the design parameters. In the following ratio, the parameters optimize the coefficient of performance (β):

$$\frac{\gamma_n}{\gamma_p} = \left(\frac{\rho_n \lambda_p}{\rho_p \lambda_n} \right)$$

The figure of merit for the junction is given by this equation:

$$Z = \frac{\alpha^2}{RK}$$

where R is the device resistance and K is the device thermal conductance.

$$R = \frac{\rho_n}{\lambda_n} + \frac{\rho_p}{\lambda_n}$$

$$K = \lambda_n \gamma_n + \lambda_p \gamma_p$$

The optimized figure of merit is given by this equation:

$$Z^* = \frac{\alpha^2}{[(\rho_n \lambda_n)^{1/2} + (\rho_p \lambda_b)^{1/2}]}$$

The driving current is another design parameter, and the value that optimizes the coefficient of performance is derived by this equation:

$$I = \frac{\alpha \Delta T}{R\left[(1 + Z^* T_{av})^{1/2} - 1\right]}$$

where T_{av} is the average and ΔT is the temperature difference of the hot (T_h) and cold (T_c) junction temperatures.

The heat pumping rate from the cold junction is as follows:

$$q = \alpha T_c I - \tfrac{1}{2} I^2 R - K \Delta T$$

The coefficient of performance is the ratio of the heat pumped from the cold junction to the electrical energy required to pump it:

$$\beta = \frac{\alpha T_c I - \tfrac{1}{2} I^2 R - K \Delta T}{\alpha I \Delta T + I^2 R}$$

The maximum value of β is found by inserting the optimized values of I, K, and R:

$$\beta_{max} = \frac{T_c}{\Delta T} \left[\frac{\left(1 + Z^* T_{av}\right)^{1/2} - T_h/T_c}{\left(1 + Z^* T_{av}\right)^{1/2} + 1} \right]$$

Finally, the power input into the device is as follows:

$$P = \alpha I \Delta T + I^2 R$$

If the device was completely optimized, this would equal the optimized power input:

$$P = \frac{q}{\beta_{max}}$$

Using these equations, create a function calculator that calculates all the device parameters. Calculate two sets of values: one for input device parameters, and the other for the optimized values of the device parameters. Begin by entering the material type and material parameters described above.

1. Start with a new worksheet, name it **fig. 2.18**

2. Set the widths of columns A through E as follows:

Column	Width	Column	Width
A	16	D	12
B	12	E	9
C	12		

3. In cell A1, enter **Thermoelectric Cooler Calculator**

4. In cell A2, enter the following text:

    n-type: 75% Bi_2Te_3 25% Bi_2Se_3 p-type: 25% Bi_2Te_3 75% Sb_2Te_3

5. Enter the following values into the indicated cells:

Cell	Contents	Cell	Contents
A3	alpha =	C5	1/K
A4	Rho =	D3	2.1E–4
A5	Z =	D4	9.8E–4
B3	–1.65E–4	D5	3.5E–3
B4	1.05E–3	E3	V/K
B5	2.0E–3	E4	ohm-cm
C3	V/K	E5	1/K
C4	ohm-cm		

Next enter the calculations for the thermal conductivities, and the hot and cold junction temperatures. Assume that you want to keep the cold junction at freezing (273 K) and the hot junction at 327 K, so that the average is at room temperature (300 K). Enter the area-to-length ratios, also. The optimized value of γ_p will be calculated in cell D11.

6. Enter the following values into the indicated cells.

Cell	Contents	Cell	Contents
A6	lambda =	D7	273
B6	=B3^2/(B4*B5)	E7	K
C6	watt/cm–K.	A8	gamma =
D6	D3^2/(D4*D5)	B8	1
E6	watt/cm–K.	C8	cm
A7	T-hot, T-cold=	D8	1
B7	327	E8	cm
C7	K		

Now calculate all the figures of merit, heat pumping rates and currents. Place the optimized calculations on the right side of the table and the actual values on the left, so you can adjust the actual values to see how close you can come to the optimized values. You often can't use the optimized values because they aren't practical; for example, having the hot leg and cold leg of two different lengths is not practical even though the optimized parameters say they should be different. Use this calculator to see how much difference there is in the final efficiency if you don't use the optimized values.

7. Enter the following values into the indicated cells.

Cell	Contents
A9	Tav =
B9	=(B7+D7)/2
C9	K Alpha =
D9	=ABS(B3)+ABS(D3)
B10	General Values

Cell	Contents
D10	Optimized Values
A11	gamma p opt =
D11	=SQRT(D4*B6/(B4*D6))
E11	cm
A12	Z =
B12	=D9^2/(B13*B14)
C12	1/K
D12	=D9^2/((SQRT(B4*B6)+SQRT(D4*D6))^2)
E12	1/K
A13	K =
B13	=B6*B8+D6*D8
C13	watt/K
D13	=B6*B8+D6*D11
E13	watt/K
A14	R =
B14	=B4/B8+D4/D8
C14	ohm
D14	=B4/B8+D4/D11
E14	ohm
A15	I =
B15	29
C15	amps
D15	=D9*(B7–D7)/(D14*(SQRT(1+D12*B9)–1))
E15	amps
A16	qc =
B16	=D9*D7*B15–0.5*B15^2*B14–B13*(B7–D7)
C16	watts
D16	=D9*D7*D15–0.5*D15^2*D14–D13*(B7–D7)
E16	watts

Cell	Contents
A17	beta =
B17	=(D9*D7*B15–0.5*B15^2*B14–B13*(B7–D7))/(D9*B15*(B7–D7)+B15^2*B14)
D17	=(D7/(B7–D7))*(SQRT(1+D12*B9)–B7/D7)/(SQRT(1+D12*B9)+1)
A18	P =
B18	=D9*B15*(B7–D7)+B15^2*B14
C18	watts
D18	=D16/D17
E18	watts

8. Right-align cells A3:A18, then format the following cells as Scientific, 3 decimal places.

   B3:B6

   B12:B14

   D3:D6

   D9

   D12:D14

SHORTCUT Another way to quickly apply a format to several groups of cells is to use the Format Painter. Format the first group, then select the group and click the Format Painter button. You can now select any other group of cells and they will be given the same formatting as the first selection.

9. Format these cells as Number, 3 decimal places:

   B15:B18

   D11

   D15:D18

10. Unprotect the following cells by selecting them, choosing the Format ➤ Cells command, Protection tab, and clearing the Locked checkbox; then format the cells bold by clicking the Bold button.

> A2
>
> B15
>
> B3:B5
>
> D3:D5
>
> B7:B8
>
> D7:D8

11. Turn off the worksheet gridlines.

12. Select cells A2:F2 and underline them by using the heavy bottom border from the Border palette (on the Formatting toolbar). Do the same for cells A9:F10.

It can be difficult to remember the name of the engineering quantity designated by the variables in column A, so create a series of cell notes containing the full name of the quantity. To add a note to a cell, select the cell and choose the Insert ➤ Note command. The Cell Note dialog box appears.

Enter the text of the note in the Text Note field and click Add. If you are adding notes to several cells, select the Cell box, enter the cell name, press Tab twice to move to the Text Note box, type the note and click Add. When you are finished with all your notes, choose OK. Cells with notes added have a small red note indicator in the upper right corner.

Now, whenever the cursor is over a cell containing a note (in Excel for Windows 95), the contents of the note pops up as shown here.

	A	B	C
1	Thermoelectric Cooler Calculator		
2	n-type: 75% Bi$_2$Te$_3$ 25% Bi$_2$Se$_3$		
3	alpha =	-1.650E-04 V/K	
4	Rho =	1.050E-03 ohm-cm	
5	Z =	2.000E-03 1/K	
6	Material	1.296E-02 watt/cm-K	
7	T-F Figure of	327 K	
8	Merit	1 cm	
9	Tav =	300 K Alpha =	
10	General Values		

13. Insert the following notes in the indicated cells.

Cell	Note
A3	**Material Seebeck Coefficient**
A4	**Material Resistivity**
A5	**Material Figure of Merit**
A6	**Material Thermal Conductivity**
A7	**Hot Leg and Cold Leg Temperatures**
A8	**Ratio of the Leg Area to Leg Length**
A9	**Average Temperature**
C9	**Junction Seebeck Coefficient**
A11	**Optimized p–type A/l Ratio Using the n–type A/l**
A12	**Junction Figure of Merit**
A13	**Device Thermal Conductance**
A14	**Device Resistance**
A15	**Device Current**
A16	**Heat Flow into the Cold Side**
A17	**Coefficient of Performance**
A18	**Input Power**

14. Protect the worksheet by choosing Tools ➤ Protection ➤ Protect Sheet and choosing OK in the Protect Sheet dialog box.

15. Save the workbook.

Your worksheet should now look like Figure 2.18. The unprotected cells (the ones whose values you can change) stand out because they are in a bold font. You could also color them using the Format ➤ Cells command, Font tab.

FIGURE 2.18:

A function calculator for analyzing a thermoelectric cooler

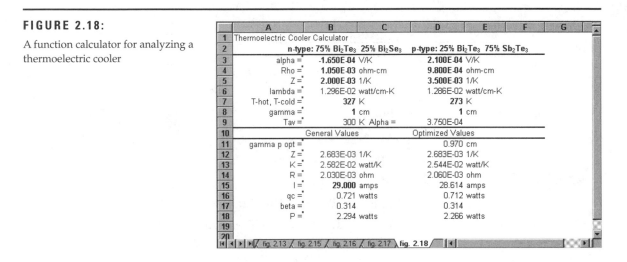

To use the worksheet, adjust the design values in the unprotected cells to see how making changes in the cooler's design changes the efficiency and power requirements. You can also compare the design parameters with the optimized parameters to see how far from an optimum design you are.

Summary

This chapter covered at least 50 percent of the worksheet techniques that a practicing scientist or engineer uses in the course of his or her daily work. Much of the numerical work that we do involves putting simple numbers into relatively simple equations and calculating the results. As you have seen, the worksheet format is quite suitable for this type of work. All that is missing is a graphical presentation of the data, which is discussed in the next chapter.

In this chapter, you explored the various ways to create engineering tables and function calculators with Excel. Engineering tables allow you to calculate single or multiple values from scientific and engineering equations. Function calculators calculate values for complex sets of equations; with them, you can model a complex system, and then perform what-if analyses with the system parameters and see the results immediately. While creating these tables and calculators, you have used many of the commands and techniques that simplify the creation of a worksheet and define how the completed worksheet will look. As you use the program to solve your own problems and gain experience in building worksheets, you will find many more ways to calculate and present useful results.

For More Information

Thermal Conductivity

L. Heasell, "The Heat Flow Problem in Silicon," *IEEE Trans. on Elec. Dev., ED-25*, 12 (Dec. 1978):1382.

Precession of the North Celestial Pole

A. E. Roy, *The Foundations of Astrodynamics* (New York: Macmillan, 1969), p. 53.

Temperature Dependence of the Intrinsic Carrier Density

S. M. Sze, *Physics of Semiconductor Devices*, 2nd. ed. (New York: Wiley, 1981), p. 19.

van der Waals Equation of State

D. Halliday, R. Resnick, *Physics* (New York: Wiley, 1967), pp. 611-615.

Absolute Magnitude of a Star

D. S. Birney, *Modern Astronomy* (Boston: Allyn and Bacon, 1969), pp. 168-174.

Electron Mobility in Silicon

W. J. Orvis, *Semiconductor Device Modeling with BURN42; a One-Dimensional Code for Modeling Solid State Devices*, UCID-20602 (Livermore, CA: Lawrence Livermore National Laboratory, 1985), p. 8.

D. M. Canghey, R. E. Thomas, "Carrier Mobilities in Silicon Empirically Related to Doping and Field," *Proc. IEEE* (Dec. 1967): 2192.

C. Jacoboni, C. Canali, G. Ottaviani, A. A. Quaranta, "A Review of Some Charge Transport Properties of Silicon," *Solid State Electronics*, 20 (1977): 77.

Stress and Deflection in a Cantilever Beam

E. Oberg, F. D. Jones, H. L. Horton, *Machinery's Handbook*, 20th ed. (New York: Industrial Press, 1978).

T. Baumeister, E. A. Avallone, T. Baumeister III, *Standard Handbook for Mechanical Engineers* (New York: McGraw-Hill, 1979).

Julian Days

G. Ottewell, *The Astronomical Companion* (Greenville, SC: Furman University, 1979), p. 23.

Thermoelectric Coolers

S. W. Angrist, *Direct Energy Conversion*, 4th. ed. (Boston: Allyn and Bacon, 1982), pp. 148-153.

Review Problems

1. Create a table of sine, cosine, tangent, arc sine, arc cosine, and arc tangent for the angles 0 through 180 degrees in steps of 10 degrees. Use degrees instead of radians.

2. Create a table of common logarithms, $\log(x)$; natural logarithms, $\ln(x)$; exponentials, e^x; and powers of ten, 10^x for the values 0, .1, .3, .5, .9, 1.0, 2.0, 5.0, 8.0, and 10.0. Automatically insert the text *INF* for $\log(0)$ and $\ln(0)$ by testing the argument with an IF statement.

3. Create a simple function calculator that, when you input an angle in degrees, will calculate all six of the trigonometric functions (sine, cosine, tangent, secant, cosecant, and cotangent) and their logarithms.

4. The Lemniscate of Bernoulli, also known as a two-leaf rose curve, is a figure-eight shaped curve aligned with the x axis. It is defined by the equation

$$\left(x^2 + y^2\right) = a^2\left(x^2 - y^2\right) \qquad \text{or} \qquad r^2 = a^2\cos(2\theta)$$

Let $a = 2$ and calculate a table of 50 values of x and y to use to draw the complete curve (that is, let θ range from 0 to 2π).

5. Create a table comparing the pressure for a given temperature and volume of gas using the Van der Waals equation of state for nitrogen, ammonia, and helium. Make the table for 10 different combinations of temperature and volume.

Gas	a $(l^2$–atm/mol$^2)$	b (l/mol)
N_2	1.39	0.0391
NH_3	4.17	0.037
He	0.0341	0.0237

6. Create a function calculator for a thermoelectric cooler that uses 75%–PbTe 25%–SnTe and AgSbTe$_2$

	75%–PbTe 25%–SnTe	AgSbTe$_2$	
type	n	p	
α	80	240	μV/K
ρ	0.8×10^{-3}	4.3×10^{-3}	ohm–cm
Z	0.8×10^{-3}	1.8×10^{-3}	K^{-1}

7. The bending (stress and deflection) of a uniformly loaded (W/l pounds/unit length) cantilever beam is described in the equations

$$S = \frac{W}{2Zl}(l - x)^2$$

$$y = \frac{Wx^2}{24 EIl}\left(2l^2 + (2l - x)^2\right)$$

Use the same beam as the example with the cantilever beam loaded at a single point. Using the Data ➤ Table command, create a single-input table that shows the stress and deflection along the beam for different total loadings. Include the weight of the beam in the loading.

8. Create a function calculator that converts ecliptic coordinates (ecliptic latitude β and ecliptic longitude λ) to equatorial coordinates (right ascension α and declination δ). Input the date and the ecliptic coordinates and output the equatorial coordinates. Don't forget to convert degrees to hours for the right ascension. (Use the ATAN2 function to get the quadrant correct.)

$$\delta = \arcsin\left[\sin(\beta)\cos(\varepsilon) + \cos(\beta)\sin(\varepsilon)\sin(\lambda)\right]$$

$$\cos(\alpha) = \left[\frac{\cos(\beta)\cos(\lambda)}{\cos(\delta)}\right]$$

$$\sin(\alpha) = \left[\frac{\cos(\beta)\cos(\varepsilon)\sin(\lambda) - \sin(\beta)\sin(\varepsilon)}{\cos(\delta)}\right]$$

$$\alpha = \arctan\left(\frac{\sin(\alpha)}{\cos(\alpha)}\right)$$

9. The escape velocity (v) is calculated with the equation

$$v^2 = G(m_1 + m_2)\frac{2}{r}$$

where
G = gravitational constant (6.67×10^{-11} nt–m^2/kg^2)
m_1 = mass of planet (kg)
m_2 = mass of escaping body (kg)
r = radius of planet (m)

Create a table of escape velocities for a rifle bullet escaping from the following bodies ($m_1 \gg m_2$; that is, ignore m_2).

	Radius (km)	Mass (kg)
Sun	695,300	1.97×10^{30}
Mercury	2,439	2.39×10^{23}
Venus	6,050	4.91×10^{24}
Earth	6,378	5.98×10^{24}
Moon	1,738	7.35×10^{22}
Mars	3,396	6.58×10^{23}

	Radius (km)	Mass (kg)
Jupiter	71,398	1.90×10^{27}
Saturn	60,330	5.70×10^{26}
Uranus	25,900	8.80×10^{25}
Neptune	24,750	1.04×10^{26}
Pluto	1,500	1.41×10^{22}

10. Make a table of drift velocities (v) and mobility (μ) for electrons in GaAs moving under applied fields (E) ranging from 0 to 10 KV/cm.

$$v = \frac{\mu_1 E \left(1 + BF^k\right)}{1 + F^k}$$

$$\mu = \frac{v}{E}$$

$$F = \frac{E}{E_0}$$

where
$E_0 = 4,000$ V/cm
$\mu_1 = 8,000$ cm^2/V–s
$k = 4$
$B = 0.05$

Exercises

1. A water tank 10 feet in diameter holds 30,000 gallons of water. Create a table of water level versus time for an outflow of 5 gpm, 10 gpm, and 50 gpm.

2. A rock falling under the force of gravity has a position given by ½ gt^2 and a velocity given by gt where $g = 980$ m/s^2 and t is the time. Create a table of position and velocity for every second for the first 20 seconds.

3. Create a function calculator for a surveyor. The surveyor draws a baseline and measures the angle to a hilltop from two points on that baseline. For the two angles and the distance between where they were measured, calculate the shortest distance between the baseline and the top of the hill.

4. The average speed (c) of an ideal gas molecule is given by the following equation:

$$c = \sqrt{\frac{3P}{\rho}}$$

where P is the pressure and ρ is the density. Create a table of velocities for hydrogen gas ($\rho = 0.09$ kg/m^3) at the pressures 100 Atm, 10 Atm, 1Atm, 0.1 Atm, 0.01 Atm and 0.001 Atm (1Atm = 1.01325 x 10^5 N/m^2.)

5. Create a function calculator that calculates the average velocity of an ideal gas molecule (see exercise 4) for different values of the density and pressure input by the user. Let the user input the pressure in Torr (1 Atm = 760 Torr).

6. Poiseuille's law for viscous fluid flow through a pipe of radius a is

$$Q = \frac{\pi a^4 P}{8\eta l}$$

where Q is the flow rate (m^3/s), P/l is the pressure gradient down the pipe (N/m^3), and η is the viscosity (kg/m-s). Create a two-input table using copied formulas for water ($\eta = 100 \times 10^{-5}$ Kg/m-s) for 10 pipe diameters between 0.5 cm and 5 cm, and 10 pressure gradients between 10^5 and 10^6 N/m^3 (1 to 10 Atm through a 1 m pipe.)

7. Do problem 6 again but use the Data ➤ Table command and do it for oil ($\eta = 8400 \times 10^{-5}$ kg/m-s).

8. The average velocity of a viscous fluid in a pipe (see exercises 6 and 7) is given by

$$\bar{v} = \frac{a^2 P}{8\eta l}$$

and the Reynolds number is

$$Re = \frac{2\bar{v}a\rho}{\eta}$$

where ρ is the density (water $\rho = 1000$ kg/m^3, oil $\rho = 900$ kg/m^3). The flow rates calculated in problems 3 and 4 depend on the flow being laminar in the pipe. If the Reynolds number is greater than 2000 then the flow is turbulent and the formulas don't apply. Calculate the Reynolds number for the pressures and pipe diameters in problems 3 and 4 to see if any of the calculations are invalid.

9. Create a function calculator for a thermoelectric generator that uses 75%–PbTe 25%–SnTe and AgSbTe$_2$. See review problem 6 for the material values.

10. The deflection at the center of a beam loaded at the center and simply supported at the ends is given by

$$f = \frac{Wl^3}{48EI}$$

Use the same beam as the example problem and calculate the deflection for different applied weights. How much weight does it take to get a deflection of 1 inch?

CHAPTER

THREE

3

Charting Data and Functions

- Excel's chart types and their uses

- Using the ChartWizard

- Charting data from a table

- Attaching and editing labels

- Drawing with the drawing tools

- Drawing with data

Once you have generated a list of numbers, your next task is to analyze them. The simplest form of analysis is to plot the numbers and see what kind of curve they form. A lot of good scientific insight has resulted from simply looking at the shape of a plot of data. In this chapter, you will examine the plotting capabilities of Excel and learn how to adapt them to scientific and engineering uses.

Creating a Chart

Two types of charts exist in Excel: charts embedded in worksheets and those on separate chart sheets. Embedded charts are attached to a worksheet. They are a part of a worksheet in the same way that a table of values is a part of the worksheet. Chart sheets are separate sheets in a workbook, and contain a single chart. In both types of charts, the points plotted on the chart are linked to the cells of a worksheet. Which type you use depends on what you are doing.

When you are analyzing data on a worksheet, you most likely will use small embedded charts. You can place a chart on the worksheet, near the data used to create it. Embedded charts are usually too small for a printed presentation, but they are more than sufficient for analysis purposes. When you are preparing a chart for a presentation or document, you will probably use a chart sheet to create a large, good-quality graph.

Embedding a Chart on a Worksheet

Creating a chart in Excel generally involves executing four or five different commands to create the basic chart, set its type, add labels, and so on. To simplify this process, Excel provides the ChartWizard, a single command that walks you through most of the steps needed to create a chart.

Selecting the Data and Chart Location

The ChartWizard has five dialog boxes, each of which gathers more of the information needed to create a chart. The first step in creating a chart is to select the data to be plotted, as follows:

- If x-data and one or more columns of y-data are in adjacent columns on a worksheet, select those columns.

- If the first cell in each column contains the text to use in a legend, select those cells as well.

- If the columns of data are not adjacent, select the column of x-data first, then hold down the Ctrl key (Cmd on the Macintosh) and select the first column of y-data. Continue until you have selected all the data to be plotted.

- If the data is in rows instead of columns, select the data as described for non-adjacent columns, but by rows instead of by columns.

The following worksheet has one column of x data and two columns of y data. The labels for the x and y data are in the first row, though only the labels in the y data columns are used on the graph.

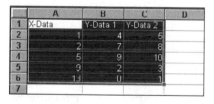

	A	B	C	D
1	X-Data	Y-Data 1	Y-Data 2	
2	1	4	5	
3	2	7	8	
4	5	9	10	
5	9	2	3	
6	13	0	1	
7				

After selecting the data, choose the ChartWizard command by clicking the ChartWizard button on the Standard toolbar. When you click the button, the cursor changes into a cross shape. Click and drag a rectangle on the current worksheet where you want the chart to appear. Don't worry if the rectangle is not exactly right; you can change its size and location later.

As soon as you select a location for the chart, the ChartWizard's first dialog box appears. The first dialog box asks you to verify that the selected data is the data you want to plot. If the data is correct, click the Next button to move to the second dialog box.

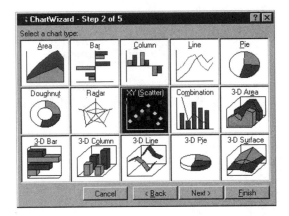

Selecting the Chart Type

In the ChartWizard's second dialog box, choose a chart type from the 15 types available. Of all the chart types, only the XY (Scatter) and 3-D Surface charts are really useful for science and engineering purposes.

The XY chart type is a true x-y chart, with linear or logarithmic scales on both axes. The XY chart type is the only type that actually plots the *x* range of data. All the other chart types use the *x* data for labels, so no matter what values you use for the *x* data, the plotted points are always equally spaced in the *x* direction. Unless all of your data is equally spaced and ordered, the other chart types are not particularly useful for science and engineering tasks.

A 3-D surface chart plots a rectangular grid of data as a 3-D surface. The data for the x- and y-axes is above and to the right of the grid of *z* data. The chart plots only the values of the *z* data, and equally spaces the plotted points along the *x* and *y* directions. The *x* and *y* data are used only for labels.

Click on the type of chart you want to create, and then click Next to continue.

Selecting the Chart Style

When you choose the XY chart type, the dialog box shown below appears. It shows six standard styles for XY charts: data markers only, markers and lines, markers and grids, markers and vertical semilog grids, markers and logarithmic grids, and lines only.

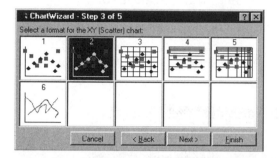

NOTE The chart styles shown in Step 3 of the ChartWizard are the most common styles. You are not constrained to only those styles, but can individually change any of the properties of a chart. Pick the style that is closest to the final result you desire, then modify it later to exactly what you want.

If you select a 3-D Surface chart type, the dialog box shown below appears. It shows the four standard styles for 3-D charts: 3-D surface, 3-D wire-frame, colored contour chart (looking straight down on a surface chart), and wire-frame contour chart.

Select the style that most closely resembles how you want your final chart to appear and click Next to continue.

Determining the Data Layout

The data for an XY chart type is normally organized in adjacent columns or rows. If the data is in columns, the first column contains the x data and the columns to the right contain the y data for one or more plots. The y data for each plot on a chart is known as a data series and may also include the x data and a label for a legend. If the x data is missing, the values 1, 2, 3, … are used.

The fourth ChartWizard dialog box, shown below, displays a sample chart and asks for information about how the data is organized on the worksheet. With this information, the ChartWizard combines the x and y data and the labels and produces the chart.

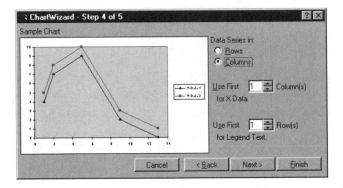

For the XY chart type, there are three questions to answer:

- How is the data organized, by columns or by rows?
- Does the first column or row contain x data, or is it the first series of y data?
- Does the first cell in each column or row contain a label for the series, or does it contain the first data point?

The organization of 3-D chart types is quite different from the 2-D chart types. In a 3-D chart, the z data forms a rectangular region on the worksheet. The first row above this rectangular region can contain the x data, and the first column to the left can contain the y data. The x and y data values that apply to a z value are the ones that are in the same row and column as the z value. If the y values are omitted, the labels s1, s2, s3,… are used. If the x values are omitted, the values 1, 2, 3,… are used as labels. For 3-D charts, the ChartWizard asks similar questions as those for the XY chart type:

- Is the data in columns or rows? This option does not make a lot of difference in a 3-D chart type, but serves to identify whether the *x* data is in the first column or the first row.

- Does the first column or row contain *x* data, or is it the first series of *z* data?

- Does the first row or column contain the *y* data, or is it the first data point in each series?

Click the option buttons next to the correct answers, then on Next to continue.

Adding Titles

The last ChartWizard dialog box, shown below, lets you add a title, axis labels, and a legend to the chart. In XY charts, the legend shows the series name and samples of the line and marker used to represent it. Use a legend on multiseries XY charts to mark the different series. In 3-D charts, the legend shows the range of *z* values that apply to a color on the chart.

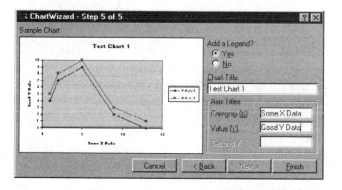

Type the text you want for the title and axes labels into the text boxes. Click Finish to complete the chart and draw it on the worksheet.

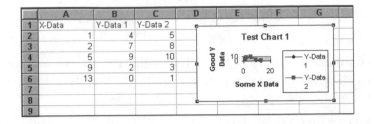

Well, that isn't exactly what I had in mind. When all the labels and legend are inserted, there is no room left for the chart. Select the chart and enlarge it by dragging one of the handles around its edge. Figure 3.1 shows the result after enlarging the graph.

FIGURE 3.1:

A chart embedded in a worksheet

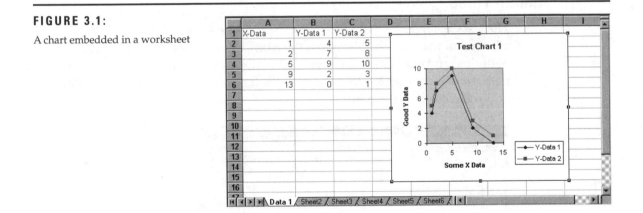

Editing the Chart

After creating a chart on a worksheet, you may need to edit the chart elements to change its appearance. To edit an existing chart, double-click on the chart. Double-clicking activates the chart so that you can edit its elements. In the case of the chart in Figure 3.1, the legend is in a bad place, and the plot area does not make good use of the chart area. Click on the legend to select it, then drag it up and to the right. Next, click on the plot area and enlarge it by dragging one of its selection handles to the right. Click anywhere on the worksheet to deactivate the chart and make the worksheet active again. The result is shown in Figure 3.2.

Embedding a Chart on a Worksheet

FIGURE 3.2:

The completed chart on a worksheet.

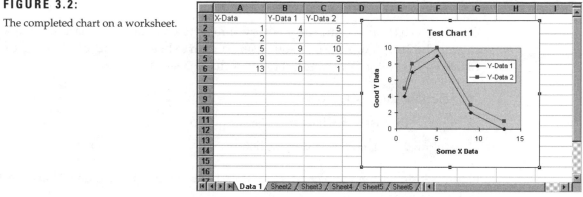

Making Higher-Quality Charts

While Excel's charts are more than adequate for most research purposes, they are not sufficient for most journals. To create a chart that a journal will except, you have two choices: edit an image of the chart with a drawing program, or get a companion program that creates better charts.

In general, the chart is sufficient for a publisher, but the axes and data labels are not. With a drawing program, you can change the labels by simply deleting the old ones and typing new ones in their places.

A good companion program for plotting Excel data is DeltaGraph® Pro. To create a chart in DeltaGraph® Pro, simply copy the data in the worksheet, switch to DeltaGraph® Pro and paste the data into its data sheet. DeltaGraph® Pro has many more chart types, and it formats numeric labels in scientific (2.3×10^5) **or engineering (230.0×10^3)notationinsteadofthecomputernotation(2.3E5)usedby Excel.**

DeltaGraph® Pro is available for both the Mac and PC platforms from DeltaPoint Inc. See Appendix A for more information.

Creating a Chart Sheet

Creating a chart on a chart sheet is very similar to embedding a chart in a worksheet. The difference is that you insert a chart sheet instead of clicking the ChartWizard button. To create a chart on a chart sheet:

1. Select the data to be plotted.

2. Choose the Insert ➤ Chart ➤ As New Sheet command.

3. Follow the ChartWizard steps as before.

Figure 3.3 shows the same chart as was created in Figure 3.2, but on a chart sheet instead of embedded in a worksheet.

FIGURE 3.3:

A chart created on a chart sheet

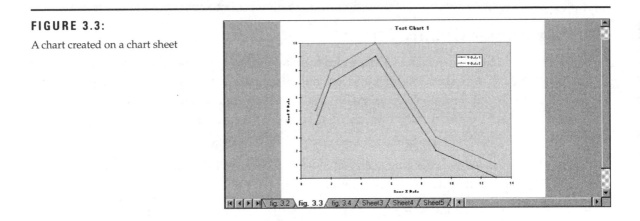

Plotting an Engineering Table

The following example demonstrates how to create charts of engineering functions. First, calculate a list of values from an equation; then create an XY chart from the data.

Resistivity of Silicon

A plot of the resistivity of silicon versus temperature is a multivalued curve that peaks at some temperature between 300 and 1000 K, depending on the doping density. This curve is important to solid-state device engineers because devices that operate beyond the peak are likely to fail.

At low temperatures, the resistance of silicon increases with temperature. Thus, any heating of a device due to high currents is self-limiting; the increasing resistance reduces the current, which reduces the heating. If, on the other hand, the temperature of a device passes a threshold value, the resistance starts to decrease with temperature. As the resistance decreases, more current flows, which increases the heating and decreases the resistance even more. The effect grows exponentially until the device melts. This is the thermal-runaway state known as thermal second breakdown in semiconductor devices.

The resistivity of silicon due to electron motion (ignore hole motion for this example) is defined with the following equation:

$$\rho = \frac{1}{qn\mu}$$

where ρ is the resistivity in ohm-meters, q is the charge on an electron, n is the electron density, and μ is the electron mobility. The electron equilibrium density in doped silicon is obtained from this equation:

$$n = \frac{1}{2}\left[N + \sqrt{N^2 + 4n_i^2} \right]$$

where N is the doping density in m^{-3}, and n_i is the intrinsic carrier density. In Chapter 2, you calculated the intrinsic carrier density, as well as the mobility for all fields, temperatures, and doping densities; however, for this problem, you will be dealing with low fields and doping densities, so the mobility equation can be approximated with:

$$\mu = \mu_0 \left(\frac{T}{T_0} \right)^{-2.42}$$

which is much simpler than the formula used in the previous chapter. If you still have the intrinsic carrier density problem available, you can use it as a starting point for this problem. Otherwise, you will need to type it all in again.

Creating the Table

Calculate the resistivity of silicon versus temperature for three doping densities: 1.0×10^{13}, 1.5×10^{13}, and 1.0×10^{14} cm^{-3}.

1. Start with a new worksheet, and name it **fig. 3.4**

2. Enter the following values into the indicated cells (use Alt-230 on the numeric keypad to type the μ).

Cell	Contents	Cell	Contents	Cell	Contents
A1	**Resistivity of Silicon vs. Temperature**	C2	**EG2=**	F2	**1.6E-19**
		C3	**Cons=**	F3	**1330**
A2	**EG0=**	D2	**636**	G2	**T0=**
A3	**EG1=**	E2	**Q=**	G3	**GAMMA=**
B2	**1.17**	E3	**μ0=**	H2	**300**
B3	**4.73E-4**			H3	**2.42**

3. In cell D3, type the following formula:

    =SQRT(4*6*(2*PI()*0.91095E–30*1.38066E–23/(6.62618E–34)^2)^3)
    *(0.33*0.56)^(0.75)*1E–6

4. Select cells A2:B3, choose the Insert ➤ Name ➤ Create command, make sure the Left Column option is checked, and choose OK. This names cells B2 and B3 as EG0 and EG1_, respectively. The name for cell EG1 is followed by an underscore to differentiate it from the valid cell reference for cell EG1. Follow the same procedure to name cells C2:D3, E2:F3, and G2:H3.

5. Select and right-align cells A2:A3, C2:C3, E2:E3, and G2:G3.

6. Excel does not know how to handle the μ in cell E3, so the symbol was replaced with an underscore when creating a name for cell F3. Select cell F3, choose the Insert ➤ Name ➤ Define command, name the cell **u0**, and delete the name _0.

7. Type the following values into the indicated cells.

Cell	Contents	Cell	Contents	Cell	Contents	Cell	Contents
D5	**Doping:**	E5	**1E13**	F5	**(cm^{-3})**	G5	**1.5E13**
H5	**(cm^{-3})**	I5	**1E14**	J5	**(cm^{-3})**		
A6	**T**	B6	**Eg**	C6	**ni**		
D6	**μ**	E6	**n**	F6	**rho**		
A7	**(K)**	B7	**(eV)**	C7	**(cm^{-3})**		
D7	**$(cm^2/V\text{-}s)$**	E7	**(cm^{-3})**	F7	**(ohm-cm)**		

8. Center the contents of cells F5, H5, J5, and A6:F7, and right-align the contents of cells A2:A3, C2:C3, E2:E3, and G2:G3.

9. Copy cells E6:F7 to G6:H7 and again to I6:J7.

SHORTCUT You can quickly perform step 9 by selecting cells E6:F7, holding down the Ctrl key (Cmd on the Macintosh) and dragging the two cells to G6:H7, and then to I6:J7.

10. In cell A8, enter **300**, and in cell A9, enter **320**. Then select A8:A9 and drag the fill handle down to cell A18.

11. In cell B8, enter the formula:

    =EG0–EG1_*A8^2/(A8+EG2_)

12. In cell C8, enter the formula:

    =Cons*SQRT(A8^3)*EXP(–B8*1.60219E–19/(2*1.38066E–23*A8))

13. In cell D8, enter the formula:

    =u0*(A8/T0)^(–GAMMA)

14. In cell E8, enter the formula:

    =0.5*(E$5+SQRT(E$5^2+4*$C8^2))

15. In cell F8, enter the formula:

    =1/(Q*E8*$D8)

16. Format cell B8 as Number, 2 decimal places.

17. Format cells C8:F8 as Scientific, 1 decimal place.

18. Copy cells E8:F8 into cells G8:H8 and I8:J8.

19. Select cells B8:J8, then drag the fill handle down to cell J18. This copies the formulas down into the body of the table.

20. Outline the table as shown in Figure 3.4.

21. Turn off the gridlines.

Your worksheet should look like Figure 3.4, with three sets of data that need to be plotted.

Creating the Chart

To plot this data, first move the table out of the way to make room for the chart, then use the ChartWizard to plot the three mobility curves versus temperature.

1. Start with the worksheet in Figure 3.4.

2. Select cells A5:J18, grab the top edge of the selection rectangle with the mouse and drag so that the upper-left corner moves down to cell A18. This moves the whole table down.

FIGURE 3.4:

Table for calculating the resistivity of silicon versus temperature

	A	B	C	D	E	F	G	H	I	J
1	Resistivity of Silicon vs. Temperature									
2	EG0=	1.17	EG2=	636	Q=	1.60E-19	T0=	300		
3	EG1=	4.73E-04	Cons=	3.3E+15	μ0=	1330	GAMMA=	2.42		
4										
5				Doping:	1.00E+13	(cm^{-3})	1.50E+13	(cm^{-3})	1.00E+14	(cm^{-3})
6	T	Eg	ni	μ	n	rho	n	rho	n	rho
7	(K)	(eV)	(cm^{-3})	(cm^2/V-s)	(cm^{-3})	(ohm-cm)	(cm^{-3})	(ohm-cm)	(cm^{-3})	(ohm-cm)
8	300	1.12	6.2E+09	1.3E+03	1.0E+13	4.7E+02	1.5E+13	3.1E+02	1.0E+14	4.7E+01
9	320	1.12	2.9E+10	1.1E+03	1.0E+13	5.5E+02	1.5E+13	3.7E+02	1.0E+14	5.5E+01
10	340	1.11	1.2E+11	9.8E+02	1.0E+13	6.4E+02	1.5E+13	4.2E+02	1.0E+14	6.4E+01
11	360	1.11	4.0E+11	8.6E+02	1.0E+13	7.3E+02	1.5E+13	4.9E+02	1.0E+14	7.3E+01
12	380	1.10	1.2E+12	7.5E+02	1.0E+13	8.2E+02	1.5E+13	5.5E+02	1.0E+14	8.3E+01
13	400	1.10	3.3E+12	6.6E+02	1.1E+13	8.6E+02	1.6E+13	6.0E+02	1.0E+14	9.4E+01
14	420	1.09	8.2E+12	5.9E+02	1.5E+13	7.3E+02	1.9E+13	5.7E+02	1.0E+14	1.1E+02
15	440	1.08	1.9E+13	5.3E+02	2.4E+13	4.8E+02	2.8E+13	4.3E+02	1.0E+14	1.1E+02
16	460	1.08	4.1E+13	4.7E+02	4.6E+13	2.9E+02	4.9E+13	2.7E+02	1.1E+14	1.2E+02
17	480	1.07	8.2E+13	4.3E+02	8.7E+13	1.7E+02	9.0E+13	1.6E+02	1.5E+14	1.0E+02
18	500	1.07	1.6E+14	3.9E+02	1.6E+14	9.9E+01	1.7E+14	9.7E+01	2.2E+14	7.5E+01

fig. 3.2 / fig. 3.3 \ **fig. 3.4** / fig. 3.5 \ Sheet4 \ Sheet5

SHORTCUT

A quick way to select a range of non-blank cells is to select a cell, hold down the Shift key, and double-click on the border of the selected cell in the direction you want to extend the selection. The selection rectangle extends in that direction until it hits a blank cell. For example, to select the cells in step 2: select cell A5, hold down the Shift key and double-click the bottom border of the cell. This extends the selection down to the next nonblank cell. Continue holding down the Shift key down and double-click on the right border of the selected cells. This extends the selection right-ward to the first nonblank cell, which selects the rest of the table. This technique is especially useful when you need to select a range of cells that extend off the edge of the screen.

3. Select cells A21:A31 (the x data), then hold down the Ctrl key and select cells F21:F31 (the first set of y data.)

4. Select the ChartWizard command by clicking the ChartWizard button on the Standard toolbar. Drag approximately over cells C5:H16 to draw the chart area. You should see the Step 1 of the ChartWizard. Click Next to continue.

5. In Step 2 of the ChartWizard, select the XY (Scatter) chart type, then click Next.

6. In Step 3, select number 2, lines and symbols, and click Next.

7. Step 4 appears, showing a sample chart. Click Next to accept the default settings and go to the next dialog box.

8. In the last ChartWizard Step, type **Resistivity of Silicon** in the Chart Title box, **Temperature (K)** in the Category (X) box, and **Resistivity (ohm-cm)** in the Value (Y) box.

9. Click Finish to leave the ChartWizard and create the chart on the worksheet.

Your worksheet should look like Figure 3.5, with a chart below the list of coefficients. If you change any of the coefficients, Excel automatically recalculates the worksheet and changes the chart to reflect the changed value.

Notice that the chart created by the ChartWizard isn't quite right. The y-axis crosses the x-axis at a bad spot, it needs two more curves, and it needs the legend moved to a better location. You will modify the chart after reviewing the techniques for editing Excel charts.

The Resistivity of Silicon versus
Temperature worksheet with an
embedded chart

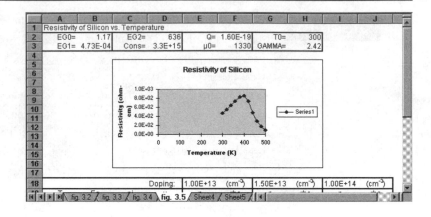

Editing Charts

To edit an embedded chart, double-click it first to activate it for editing. When you are finished editing the chart, click anywhere on the worksheet to update the chart on the worksheet. A chart on a chart sheet does not need to be activated before editing.

In an activated chart or in a chart sheet, you can select elements of the chart and edit them individually, as follows:

- Click on the plotted points (the data markers) to change the cells being plotted, the symbols and lines being used, and any attached text.

- Click on an axis to change its style, limits, and label text format.

- Click on the whole chart (click an empty space in the chart area) to change all the text styles and the background and foreground colors and patterns.

- Click and drag the legend or on any of the labels to move them to a new location.

- Click on the plot area and drag the handles to change the size of the plot area in the graph area.

When an embedded chart is activated or a chart sheet is open, the Insert and Format menus display commands for editing charts.

NOTE

> If you are not sure what you have selected, check the Name box on the left side of the formula bar. The Name box contains the name of the current selection. If you are having trouble selecting some part of a chart, select any object on the chart and use the arrow keys to cycle through all the other parts. The up and down arrows cycle through the objects on a chart and the left and right arrows cycle through the parts of an object.

Adding and Changing Objects on a Chart

Use the Insert menu to add or change objects attached to a chart, as follows:

- The Titles command determines what titles and axis labels are visible. You can select a label (a title) and edit it directly to change its value.
- The Data Labels command attaches labels to each of the data points on the selected chart. Again, to change a label, select it and edit it directly.
- The Legend command places a legend on the chart. To remove a legend, select it and press Del.
- The Axes command determines which of the two (x, y) or three (x, y_1, y_2) axes are displayed on the screen.
- The Gridlines command sets the gridline display within the body of the chart.
- The New Data command allows you to add a new data series to the chart.

To add unattached text: click on the chart, then click in the formula bar, and type. Whatever you type appears on the chart as a floating label, which you can drag anywhere on the chart. To edit the axis labels or the series names, double-click the label or name and edit it in place.

Formatting a Chart

The Format menu contains commands to change the format or style of objects on a chart. The commands available depend on the object selected on the chart. The command you choose is applied to the selected chart object.

The Format ➤ Selected (Data, Series, Chart Area, and so forth) command displays different dialog boxes depending on which object is selected. If a data series is selected, the command controls the color and shape of the data marker lines and symbols. If the chart area is selected, the command changes the foreground and background colors and the border style and color for the entire chart.

The Format ➤ Chart Type command displays the Chart Type dialog box, which lists all the standard chart types. You can select one of these options to change the type of the entire chart, or to change the type for a selected data series.

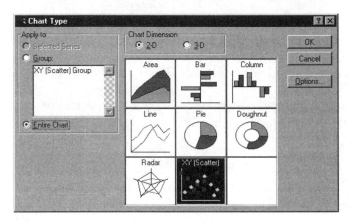

On the Chart Type dialog box, click the Options button to see the list of chart sub-types. Use the Tools ➤ Options command, Chart tab to make the current chart layout the default. This is especially useful if you are plotting many similar charts.

You can also drag an embedded chart to another location on the worksheet, or drag the chart by its border handles to change its size and shape. You can reorient a 3-D chart by selecting the corners of the chart floor and walls, then dragging a corner with the mouse to rotate the chart to the orientation that most suits its purpose.

Adding Curves to a Chart

The simplest way to add more curves to an embedded chart is to select the data, then drag it onto the chart and drop it. If you are adding data to a chart sheet, copy the data using the Edit ➤ Copy command, then select the chart and paste the data using the Edit ➤ Paste Special command. You need to use the Paste Special command so that you can designate the first column of data as the x data. If you use

Paste instead of Paste Special, Excel plots both the x and y data as two separate curves, with the integers 1, 2, 3, ... as the x data. Alternatively, use the Insert New Data command, which gives the same results.

Excel attaches curves to charts with series formulas. To see a series formula, activate a chart (double-click on the chart) and click on the curve. The series formula appears in the formula bar where it can be edited. A series formula has four arguments separated by commas: the name of the series, surrounded by double quotation marks, which is used in a legend; a range reference to the x data; a range reference to the y data; and a series number, which determines the order in which the data is plotted. In most cases, the first argument is blank until you insert some text there to use in the legend. If the x data is omitted, the integers 1, 2, 3, ... are used.

You can edit a series formula to change the data that is plotted. If you paste a series formula into the formula bar, the data the formula points to is plotted on the current chart. To quickly add names to a legend, click before the first comma in the series formula and type a quoted string or a range reference to a string containing the text of the legend.

Freezing a Chart's Contents

One reason to edit a series formula is to prevent the chart from being updated when you change the data being plotted. Normally, a chart displays the contents of the attached cells; if the contents of the cells change, the chart changes to reflect the new values. If you have a chart that you want to keep, but you want to continue changing the data on the worksheet, you need to change the references in the chart's series formula into values.

You could explicitly type all the values in the curve into the series formula, but Excel can do this for you. Simply select the reference in the series formula, press Ctrl+= (Cmd+= on the Macintosh) to replace the reference with its values, and click on the check button. After you change the data to values, you can continue to work with the worksheet without affecting that chart. You can develop some new data and plot another chart, or add another curve to an existing chart.

Modifying an XY Chart

Now you are ready to edit the Resistivity of Silicon chart created earlier in this chapter. The first step toward improving this XY chart is to plot the other two curves.

1. Save the current worksheet for later reference, by selecting it and copying it to a new worksheet named **fig. 3.6**

> **NOTE**   To quickly copy a worksheet, hold down the Ctrl key and drag the sheet tab to where you want the copy.

2. Select the two other series to be plotted: first select the *x* data in the range A21:A31, then hold down the Ctrl key and select H21:H31 and J21:J31.

3. Choose the Edit ➤ Copy command.

4. Double-click on the chart to activate it.

5. Choose the Edit ➤ Paste Special command. Select the Columns option to indicate the data is in columns, click the Categories (X Values) in First Column checkbox to indicate that the first column contains *x* data, and then click OK.

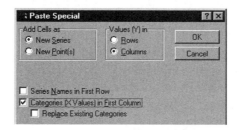

All three series are now on the chart. Now adjust the point where the y-axis crosses the x-axis. Make the chart taller so the *y* legend fits and wider so the chart can be seen better.

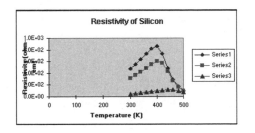

6. Click on the x-axis to select it.

7. Choose the Format ➤ Select Axis command, Scale tab, and change the value in the Minimum box to **300**, then click OK.

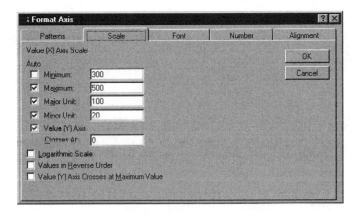

8. Select the plot area and drag the top border up to make the plot area taller; select the right side of the plot border and make the plot area wider.

9. Select the legend and move it up, out of the way. Move any labels that are out of place.

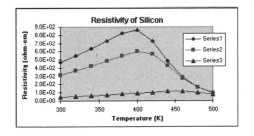

The chart now looks like the one shown above. The next task is to fix the labels that identify the three curves. You can add a label as a legend, as data labels, or as unattached text. First try a legend to see how it looks.

The series formulas for the three curves do not contain series names for the curves. You'll begin by adding the series names to the series formulas.

10. Select the upper curve.

11. In the series formula (in the formula bar), before the first comma, type **"1.0E13 (cm^{-3})"**

| S1 | ▼ | =SERIES("1.0E13 (cm^-3)",'fig. 3.6'!$A$21:$A$31,'fig. 3.6'!$F$21:$F$31,1) |

NOTE Another way to add a series name is to use the Format ➤ Selected Data Series command, Names and Values tab, but I find it faster to simply edit the series formula.

12. Select the middle curve and type **"1.5E13 (cm^–3)"** in the series formula.

13. Select the lower curve and type **"1.0E14 (cm^-3)"** in the series formula.

14. Move the legend again if necessary.

The modified chart looks like the one in Figure 3.6. If you don't like the way the legend appears, select it and use the Format ➤ Legend command to change its layout, or drag the legend to a new location.

The second method for labeling the curves on a chart is by using data labels. You attach a data label to a data point with the Data Labels command on the Insert menu. Any data label attached to a data point appears near that data point (but the labels can be repositioned independently). If you move the data point, the data label moves along with it. Now replot your data using data labels instead of a legend.

1. Copy the worksheet, and rename it **fig. 3.7**

2. Double-click on the chart to activate it.

3. Select the legend and press Del to remove the legend.

The Resistivity of Silicon chart with a legend

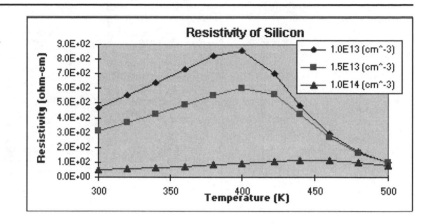

4. Select the top curve, then choose Insert ➤ Data Labels, select the Show Value option and choose OK.

5. Delete all but the seventh label (click one label to select the entire set of series labels, then click one of the labels to select and delete it alone); select the seventh label and type, **1.0E13 (cm^-3)** then press Enter.

6. Do the same to the center curve, but change the label of the fourth point to, **1.5E13 (cm^-3)**

7. Do the same for the bottom curve, and type **1.0E14 (cm^-3)** into the data label.

8. Click anywhere on the worksheet to deactivate the chart.

9. Turn off the gridlines.

The worksheet and chart should now look like Figure 3.7, with the three data series labeled with attached text.

Now see how the chart looks with unattached text and arrows.

To add unattached text, type it into the formula bar while the chart is active, and then drag it to where you want it to appear. You can make the label multilinear by simply typing Enter.

1. Copy the current worksheet and rename it **fig. 3.8**

2. Double-click on the chart to activate it.

FIGURE 3.7:

The Resistivity of Silicon chart with
the curves labeled with data labels

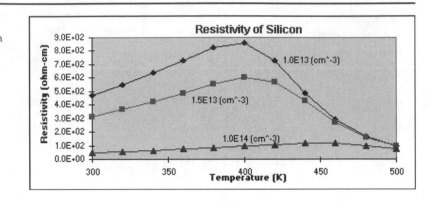

3. Select one of the attached data labels and press the Delete (Backspace on the Macintosh) key to remove it. Delete the other two labels in the same way.

4. Click in the formula bar and type **1.0E13 (cm^-3)**, then press Enter. The text box appears in the chart.

> **NOTE**   You can also create unattached text using the Text box tool on the Drawing toolbar.

5. Click in the new text box, at the end of the text, and press Enter again to move down a line. Then type **1.5E13 (cm^-3)**, press Enter, and type **1.0E14 (cm^-3)**

6. Drag the unattached text from the center of the chart to the open area in the upper-right corner of the chart.

7. Display the Drawing toolbar by using the View ➤ Toolbars command and checking the Drawing checkbox.

8. Click the Arrow button on the Drawing toolbar and draw three arrows on the chart, from the labels to the curves.

9. Double-click on one arrow, or select it and choose Format ➤ Selected Object to display the Format Object dialog box. On the Patterns tab, in the Width and Length dropdown lists, select the smallest arrow head.

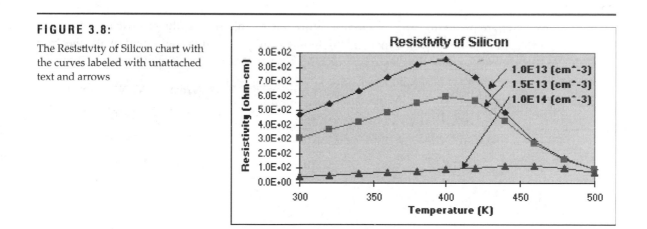

10. Format the other two arrows the same way.

11. Click on the worksheet to deactivate the chart.

12. Turn off the gridlines.

Your worksheet should now look like Figure 3.8. Unattached text is also useful for placing notes and other information on a chart.

FIGURE 3.8:

The Resistivity of Silicon chart with the curves labeled with unattached text and arrows

Creating Log and Semilog Charts

The XY chart type includes both linear and logarithmic axes. To switch the axes from linear to logarithmic, select the axis, choose the Format ➤ Selected Axis command, Scale tab, and check the Logarithmic check box. In the next example, calculate another equation and graph it as a logarithmic chart.

Electron Avalanche Coefficient in Silicon

When a voltage is applied across a semiconductor device, electrons in the semiconductor material are accelerated. If the voltage is high enough, the electrons are accelerated to the point where they generate additional electrons through impact ionization. The generated electrons are accelerated until they generate more electrons, and so on. This process is known as avalanche ionization. Device designers usually like to keep avalanche out of their devices, except in special devices such as the avalanche transistor.

The avalanche rate can be calculated with empirical equations that have been fit to experimental data. For example, you can calculate the silicon avalanche coefficients versus electric field and temperature with the following equation:

$$\alpha = AVN1 \cdot \exp\left[\frac{AVN2 + AVN3(T - 300)}{|E|} \right]$$

where α is in m^{-1}, T is the temperature in Kelvin, and E is the electric field in V/m. The avalanche rate is then calculated by multiplying this coefficient by the electron density and by the electron velocity. These are the coefficients of the equation:

E (V/m)	AVN1 (m^{-1})	AVN2 (V/m)	AVN3 (V/m–K)
$E < 2.4 \times 10^7$	2.6×10^8	1.43×10^8	1.3×10^5
$2.4 \times 10^7 < E < 4.2 \times 10^7$	6.2×10^7	1.08×10^8	1.3×10^5
$E > 4.2 \times 10^7$	5.0×10^7	9.90×10^7	1.3×10^5

Creating the Table

In this example, calculate the avalanche coefficients versus electric field at 300, 600, and 900 K.

1. Start with a new worksheet, and name it **fig. 3.9**

2. Set the column widths as follows:

Column	Width	Column	Width
A	2	D	12
B	12	E	12
C	12		

3. In cell A1, type **Electron Avalanche Coefficients in Silicon**

   First, create the table of values for the avalanche coefficient equation. Each set of coefficients is for a different range of electric field values.

4. In cells B3:E6, enter the following data:

Cell	Contents	Cell	Contents	Cell	Contents
B3	E (V/m)	C5	6.2E7	E3	AVN3 (V/m–K)
B4	0	C6	5.0E7	E4	1.3E5
B5	2.4E7	D3	AVN2 (V/m)	E5	1.3E5
B6	4.2E7	D4	1.43E8	E6	1.3E5
C3	AVN1 (1/m)	D5	1.08E8		
C4	2.6E8	D6	9.9E7		

5. Right-align the contents of cells B3:E3.

6. Name cells in the table as follows:

Cell	Contents	Cell	Contents	Cell	Contents	Cell	Contents
		C4	AVN11	D4	AVN21	E4	AVN31
B5	ECUT1	C5	AVN12	D5	AVN22	E5	AVN32
B6	ECUT2	C6	AVN13.	D6	AVN32	E6	AVN33

7. Name the whole table, B4:E6, **COEFFS**

Next, create the avalanche coefficient table.

8. In cell B8, enter **T (K) =** and right-align it.

9. In cells C8:E8, enter **300**, **600**, and **900**

10. In cell B9, enter **E (V/m)** and right-align it.

11. In cell C9, enter **alpha (1/m)** and right-align it.

12. Select cell C9 and copy it into cells D9:E9 by dragging its fill handle right to cell E9.

13. In cell B10, enter **5.0E+06**, in cell B11, enter **1.0E+07**. Select cells B10:B11, and drag the fill handle down to cell B29.

You can choose the correct values from the table according to the applied field in two ways. The first is to use nested IF functions. Two nested IF functions will divide the problem into three ranges. The second method is to use the VLOOKUP function, which scans the table automatically. You'll use both methods in this example. First, use the nested IF function method.

1. In cell C10, enter the following formula:

=IF($B10>ECUT1,IF($B10>ECUT2,AVN13,AVN12),AVN11)
*EXP(–(IF($B10>ECUT1,IF($B10>ECUT2,AVN23,AVN22),AVN21)
+IF($B10>ECUT1,IF($B10>ECUT2,AVN33,AVN32),AVN31)
*(C$8–300))/$B10)

The lookup functions result in a more compact formula than the nested IF functions, especially if there are more than two ranges in the table. The next step uses the VLOOKUP function method.

2. In cell D10, enter the following formula:

=VLOOKUP($B10,COEFFS,2)*EXP(–(VLOOKUP($B10,COEFFS,3)
+VLOOKUP($B10,COEFFS,4)*(D$8–300))/$B10)

Use the lookup function method for the rest of the worksheet.

3. Select cell D10, and drag its fill handle right to E10.

4. Select cells C10:E10, and drag the fill handle down to E29.

5. Format cells B4:E6 and B10:E29 as Scientific, 2 decimal places.

6. Outline the cells as shown in Figure 3.9.

7. Turn off the worksheet gridlines.

8. Save the workbook.

This completes the worksheet, which should look like Figure 3.9. This worksheet calculates the electron avalanche coefficient versus electric field for the temperatures 300, 600, and 900 K, listed along the top.

FIGURE 3.9:

Electron avalanche coefficients in silicon versus electric field and temperature. View ➤ Full Screen was used to show more of the worksheet.

	A	B	C	D	E	F	G	H	
1		Electron Avalanche Coefficients in Silicon							
2									
3		E (V/m)	AVN1 (1/m)	AVN2 (V/m)	AVN3 (V/m-K)				
4		0.00E+00	2.60E+08	1.43E+08	1.30E+05				
5		2.40E+07	6.20E+07	1.00E+00	1.30E+05				
6		4.20E+07	5.00E+07	9.90E+07	1.30E+05				
7									
8		T (K) =	300	600	900				
9		E (V/cm)	alpha (1/m)	alpha (1/m)	alpha (1/m)				
10		5.00E+06	9.87E-05	4.04E-08	1.66E-11				
11		1.00E+07	1.60E+02	3.24E+00	6.56E-02				
12		1.50E+07	1.88E+04	1.40E+03	1.04E+02				
13		2.00E+07	2.04E+05	2.90E+04	4.13E+03				
14		2.50E+07	8.25E+05	1.73E+05	3.64E+04				
15		3.00E+07	1.69E+06	4.62E+05	1.26E+05				
16		3.50E+07	2.83E+06	9.30E+05	3.05E+05				
17		4.00E+07	4.17E+06	1.57E+06	5.90E+05				
18		4.50E+07	5.54E+06	2.33E+06	9.79E+05				
19		5.00E+07	6.90E+06	3.16E+06	1.45E+06				
20		5.50E+07	8.26E+06	4.07E+06	2.00E+06				
21		6.00E+07	9.60E+06	5.01E+06	2.62E+06				
22		6.50E+07	1.09E+07	5.98E+06	3.28E+06				
23		7.00E+07	1.22E+07	6.96E+06	3.99E+06				
24		7.50E+07	1.34E+07	7.94E+06	4.72E+06				

fig. 3.4 / fig. 3.5 / fig. 3.6 / fig. 3.7 / fig. 3.8 / fig. 3.9

Creating the Chart

The values of the avalanche coefficient span many orders of magnitude, which is difficult to plot on a linear scale. A logarithmic scale gives a much more reasonable chart. This time, create a chart on a separate sheet.

1. Select cells B10:E29.

2. Choose the Insert ➤ Chart ➤ As New Sheet command.

3. Follow the steps in the ChartWizard to create a new chart.

>   Chart Type: **Scatter Chart**
>
>   Chart subtype: **2**
>
>   Data in **columns**
>
>   Use first **1** column(s) for x data
>
>   Use first **0** row(s) for legend text
>
>   Chart Title: **Electron Avalanche Coefficient in Silicon**
>
>   X axis label: **Electric Field (V/m)**
>
>   Y axis label: **Avalanche Coeff. (1/m)**

4. Choose the View ➤ Sized With Window command to make the chart easier to read.

5. Click on the y-axis and choose the Format ➤ Selected Axis command, Scale tab; check the Logarithmic Scale box.

6. Change the Category (X) Axis Crosses At box to **1E-11** and click OK.

7. Drag the legend to position it under the curve.

8. Select the top curve on the graph and choose the Format ➤ Selected Data Series command, Names and Values tab. In the Name field, type **T = 300 K** and choose OK.

9. Select the center curve on the graph and do the same, changing its name to **T = 600 K**, and change the name of the bottom curve to **T = 900 K**

10. Select the x-axis and choose the Format ➤ Selected Axis command, Scale tab. Change the major unit to **2E7** and choose OK.

11. The Insert ➤ Chart ➤ As New Sheet command inserted the chart sheet to the left of the sheet with the data. Move the chart sheet to the right by using the

mouse to drag the chart tab at the bottom of the screen (named Chart1) to the right of the fig. 3.9 tab.

12. Double-click on the Chart1 tab and change its name to **fig. 3.10**

13. Save the workbook.

The completed chart is shown in Figure 3.10. This chart is currently on a separate chart sheet. If you want to embed the chart in the worksheet, select the chart area, choose Copy on the Edit menu, select a cell on the worksheet, and then choose Paste. A copy of the chart will be embedded in the worksheet.

FIGURE 3.10:

Electron avalanche coefficient in silicon for three different temperatures: a semilog plot.

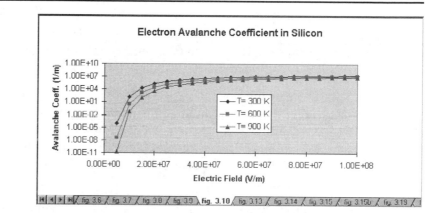

Creating Three-Dimensional Charts

Excel's three-dimensional charts all have equally spaced grids in both the x and y directions, so that the gridding is uniform no matter what values you supply for the x- and y-axes. This uniform gridding can be a problem in some cases, such as when the gridding distorts the results; however, by plotting consecutive slices through the data and offsetting them by an appropriate amount, you can produce a reasonable three-dimensional wire-frame plot using the two-dimensional XY chart type.

First, you need to define a new rectangular coordinate system u, v, and w. Plot the u axis horizontally, the v axis at an angle ϕ, and the w axis vertically, as illustrated in

Mapping the three-dimensional axes
onto the two-dimensional surface

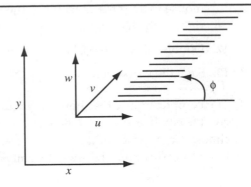

Figure 3.11. Next, you map these three axes onto the two-dimensional plane, with these transform equations: $x = u + v\cos(\phi)$ and $y = w + v\sin(\phi)$. To plot a three-dimensional data point (u, v, w), insert it into the transform equations and calculate the two-dimensional (x,y) data point.

To create the worksheet, you need to put the three-dimensional data into three columns so that you can map them into two columns that can then be plotted on an XY chart. Data for this type of chart usually appears as slices through the domain to be plotted. Each slice goes from one boundary to the other. You stack these data sets, so that the first data point of one section comes after the last data point of the previous section.

A problem with the layout of the chart is that a line will be drawn from the last data point of each section to the first data point of the next section. These lines cut across the middle of the chart, which is definitely not what you want. But you can stop Excel from drawing the return lines by inserting a blank row between each section of data. Excel considers the blank line as a data point missing from the middle of a data range, and will not draw a data marker or lines to that point.

Temperature Profile in an Overstressed Silicon Diode

When a small silicon diode is pulsed with a high-power pulse of electricity, it heats up. If it heats up too much, it is damaged. Of course, if you really pour on the power, you will see smoke and fire where the diode used to be, and there will not be much question that it failed. On the other hand, if you use only a small amount of power, the diode may only be degraded and may still operate, at least for a while.

One way to evaluate the type of damage that a diode may sustain is to mathematically model its operation and see where the damaging heating occurs. This type of modeling is usually done on a supercomputer, but the analysis of the results can be done with Excel. The data in Table 3.1 comes from just such a diode simulation, and it shows the temperature at different positions in the diode. The data is in the form of y and z position data, and T temperature data.

The data at $y = 0$ is the centerline of the device (that is, only half of the diode was modeled). The bottom conductor is at $z = 130$ microns, and it covers the whole bottom of the diode. The top conductor is at $z = 0$, and it extends from $y = 0$ to $y = 40$ microns. The diode junction, where all of the action takes place, is at $z = 10$ microns, and extends from $y = 0$ to about 50 microns. The layout of the diode is illustrated in Figure 3.12.

FIGURE 3.12:

The layout of the small signal diode used to generate the temperature data

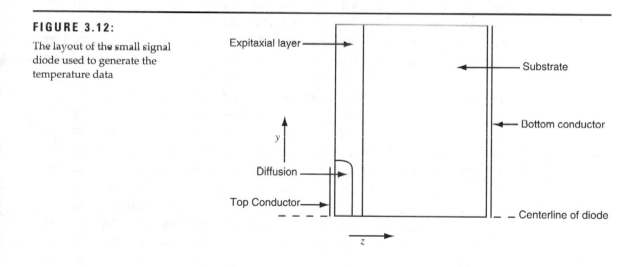

TABLE 3.1: Temperature Data Versus Position in a Small Signal Diode

T(K)	$y(\mu)$ 0	10	20	30	35	40	43.3	46.6	50	55	60	110	155	200	250
0	300	300	300	300	300	300	486	329	308	303	301	300	300	300	300
1	425	429	441	474	528	779	414	327	307	302	301	300	300	300	300
2	462	465	478	512	569	766	419	332	309	303	301	300	300	300	300
3	463	465	476	505	554	659	448	342	312	303	301	300	300	300	300
4	453	456	466	495	542	659	461	352	316	304	301	300	300	300	300
5	440	443	453	480	522	617	459	360	320	305	301	300	300	300	300
6	424	426	435	460	497	572	451	365	324	306	301	300	300	300	300
7	405	407	415	436	467	527	443	370	328	308	301	300	300	300	300
8	389	390	397	416	443	496	440	377	333	309	301	300	300	300	300
9	380	382	388	406	430	482	442	384	338	311	301	300	300	300	300
10	381	383	389	407	430	480	448	392	344	313	302	300	300	300	300
11	385	387	395	413	435	480	452	398	350	316	302	300	300	300	300
12	391	393	401	420	439	476	451	403	356	319	302	300	300	300	300
13	376	378	384	400	415	449	440	404	360	322	303	300	300	300	300
14	444	447	457	477	494	518	492	442	385	333	305	300	300	300	300
15	444	448	459	484	503	520	493	449	399	349	323	301	300	300	300
16	344	346	354	373	391	414	410	397	376	352	338	302	300	300	300
17	331	333	339	354	369	386	386	378	365	348	335	302	300	300	300
18	330	332	337	351	363	375	375	369	359	344	333	302	300	300	300
19	330	331	337	349	359	368	367	362	353	341	331	302	300	300	300
20	330	331	336	347	355	362	361	356	348	337	328	302	300	300	300
31	325	325	327	329	330	329	328	326	323	319	314	302	300	300	300
42	319	319	319	319	318	317	316	315	314	312	309	302	300	300	300
53	315	315	314	314	313	312	311	311	310	309	307	302	300	300	300
64	312	312	311	310	310	309	309	308	308	307	306	301	300	300	300
75	310	310	309	308	308	308	307	307	306	306	305	301	300	300	300
86	308	308	308	307	307	307	306	306	306	305	305	301	300	300	300
97	307	307	307	306	306	306	306	305	305	305	304	301	300	300	300
108	307	307	306	306	306	305	305	305	305	304	304	301	300	300	300
119	306	306	306	306	305	305	305	305	305	304	304	301	300	300	300
130	300	300	300	300	300	300	300	300	300	300	300	300	300	300	300

$z(\mu)$

Creating the Table

As you can tell from Table 3.1, a large amount of data has to go into this worksheet; however, it does not take too much time to enter it. Now create the table, and then use the data in a three-dimensional chart.

1. Start with a blank worksheet, and name it **fig. 3.13**

2. Select columns B:AG and change their width to 4. Set the width of column A to 10.

3. In cell A1, enter **Temperature Profile in an Overstressed Silicon Diode**

4. Enter the values in the indicated cells.

    B3   **T (K)**

    J2   **Z (microns)**

    A10 **y (microns)**

5. In cells B4:B18, enter the y values (from Table 3.1):

Cell	Contents	Cell	Contents	Cell	Contents
B4	0	B9	40	B14	60
B5	10	B10	43.3	B16	110
B6	20	B11	46.6	B17	155
B7	30	B12	50	B18	200
B8	35	B13	55	B19	250

6. In cells C3:AG3, enter the z values (from Table 3.1):

Cell	Contents	Cell	Contents	Cell	Contents	Cell	Contents
C3	0	K3	8	S3	16	AA3	64
D3	1	L3	9	T3	17	AB3	75
E3	2	M3	10	U3	18	AC3	86
F3	3	N3	11	V3	19	AD3	97
G3	4	O3	12	W3	20	AE3	108
H3	5	P3	13	X3	31	AF3	119
I3	6	Q3	14	Y3	42	AG3	130
J3	7	R3	15	Z3	53		

FIGURE 3.13:

The worksheet for the temperature profile in an overstressed silicon diode

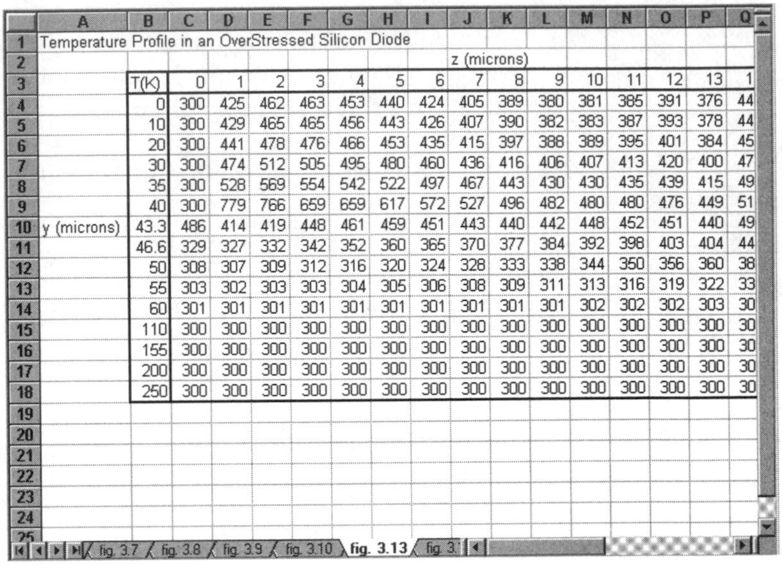

	A	B	C	D	E	F	G	H	I	J	K	L	M	N	O	P	Q
1	Temperature Profile in an OverStressed Silicon Diode																
2										z (microns)							
3		T(K)	0	1	2	3	4	5	6	7	8	9	10	11	12	13	1
4		0	300	425	462	463	453	440	424	405	389	380	381	385	391	376	44
5		10	300	429	465	465	456	443	426	407	390	382	383	387	393	378	44
6		20	300	441	478	476	466	453	435	415	397	388	389	395	401	384	45
7		30	300	474	512	505	495	480	460	436	416	406	407	413	420	400	47
8		35	300	528	569	554	542	522	497	467	443	430	430	435	439	415	49
9		40	300	779	766	659	659	617	572	527	496	482	480	480	476	449	51
10	y (microns)	43.3	486	414	419	448	461	459	451	443	440	442	448	452	451	440	49
11		46.6	329	327	332	342	352	360	365	370	377	384	392	398	403	404	44
12		50	308	307	309	312	316	320	324	328	333	338	344	350	356	360	38
13		55	303	302	303	303	304	305	306	308	309	311	313	316	319	322	33
14		60	301	301	301	301	301	301	301	301	301	301	302	302	302	303	30
15		110	300	300	300	300	300	300	300	300	300	300	300	300	300	300	30
16		155	300	300	300	300	300	300	300	300	300	300	300	300	300	300	30
17		200	300	300	300	300	300	300	300	300	300	300	300	300	300	300	30
18		250	300	300	300	300	300	300	300	300	300	300	300	300	300	300	30

fig. 3.7 / fig. 3.8 / fig. 3.9 / fig. 3.10 \ **fig. 3.13** / fig. 3

7. In cells C4:AG18, enter the temperature values from Table 3.1. Note that the values you are typing in the worksheet are the transpose of the values in the table (that is, as you move across the table you move down the worksheet).

Your worksheet should now look like Figure 3.13.

Creating the Chart

Now see how Excel's built-in 3-D wire-frame chart does with the data.

1. Select cells B3:AG18 and choose the Copy command on the Edit menu.

2. Choose the Insert ➤ Chart ➤ As New Sheet command to create a new chart sheet.

3. Follow the five ChartWizard steps to create the chart. Use the following options in the ChartWizard:

   Chart Type: **3D-Surface**

   Chart subtype: **2 (wire frame)**

   Data in **rows**

   Use first **1** row(s) as x data

Use first **1** column(s) as y data

Legend: No

Category (x): **z (microns)**

Value (Z): **T (K)**

Series (Y): **y (microns)**

4. Drag the chart sheet tab to the right of sheet fig. 3.13 and change its name to **fig. 3.14**

5. Click on a wall, floor, or corner so that the black squares appear on the corners of the 3-D box surrounding the plot. Drag one of these corners and rotate the plot to the left a little until it looks better.

6. Select the vertical axis, choose the Format ➤ Selected Axis command, and change the Minimum to **300**

This chart, shown in Figure 3.14, is not bad. The only problem is that the uniformly spaced grids cause the temperature data in the upper-left corner of the plot to be spread out over most of the plot. It is a bit difficult to get a good idea of where the heating is taking place because of the distortion in the chart. Plot this data again, but this time calculate your own lines and correctly space the gridlines.

FIGURE 3.14:

The 3-D wire-frame chart of the temperature profile in an overstressed silicon diode

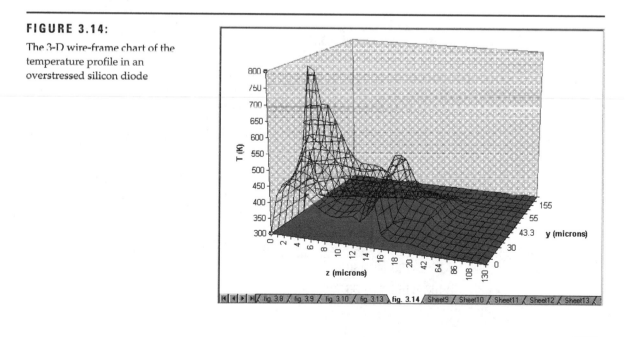

Creating the Table with Proportionally Spaced Gridlines

First place the y, z and T data into three parallel columns on a worksheet, and then map this data onto the x-y plane in two more columns.

1. Open a new worksheet, and name it **fig. 3.15**

2. In cell A1, enter **Temperature Profile in an Overstressed Silicon Diode**

You need a rotation angle to rotate the chart, and both the sine and cosine of that angle in every mapping. Instead of recalculating them again and again, calculate them here and use the numbers in the rest of the worksheet. First convert the degrees to radians, and then use them in the functions.

3. Enter the following values in the indicated cells:

Cell	Contents	Cell	Contents
D2	**Plot Angle:**	E2	60
F2	**=SIN(RADIANS(E2))**	G2	**=COS(RADIANS(E2))**
A3	**Y (μ)**	B3	**Z (μ)**
C3	**T (K)**	D3	x
E3	y		

4. Right-align cells D2 and A3:E3

Now you are ready to enter the y values. Fill the cells by entering the first value and then copying it to the rest of the range. You can use the Copy and Paste commands, the Fill Down command, or the fill handle to copy the values.

5. In the following ranges, enter the value in the first cell and copy it into the other cells in the range:

Cell	Contents	Cell	Contents
A4:A34	**0**	A260:A290	**50**
A36:A66	**10**	A292:A322	**55**
A68:A98	**20**	A324:A354	**60**
A100:A130	**30**	A356:A386	**110**
A132:A162	**35**	A388:A418	**155**

Cell	Contents	Cell	Contents
A164:A194	40	A420:A450	200
A196:A226	43.3	A452:A482	250
A228:A258	46.6		

Next put in the z data values. Again, you enter the data once and then copy it into ranges. You can either type the first set or copy it from the other 3-D chart worksheet. To copy the first data set, switch to the worksheet for the last example, copy the data there, switch back to this worksheet, select the range, use the Paste Special command on the Edit menu, and check the Transpose box.

After the first set of values is on the worksheet, copy the values into the other ranges by dragging the border of the range to a new position while holding down the Ctrl key (Option on the Macintosh).

6. Enter the data into the following ranges:

B4:B34	B164:B194	B324:B354
B36:B66	B196:B226	B356:B386
B68:B98	B228:B258	B388:B418
B100:B130	B260:B290	B420:B450
B132:B162	B292:B322	B452:B482

Enter this list of data into the first cell range, and then copy it to the others:

0	8	16	64
1	9	17	75
2	10	18	86
3	11	19	97
4	12	20	108
5	13	31	119
6	14	42	130
7	15	53	

Now put in the temperature data. Be sure that you put the correct temperature value with each y, z value and don't forget to insert blank lines between the sets of data. The quickest way to do this is to copy this data from the last example. Select a row of data in the last example, copy it, switch to this worksheet, select the first cell of the range, and use the Paste Special command on the Edit menu with the Transpose box checked. If you don't want to type the 464 data values (it only takes about 15 minutes), you can plot the formula shown in the next step instead. The formula has no special significance other than it makes an interesting chart.

7. Using the data in Table 3.1, enter or copy the 464 temperature values in cells C4:C482. Alternatively, you can type and then copy this formula into the same cells:

$$=300+500*COS(A4*3*PI(\ )/250)*COS(B4*3*PI(\ )/130)$$
$$*EXP(-A4/62)*EXP(-B4/33)$$

The next step is to insert the mapping functions.

8. In cells D4:D482, enter and copy =B4+A4*$G$2

9. In cells E4:E482, enter and copy =C4+A4*$F$2

10. Select the following rows, then click the right mouse button on the selection and choose Clear Contents from the shortcut menu: 35, 67, 99, 131, 163, 195, 227, 259, 291, 323, 355, 387, 419, and 451.

Insert some extra data values that will draw lines around the edges of the plot at the minimum temperature (300 K), to provide a visual cue to the perspective of the chart.

11. Enter the following values in the indicated cells:

Cell	Contents	Cell	Contents
D483	130	E483	300
D484	0	E484	300
D485	=0+250*$G$2	E485	=300+250*$F$2
D486	=130+250*$G$2	E486	=300+250*$F$2

12. Turn off the gridlines.

The worksheet should now look like Figure 3.15.

FIGURE 3.15:

The remapped worksheet for the temperature profile in an overstressed silicon diode

	A	B	C	D	E	F	G	H	I
1	Temperature Profile in an Overstressed Silicon Diode								
2			Plot Angle:		60	0.866025	0.5		
3	Y (µ)	Z (µ)	T (K)	x	y				
4	0	0	300	0	300				
5	0	1	425	1	425				
6	0	2	462	2	462				
7	0	3	463	3	463				
8	0	4	453	4	453				
9	0	5	440	5	440				
10	0	6	424	6	424				
11	0	7	405	7	405				
12	0	8	389	8	389				
13	0	9	380	9	380				
14	0	10	381	10	381				
15	0	11	385	11	385				
16	0	12	391	12	391				

fig. 3.9 / fig. 3.10 / fig. 3.13 / fig. 3.14 / **fig. 3.15** / Sh

Creating the Chart with Proportionally Spaced Gridlines

Plot the data in columns D and E.

1. Select cells D4:E486.

2. Click the ChartWizard button and draw a chart on cells K2:R16.

3. Follow the ChartWizard steps and enter the following information:

Chart Type: **XY (Scatter)**

Chart subtype: **6 (lines, no symbols)**

Data in **Columns**

Use first **1** column(s) as x data

Use first **0** row(s) as Legend Text

Legend: No

Title: **Temperature Profile in a Silicon Diode**

Category (x): **z (microns)**

Value (Z): **T (K)**

Series (Y): **y (microns)**

4. Click Finish to display the chart.

5. Double-click the chart to activate it, then select the plot area, and click the Fill Color button on the Formatting toolbar. On the dropdown palette, select the white color.

Now mark the y-axis with labels. Add the labels by creating a new hidden plot and attaching a label to each point.

6. Copy the contents of cells A354:E354 to L19:P19.

7. Copy the contents of cells A418:E418 to L20:P20.

8. Copy the contents of cells A482:E482 to L21:P21.

9. Select the range O19:P21 and choose Copy from the Edit menu.

10. Double-click the chart to activate it.

11. Choose the Paste Special command on the Edit menu, select Columns, select Categories (X) in First Column, and then click OK.

12. Select the new curve, and choose the Insert ➤ Data Labels command. Check the Show Value checkbox and click OK.

13. Select the front-most data label and change its value to ------60

14. Select the middle data label and change its value to ------155 **(microns)**

15. Select the back data label and change its value to ------250

16. Click the curve line, choose the Format ➤ Selected Data Series command, Patterns tab, and select None under Lines and None under Marker.

17. Select the horizontal axis, choose the Format ➤ Selected Axis command, Scale tab, and set the minimum value to 0. Choose OK.

18. Save the workbook.

Your 3-D chart should look like the one in Figure 3.16, unless you plotted the formula (in step 7) instead of the data. If you plotted the formula, your chart should look like the one in Figure 3.17. You can change the value of the plot angle and see how it changes the view of the chart.

FIGURE 3.16:

The replotted 3-D chart of the temperature profile in an overstressed silicon diode

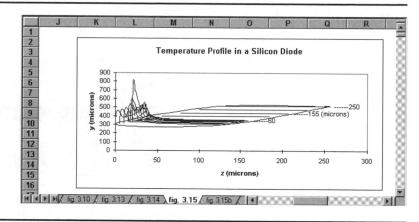

FIGURE 3.17:

The 3-D chart of the alternative formula

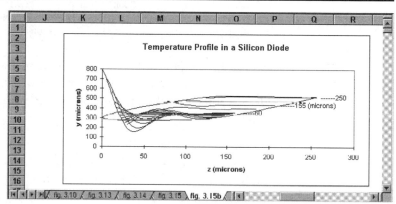

Drawing Pictures

Along with its charting tools, Excel also provides tools for drawing shapes. If you activate the Drawing toolbar, you can draw lines, circles, and boxes in various colors to highlight different results and calculations on your worksheets. To display the Drawing toolbar, click the Drawing button on the Standard toolbar, or choose the View ➤ Toolbars command and select the checkbox for the Drawing toolbar. The Drawing toolbar and its tools are shown in Figure 3.18.

In addition, you can use Excel's data-plotting capability to draw complex figures on the screen. Figure 3.19 shows a segmented line drawing created with approximately 425 data pairs that form 53 discrete line segments. Digitizing the drawing

FIGURE 3.18:

The Drawing toolbar and its tools

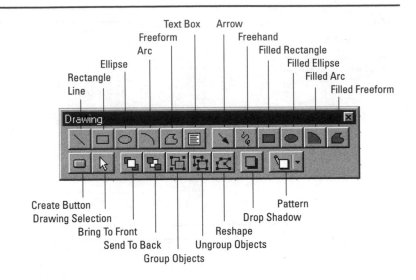

by hand and typing the data pairs into the worksheet took an evening, which is not an unreasonable amount of time to produce a figure of this complexity. Of course, this does not include the amount of time that Julie, my wife, spent drawing the original figure.

A drawing on a chart helps illustrate the function being plotted. For example, if you are plotting the output of an electronic circuit, adding a simple drawing of the circuit in the corner of your chart makes the results more meaningful to a reader. You can either use the drawing tools to add a graphic, or you can place a drawing on a chart sheet by using line segments, as in Figure 3.19.

FIGURE 3.19:

A drawing created as line segments with Excel's data plotter (an osprey in flight, by Julie Stephens Orvis, D.V.M)

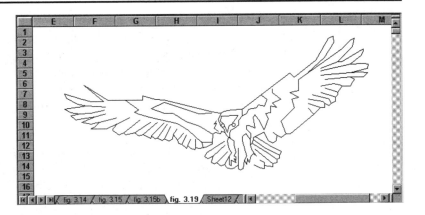

A diagram of the Delyiannis
bandpass circuit

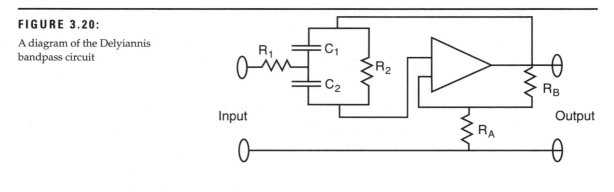

Delyiannis Bandpass Filter

The Delyiannis bandpass filter is an active electronic filter network that passes frequencies within a particular range and filters out all others. Figure 3.20 shows the circuit diagram. The transfer function (the ratio of the output to the input) is defined with this equation:

$$\left|G(i\omega)\right| = \frac{\dfrac{\omega}{R_1 C_2 \left(1 - 1/k\right)}}{\sqrt{\left(\omega_p^2 - \omega^2\right)^2 + \omega^2 \left(\omega_p / Q_p\right)^2}}$$

Here, ω is the angular frequency:

$$k = 1 + \frac{R_A}{R_B}$$

$$\omega_p^2 = \frac{1}{R_1 R_2 C_1 C_2}$$

$$\frac{\omega_p}{Q_p} = \frac{1}{R_2 C_1} + \frac{1}{R_2 C_2} - \frac{1}{k-1}\frac{1}{R_1 C_2}$$

Creating the Table

Let $C_1 = C_2 = 1$ µf, $R_1 = R_2 = R_B = 10$ ohms and $R_A = 32$ ohms, which yields a bandpass frequency centered on 100 kHz. Plot the transfer function and then draw the circuit on the graph.

1. Start with a new worksheet, and name it **fig. 3.21**

2. Set the column widths as follows:

A	3	E	9
B	10	F	9
C	10	G	9
D	20		

3. In cell A1, type **Delyiannis Bandpass Circuit**

4. Enter the following values in the indicated cells:

Cell	Contents	Cell	Contents	Cell	Contents
B3	**RES1**	C3	**10**	D3	**CAP1**
B4	**RES2**	C4	**10**	D4	**CAP2**
B5	**K**	C5	**=1+RESA/RESB**	D5	**WP**
E3	**1E-6**	F3	**RESA**	G3	**32**
E4	**1E-6**	F4	**RESB**	G4	**10**
		F5	**WPQP**		

5. In cell E5, enter this formula:

   =SQRT(1/(RES1*RES2*CAP1*CAP2))

6. In cell G5, enter this formula:

   =1/(RES2*CAP1)+1/(RES2*CAP2)–(1/(K–1))*1/(RES1*CAP2)

7. Right-align cells B3:B5, D3:D5, and F3:F5.

8. Select cells B3:C5, choose Insert ➤ Name ➤ Create, make sure the Left Column option is selected and click OK. Do the same for cells D3:E5, and F3:G5.

9. Enter the following values in the indicated cells:

Cell	Contents
B8	**Frequency**
C8	**|G(s)|**
D8	**Comments**

10. In cells B9 and B10, enter **1E4** and **2E4**. Select B9:B10 and drag the fill handle down to cell B49.

11. In cells C9:C49, enter and copy the following formula:

    =(B9/(RES1*CAP2*(1–1/K)))/SQRT((WP^2–B9^2)^2+WPQP^2*B9^2)

12. In cell D9, enter **Begin filter calculation**

13. In cell D49, enter **End filter calculation**

14. Format cells B9:B133, E3:E5, and G5 as Scientific, 2 decimal places; format cells C9:C135 as Numeric, 2 decimal places.

15. Outline the cells as shown in Figure 3.21.

16. Turn off gridlines.

FIGURE 3.21:

The Delyiannis Bandpass Circuit worksheet

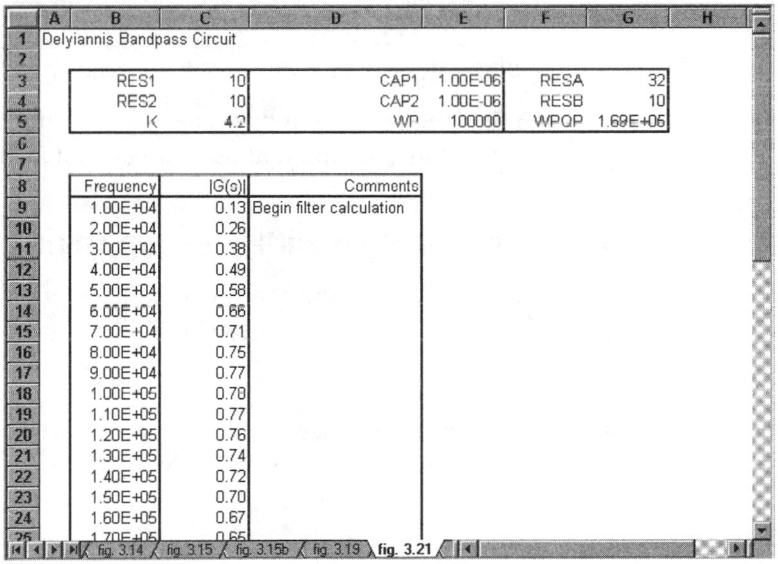

This completes the data for the transfer function. Your worksheet should look like Figure 3.21.

Creating the Chart

Now you'll create a chart of the transfer function versus frequency.

1. Select cells B9:C49, click on the ChartWizard button, and draw the chart on cells I1:Q18.

2. Follow the ChartWizard steps and enter the following information:

> Chart Type: **XY (Scatter)**
>
> Chart subtype: **6 (lines, no symbols, smoothing)**
>
> Data in **Columns**
>
> Use first **1** column(s) as x data
>
> Use first **0** row(s) as Legend Text
>
> Legend: No
>
> Title: **Delyiannis Bandpass Circuit**
>
> Category (x): **Angular Frequency (Rad/s)**
>
> Value (Y): **Transfer Function**

3. Double-click the chart to activate it. Click on the plot area and choose the Format ➤ Selected Plot Area command, then set the Area pattern to none. Click OK, and then click on the worksheet to deactivate the chart.

4. Select the chart, hold down the Ctrl key and drag a new copy of the chart below the first. You will use this copy later.

Drawing the Diagram with Drawing Tools

In the first copy of the chart, draw the circuit diagram using the drawing tools. First, display the Drawing toolbar and magnify the image to make the drawing tools easier to use.

1. Scroll the worksheet until the upper chart is visible, and double-click on the chart to activate it.

2. Click the Drawing button on the Standard toolbar to display the Drawing toolbar.

3. Drag the Drawing toolbar to a convenient location.

4. Use the Zoom Control box on the Standard toolbar to set 200% magnification.

5. Use the drawing tools to draw the circuit as shown in Figure 3.20. Most of this is done with the Line tool. Use the Ellipse tool to draw the four circles, and the Text Box tool to label the parts. Use the Format ➤ Object command, Patterns tab to set no border and no fill for the text boxes. Use the Font tab to set the font size to 8 points and to set the subscript text.

SHORTCUT You can speed the drawing by drawing an object such as a resistor, and then make copies of it for the other resistors. To copy an object, select it, hold down Ctrl, and drag the copy to the new location.

6. Use the Zoom Control box to change back to 100% magnification.

7. Use the Selection tool on the Drawing toolbar to select the whole drawing.

8. Click the Group tool to combine all the lines in the drawing into a single object so that they move together. You must ungroup them if you want to edit the drawing.

The chart should look like the one shown in Figure 3.22.

Drawing the Diagram with Data

Now try the same thing with the copy of the chart, but do the drawing with a second data set. I sketched the circuit on grid paper to determine the x-y coordinates of the lines to type into the worksheet. All of the drawing must be done in the scale of the plot already on the graph, so draw the circuit on a regular grid and then use a simple function to map the values onto the scale of the plot on the chart.

FIGURE 3.22:

The Delyiannis Bandpass Transfer function chart with a circuit drawn with the drawing tools

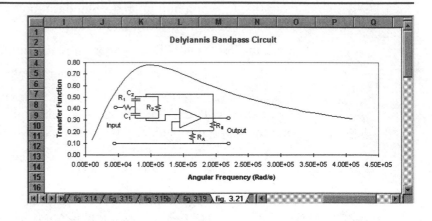

1. In cells B52:D133, enter the following table of values:

Row	Col. B	Col. C	Col. D
53			**Begin circuit plot**
54	**0.5**	**1.0**	**Ground line**
55	**3.0**	**1.0**	
56			
57	**2.3**	**1.0**	**Resistor A**
58	**2.3**	**1.2**	
59	**2.35**	**1.3**	
60	**2.25**	**1.4**	
61	**2.35**	**1.5**	
62	**2.25**	**1.6**	
63	**2.35**	**1.7**	
64	**2.35**	**1.8**	
65	**2.3**	**2**	
66			
67	**2.0**	**2.4**	**Operational amplifier**
68	**2.5**	**3.0**	
69	**2.0**	**3.6**	

Row	Col. B	Col. C	Col. D
70	2.0	2.4	
72	2.0	2.6	Resistor B and wire
73	1.9	2.6	from input network
74	1.9	2.0	to operational amplifier
75	2.8	2.0	
76	2.8	2.2	
77	2.85	2.3	
78	2.75	2.4	
79	2.85	2.5	
80	2.75	2.6	
81	2.85	2.7	
82	2.8	2.8	
83	2.8	4.2	
84	1.25	4.2	
85	1.25	3.9	
86			
87	1.0	3.5	Resistor 2
88	1.0	3.9	
89	1.5	3.9	
90	1.5	3.3	
91	1.45	3.2	
92	1.55	3.1	
93	1.45	3.0	
94	1.55	2.9	
95	1.45	2.8	
96	1.5	2.7	
97	1.5	2.1	
98	1.0	2.1	
99	1.0	2.5	

Row	Col. B	Col. C	Col. D
100			
101	0.85	2.5	Capacitor 1
102	1.15	2.5	
103			
104	0.85	2.6	
105	1.15	2.6	
106			
107	0.85	3.4	Capacitor 2
108	1.15	3.4	
109			
110	0.85	3.5	
111	1.15	3.5	
112			
113	0.5	3.0	Resistor 1
114	0.6	3.0	
115	0.65	3.1	
116	0.7	2.9	
117	7.5	3.1	
118	0.8	2.9	
119	0.85	3.1	
120	0.9	3.0	
121	1.0	3.0	
122			
123	2.5	3.0	Output terminal
124	3.0	3.0	
125			
126	1.0	2.6	Wire from C1 to C2
127	1.0	3.4	
128			

Row	Col. B	Col. C	Col. D
129	1.25	2.1	**Wire from input network**
130	1.25	1.8	**to operational amplifier**
131	1.8	1.8	
132	1.8	3.3	
133	2.0	3.3	

Now create the mapping function to map the values in columns B and C into the units used on the chart. Apply a simple linear transform to convert each value.

2. Enter the following values in the indicated cells:

Cell	Contents	Cell	Contents	Cell	Contents
D51	**Offset**	E51	0	F51	0
D52	**Multiplier**	E52	1E5	F52	0.1
		E53	x	F53	y
		E54	=E$51+E$52*B54	F54	=F$51+F$52*C54

3. Select cells E54:F54, then drag the fill handle down to F133.

4. Scan down the column and delete the contents of any cells in columns E and F that correspond to blanks in columns B and C.

5. Outline the cells as shown in Figure 3.23. Select cells E54:F133 and choose the Edit ➤ Copy command.

6. Select the copy of the chart you made earlier and double-click it to activate it.

7. Choose the Edit ➤ Paste Special command, select Values (Y) in Columns and Categories (X Values) in First Column, and click on OK.

8. Select the circuit drawing and choose the Format ➤ Selected Data Series command, Patterns tab; set Marker to None, Line to Black, and uncheck the Smoothed line checkbox. Then click OK.

9. Use unattached text (type in the formula bar while the chart is active) to create the four circles at the left and right (use a lowercase *o*) and to label the resistors and capacitors. Use the Format ➤ Selected Object command, Font

FIGURE 3.23:

The data for drawing the circuit and the linear transform

	A	B	C	D	E	F	G	H
49		4.10E+05		0.31	End filter calculation			
50								
51					Offset	0	0	
52					Multiplier	1.00E+05	0.1	
53					Begin circuit plot	x	y	
54		0.50		1.00	Ground Line	5.00E+04	0.10	
55		3.00		1.00		3.00E+05	0.10	
56								
57		2.30		1.00	Resistor A	2.30E+05	0.10	
58		2.30		1.20		2.30E+05	0.12	
59		2.35		1.30		2.35E+05	0.13	
60		2.25		1.40		2.25E+05	0.14	
61		2.35		1.50		2.35E+05	0.15	
62		2.25		1.60		2.25E+05	0.16	
63		2.35		1.70		2.35E+05	0.17	
64		2.30		1.80		2.30E+05	0.18	
65		2.30		2.00		2.30E+05	0.20	
66								
67		2.00		2.40	Operational amplifier	2.00E+05	0.24	
68		2.50		3.00		2.50E+05	0.30	
69		2.00		3.60		2.00E+05	0.36	
70		2.00		2.40		2.00E+05	0.24	
71								
72		2.00		2.60	Resistor B and wire	2.00E+05	0.26	
73		1.90		2.60	from input network	1.90E+05	0.26	

fig. 3.14 / fig. 3.15 / fig. 3.15b / fig. 3.19 \ **fig. 3.21** /

tab to reduce the size of the text to 8 points. Use the Patterns tab to set the Border and Fill to none.

10. Click on the worksheet to activate the worksheet.

The chart should look like Figure 3.24.

FIGURE 3.24:

The Delyiannis Bandpass Transfer function chart and circuit drawn with worksheet data

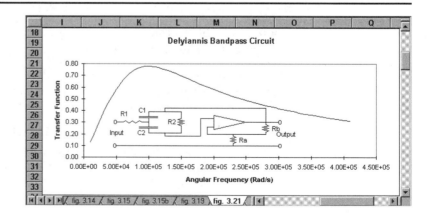

fig. 3.14 / fig. 3.15 / fig. 3.15b / fig. 3.19 \ **fig. 3.21** /

> **TIP**
> There is actually a much easier way to place a graphic on a chart: use a drawing program to draw it, copy the drawing, and paste it on the worksheet or chart. The features in most drawing programs are easier to use than the drawing tools in Excel.

Summary

In this chapter, you created charts of worksheet data and enhanced those charts with data labels, markers, legends, and titles. In addition to these normal plotting functions, you investigated ways to use Excel's graphics capabilities to perform other common science and engineering graphics tasks, such as creating log or semi-log charts and three-dimensional plots, and enhancing those charts with simple drawings.

Using the techniques presented in this chapter plus a little ingenuity, you should be able to manage most of your data-plotting and presentation tasks. For any new plot type, such as polar, create a linear transform to transform your data onto the linear x- and y-axes in Excel. Plot your data, and then use Excel's tools to add any required axis lines or labels.

For More Information

Resistivity of Silicon

S. M. Sze, *Physics of Semiconductor Devices*, 2nd ed. (New York:Wiley, 1981), Ch. 1.

Electron Avalanche Coefficient in Silicon

W. N. Grant, "Electron and Hole Ionization Rates in Epitaxial Silicon at High Electric Fields," *Solid State Electronics 16* (1973):1189-1203.

Delyiannis Bandpass Filter

D. G. Fink and D. Christiansen, *Electronics Engineers' Handbook* (New York: McGraw Hill, 1982).

Review Problems

1. Plot the results of the first engineering table in the previous chapter (thermal conductivity of silicon). Don't forget to label the axes.

2. The hyperbolic sine (sinh) of an angle in radians is calculated by

$$\sinh(x) = \frac{e^x - e^{-x}}{2}$$

   a. Using this equation, calculate the value of the sinh of x for 40 values of x between 0 and 2π radians. Plot those values and label the axes.

   b. Add plots of the hyperbolic cosine (cosh) and hyperbolic tangent (tanh) to the plot of the hyperbolic sine. Label the curves with a legend.

$$\cosh(x) = \frac{e^x + e^{-x}}{2} \qquad \tanh(x) = \frac{\sinh(x)}{\cosh(x)}$$

   c. Label the curves with data labels attached to the respective curves instead of the legend.

3. Modify the van der Waals example from the previous chapter to calculate a table of three isotherms of the van der Waals equation of state for carbon dioxide. Let the volume range from 0.06 to 0.4 1/mole in steps of 0.01. In three columns, calculate the pressure for the temperatures 264 K, 304 K, and 344 K. Plot the pressure versus volume for these three isotherms, and label them with the temperature.

4. Complete problem 3 using the ideal gas law instead of the van der Waals equation.

5. Complete problem 2 as a semilog plot. Plot the log of the hyperbolic functions for x ranging from 0 to 10.

6. Create a template for polar plots. On the screen, draw x- and y-axes that range from −2.5 to +2.5 with the origin at the center. Draw a circle of radius 1 and a circle of radius 2, centering both on the origin. Create a transfer function to convert a function of r and v to x and y values that can be plotted on the template.

7. Plot the four-leaved rose function on the polar template created in problem 6:

$$r = a\sin(2\theta) \quad 0 < \theta < 2\pi \quad a = 2$$

8. For the bending beam example in Chapter 2, plot the stress as a function of the position along the beam. Draw a picture of a cantilever beam (see Figure 2.14) in the corner of the plot. (Draw a straight beam instead of the curved one shown in the figure.)

9. For the LVDT (linear variable differential transformer) calibration table in Chapter 2, plot the four calibration curves versus the transducer voltage. Label the curves on the plot with a legend.

10. For the intrinsic carrier density example in Chapter 2, plot the energy gap and the log of the intrinsic density as a function of the temperature. Label the curves.

11. Make a three-dimensional plot of the function $\sin(x \times y)$ for x and y ranging from π to $+\pi$.

12. Make a wire-frame plot of the three-dimensional plot example in the text. (On a wire-frame plot, the data points are connected in both directions, rather than in just the one illustrated in the example.) Plot the data first along the y direction, as in the example, and then again along the z direction. The result should look like a net draped over the data points, creating a surface in three-dimensional space.

Exercises

1. The average velocity (c) of an ideal gas molecule is given by:

$$c = \sqrt{\frac{3P}{\rho}}$$

   where ρ is the density (water $\rho = 1000$ kg/m^3) and P is the pressure (N/m^2). Calculate and chart the velocity for pressures ranging from 0.001 to 100 Atm. Use logarithmic axes if necessary.

2. In Chapter 2, a table of distance to a star versus relative and absolute magnitudes was calculated (Figure 2.12). Calculate that table and chart it as a two-dimensional wire frame chart using the built-in 3D charting routines.

3. Chart the data in problem 2 again, but use the 3-D surface charts this time. Compare the results to those in problem 2.

4. The data in problem 2 should really be charted with a logarithmic axis in the vertical direction. Change the vertical to logarithmic and chart it again as a wire frame and as a 3-D surface plot.

5. The change in the ecliptic longitude (X) and the value of the obliquity of the ecliptic (ε) are given by.

$$X = 50.2564'' + 0.00222''t$$
$$\varepsilon = 23^{0}27'8.26'' - 0.4684''t$$

   where t is the number of years since 1900. Calculate X and ε for t ranging from 0 to 100 and chart the results. Draw the parts of Figure 2.7 that illustrate X and ε on the chart.

6. A water tank 10 feet in diameter and 10 feet tall is filled with water. It has a 2-inch pipe at the bottom that is 1 foot long. Assuming water gives a pressure of 2 psi per foot of depth, chart the flow rate through the pipe for different depths of water in the tank. See Poiseuille's law in exercise 6, Chapter 2.

7. Do problem 6 again, but sketch the tank, pipe, and outflowing water in the margin of the chart.

8. Calculate the sine, cosine, tangent, secant, cosecant, and cotangent for angles ranging from -2π to 2π, and chart the results. Be sure to label all the curves.

9. Using the water tank in exercise 6, calculate and chart the flow rate (Q) versus time (t) for the water tank. Poiseuille's law gives the flow rate versus pressure, pressure is a constant times the depth, and depth is volume of the tank divided by the area. Put this all together and you have a simple differential equation that can be solved analytically as follows:

$$Q = KV_0\, e^{-Kt}$$

where

$$K = \frac{\pi a^4 u}{8\eta l A}$$

and a is the pipe radius, u is the pressure drop per unit depth (water 0.433 psi/ft,) v is the viscosity, l is the length of the pipe, and A is the cross-sectional area of the tank.

10. For the thermoelectric cooler example created in Chapter 2 (Figure 2.18), turn the function calculator into a table, then calculate and chart the thermoelectric efficiency and the heat pumping rate for input currents ranging from 20 to 40 amps.

CHAPTER

FOUR

Using Visual Basic for
Applications

4

- Recording command procedures

- Creating custom functions

- Creating applications

In 1994, Microsoft made a significant change to its macro capability; it specified the goal to make Visual Basic the macro language for all its standard applications, and Excel became the first of those applications to be changed. Visual Basic is very successful as a language for developing Windows applications by virtue of its visual interface (you draw your application) and the relative simplicity of its modern Basic language. Many people scoff at Basic as a language, but Visual Basic is a modern programming language, containing block structuring, procedures, and programming objects. Excel contains a variation of Visual Basic called Visual Basic, Applications Edition, or Visual Basic for Applications. It is not the full Visual Basic language, but it contains most of the procedures. In addition, it contains special programming objects that allow it to access the cells on a worksheet and control Excel.

If you have programmed before using one of the modern versions of Basic or FORTRAN, you will be very comfortable with the Visual Basic language. If you are a C or Pascal programmer, the change will not be difficult. On the other hand, if you are a GW-BASIC or BASICA programmer, you will recognize the language, but you have a lot to learn. The modern Basic language is significantly different from those early versions.

The Visual Basic for Applications language is a fully functional programming language, and deserves a separate book all its own to describe all its capabilities (I know, I wrote one.) This chapter will give a good overview of the capabilities that you are most likely to use as a scientist or engineer, but it is just not possible to give a complete description of the language in a single chapter. If you need to learn more about the language, see one of the books listed in the For More Information section at the end of this chapter. See also the *Visual Basic User's Guide* included in the Excel 5 package, and the online references in both Excel 5 and Excel for Windows 95, for a complete description of the available functions and all their capabilities.

Creating Visual Basic Procedures

A Visual Basic for Applications procedure is a block of Visual Basic code that is executed as a unit. It is identified by a procedure header and footer that surround the block of code to be executed. The procedure header has the following syntax:

```
Sub ProcName(arguments)
```

where *ProcName* is replaced with the name of the procedure and *arguments* are any arguments to be passed to or from the procedure. The procedure footer is simply:

End Sub

which follows the last statement of the procedure.

Procedures are placed on a separate module sheet within an Excel workbook. You add a module sheet to an existing Excel workbook using the Insert ➤ Macro ➤ Module command. When you choose that command, a new Excel module sheet is inserted into the current notebook, and the Visual Basic toolbar is displayed. The Visual Basic toolbar contains commands to run, stop, and pause a Visual Basic program. Figure 4.1 shows the Visual Basic toolbar and lists the functions of the buttons. In addition to the toolbar, the Run and Tools menus also contain commands for running and debugging procedures.

FIGURE 4.1:

The Visual Basic toolbar contains buttons for running and debugging a procedure.

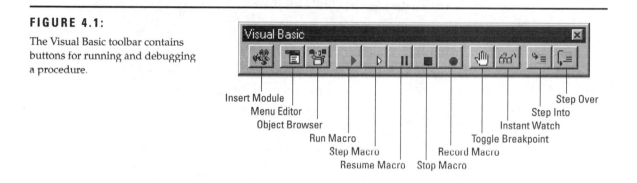

In addition to module sheets, there are dialog sheets for creating dialog boxes complete with buttons, labels, check boxes, lists, and edit boxes. You can add a new dialog sheet by choosing the Insert ➤ Macro ➤ Dialog command. The dialog sheet contains a blank dialog box with only OK and Cancel buttons (see Figure 4.2). Next to the dialog box is the Forms toolbar containing buttons to create buttons, edit boxes, labels, lists and other objects on the form (see Figure 4.3). To create an object, simply click a button in the toolbar and draw the object on the dialog box.

Once you create an object on a dialog box, you must assign a Visual Basic procedure to it. Select an object on the dialog box, such as a button, and choose the Tools ➤ Assign Macro command. The Assign Macro dialog box displays a list of all

FIGURE 4.2:

A new Visual Basic dialog sheet and the Forms toolbar

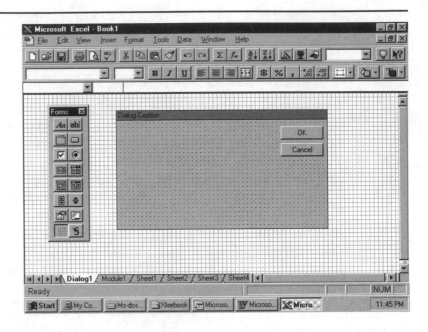

FIGURE 4.3:

The Visual Basic Forms toolbar contains buttons for placing new objects on a dialog box.

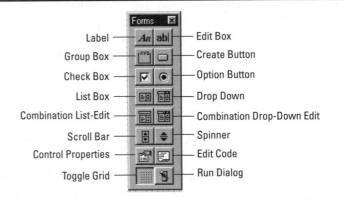

the procedures available in this workbook, from which you select the one to assign to your object. From then on, when you click on that object, the Visual Basic procedure is executed.

Object-Oriented Programming

Object-oriented programming is a programming paradigm in which data (properties) and the code that manipulates that data (methods) are combined in a container called an object. In Visual Basic, a button is an object. It contains the data that describes where it is on the dialog box, how large it is, what color it is, and the text displayed on top. It also contains the code to draw the button on the screen, to simulate a button being pressed and start a user-defined procedure when you click it.

To use an object, you either read or change its Properties, or you execute its attached code by calling its Methods. For example, a Button object has Top and Left properties that set its position relative to the top-left corner of the dialog box. A program can read those properties to see where a button is, or change them to move a button to a different location. A button also has a Copy method that, if executed, puts a copy of the button object on the clipboard.

Objects are combined into new objects using the container model. In the container model, each instance of an object is contained in a larger object, and the larger object is contained in an even larger object. Thus, the buttons on a dialog box are contained in the dialog box object. The dialog box is contained in the workbook object along with the worksheet and module objects. All open workbook objects are contained in the application object, and so on. When you access an object, you use this hierarchy of containers to specify exactly which object you are accessing.

Accessing Objects with Visual Basic

Visual Basic for Applications is not fully object-oriented, in that you cannot create new objects, but it contains and uses objects, and you use objects when accessing Excel. Each item in Excel is an object, and is accessible by a Visual Basic program. Not only are cells and worksheets objects, but all the commands and worksheet functions as well.

In Visual Basic for Applications, a cell or group of cells is a Range object contained in a Worksheet object. Accessing a property of an object follows this hierarchy of containers to specify what object and property you are interested in. For example, to access the value of cell A1 on the worksheet named FlowCalc in the Design workbook, you would use the following syntax.

```
Application.Workbooks("Design").Sheets("FlowCalc").Range("A1").Value
```

This syntax follows each container object with a dot, followed by the object contained in it. The exclamation point (!) is also used to separate objects when an object and property have the same name. If a dot is used, the property is selected, if the exclamation point is used, the object is selected.

You don't always have to type all the links shown above. If you leave off links on the left side of the hierarchy of containers, the currently active object is assumed to be there. Thus, you normally need only to specify the Sheet and Range for a cell or range of cells. For example, the following would work in most situations.

```
Sheets("FlowCalc").Range("A1")
```

In addition, there are some special objects that always select the currently active object. ActiveSheet selects the active sheet, ActiveCell selects the active cell, and Selection returns the selected objects on the selected container object. For example, ActiveSheet.Selection accesses the selected cells (Range object) on the currently active sheet, ActiveSheet.ActiveCell accesses the active cell within that selection, and ActiveDialog.Selection accesses the currently selected control on the active dialog box.

NOTE   To learn what Properties and Methods an object has, use the Object Browser (click the Object Browser button on the Visual Basic toolbar). In the Object Browser dialog box, select the library (Excel or VBA) and the object. A list of the available Properties and Methods appears. Selecting a particular Property or Method displays its syntax and pressing the question mark button (?) displays the help topic describing it.

Creating Command Procedures to Automate Worksheets

The most elementary Visual Basic procedures are for automating repetitive actions on a worksheet. Procedures of this type are known as command procedures, because they are executed like menu commands. Almost every repetitive task can be performed by a procedure. The main uses for these procedures are to save you time when you have to perform repetitive actions and to create automated worksheets for people who are not experts at Excel. They are also good for amazing your friends, because worksheets appear to create themselves without your touching the keyboard.

Recording a Procedure

Command procedures are simple to create and even simpler to use. To create a command procedure, set up a worksheet as it will be before the procedure is executed, and choose the Tools ➤ Record Macro ➤ Record New Macro command. The Record New Macro dialog box appears—click the options button, and the dialog box expands as shown here.

In this dialog box, you type a name for your procedure and, optionally, place it on the Tools menu and assign it a shortcut key used in combination with the Ctrl key (Option+Cmd on the Macintosh) as a shortcut for playing back the procedure. You don't need to specify a menu name or shortcut key—you can assign them later, or assign the procedure to a button. The Record New Macro dialog box also includes the choice between recording the procedure in the current workbook, a personal workbook, or a new workbook. Put procedures that you intend to use on many different workbooks in the personal workbook, because that workbook is opened whenever you run Excel. Put project-specific procedures in the same workbook as the project.

The language option should be Visual Basic. Excel is capable of creating macros in the earlier Excel Macro language, but you should only use that if there is some specific reason to do so, such as creating a procedure for users who do not have the more recent versions of Excel.

 As soon as you click OK, the Stop toolbar appears containing the Stop Macro button, and Excel begins recording your actions. Everything you do is recorded on the macro sheet: opening and closing files, typing formulas, and so on. When you are finished, choose the Tools ➤ Record Macro ➤ Stop Recording command or press the Stop Macro button.

If you recorded your procedure on a module sheet, switch to that sheet using the sheet tabs at the bottom of the worksheet window, and you will see your new procedure. If your procedure is on the personal workbook, use the Unhide command on the Window menu to make the personal workbook visible.

Adding to an Existing Recording

To record a second procedure on the same module sheet, or to add to an existing procedure, select the place where you want to start recording and choose Tools ➤ Record Macro ➤ Mark Position for Recording command. Then use the Tools ➤Record Macro ➤ Record at Mark command to start recording. When you are finished recording, use the Tools ➤ Record Macro ➤ Stop Recording or the Stop Macro button as before.

The Tools ➤ Record Macro ➤ Record at Mark command does not insert a procedure header for the recorded code and does not name them. It simply inserts the recorded code at the marked location. Unless this code is inserted within an existing procedure, you must name the code so you can access it. To name the recorded code, insert a procedure header and footer above and below the recorded code. The name used in the procedure header is the name used to access the code.

NOTE When you are recording macros, cell references are recorded in absolute mode, which makes them access the same cells every time. For example, if you create a macro that formats a cell, you want the macro to format the currently active cell, not the cell that was active when you recorded the macro. To change to recording in Relative mode, choose the Tools ➤ Record Macro ➤ Use Relative References. Choose the command again to change back.

Assigning a Procedure to an Object

Instead of giving a procedure a shortcut key or executing it from the Tools menu, you can assign a procedure to an object, such as a button, and execute it by clicking on the object. You can create a button with the Create Button tool on the Forms or Drawing toolbar, but any object on a worksheet can have a procedure assigned to it, including an embedded chart or a drawing element (such as a rectangle or line). To assign a procedure to an object, select the object, choose the Tools ➤ Assign Macro command, select the procedure to assign from the Assign Macro dialog box, and click OK.

Assign Macro

Macro Name/Reference:
CloseFile

CancelBtn_Click
CloseFile
closeit
Excel2For
OkBtn_Click
SelectBox
ToFortran

OK
Cancel
Edit
Record...

Description

To change the procedure assigned to a button, you need to first select the button, but selecting the button executes the procedure. To select a button without executing the assigned procedure, hold down the Ctrl key when selecting it. In addition, you can use the Drawing Selection tool on the Drawing toolbar to select an object without executing the assigned procedure. This method works for all objects that have procedures assigned to them.

Running a Command Procedure

To run a command procedure, hold down Ctrl (Option+Cmd on the Macintosh) and press its shortcut key (if you assigned one), click on its object (if you assigned a procedure to an object), or select Tools ➤ Macro and choose its name from the Macro dialog box.

Cell Formatting Procedure   As an example, create a command procedure to format and outline cells. This is a simple procedure that formats the contents of the selected cell or cells as scientific with two decimal places and draws a box around the cells. Assign the procedure to a button on the worksheet.

1. Start with a new worksheet, and name it **fig. 4.4**

2. Select cell B7 (actually, any cell will do) and enter any number in it to use while recording the procedure.

3. Choose the Tools ➤ Record Macro ➤ Record New Macro command.

4. In the Record New Macro dialog box, click the Options button.

5. Name the macro **FormatIt**, type a description, place it on the Tools menu, set the shortcut key to **f**, and click OK to start recording.

Record New Macro

Macro Name:
FormatIt

Description:
Procedure to format a cell as 0.00E00 and outline it.

OK
Cancel
Options >>

Assign to
☑ Menu Item on Tools Menu:
Format It
☑ Shortcut Key:
Ctrl+f

Store in
○ Personal Macro Workbook
◉ This Workbook
○ New Workbook

Language
◉ Visual Basic
○ MS Excel 4.0 Macro

6. Choose the Tools ➤ Record Macro ➤ Use Relative References command (this places a checkmark next to the command). If it is already checked, leave it alone, because the recorder is already in Relative mode.

7. Click on the cell containing the number, choose the Format ➤ Cells command, Number tab, select Scientific format with two decimal places, and click OK.

8. Click the down arrow on the Borders button, and select the outline button from the palette.

9. Click the Stop Macro button.

10. Select the Module1 sheet tab.

The macro appears on the macro sheet, as shown in Figure 4.4. The recorder automatically inserted some comments at the top along with the procedure header and footer, and recorded all the actions taken on the selected cell.

NOTE Comments in Visual Basic are any text on a line that follows a single quote. Comments can appear on a single line, or may appear to the right of an executable statement. Use comments liberally in your codes to make them more meaningful.

FIGURE 4.4:

The FormatIt macro recorded on the macro sheet

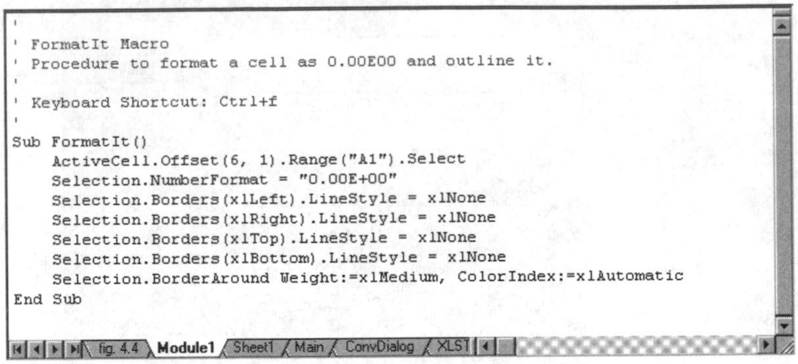

```
'
' FormatIt Macro
' Procedure to format a cell as 0.00E00 and outline it.
'
' Keyboard Shortcut: Ctrl+f
'
Sub FormatIt()
    ActiveCell.Offset(6, 1).Range("A1").Select
    Selection.NumberFormat = "0.00E+00"
    Selection.Borders(xlLeft).LineStyle = xlNone
    Selection.Borders(xlRight).LineStyle = xlNone
    Selection.Borders(xlTop).LineStyle = xlNone
    Selection.Borders(xlBottom).LineStyle = xlNone
    Selection.BorderAround Weight:=xlMedium, ColorIndex:=xlAutomatic
End Sub
```

The first statement in the procedure following the procedure header is a select statement. The statement itself is a result of setting relative recording and selecting cell B7.

```
ActiveCell.Offset(6, 1).Range("A1").Select
```

The ActiveCell object resolves to the currently selected cell in the topmost worksheet. In this case, it was cell A1. The Offset(6,1) method moves the origin for a selection 6 rows down and 1 column right (cell B7). The Range("A1") method returns the top-left cell in the offset range it is applied to. In this case, the Offset command made cell B7 the top-left cell so selecting the top-left (A1) cell in this range selects cell B7. If more than one cell were selected, the Range method would have a range of cells in the argument. The Select method selects that cell, making it the new active cell.

Following the Select statement are five lines set by the Borders command. When you select a border using either the Border dialog box or the Borders button, you set one or more of five options: Left, Right, Top, Bottom, or Outline. Each of those five options results in a line in the recorded procedure, even if you don't change the option from its default setting. In the example, the outline border was selected, so all the options are set to none, except for the BorderAround option, which is set to be a medium weight line.

The seven variables in Figure 4.4 that start with xl (xlLeft, xlRight, xlTop, xlBottom, xlNone, xlAutomatic, and xlMedium) are globally defined constants for use with Visual Basic applications. The available constants are listed in the online help, and are also listed in the Object Browser under the Constants object in the Excel and Visual Basic libraries. You can use these constants wherever the value would be used to make your code more readable.

This procedure is intended to format whatever cell or cells you have selected (not necessarily the cell 6 rows down and 1 column right from the active cell), so you must remove the selection statement. Next, create a button on the worksheet and assign the procedure to it.

1. Delete the first line of the procedure, or change it into a comment by typing a single quote at the far left side.

2. Select the sheet tab for worksheet fig. 4.4.

3. Click on the Drawing button on the Standard toolbar to display the Drawing toolbar.

4. Click on the Create button tool and draw a button on the worksheet by clicking and dragging in a convenient place.

5. In the Assign Macro dialog box that appears, select the FormatIt macro and click OK.

6. Use the mouse pointer to select the text on the face of the button, then type **Format It**. If you have de-selected the button for any reason, hold down the Ctrl key when selecting it again so you don't execute the assigned procedure.

The procedure is now ready to use. Type some numbers in some cells, then select the cells and click on the Format It button to see what happens. Select some other cells and choose the Tools ➤ Format It command. The same procedure is executed. Select a third set of cells and press Ctrl+F, and again the procedure is executed.

Once created, a module sheet is saved or opened just like a worksheet. To use a procedure, the module sheet that contains it must be open. The procedures you create are portable; you can use the procedures on an open module sheet with any open worksheet, not just the one that was active when they were created.

Programming with Visual Basic for Applications

Procedures need not be as simple as the one in the last example. You can write complete programs that include custom dialog boxes and menus, repetitive calculations, file access and creation, and custom control of a worksheet using Visual Basic. In addition, if you have a custom function that needs the speed of a compiled language, create it as a module in a Dynamic Link Library (DLL, or a CODE resource on the Macintosh) and then use the Declare statement to register it with Excel. Any external procedure can be used much like a built-in procedure once it is registered with Excel. Appendix D describes how to create and use an external function in a worksheet.

Manipulating Cell References

When you use Visual Basic to manipulate Excel, you generally access worksheet cells and ranges of cells. Any range of cells on a worksheet, from a single cell to a large area, is a Range object. A range is accessed using the Range method, with the cells to access listed in the Range method's argument. Thus Range("B7:F9") selects the cells in the rectangular cell range B7:F9. If you apply another range method to an existing range, the selectors refer to the range as they receive it and not to the worksheet as a whole. For example,

```
ActiveSheet.Range("B7:F9").Range("B2")
```

accesses cell C9, even though the reference specified in the last range method is B2. The first Range method returns the range B7:F9, The second extracts the cell that is two rows down and two rows below the top-right corner of the range it is being applied to.

Another useful range method is Cells( ). The Cells method takes two integer arguments for the row and column, and returns a reference to the cell at the intersection of the indicated row and column. The Cells method's biggest use is in a loop or other structure where you need to access the cells in a range using integer indices. For example,

```
ActiveSheet.Range("B7:F9").Cells(2,2)
```

accesses the same cell as the previous range method, and

```
ActiveSheet.Range(Cells(7, 2), Cells(9, 6))
```

is the same as

```
ActiveSheet.Range{"B7:F9")
```

Visual Basic Variables

Variables in Visual Basic don't have to be declared but are automatically created the first time you use them. You should, however, declare them anyway to help locate misspellings and other problems. You can force yourself to declare everything by using the Option Explicit statement at the top of all your modules. If a variable is not defined, a compile time error results from Visual Basic. This error is usually caused by misspelling an existing variable name.

Variables are declared using the Dim, Internal, External, Const, and Static statements. The Dim statement declares a variable for the current procedure if it is used within that procedure, or for all procedures in a module if it is declared at the top of the module, outside of any procedure. The syntax of the Dim statement is,

Dim *Variable* **As** *Type*

The word *Variable* is replaced with the name of the variable you are declaring and *Type* is replaced with the Type declaration to apply to the variable.

> **TIP**
>
> There are several conventions for naming variables. One of the most readable, prefixing the variable name with its type, makes it easy to remember the variable's type. For example, intCounter for an integer counter or strFileName for a string.

There are ten data types built into Visual Basic. The following list shows the types and the suggested prefixes for variables of that type.

Type	Prefix	Description
Integer	int	16-bit integer value
Long	lng	32-bit integer value
Single	sng	Single-precision floating point (32 bits)
Double	dbl	Double-precision floating point (64 bits)

Currency	cur	64-bit integer type for calculating currency
Date	date	A date or time
String	str	Text strings
Variant	var	Any data type, the actual type is determined at runtime
Boolean	f	Logical True or False
Object	depends on the object	An object variable of some type

Additionally, there is an Array variable type, which is a group of variables with the same name and accessed using an integer index.

> **NOTE**
>
> The Variant data type is special, in that it can be assigned a value of any type. The apparent type of a Variant is assigned at runtime, when it is assigned a value. Variant types also store special data types such as database tables. The drawback in using Variants is that their type is not checked at compile time, but at runtime where they cause runtime errors. There is also extra overhead involved in figuring out what a Variant's type is, and in storing it.

The Internal statement works identically to the Dim statement, but is more meaningful, because it better expresses the actual scope of variables declared with the statement. It is seldom used, however, because Dim has been in common use for many years.

The External statement has the same syntax as a Dim statement, but its scope is much wider. An External statement is used to declare a variable at the top of a module. In this case, though, it is not just available within that module, it is available to all modules in an application (that is, it is a global variable).

> **WARNING**
>
> While global variables are useful because they are available everywhere, be careful because they can also be changed anywhere. If you reuse a global variable in another procedure without declaring it there, you will change the value of the global variable.

The Const statement does not really declare a variable, but declares a constant value. The syntax of the Const statement is,

```
Const Variable = Value
```

When a constant is declared in a program, wherever the *Variable* name is found in the program, it is replaced with the *Value*. Because constants are inserted as literal values at compile time, they cannot be changed while a program is running. Constants are primarily used to set flags, and to make Visual Basic statements more meaningful. By declaring and using constants, you make your code much easier to read than code that contains the literal values.

The Static type is used like Dim within a procedure, but allocates static storage for a variable. The syntax for the Static statement is as follows:

```
Static Variable As Type
```

Normally, memory for variables is allocated when a procedure starts running and disappears when the procedure completes. The Static declaration allocates storage at compile time, so the contents of Static variables do not disappear when a procedure completes, but are available for future calls to that procedure.

> **TIP**
>
> It is common practice to group all global declarations and constants into a single module all by themselves. In this way, they are easy to locate and change if necessary.

Creating Mathematical Statements with Visual Basic

Mathematical assignment statements (those that calculate a value and store it in a variable) are almost identical to their algebraic equivalents. On the left is a variable that is to receive the calculated value, followed by an equal sign and the formula for calculating the value on the right. Addition, subtraction, multiplication and division are identical. Exponentiation is done with the up arrow (^) operator.

Mathematical functions are similar in name and function to the worksheet functions. In fact, worksheet functions can be used in Visual Basic statements.

For example, the mobility equation from Chapter 2,

$$\mu = \frac{\mu_0 \,(T/T_0)^{-\delta}}{(1 + (E/E_c)^\beta)^{1/\beta}}$$

would convert to the Visual Basic statement

```
u = (u0*(T/T0)^(-delta))/((1+(E/Ec)^beta)^(1/beta))
```

Note the use of parentheses to insure that the statement is calculated in the correct order.

> **WARNING**
>
> The precedence of the operators in Visual Basic for Applications is slightly different from that of formulas on the worksheet. The precedence of the operators determines which operations are carried out first. In Visual Basic for applications, exponentiation comes before negation, while on the worksheet, negation comes first. For example, -1^2 returns 1 on the worksheet and -1 from Visual Basic for Applications. To get the same result in Visual Basic for Applications as for the worksheet, use parentheses to force the order of calculation:(-1)^2.

The types of the variables are important in Visual Basic. If you create a formula that includes different types of variables, Visual Basic will convert all the values to the most accurate type before performing the calculations. The final result is then converted to the type of the variable on the left side of the formula. In most cases, the conversions should have no effect on the results. If it will effect the results, convert all the variables to a single type before calculating the formula. Functions are available to do these conversions for you.

Handling Input and Output

To get a single item of input from the user, use the InputBox function. To simply send the user a message, use the MsgBox function. Both of these functions display a dialog box containing text and buttons. The MsgBox function displays a message to the user. The InputBox function both displays a message and has an Edit Box for the user to enter information. In addition to these built-in dialog boxes, you can create your own custom dialog boxes. To create a custom dialog box, open a dialog sheet and use the Forms toolbox to draw the buttons and boxes you need.

To access external disk files, use the standard dialog functions to display the standard Windows Open and Save As dialog boxes for you to select or enter the file name you want. The standard-dialog dialog boxes do not actually open a file, but only return the validated name and path of a file. The two standard dialog boxes are used as follows:

```
answer = Application.GetSaveAsFilename(strFileName, strFilter)
answer = Application.GetOpenFilename(strFilter)
```

There are more arguments, but these few are all that are needed to use the functions. The result of the functions, which is stored in the variable *answer*, is the name and path to the file to be opened. strFileName contains a suggested file name that is inserted into the Save As dialog box. The user does not have to use that suggestion, but can if he wants to. The strFilter variable contains a file filter to control what files are listed in the dialog box. If no filter is included, all the files are displayed.

When you have a name and path, use the Open statement to prepare a file for access. The basic syntax of an Open statement is

```
Open fileName For inputType As #1
```

The fileName argument is, again, the file's name and path. The inputType argument takes four values: Input, Output, Append, and Random. The #1 is a number that identifies the file and connects the Open command to the Input and Write commands that access the open file. There are a lot more options available to the Open command, but this simple syntax will handle most situations.

Writing to an open file is done with Write and Print statements. The syntax of Write and Print are

```
Write #1, Variable, Variable,...
Print #1, Variable, Variable,...
```

where *Variable, Variable,...* is a list of one or more variables whose contents you want to write to the file and #1 is the file number used to open the file. The difference between Write and Print is significant. Print produces output that could be printed on the screen or on a printer. Values are printed in columns and can be formatted, and the contents of string variables are printed without delimiters. Write, on the other hand, is for producing files that are easier to be read back into a

Visual Basic program. Write places delimiters around everything written to the file to make it easy to separate one written value from another. Quotes surround printed strings and commas are placed between each printed item.

To read information from a file, use the Input and Line Input statements. Input and Line Input have the following syntax:

```
Input #1, Variable, Variable,...
Line Input #1, StringVariable
```

Input reads data from a file until all its variables are filled. Line Input reads one line of text into a string variable, up to but not including the return linefeed at the end of the line. The Input statement complements the Write statement, and can retrieve the exact items that were written with Write. It can also be used to read information written with the Print statement, but may read strings differently. For example, a single string containing a comma could be written with either Write or Print. Write would place quotation marks around the string, so Input would know to include the comma when it reads the string back into the computer. Print would not surround the string with quotation marks, so the Input statement would assume the comma was a delimiter, and would stop inputting the string at the comma.

Use Line Input to get a complete line of text from a file. Line Input ignores all delimiters in a file except the newline character and the end of file. Commas, quotation marks, everything is included in the string read into the program, up to but not including the newline character.

NOTE On an MS-DOS or Windows computer, the newline character is a carriage return, linefeed pair. On the Macintosh it is a carriage return, and on a UNIX machine it is a linefeed.

When you are done with a file, close it with the Close statement. The syntax is

```
Close #1
```

where the #1 again is the file number the file was opened with.

<table>
<tr><td>WARNING</td><td>If you open a file in a program and the program crashes before you execute the Close statement, the file remains open until you quit Excel. If you run your program again, it will crash when trying to open the file with a File Open error. To close the file, execute the Close statement in the Immediate pane of the Debug window. You can also create a simple procedure with a single Close statement in it. When you run the procedure, it closes any open files.</td></tr>
</table>

Controlling Program Flow

The flow of operations in a running program is controlled with loops, jumps, conditionals, functions, and sub procedure calls. Loops are implemented with For/Next, Do Loop, and For Each/Next statements. The For/Next statements create a counted loop. The syntax of the For/Next loop is as follows,

```
For loopCounter = start To end Step step
  .
  Block of Code
  .
Next loopCounter
```

Here, *loopCounter* is a variable that changes for each loop through the block of code, *start* is the beginning value of the loop counter and *end* is the ending value. *Step* is the amount to change the loop counter during each iteration. For example, the following loop iterates the block of statements 10 times with the loop counter, I, taking the values 2, 4, 6, 8, 10, 12, 14, 16, 18 and 20.

```
For I = 2 To 20 Step 2
  .
  Block of Statements
  .
Next I
```

The For statement specifies the starting value for the loop counter, the ending value and the step. If the step is 1, the Step 1 clause is optional. You use a counted loop when you want to execute a block of statements a specific number of times.

The Do/Loop statements implement a logically terminated loop. That is, a logical value determines when the loop stops executing. Another loop While/Wend is a special case of the Do/Loop statements, and is included for compatibility. The Do/Loop statements have the following syntax,

```
Do [While (logical)│Until (logical)]
  .
  Block of Code
  .
Loop [While (logical)│Until (logical)]
```

Only one of the four While and Until clauses is used in an actual statement. The Placement of the While or Until clause determines when the logical value is tested. Placing it at the top of the loop causes it to be checked before running the loop for the first time. Placing it at the end causes the loop to be calculated at least once before checking the value of the logical statement. When the While clause is used, the loop is executed as long as the logical expression is True, and stops when it changes to False. The Until clause is just the opposite, causing the loop to be executed until the logical value becomes True.

For example, the following loop is calculated until the value of A is equal to 10. Presumably, there is some calculation within the block of code that is changing the value of A and will eventually make it 10, otherwise this loop will run forever.

```
Do Until (A = 10)
  .
  Block of Code
  .
Loop
```

The For Each/Next statements are a special loop created for collections of objects and array variables. All the plural object names are collections, such as Worksheets and TextBoxes. The Worksheets collection contains all the Worksheet objects in a workbook. Normally, you would extract a particular worksheet by applying the sheet's name to the Worksheets collection. If you want to do something to every member of a collection, or every element of an array, use the For Each/Next loop. The syntax of the loop is:

```
For Each object In collection
  .
  Block of Code
  .
Next object
```

where *object* is an object variable of the type contained in the *collection* and *collection* is the collection of objects. *Collection* could also be an array variable—then the object would be an element of the array. The loop calculates once for each object in the collection, with the object variable taking the value of a different object during each pass through the loop.

In addition to loops are the If statements. An If statement tests a logical value and either executes or does not execute the following block of code, depending on the value of the logical value. The syntax of the block If statement is:

```
If (logical1) Then
  .
  Block of Code 1
  .
ElseIf (logical2)
  .
  Block of Code 2
  .
Else
  .
  Block of Code 3
  .
End If
```

When the block If statement is first executed, the value of *logical1* is tested. If it is True, then *Block of Code 1* is executed. If not, the value of *logical2* is tested, and if it is True, *Block of Code 2* is executed. There can be many ElseIf clauses in a block If statement to test for different situations, but only the first block of code with a True logical value is executed. All the others are skipped, even if their logical values are also True. The last block can be an Else clause. If none of the other logical values are True, *Block of Code 3* is executed. The ElseIf and Else clauses are optional.

The Select Case statement allows you to select a single block of code from a list according to a value. The Syntax is:

```
Select Case value
        Case compare1
                Block of Code 1
        Case compare2
                Block of Code 2
        Case Else
                Block of Code 3
End Select
```

The *value* argument is compared to *compare1* and if they match, *Block of Code 1* is executed. If *compare2* matches instead, *Block of Code 2* is executed. If nothing matches, the optional Case Else clause is selected and *Block of Code 3* is executed. Only the first block of code with a compare value that matches the value argument is actually executed. All the others are skipped.

Calling Other Procedures

Procedures can be independent programs, or they can be part of larger, segmented programs. If a particular task is performed at multiple places in a program, you could copy the block of code that performs that task to each of those locations, or you could create a new procedure containing that block of code and call that procedure wherever it is needed. Segmenting repeated tasks reduces the amount of code you have to write and simplifies debugging of that code. In addition, segmenting a program into parts that perform simple, straightforward tasks, makes it easier to understand.

To call a Sub procedure from within another procedure, simply insert the procedure's name where you want its task performed. If the procedure has arguments, insert them as a comma-separated list after the procedure name. Don't surround the arguments with parentheses when you call a procedure, even though they are surrounded with parentheses in the procedure header.

> **NOTE**   You can also call a procedure using the Call statement. The Call keyword is followed by the procedure name and its arguments. In this case, the arguments must be surrounded by parentheses.

You call a function procedure in exactly the same way that you call one of the built-in functions. On the right side of a formula, type the procedure name followed by a left parenthesis, followed by the procedure arguments, followed by a right parenthesis. The result of the function procedure is returned in the procedure's name and possibly also in the procedure's arguments.

Creating Dialog Boxes

Dialog boxes other than the built-in ones are created on a dialog sheet. When you insert a dialog sheet into a workbook using the Insert ➤ Macro ➤ Dialog command, you see a new dialog box and the Forms toolbar, as shown in Figure 4.2. Each of the buttons on the Forms toolbar (see Figure 4.3) creates a different object on the new dialog box. The new dialog box comes with the OK and Cancel buttons already inserted.

Drawing a Dialog Box

You create additional objects on the dialog box by clicking one of the buttons on the Forms toolbar and then drawing the object on the dialog box. Once an object is drawn on a dialog box, you can edit the object's properties to change how it looks or operates. Properties are changed either by selecting and directly editing the property on the object, as with the caption text, using the Format ➤ Object command or the Control Properties button on the Forms toolbar; or by using the Name box on the formula bar. In addition, many of the properties can be changed by an operating program, by setting the value of the property with an assignment statement.

> **NOTE** Naming objects on a dialog box must be done with the Name box on the formula bar. This changes the actual name of the object. If you use the Insert ➤ Name ➤ Define command, you create a name that refers to the name of the object instead of changing the name of the object itself.

Each button on the Forms toolbar either creates a new object or allows you to edit or test the dialog box.

 Label — A label is text that cannot be edited. It is usually used to annotate a dialog box, or to send a message to the user.

 Edit Box — A box where the user can input information. The type of information the box accepts is set with the Format ➤ Object command, Control tab.

 Group Box — A box for visually grouping controls. It also specifies the control group for option buttons.

 Create Button — A command button for starting a procedure. One command button is the default button, which is pressed if the user presses Enter. Another is the Cancel button, which is pressed if the user presses Esc. There can be only one default and one Cancel button on a dialog box.

	Check Box	A control for setting options by clicking the box.
	Option Button	A control for selecting one of a set of mutually exclusive options. Clicking one option button in a group de-selects all the others. A group consists of all the option buttons directly attached to a dialog box, or all the option buttons attached to a single Group Box.
	List Box	A box containing a list of values from which the user can select one.
	Drop-Down	A list box with a list that is not displayed until the user clicks on it. Only the current selection is displayed.
	Combination List-Edit	The combination of a List Box and an Edit Box. The user can either select from the list, or type in a value in the Edit Box.
	Combination Drop-Down Edit	A combination of a Drop-Down and an Edit Box. The user can either drop down the list and select a value, or type a value in the Edit Box.
	Scroll Bar	A standard scroll bar. It has a value, depending on the location of the thumb (the slider.)
	Spinner	A control whose value changes by one each time you click on it.
	Control Properties	Displays the Format Object dialog box for the selected control.
	Edit Code	Displays the procedure assigned to the OnAction property of a control or creates a new procedure if one is not assigned.
	Toggle Grid	Turns the background grid on the Dialog sheet on and off. If a worksheet is visible, it turns the worksheet grid on and off as well.
	Run Dialog	Starts Visual Basic executing, with the dialog box active. Clicking a button runs the assigned procedure instead of selecting the button. Use to test a dialog box.

NOTE · The OnAction property contains the name of the procedure to execute when the control is used.

Displaying a Dialog Box

When you have drawn a dialog box, you need a way to display it with a running program. A dialog box is displayed using the Show method of the Dialog box object. The Syntax is

```
Sheets("SheetName").Show
```

where *SheetName* is the name of the dialog sheet.

Hiding a Dialog Box

When you are done with a dialog box, you need to get rid of it so you can continue with whatever else your program is going to do. To hide a dialog box, use the Hide method, or set the Dismiss property of a button on the dialog box. The Hide method is usually inserted in the procedure assigned to the dialog box's OK button. The syntax of the Hide method is as follows:

```
Sheets("SheetName").Hide
```

The Dismiss property of a command button closes the dialog box if the button is pressed.

Assigning Procedures to the Dialog Box's Controls

To make a dialog box do something, you need to assign procedures to the controls on the dialog box. You do this with the OnAction property. The OnAction property of a control contains the name of the procedure to execute when the control is accessed. The action that triggers the property depends on the control. A command button triggers the property when it is pressed. An edit box triggers the property when its contents change.

To set the procedure assigned to the OnAction property, select the control, choose the Tools ➤ Assign Macro command, and select the procedure to run from the list. Use the same procedure to change the contents of the OnAction property. The

OnAction property can also be changed by a running program using a statement like the following:

```
Sheets("SheetName").OnAction = ProcedureName
```

where SheetName is the name of the dialog sheet and ProcedureName is the name of the procedure to run.

> **NOTE** A procedure assigned to a control is usually named with the control's name and the action. For example, Button1_Click is the name of the procedure that is executed by clicking Button1.

Creating Function Procedures

When you define a procedure, the procedure header specifies either a Sub procedure or a Function procedure. Where Sub procedures usually perform actions, Function procedures return values. That does not mean that a Function procedure cannot perform an action, only that it can also return a value and be used in a formula. The simplest and most common type of function procedure returns a single value; however, function procedures can return an array of values, and they are treated in the same manner as any of the other Excel functions that return an array.

Function Macro—Energy Gap in Silicon

Use function procedures to provide functions that are not available in Excel and for special-purpose functions that cannot be easily constructed with Excel functions. In Chapter 2, you needed the energy gap in silicon in order to calculate the intrinsic carrier density. The energy gap in silicon is not a built-in Excel function, although it would be handy for those of us doing a lot of solid-state physics. In Chapter 2, you calculated it in one column of a worksheet and used it in the adjacent column. If it were available as a function, however, you could eliminate a whole column of data on the worksheet.

Referring to the equations in the last chapter, the energy gap in silicon is a simple function of the temperature. Create a function macro that returns the energy gap for any temperature used as an argument. Omit the q from the equation to return the value in electron volts instead of Joules.

1. Choose the Insert ➤ Macro ➤ Module command to insert a new module.

2. Double-click the module's tab to display the Rename Sheet dialog box, then change the sheet name to **MyFunctions**

3. Type the following code on the Module sheet:

```
'
' Energy Gap function
'
Function EnergyGap(T As Double) As Double
Const Eg0 = 1.17
Const Eg1 = 0.000473
Const Eg2 = 636
EnergyGap = Eg0 - (Eg1 * T ^ 2) / (T + Eg2)
End Function
```

That's all there is to it. The function named EnergyGap is now available for use on a worksheet. The procedure itself starts with three lines of comments to identify the procedure, followed by the procedure header. The procedure header identifies the procedure as a function, so Excel knows it returns a value and can be used on the worksheet. The header also defines the function name, the name and type of its one argument and the type of the data returned by the function. Next are three Const statements that define the three constants used in the equation, and then the energy gap equation. The variable on the left side of the equation must be the name of the function, indicating that this is the value to be returned by the function. Finally, the function footer ends the function.

To use this function in a worksheet, simply enter its name, followed by its argument enclosed in parentheses. If cell A3 contains a temperature, the following formula in some other cell executes the procedure and returns the energy gap in eV:

```
=EnergyGap(A3)
```

If the function is in another workbook, you must insert it as an object reference, including the name of the workbook that contains it. For example, to reference this function in another workbook, use a formula like the following.

```
=ch4.xls!EnergyGap(A3)
```

The simplest and most accurate way to insert a function in a formula is to use the Function Wizard. With the cursor in an open formula, press the Function Wizard button (on the Standard toolbar or the formula bar) and scroll down to the list of all User Defined functions in currently open workbooks.

```
Function Wizard - Step 1 of 2                    ? X

Choose a function and press Next to fill in its arguments.

Function Category:              Function Name:
All                             ch4.xls!ArrayTest
Financial                       ch4.xls!EnergyGap
Date & Time
Math & Trig
Statistical
Lookup & Reference
Database
Text
Logical
Information
User Defined

ch4.xls!EnergyGap(T)

No help available.


   Help      Cancel      < Back    Next >     Finish
```

Click Finish to insert the function with a dummy argument, or Next to insert the correct argument. The function can be used like any built-in Excel function.

Building An Array Function   As mentioned, functions can also return arrays to the worksheet. The following simple function returns an array of numbers based on the argument.

```
'
' Array function
' This is an example of returning an array.
'
Function ArrayTest(n As Integer) As Variant
Dim A(2, 3) As Integer
A(0, 0) = n
A(1, 0) = n + 1
A(0, 1) = n + 2
A(1, 1) = n + 3
A(0, 2) = n + 4
A(1, 2) = n + 5
ArrayTest = A
End Function
```

As before, the function begins with some comments and the function header. Note that the type of value returned by the function is a Variant—the type must be

Variant to return an array. Next an array is defined and filled with data based on the function argument, and the function name is then equated to the array, completing the function.

To use this function in a worksheet, select a two-cell by three-cell area on a worksheet, type the function name in a formula, and hold down Ctrl+Shift (Cmd+Shift on the Macintosh) while pressing Enter. The function is entered in an array of values. For example, enter the following formula as an array in cells D2:F3:

```
=ArrayTest(5)
```

and the following range of values results:

D	E	F	G
5	7	9	
6	8	10	

Creating a Visual Basic Program

In addition to calculating simple functions, you can create complete programs with Visual Basic. The programs can pause for keyboard input, store values, calculate values, test for errors, print error messages, and so on. In the next example, create a program that converts worksheets to another format.

A Program to Convert Excel to FORTRAN

The work involved in converting a large worksheet into another program format is tedious, time-consuming, and prone to error. Suppose that you need to convert a worksheet with several thousand filled cells into a compiled FORTRAN program. Instead of doing it by hand, you can create a Visual Basic program to do the job for you. The procedures in this example do not completely convert a worksheet to FORTRAN, but they come close.

The program creates and opens a text file, and then displays a custom dialog box that asks the user to select the cells to convert. After the cells are selected, the macro scans the cells row by row looking for cells with numeric values, formulas, or text.

If a cell contains text, the macro converts it to a FORTRAN comment (a c in column 1). If a cell contains a value or a formula, the macro creates a FORTRAN statement by inserting six spaces, followed by the cell reference and finally the formula or value. The new statement is then scanned for an up arrow (for exponentiation), which must be replaced with the ** used in FORTRAN. Finally, the statement is written to the text file.

One thing this program does not do is make sure that values are defined prior to use; however, since most worksheets are generated down and to the right, the statements are usually in the correct order. When the conversion is complete, you must check the results to see that everything is in the correct order and that array variables are declared.

Create the Dialog Box and Controls   Begin by drawing the custom dialog box shown in Figure 4.5 on a dialog sheet.

FIGURE 4.5:

A custom dialog box for the Excel to FORTRAN program

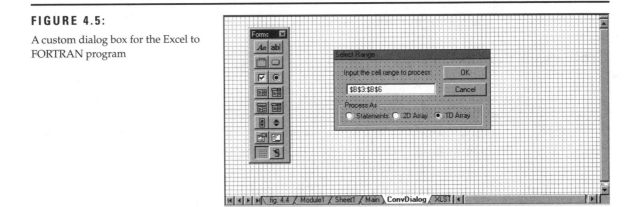

1. Start with a new dialog sheet, and name it ConvDialog.

2. Select the words "Dialog Caption" at the top of the dialog box, then type **Select Range**

3. Using Figure 4.5 as a guide, select the Label tool and draw a label across the top of the dialog box. Select the contents of the label and type **Input the cell range to process**

4. Select the Edit Box tool and draw an edit box as shown in the figure.

5. With the edit box selected, change its name by typing **SelectionBox** in the Name box and then pressing Enter. If you don't press Enter, the name will not be changed.

The procedure allows for three types of formulas: normal assignment statements, 2-D array assignment statements, and 1-D array assignment statements. Add option buttons for selecting the type of conversion.

6. Select the Group Box tool and draw a group box across the bottom of the dialog box. Select the title of the group box and type **Process As**

7. Select the Option Button tool and draw three option buttons on the group box. Select their labels one at a time and change them to **Statements**, **2D Array**, and **1D Array**

8. Select each option button and change the object names by typing a new name into the Name box and pressing Enter. Change the names to **Statements**, **As2D**, and **As1D**

9. Select the OK button and change its name to **OKBtn**. With the OK button still selected, click the Control Properties button and clear the Dismiss checkbox on the Control tab.

10. Select the Cancel button and change its name to **CancelBtn**

11. Adjust the sizes of the boxes and their locations, as shown in Figure 4.5.

12. Choose the Tools ➤ Tab Order command. In the Tab Order dialog box, select SelectionBox. Using the Move arrows, move it to the top of the list.

```
Tab Order                          [?][X]
 Tab Order:
┌──────────────────────────────┐   ┌──────┐
│SelectionBox                  │▲  │  OK  │
│Group Box 9 [Process As]      │   └──────┘
│OkBtn [OK]                    │   ┌──────┐
│CancelBtn [Cancel]            │   │Cancel│
│Label 4 [Input the cell range to process]│ └──────┘
│Statements [Statements]       │
│As2D [2D Array]               │   ┌──┐
│As1D [1D Array]               │   │▲ │
│                              │   └──┘
│                              │   Move
│                              │   ┌──┐
│                              │▼  │▼ │
└──────────────────────────────┘   └──┘
```

The preceding step set the tab order for the controls in the dialog box. The tab order is the order in which the controls are selected when you press the Tab key. You want the SelectionBox to be at the top of the list so that it and its contents are automatically selected whenever the dialog box is made active. This completes the dialog box.

Create Procedures for the Controls   Now you'll create the procedures on a module sheet and assign them to the controls on the dialog box.

1. Open a new module sheet with the Insert ➤ Macro ➤ Module command and change its name to **Main**

2. Type the following code into the Main module sheet (the code consists of a module header and the main procedure):

```
Option Explicit                     'Force all variables to be declared.
Public fCancelNotPushed As Boolean 'Test for cancel button pressed.
Base Excel to Fortran
Sub Excel2For( )                    'This is the start of the program.
Dim strFilter As String
Dim strFileName As String
Dim answer As Variant
'Set the Fortran filter and the default file name.
strFilter = "Fortran Source (*.FOR),*.FOR"
strFileName = "prog.for"
'Display the SaveAs dialog box.
answer = Application.GetSaveAsFilename(strFileName, strFilter)
If answer = False Then Exit Sub  'The user clicked cancel, so quit.
'Clean up the file name then open the file.
strFileName = Trim(answer)
Open strFileName For Output As #1
fCancelNotPushed = True
'Continue displaying the dialog box until the user presses Cancel.
Do While fCancelNotPushed = True
  Sheets("ConvDialog").Show
Loop
'We are done, close the file and quit.
Close #1
End Sub
'
```

In the module header, the Option Explicit statement is used to force every variable in the module to be declared. The flag fCancelNotPushed is declared a Public variable, making it available everywhere.

The Excel2For procedure is the main procedure for this program. It is where the program begins. First, use the common dialog GetSaveAsFilename to get a name for the text file to use to store the code. Before calling the procedure, setup the file filter and a suggested file name for the file. The filter contains two parts, separated with a comma, for each file type. The first part contains the text displayed in the filter dialog box on the Save As dialog sheet. The second part contains the actual filter that is used to select the file names. The filter is the same as is used in DOS to select files.

```
strFilter = "Fortran Source (*.FOR),*.FOR"
```

If the user clicks Cancel, the dialog box returns with a value of False. Check that with an If statement, and end the procedure if it is False. Otherwise, continue with the program. Trim off any extra spaces on the file name, and use it to open or create the new text file.

With the text file open as file number 1, the procedure sets the value of the flag fCancelNotPressed and starts a loop over the Show statement that displays the custom dialog box. This loop continues until the FCancelNotPressed flag changes to False. A Close statement then closes the text file and the program ends.

3. Type the following procedure into the Main module sheet:

```
'Begin sub procedures.
'
' CancelBtn_Click Macro
'
'
Sub CancelBtn_Click( )
'The user pressed cancel, so set the flag, and hide the dialog.
fCancelNotPushed = False
Sheets("ConvDialog").Hide
End Sub
```

The CancelBtn_Click procedure will be assigned to the cancel button on the dialog box. When the cancel button is pressed, the procedure clears the fCancelNotPressed flag and hides the dialog box.

4. Type the following procedure into the Main module sheet:

```
'
' OKBtn_Click Macro
'
' This procedure processes the selected cells into FORTRAN.
```

```
'
Sub OkBtn_Click( )
Dim rngSelArea As Range
Dim intConvType As Integer
Dim strAddress As String
Dim strCellAddress As String
Dim rngCell As Range
Dim strFormula As String
Dim strFormula2 As String
Dim intRows As Integer
Dim intCols As Integer
Dim intI As Integer
Dim intJ As Integer
Dim intCellType As Integer
Dim strNote As String
Dim strName As String
Const AsStatements = 1                        'Conversion types
Const As2DArray = 2
Const As1DArray = 3
Const AFormula = 1                            'Cell contents types
Const AValue = 2
Const ALabel = 3
'Set the CancelNotPushed Flag
fCancelNotPushed = True
'Hide the dialog box.
Sheets("ConvDialog").Hide
'Select the range indicated in the dialog box.
ActiveSheet.Range(Sheets("ConvDialog").EditBoxes("SelectionBox")
        ➡.Text).Select
'Store the selection as a Range object.
Set rngSelArea = Selection
'Get the conversion type from the option buttons on the dialog box.
If Sheets("ConvDialog").OptionButtons("Statements").Value = 1 Then
    intConvType = AsStatements
ElseIf Sheets("ConvDialog").OptionButtons("As2D").Value = 1 Then
    intConvType = As2DArray
Else
    intConvType = As1DArray
End If
'Get the address of the top-left cell in the selection as a string.
strAddress = rngSelArea.Cells(1, 1).Address(False, False)
'Get the number of rows and columns in the slection.
intRows = rngSelArea.Rows.Count
intCols = rngSelArea.Columns.Count
'Loop over all the cells in the selection.
```

```
For intI = 1 To intRows
    For intJ = 1 To intCols
        'Get a reference to the selected cell.
        Set rngCell = rngSelArea.Cells(intI, intJ)
        'Get the formula in the cell.
        strFormula = rngCell.Formula
        'Get the address of the cell as a string, and if the
        'conversion type is statement by statement, change the
        'address to point to the cell instead of to the selection.
        strCellAddress = rngCell.Address(False, False)
        If intConvType = 1 Then
            strAddress = strCellAddress
        End If
        'Get the type of cell contents
        If rngCell.HasFormula Then
            intCellType = AFormula
        ElseIf Application.IsNumber(rngCell.Value) Then
            intCellType = AValue
        Else
            intCellType = ALabel
        End If
        'Get any note assigned to the cell and convert it
        'into a comment.
        strNote = rngCell.NoteText
        If strNote <|> "" Then
            Print #1, "c     " + strAddress + ": Note:" + strNote
        End If
        'Convert the cell contents into Fortran statements.
        If intCellType = AFormula Then
            'It is a formula, change to a statement
            Select Case intConvType
            Case AsStatements
                strFormula = "      " + strAddress + strFormula
                strFormula2 = ""
            Case As2DArray
                strFormula = "      " + strAddress + "(" + Str(intI) +
                    ➡ "," + Str(intJ)+ ")" + strFormula
                'Add a cross reference formula in case the cell is
                'referenced directly.
                strFormula2 = "        " + strCellAddress + "=" + strAddress
                    ➡ + "(" + Str(intI) + "," + Str(intJ) + ")"
            Case As1DArray
                strFormula = "      " + strAddress + "(" + Str(intI +
                    ➡ (intJ - 1) * intRows) + ")" + strFormula
```

```
                    strFormula2 = "        " + strCellAddress + "=" +
                    ➡ strAddress + "(" + Str(intI+ (intJ - 1) *
                    ➡ intRows) + ")"
            End Select
        ElseIf intCellType = AValue Then
            'It is a Value, change to a statement
            Select Case intConvType
            Case AsStatements
                strFormula = "       " + strAddress + "=" + strFormula
                strFormula2 = ""
            Case As2DArray
                strFormula = "       " + strAddress + "(" + Str(intI) +
                    ➡ "," + Str(intJ) + ")=" + strFormula
                strFormula2 = "        " + strCellAddress + "=" +
                    ➡ strAddress + "(" + Str(intI) + "," +
                    ➡ Str(intJ) + ")"
             Case As1DArray
                strFormula = "        " + strAddress + "(" + Str(intI +
                    ➡ (intJ - 1) * intRows) + ")=" + strFormula
                strFormula2 = "        " + strCellAddress + "=" +
                    ➡ strAddress + "(" + Str(intI + (intJ - 1) *
                    ➡ intRows) + ")"
            End Select
        Else 'A label
            strFormula = "c    " + strCellAddress + ": " + strFormula
        End If
        'Convert any known syntax to Fortran syntax.
        If intCellType = AFormula Then
            strFormula = Application.Substitute(strFormula, "^", "**")
            'Replace ^ with **
        End If
        'Print the results.
        Print #1, strFormula
        If strFormula2 <> "" Then Print #1, strFormula2
        'If the cell is named, create another cross reference formula.
        'Use an error trap because testing for a name results in
        'an error if the cell is not named.
        On Error Resume Next
        strName = rngCell.Name.Name
        If Err = 0 Then
            Print #1, "       " + strName + " = " + strCellAddress
        End If
        'If IsNull(rngCell.Name!Name) Then
        ' Print #1, "        " + rngCell.Name.Name + "=" + strAddress
        ' End If
```

```
        'Put in a comment separator between this and the next section.
    Next intJ
Next intI
Print #1, "C ****************************"
End Sub
```

The OKBtn_Click procedure is assigned to the OK button on the dialog box. This is where the contents of the worksheet cells are actually converted into FORTRAN code.

To make things easier to see, blocks of the code will be repeated after the paragraphs that describe them. The first block of code contains the procedure header and the variable and constant declarations.

NOTE The constants declare names to use that are more meaningful than the numbers they represent. Using constants in this way makes the code much easier to understand.

```
'
' OKBtn_Click Macro
'
' This procedure processes the selected cells into Fortran.
'
Sub OkBtn_Click( )
Dim rngSelArea As Range
Dim intConvType As Integer
Dim strAddress As String
Dim strCellAddress As String
Dim rngCell As Range
Dim strFormula As String
Dim strFormula2 As String
Dim intRows As Integer
Dim intCols As Integer
Dim intI As Integer
Dim intJ As Integer
Dim intCellType As Integer
Dim strNote As String
Dim strName As String
Const AsStatements = 1                    'Conversion types
Const As2DArray = 2
Const As1DArray = 3
```

```
Const AFormula = 1                    'Cell contents types
Const AValue = 2
Const ALabel = 3
```

The next block of code hides the dialog box and gets the settings of all the controls on the dialog box. After hiding the dialog box, the procedure selects the cells on the worksheet that were selected in the in the edit box, and then stores a Range object containing the selection. Next is a block If statement that tests each of the option buttons to see which one is selected. The variable intConvType is set to the type of conversion to be performed on the selection.

```
'Set the CancelNotPushed Flag
fCancelNotPushed = True
'Hide the dialog box.
Sheets("ConvDialog").Hide
'Select the range indicated in the dialog box.
ActiveSheet.Range(Sheets("ConvDialog").EditBoxes("SelectionBox")
              ➡.Text).Select
'Store the selection as a Range object.
Set rngSelArea = Selection
'Get the conversion type from the option buttons on the dialog box.
If Sheets("ConvDialog").OptionButtons("Statements").Value = 1 Then
 intConvType = AsStatements
ElseIf Sheets("ConvDialog").OptionButtons("As2D").Value = 1 Then
 intConvType = As2DArray
Else
 intConvType = As1DArray
End If
```

The following short block gets the address of the selection and the number of rows and columns in the selection.

```
'Get the address of the top-left cell in the selection as a string.
strAddress = rngSelArea.Cells(1, 1).Address(False, False)
'Get the number of rows and columns in the slection.
intRows = rngSelArea.Rows.Count
intCols = rngSelArea.Columns.Count
```

In the next block, two loops are started that will loop over all the cells in the selection. The body of the loop then processes each cell. The block first gets a range reference to the individual cell by extracting it from the selection using the Cells method. The reference to the cell is then used to get the formula and reference of the cell as strings. If the conversion type is statement by statement instead of as an array, the range reference is changed to point to the individual cell instead of to the top-left cell.

```
'Loop over all the cells in the selection.
For intI = 1 To intRows
 For intJ = 1 To intCols
 'Get a reference to the selected cell.
 Set rngCell = rngSelArea.Cells(intI, intJ)
 'Get the formula in the cell.
 strFormula = rngCell.Formula
 'Get the address of the cell as a string, and if the
 'conversion type is statement by statement, change the
 'address to point to the cell instead of to the selection.
 strCellAddress = rngCell.Address(False, False)
 If intConvType = AsStatements Then
  strAddress = strCellAddress
 End If
```

The next block determines the type of value stored in the cell. The HasFormula method returns True if the cell contains a formula. To test for a value, use the IsNumber worksheet function. Note the use of the Application object to identify the function as coming from outside of Visual Basic. After testing for a formula or value, whatever is left is assumed to be a label.

```
'Get the type of cell contents
 If rngCell.HasFormula Then
  intCellType = AFormula
 ElseIf
  Application.IsNumber(rngCell.Value) Then
  intCellType = AValue
 Else
  intCellType = ALabel
 End If
```

If the cell has a note assigned, convert it into a FORTRAN comment and write it out to the text file. The print statement puts a c in column one, making the line a comment, then it inserts the cell name, the text ": Note:" and the contents of the note.

```
'Get any note assigned to the cell and convert it into a comment.
 strNote = rngCell.NoteText
 If strNote <¦> "" Then
  Print #1, "c   " + strAddress + ": Note:" + strNote
 End If
```

The following block of code is where the actual conversions take place. If the cell contains a formula, all it needs is a variable name on the left hand side to make it into a FORTRAN statement. A Select Case statement is used to break the conversion into three parts according to the type of conversion to be performed. If the conversion is statement by statement, use the cell reference as the variable name. If the conversion is a one- or two-dimensional array, use the address of the upper-left cell as the array name with intI and intJ loop variables as the indices. Additionally, since a cell may be referenced directly rather than as an element of an array, create a cross-reference statement that equates the cell reference to the array reference.

```
'Convert the cell contents into FORTRAN statements.
If intCellType = AFormula Then
   'It is a formula, change to a statement
   Select Case intConvType
   Case AsStatements
      strFormula = "      " + strAddress + strFormula
      strFormula2 = ""
   Case As2DArray
      strFormula = "      " + strAddress + "(" + Str(intI) +
         ➥ "," + Str(intJ) + ")" + strFormula
      'Add a cross reference formula in case the cell is
         ➥ referenced directly.
      strFormula2 = "      " + strCellAddress + "=" +
         ➥ strAddress + "(" + Str(intI) + "," + Str(intJ) + ")"
   Case As1DArray
      strFormula = "      " + strAddress + "(" + Str(intI +
         ➥ (intJ - 1) * intRows) + ")" + strFormula
      strFormula2 = "      " + strCellAddress + "=" + strAddress
         ➥ + "(" + Str(intI + (intJ - 1) * intRows) + ")"
   End Select
```

If the cell contains a value, you need a variable on the left and an equal sign, otherwise the conversion is the same as for a formula. Again, a Select Case statement breaks the calculation according to the type of conversion.

```
ElseIf intCellType = AValue Then
   'It is a Value, change to a statement
   Select Case intConvType
   Case AsStatements
      strFormula = "      " + strAddress + "=" + strFormula
      strFormula2 = ""
```

```
Case As2DArray
    strFormula = "        " + strAddress + "(" + Str(intI) +
        ➥ "," + Str(intJ) + ")=" + strFormula
    strFormula2 = "        " + strCellAddress + "=" +
        ➥ strAddress + "(" + Str(intI) + "," + Str(intJ) + ")"
Case As1DArray
    strFormula = "        " + strAddress + "(" + Str(intI +
        ➥ (intJ - 1) * intRows) + ")=" + strFormula
    strFormula2 = "        " + strCellAddress + "=" + strAddress
        ➥ + "(" + Str(intI + (intJ - 1) * intRows) + ")"
End Select
```

The last possibility is that the cell contains a label. Convert this label into a comment statement by adding a c and the cell address and the contents of the cell.

```
Else 'A label
    strFormula = "c    " + strCellAddress + ": " + strFormula
End If
```

The next block of code checks to see if there is an up arrow (^) in any of the formulas and replaces them with **, the FORTRAN operator for exponentiation. Any other syntax conversions would be placed here.

```
'Convert any known syntax to Fortran syntax.
If intCellType = AFormula Then
    strFormula = Application.Substitute(strFormula, "^", "**")
        ➥'Replace ^ with **
End If
```

Print the new FORTRAN statements into the text file: the formula and the cross reference to the cell name.

```
'Print the results.
Print #1, strFormula
If strFormula2 <> "" Then Print #1, strFormula2
```

If a cell is named, that name may also be used in a formula and must be cross-referenced with the cell name. Unfortunately, there is no good way to see if a cell is named without causing an error. To do it, create an error trap with the On Error statement. The On Error statement sets where execution should continue if an error occurs. In this case, it is set to be at the statement following the statement that caused the error. Without this error trap, the code would end with a runtime error for any cell that does not contain a name.

> **NOTE**
>
> The On Error statement provides a way to work around a deficiency in the Visual Basic language. By providing a way to continue execution when an error occurs, we can write procedures that try to do things that may not always be allowed.
>
> With the error trap set, the next statement attempts to extract a name from the range reference. The construction Name.Name is required, because the first Name extracts a Name object and the second extracts the text of the name from the Name object. If the cell does not have a name, an error occurs and the error trap sends the execution point to the If Err = 0 statement. If an error has occurred, then the function Err returns the error value, otherwise it returns 0. If there was no error, then a name existed and the block of code creates a cross-reference between the cell name and the cell address.

```
'If the cell is named, create another cross reference formula.
'Use an error trap because testing for a name results in an
'error if the cell is not named.
On Error Resume Next
strName = rngCell.Name.Name
If Err = 0 Then
    Print #1, "         " + strName + " = " + strCellAddress
End If
```

The last block contains the bottoms of the two loops, a print statement to insert a separator bar comment at the end of each section, and the end of the procedure.

```
    'Put in a comment separator between this and the next section.
    Next intJ
Next intI
Print #1, "c ****************************"
End Sub
```

5. Type the following procedure into the Main module sheet:

```
'
'Close File procedure to close the disk file
'while debugging the program.
'
Sub CloseFile( )
Close
End Sub
```

This last short procedure is for debugging purposes. If the procedure crashes for any reason while you are testing it, it will leave the file open. If you try to open it again, you get an error. This short procedure closes all open files whenever it is run. Run it before running the Excel2For procedure again after it has an error.

The last step is to assign the procedures to the two buttons on the dialog box.

6. Switch to the ConvDialog dialog sheet and select the OK button. Choose the Tools ➤ Assign Macro command, select the OKCmd_Click procedure and click OK.

7. Select the Cancel button, choose the Tools ➤ Assign Macro command, select the CancelBtn_Click procedure and click OK.

This completes the program. You can now open a worksheet and apply the program to it. The program should work if you have not made any typing errors. If it does not work properly, you can debug it, as described in the next section.

As an example, apply this program to the Delyiannis Bandpass Circuit worksheet created in Chapter 3.

1. Open the Delyiannis Bandpass Circuit worksheet created in Chapter 3.

2. Copy the worksheet into the program's workbook (use the Edit Move or Copy Sheet command, or press Ctrl while you drag the sheet tab from one workbook to the other).

3. Choose the Tools ➤ Macro command, select the Excel2For program in the dialog box, and click on Run.

4. When the Save dialog box appears, accept the default file name and click OK to save the output in that file.

5. When the custom dialog box appears, the contents of the edit box should be selected; if they are not selected, then select them. Click and drag through cells B3:C5 on the Delyiannis Bandpass circuit worksheet, as shown in Figure 4.6.

6. Click on Statements, and then click OK.

7. When the dialog box reappears, select cells B9:C11, click on 2-D Array, and click OK.

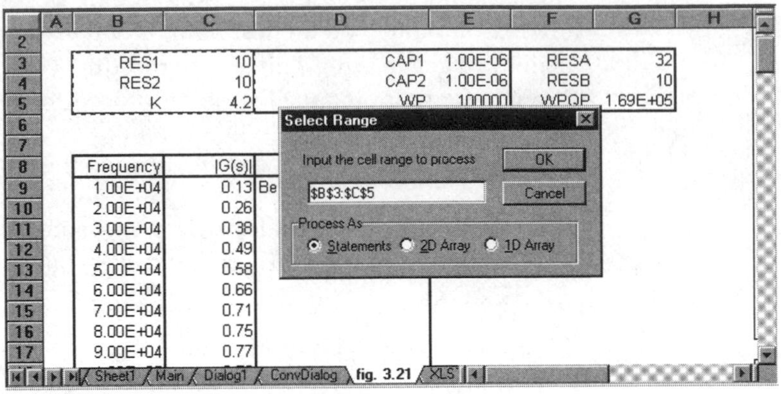

FIGURE 4.6:

Selecting cells to process into FORTRAN

8. When the dialog box reappears, click Cancel to close the file and end the program.

> **NOTE**
>
> When debugging and testing the program, use the Drawing toolbar to draw two buttons on the worksheet. Assign one to Excel2For and the other to CancelBtn_Click. That way, pressing a single button clears memory and starts the programs.

The text file created by the program contains the following:

```
c       B3: RES1
            C3=10
            RES1 = C3
c       B4: RES2
            C4=10
            RES2 = C4
c       B5: K
            C5=1+RESA/RESB
            K = C5
C *************************
c       D3: CAP1
            D3( 1, 2)=0.000001
            E3=D3( 1, 2)
            CAP1 = E3
```

```
c       D4:  CAP2
             E3=D3( 1, 2)
             D3( 2, 2)=0.000001
             E4=D3( 2, 2)
             CAP2 = E4
c       D5:  WP
             E4=D3( 2, 2)
             D3( 3, 2)=SQRT(1/(RES1*RES2*CAP1*CAP2))
             E5=D3( 3, 2)
             WP = E5
c *****************************
```

Note that it is all good FORTRAN, and could be compiled by most generic compilers. You still need to check the order of the statements to ensure that the values are not used before they are assigned. You also need to rewrite IF statements and look for lines longer than 72 characters, although your FORTRAN compiler will find most of these problems the first time you try to compile your program. Note how the labels in cells B3 and B4 are turned into comments in the program, the value in cell C3 is equated to a variable named C3, and then the name of cell C3 is equated to the name C3. All possible names are now available for formulas to use later in the program.

Cells D3:E5 were converted as a two-dimensional array; however, the first column contains only labels and is skipped. The array is then named for the cell in the top-left corner.

Debugging Macro Programs

In many cases, a Visual Basic program does not work correctly the first time. To figure out where you went wrong, you need to determine what the procedure is doing at each step. If you get a runtime error of some type, the error dialog box appears with the option to end, continue, switch to the debug window, or jump to the statement that caused the error.

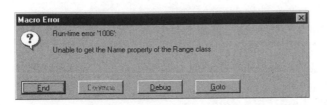

In most cases, you will switch to the Debug window.

```
Debug - ch4.xls.main

    Watch    Immediate    OkBtn_Click




    'If the cell is named, create another cross reference formula.
    'Use an error trap because testing for a name results in an error
    'if the cell is not named.
     On Error Resume Next
    strName = rngCell.Name.Name
    If Err = 0 Then
       Print #1, "        " + strName + " = " + strCellAddress
```

The Debug window displays the code in the code window at the bottom. The statement that caused the error is outlined. In this case, you notice that I commented out the On Error statement that enables the error trap. Without the error trap, you get a runtime error. At this point, you can select a variable and click the Instant Watch button (on the Visual Basic toolbar) to see the value of the variable. For example, if you select the variable Err, and click Instant Watch, you see that it has the value 1006. You have the option of making the current selection a regular watch variable by clicking the Add button on the Instant Watch dialog box.

A regular watch variable appears in the watch pane at the top of the Debug window. Click on the Watch tab if the Immediate pane is visible. The watch variable will always display the current value of the watched variable in the indicated context.

The Immediate pane of the Debug window is used to immediately execute any Visual Basic command or statement that can be placed on a single line. Multiple statements can be stacked by separating them with colons.

> **NOTE**
> The immediate pane is a good place to experiment with new code and procedures. Run a short program to set up your environment, dimension variables and so forth. Place a stop command or a breakpoint to make the code stop before finishing. You can then try out new procedures and statements without having to create a special program for them, and test them only in that code.

 Another way to trace an error is to run the code in Step mode. In Step mode, the program executes one line at a time, so you have time to examine the variables to see how they are changing, right up to the point that the program crashes. To quickly jump to the region where the problem occurred, select a statement in that area and click the Toggle Breakpoint button. When you run your code, it runs at normal speed until it reaches the breakpoint, stops and displays the Debug window. You can then continue running the program, one step at a time.

Summary

Visual Basic tremendously increases the power of Excel. With Visual Basic procedures, you can automate most repetitive worksheet tasks. You can also create custom functions for use in the worksheet, as well as complete programs to automate complex tasks.

Excel's macro recorder records every action you take as a list of Visual Basic commands. You can edit this list of commands into a macro program you can use. For debugging programs, Excel includes a Debug window that shows the values of variables and allows you to watch an executing program, one step at a time.

Visual Basic has far more capabilities than are shown in this short chapter. As mentioned before, whole books are written just on Visual Basic, so get one of them to really learn the capabilities of the language.

For More Information

Visual Basic for Applications

W. J. Orvis, *Visual Basic for Applications By Example*, Indianapolis, IN: Que, 1994.

Microsoft, *Visual Basic User's Guide*, and the online Visual Basic help, included with Excel.

Review Problems

1. Write a procedure to automatically create the worksheet shown in Figure 2.5.

2. Write a procedure to automatically create the worksheet shown in Figures 3.15 and 3.17. Use the alternative formula rather than the temperature data.

3. Write a procedure that displays the question "Do you want to save this workbook (Y or N)?" in a dialog box, and waits for you to click Yes or No. If Yes is clicked, your procedure should save the worksheet in the current directory, replacing any old version, and display "Workbook saved" in the status bar. If No is clicked, "Workbook not saved" should appear in the status bar.

4. Write a procedure that displays the question "What is your birth date?" in a dialog box, accepts the date, and then displays how many days old you are in another dialog box.

5. Write a procedure that automatically creates a table of angles x and values of the hyperbolic sine for 11 angles from 0 to 4, using the following equation:

$$\sinh(x) = \frac{e^x - e^{-x}}{2}$$

6. Write a procedure to create a plot of the data in problem 5. Label both axes and set the data ranges and plot type.

7. Write a procedure to create the worksheet shown in Figure 2.8.

8. Write a procedure to transpose a 3x3 matrix (**A**). A transposed matrix (**At**) has the values in the rows and columns exchanged. Don't use the Transpose command in the Paste Special dialog box.

$$A = \begin{vmatrix} a & b & c \\ d & e & f \\ g & h & i \end{vmatrix}, \qquad A^t = \begin{vmatrix} a & d & g \\ b & e & h \\ c & f & i \end{vmatrix}$$

9. Write a procedure that combines two numbers in two cells and creates a cell reference as a text value. The first number specifies the column, and the second specifies the row. The column numbers will need to be converted to the corresponding letter (1 to A, 2 to B, and so on). For example, for the numbers 3 and 5, your macro should produce the string C5.

10. Write a procedure to scroll a worksheet down one screen, and move the active cell down to the top of the visible screen. Write a second procedure to scroll the worksheet up one screen, again moving the active cell to the top of the screen. Write two more procedures to move the worksheet left and right by one screen, with the active cell always at the left side of the visible screen.

Exercises

1. Write a function procedure to calculate the volume of a cylindrical water tank, given the diameter and height.

2. The factorial of a number is defined as the product of all the integers that make up the number, thus:

```
5! = 1 × 2 × 3 × 4 × 5
6! = 1 × 2 × 3 × 4 × 5 × 6
```

and so on. Write a function procedure to calculate and return the factorial for any given argument.

3. Recreate the Julian Day calculator, but do it on a dialog sheet instead of on a worksheet.

4. Modify the Excel2For procedure to write Visual Basic code instead of FORTRAN.

5. Write a procedure to do the Thermoelectric Cooler example from Chapter 2 as a dialog box.

6. Write a function procedure to calculate and return a two-element array containing the ecliptic longitude (X) and the obliquity of the ecliptic (ε), given the date as an argument.

$$X = 50.2564'' + 0.00222''t$$

$$\varepsilon = 23^0 27'8.26'' - 0.4684''t$$

7. The average velocity of a viscous fluid in a pipe is given by:

$$\bar{v} = \frac{a^2 P}{8\eta l}$$

and the Reynolds number is:

$$Re = \frac{2\bar{v}a\rho}{\eta}$$

where a is the radius of the pipe, ρ is the density, P/l is the pressure gradient down the pipe, and η is the viscosity. Write a function procedure that calculates and returns the Reynolds number given the pipe radius, density, pressure gradient, and viscosity of the fluid. Recreate the table from problem 6 in Chapter 2 using the function.

8. When cutting metal with a lathe, using the proper cutting speed (the optimum speed at which the cutting tool passes through the work) is important. If you cut too slowly, you don't get as much work done; if you cut too fast, you ruin your tools or the work. The optimum cutting speed for a lathe with high-speed steel tools is given by the following empirical formula:

$$V = \frac{H \times S}{\left(\sqrt[3]{D+Y}\right)\left(\sqrt[3]{F-Z}\right)}$$

where V is the cutting speed in feet per minute, D is the depth of the cut in 64ths of an inch, and F is the feed in 64ths of an inch per revolution. H, S, Y, and Z are constants that depend on the material being cut and the size of the cutter.

Material Hardness	H
Hard	0.6
Medium	1.0
Soft	2.0

Tool Size (in)	Material	S	Y	Z
3/4	I	232	3	0
1/2	I	215	8	0.3
3/4	S	325	-2	0.3
1/2	S	288	0	0.5

I = cast iron, S = steel

Create a function that returns the optimum cutting speed given D, F, the hardness, the size of the tool, and the material. Use text flags for the hardness (H, M, S) and material (I, S).

9. Professional journals often have limits on the size of an abstract, specified as the number of words. Create a program to help you stay under the limit. The program should open a text file selected with an Open dialog box, count the number of words in it and display the total in a dialog box.

10. The built-in standard deviation function, StDev, includes blank cells in the calculation range when it calculates the standard deviation. Write a new standard deviation function that ignores any blank cells in the calculation range. The equation for the standard deviation is.

$$\sqrt{\frac{\sum_{i=1}^{N}(x_i - \bar{x})^2}{N-1}}$$

where N is the number of countable cells, the x_i are the contents of the countable cells and $\bar{x}$ is the average of the values in the countable cells.

CHAPTER

FIVE

Using a Database
to Analyze Data

5

- Importing data into a worksheet

- Parsing data

- Using an external database

- Using data filters to select data

- Using a data form to select data

- Sorting data

Analysis of experimental data can be as simple as averaging a few numbers or as complex as searching a large database for records that match some criterion. With Excel you can handle both these extremes and most cases in-between.

Your first step is to bring the experimental data into Excel. After the data is in a worksheet, you can use Excel's commands and functions to calculate averages, fit data to lines, or plot data. For example, many experimental devices output voltages and currents that are proportional to the physical quantities being measured. Using a simple equation and the engineering table format, you can easily convert those voltages and currents into the physical quantities they represent.

Bringing Experimental Data into a Worksheet

There are several methods for getting data into a worksheet; the method you choose depends on the format of the data. If it is in the form of handwritten data in an experimental notebook, your only choice is to type it directly into a worksheet. If it is already on a computer disk in some readable format, you can generally load it directly into a worksheet and separate it into cells without retyping it. If the data is in an external database, Excel can access it directly.

Manually Entering Data

Much experimental data is available only in written form. Notes in an engineering notebook and data tables in reports or journal articles are good examples of printed experimental data. You must manually type this data into the worksheet, unless you happen to have access to a scanner and optical character recognition (OCR) software (or a graduate student).

A scanner coupled with OCR software can read printed (but not handwritten) characters and turn them into editable text in a disk file. If the data is printed, even the inexpensive hand scanners and bundled OCR software do a credible job scanning in data and converting it into editable text. Make sure you carefully compare the printed data with the scanned data to ensure there are no mistakes (it's a good idea to check graduate-student-scanned data as well).

You can type data into Excel relatively quickly. Select a column in a worksheet using the mouse and begin typing. When you press Enter or Tab, the active cell moves down to the next cell so you can continue with the next number.

WARNING   Be careful that you don't reach the end of the selected range before you type the last data value, because when the active cell reaches the end of the selection, it wraps back to the top of the selection and begins overwriting the data you just typed.

If you select two or more columns and press Enter (Return on the Macintosh) after each value, the active cell moves down the first column before going down the next. Press Tab (or Enter on the Macintosh) after each value to move left to right across all the columns in the selected range before moving down to the next row. If you hold down Shift when pressing Tab or Enter, the active cell moves in the opposite direction (up for Shift+Enter and left for Shift+Tab). In Excel for Windows 95, you can set the direction the selection moves after pressing Enter, using the Tools ➤ Options command, Edit tab.

Importing Data from a Disk File

Getting data into a worksheet is much simpler if your data already exists in a disk file. This includes data created by numerical simulation programs, or data you receive from other sources. There are several methods for reading data from a disk file into a worksheet.

Excel can directly open all the file formats listed in Table 5.1. In addition, Excel can open and manipulate most popular database formats using the Query add-in. Data returned to Query flows directly into a worksheet.

Computer modeling of physical phenomena and devices produces large amounts of data that needs to be analyzed and plotted. As long as that data is written out into a text file, you can easily load it into the worksheet for further analysis.

If the data is in a binary file, you must write a small program to read that binary file and write a text file. For easy conversion, the data in the text file should be in the form of a table, with multiple columns of data values or text separated by tabs, with carriage returns at the end of each line. This is Excel's default text file format.

TABLE 5.1:   File Formats Accepted by Excel

Format	File Extension
Excel 5.0 or 7.0	.XLS, .XLT
Excel 4.0	.XLS, .XLC, .XLM, .XLW, .XLA,.XLT, .XLB, .XLL
Excel 3.0	.XLS, .XLC, .XLM, .XLW, .XLA, .XLT
Excel 2.x	.XLS, .XLC, .XLM, .XLW
Symbolic link	.SLK
Text	.TXT
Comma-separated values	.CSV
1-2-3 Release 1A	.WKS
Microsoft Works	.WKS
1-2-3 Release 2.x	.WK1, .FMT
1-2-3 Release 3.x	.WK3, .FM3, .PRN
1-2-3 for Windows	.WK3, .FM3, .PRN
Allways	.ALL
Data interchange	.DIF
dBASE II	.DBF 2
dBASE III	.DBF 3
dBASE IV	.DBF 4
Quattro Pro for MS-DOS	.WQ1, .WQS

Excel can also read text files in which the data is delimited by commas, semicolons, spaces, or any single character, but you must specify the delimiter in the Text Import Wizard dialog box.

Terminal-emulation programs make your computer behave like a terminal for communications with another computer. You can use these programs to receive the results of a simulation on a mainframe computer or to receive data from another person at a remote desktop computer. Most terminal-emulation programs have the capability to receive and store data in text files.

NOTE

Terminal-emulation programs are also useful for connecting two computers with incompatible storage media and allowing them to share files. Connect the two computers' serial ports together using a null modem cable, then transfer files using one of the standard file transfer protocols.

Importing Delimited Files

If your data is in a tab-delimited text file, simply open the file with the File ➤ Open command. This format—data values separated with tab characters (delimiters) and with a carriage return at the end of each line—is Excel's default text file format. When you open a tab-delimited text file, Excel opens a new workbook, and places characters from the file into cell A1 until it reaches the first tab character. Excel then moves the active cell right one cell and places the characters following the tab character in cell B1 until it reaches the next tab character. Excel continues moving right one cell at each tab until it reaches a carriage return, which causes the active cell to move down one row and left to column A again.

If your data is delimited with a different character, such as a comma, space, or semicolon, select the delimiter from the list displayed by the Text Import Wizard that appears while opening the file. You can also select the file origin, which corrects for different end-of-line characters used by different operating systems.

Spark Gaps—a Space-Delimited Text File

As an example, consider the text file in Figure 5.1, which consists of some spark gap data. The text file was created with the Notepad application included with Windows. On the Macintosh, use Teach Text to create the file.

1. Using the Notepad application (Teach Text on the Macintosh), create the text file shown in Figure 5.1. Use spaces to align the columns.

2. Save the file as **COLUMNS.TXT**

3. Switch to Excel and open the file using the File ➤ Open command.

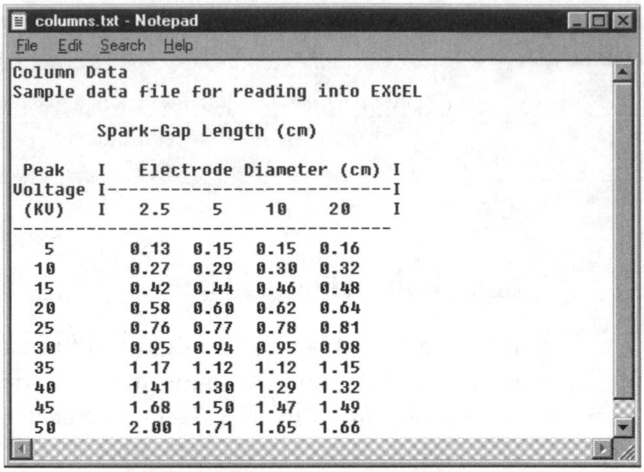

FIGURE 5.1:

Spark-gap sizes: a text file created
with the Windows Notepad
application

4. In the Open dialog box, change the Files of type: box to **All Files (*.*)**

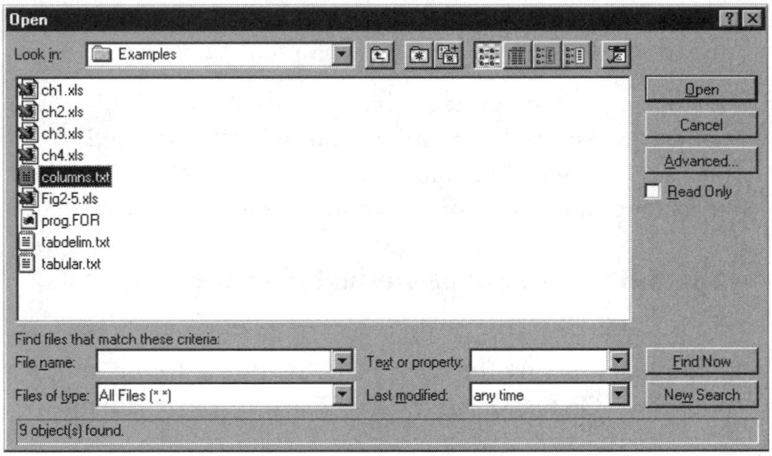

5. Select COLUMNS.TXT and click on Open.

At this point the Text Import Wizard appears, to help you import the file into Excel.
The document contains fixed-width columns delimited with spaces.

6. Click the Delimited option button and click Next.

7. In the second step of the wizard, check the Space and the Treat Consecutive Delimiters As One checkboxes. Click Next to continue. You can clear the Tab delimiter checkbox if you want to; if you leave it checked, then any Tab characters will also be used to parse the file into columns.

8. Step three of the wizard allows you to set the formatting of the data in each column. Leave the formatting as General, so Excel formats the columns as text and numbers. Click Finish to continue.

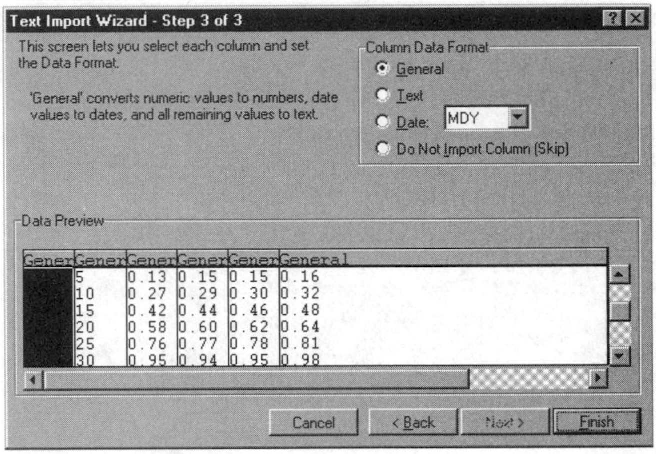

The worksheet now looks like Figure 5.2. Excel was able to separate the numeric data, but most of the labels are a mess. The titles must all be redone by hand to make the table look good.

FIGURE 5.2:

Excel's importation of a columnar text file

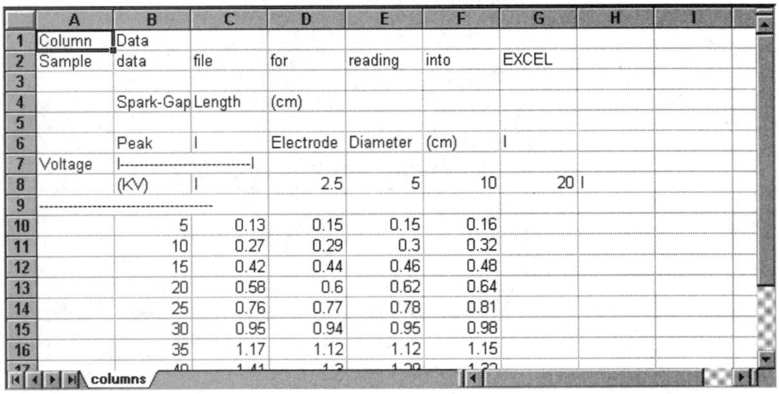

Importing a Tab-Delimited Text File   If the table is tab-delimited, Excel can generally do a better job of extracting the table from the text file. Try importing a file again, but use a tab-delimited file instead.

FIGURE 5.3:

A tab-delimited text file created in
the Notepad application

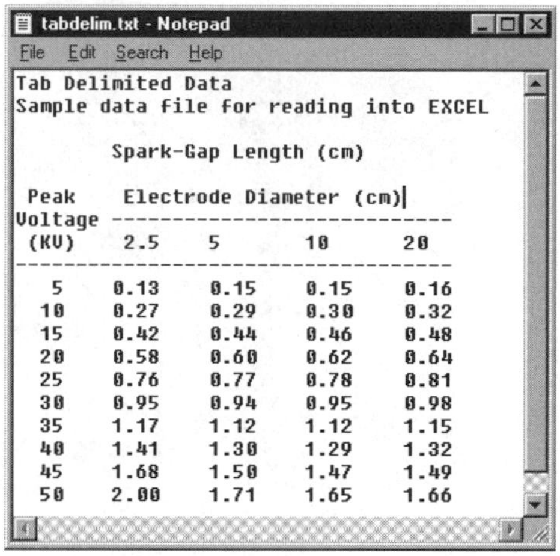

```
┌─────────────────────────────────────────────────┐
│ 📄 tabdelim.txt - Notepad              _ □ ✕      │
├─────────────────────────────────────────────────┤
│ File  Edit  Search  Help                          │
│ Tab Delimited Data                          ▲     │
│ Sample data file for reading into EXCEL           │
│                                                   │
│          Spark-Gap Length (cm)                    │
│                                                   │
│  Peak  │  Electrode Diameter (cm)│                │
│ Voltage  ------------------------------           │
│  (KV)    2.5    5      10     20                   │
│ ------------------------------------------        │
│     5   0.13   0.15   0.15   0.16                 │
│    10   0.27   0.29   0.30   0.32                 │
│    15   0.42   0.44   0.46   0.48                 │
│    20   0.58   0.60   0.62   0.64                 │
│    25   0.76   0.77   0.78   0.81                 │
│    30   0.95   0.94   0.95   0.98                 │
│    35   1.17   1.12   1.12   1.15                 │
│    40   1.41   1.30   1.29   1.32                 │
│    45   1.68   1.50   1.47   1.49                 │
│    50   2.00   1.71   1.65   1.66           ▼     │
│ ◄                                         ►       │
└─────────────────────────────────────────────────┘
```

1. Using the Notepad application (Teach Text on the Macintosh), create the text file shown in Figure 5.3; use tabs to align the columns.

2. Save the file as **TABDELIM.TXT**, then close the file.

3. Switch to Excel and open the file using the File ➤ Open command.

4. In the Open dialog box, select **All Files (*.*)** in the Files Of Type box. Select COLUMNS.TXT and click Open.

5. In the Text Import Wizard, click the Delimited option button and click Next.

6. In the second step of the wizard, check the Tab checkbox and click Next to continue.

7. In step three, leave the formatting as General and click Finish to continue.

The worksheet now looks like Figure 5.4, with most of the information in the right place. A small amount of editing results in the table shown in Figure 5.5, which is much nicer-looking than the original table.

Importing Tabular Data

If your data is in columns (as in Figure 5.1), you can still load it into Excel and place the data values in separate columns without having to change all the spaces into tabs. Many DOS applications create tabular data, using a monospaced font to make the numbers line up. To import a text file that is in columns without delimiters, use

FIGURE 5.4:

A tab delimited text file loaded into Excel

	A	B	C	D	E	F	G	H	I
1	Tab Delimited Data								
2	Sample data file for reading into EXCEL								
3									
4	Spark-Gap Length (cm)								
5									
6	Peak	Electrode Diameter (cm)							
7	Voltage	--------------------------							
8	(KV)	2.5	5	10	20				
9	--------------------------								
10	5	0.13	0.15	0.15	0.16				
11	10	0.27	0.29	0.3	0.32				
12	15	0.42	0.44	0.46	0.48				
13	20	0.58	0.6	0.62	0.64				
14	25	0.76	0.77	0.78	0.81				
15	30	0.95	0.94	0.95	0.98				
16	35	1.17	1.12	1.12	1.15				

tabdelim

FIGURE 5.5:

The Spark Gap table after being cleaned up by hand

	A	B	C	D	E	F	G	H	I
1	Tab Delimited Data								
2	Sample Data File for Reading Into Excel								
3									
4	Peak	Spark-Gap Length (cm)							
5	Voltage	Electrode Diameter (cm)							
6	(KV)	2.50	5.00	10.00	20.00				
7	5	0.13	0.15	0.15	0.16				
8	10	0.27	0.29	0.30	0.32				
9	15	0.42	0.44	0.46	0.48				
10	20	0.58	0.60	0.62	0.64				
11	25	0.76	0.77	0.78	0.81				
12	30	0.95	0.94	0.95	0.98				
13	35	1.17	1.12	1.12	1.15				
14	40	1.41	1.30	1.29	1.32				
15	45	1.68	1.50	1.47	1.49				
16	50	2.00	1.71	1.65	1.66				

columns / tabdelim \ fig. 5.5

parsing. Parsing is a method of separating fixed-width columns of data into worksheet columns, and is accomplished using the Fixed Width setting in either the Text Import Wizard when you open the file, or in the Convert Text To Columns Wizard when you use the Data ➤ Text To Columns command. Data parsing does not work correctly if the file is not created with a monospaced font.

NOTE
> A monospaced font is one in which each letter is the same width. Most computers that operate in text mode use a monospaced font to make things line up vertically. In Windows, most fonts are not monospaced; they are proportionally spaced like the text in this book. The letter *i* uses less space than the letter *w*.

When you load a text file into Excel without parsing, lines of text from the text file are placed into consecutive cells down column A of the worksheet. Each cell in the column contains a complete line of text stored as a long label.

WARNING
> Beware of text files created by word processors that word-wrap at the ends of lines. Most modern word processors store a complete paragraph as a long line with a single carriage return at the end. When you load such a file in Excel, the whole paragraph (up to the 255-character limit) is stored in a single cell. Word processors also place hidden formatting characters within a file, which cause problems when loading the file into Excel. Before opening such a file in Excel, load it into the word processor that created it and save it as text only, with line breaks (refer to the application's manual for instructions). Then the saved file will open properly in Excel.

Elementary Particles

Figure 5.6 is a table of elementary particles and some of their characteristics. This is a more complicated table, containing a mixture of text, numbers, and rational fractions.

To parse the text, open the file and use the Fixed Width option in the Text Import Wizard, or open the file as text and use the Data ➤ Text To Columns command, which opens a Wizard with the same options as the Text Import Wizard.

1. Create the text file shown in Figure 5.6 using the Notepad application (Teach Text on the Macintosh). Save the file as TABULAR.TXT, then close it.

Particle physics constants: a text file
created with Notepad

```
tabular.txt - Notepad                                                    _ □ ×
File  Edit  Search  Help
Particle Physics; A sample text file for reading into EXCEL
   Family    Particle  Mass   Spin  Strange   Charge  Lifetime (s)
------------------------------------------------------------------
             Photon      0       1       0         0    Infinite
   Electron  Electron    1     1/2       -        -e    Infinite
    Family   Neutrino    0     0.5       -         0    Infinite
   Muon      Muon      206.77  0.5       -   -1.6e-19   2.212e-6
    Family   Neutrino    0     0.5       -         0    Infinite
   Mesons    Pion +    273.2     0       0   +1.6e-19   2.55e-8
             Pion 0    264.2     0       0         0    1.9e-16
             Kaon +    966.6     0      +1    1.6e-19   1.22e-8
             Kaon 0    974.0     0       1         0    1.00e-10
   Baryons   Proton   1836.12   .5       0    1.6e-19   Infinite
             Neutron  1838.65  0.5       0         0    1013
             Lambda   2182.8   0.5      -1         0    2.51e-10
             Sigma +  2327.7   0.5      -1    1.6e-19   8.1e-11
             Sigma -  2340.5   0.5      -1   -1.6e-19   1.6e-10
             Sigma 0  2332     0.5      -1         0    1e-20
             Xi -     2580     0.5      -2   -1.6e-19   1.3e-10
             Xi 0     2570     0.5      -2         0    1e-10
```

2. In Excel, open TABULAR.TXT. In the first step of the Text Import Wizard, click the Fixed Width option and click Next to continue.

3. In the second step of the Text Import Wizard, insert delimiter lines to mark where Excel should break the text into columns. Click Next to continue.

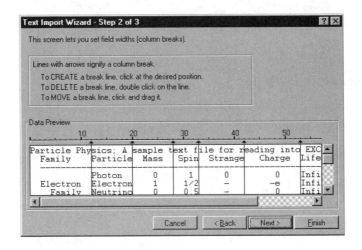

NOTE Excel makes its best guess as to where the line breaks should be. Click on the ruler to create a new delimiter line, or double-click a delimiter line to remove it. Click and drag to move a delimiter line.

4. In the third step of the Text Import Wizard, you again set the format for converting each column of data. Leave it as General format and click Finish.

5. In the worksheet, widen column A so you can see all of the text.

This is actually not too bad; the data is in columns, and only the labels are messed up a little, as shown in Figure 5.7. Two data items need to be corrected in cells D5 and F5. In cell D5, Excel interpreted the 1/2 as a Date, not a number. In cell F5, Excel was confused by the –e in that column.

6. Change the entry in cell D5 to **0.5** and change the cell format back to General.

7. Change the entry in cell F5 to **–1.6E–19**

8. Clean up the titles, delete row 3, add some outlines, and turn off the gridlines.

The worksheet now looks like Figure 5.8, with all the data laid out much like the original table, but now the individual data items are in cells, which makes them accessible to formulas elsewhere in the worksheet.

FIGURE 5.7:

Particle physics constants parsed into cells

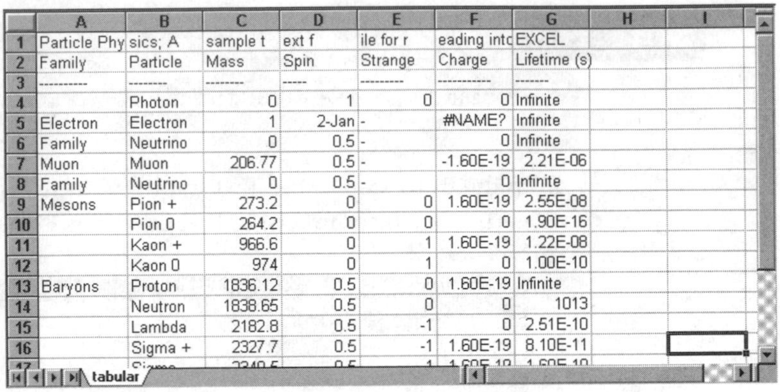

	A	B	C	D	E	F	G	H	I
1	Particle Phy	sics; A	sample t	ext f	ile for r	eading intc	EXCEL		
2	Family	Particle	Mass	Spin	Strange	Charge	Lifetime (s)		
3	---------	--------	--------	----	---------	-----------	-------		
4		Photon	0	1	0	0	Infinite		
5	Electron	Electron	1	2-Jan	-	#NAME?	Infinite		
6	Family	Neutrino	0	0.5	-	0	Infinite		
7	Muon	Muon	206.77	0.5	-	-1.60E-19	2.21E-06		
8	Family	Neutrino	0	0.5	-	0	Infinite		
9	Mesons	Pion +	273.2	0	0	1.60E-19	2.55E-08		
10		Pion 0	264.2	0	0	0	1.90E-16		
11		Kaon +	966.6	0	1	1.60E-19	1.22E-08		
12		Kaon 0	974	0	1	0	1.00E-10		
13	Baryons	Proton	1836.12	0.5	0	1.60E-19	Infinite		
14		Neutron	1838.65	0.5	0	0	1013		
15		Lambda	2182.8	0.5	-1	0	2.51E-10		
16		Sigma +	2327.7	0.5	-1	1.60E-19	8.10E-11		

tabular

FIGURE 5.8:

The cleaned up particle physics sheet

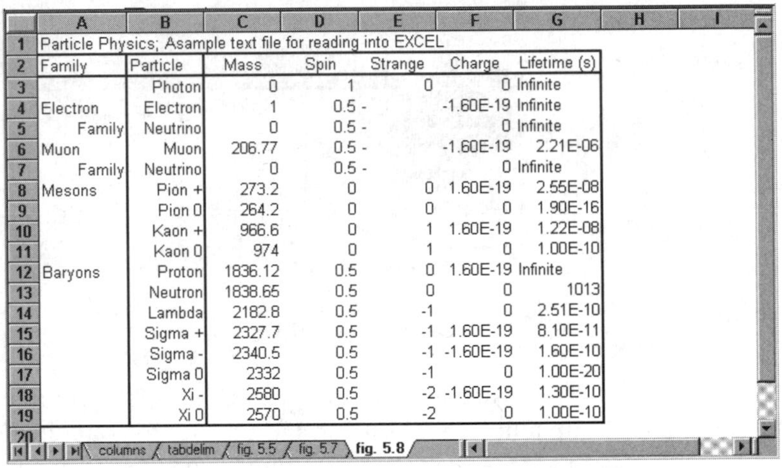

	A	B	C	D	E	F	G	H	I
1	Particle Physics; Asample text file for reading into EXCEL								
2	Family	Particle	Mass	Spin	Strange	Charge	Lifetime (s)		
3		Photon	0	1	0	0	Infinite		
4	Electron	Electron	1	0.5 -		-1.60E-19	Infinite		
5	Family	Neutrino	0	0.5 -		0	Infinite		
6	Muon	Muon	206.77	0.5 -		-1.60E-19	2.21E-06		
7	Family	Neutrino	0	0.5 -		0	Infinite		
8	Mesons	Pion +	273.2	0	0	1.60E-19	2.55E-08		
9		Pion 0	264.2	0	0	0	1.90E-16		
10		Kaon +	966.6	0	1	1.60E-19	1.22E-08		
11		Kaon 0	974	0	1	0	1.00E-10		
12	Baryons	Proton	1836.12	0.5	0	1.60E-19	Infinite		
13		Neutron	1838.65	0.5	0	0	1013		
14		Lambda	2182.8	0.5	-1	0	2.51E-10		
15		Sigma +	2327.7	0.5	-1	1.60E-19	8.10E-11		
16		Sigma -	2340.5	0.5	-1	-1.60E-19	1.60E-10		
17		Sigma 0	2332	0.5	-1	0	1.00E-20		
18		Xi -	2580	0.5	-2	-1.60E-19	1.30E-10		
19		Xi 0	2570	0.5	-2	0	1.00E-10		
20									

columns / tabdelim / fig. 5.5 / fig. 5.7 \ **fig. 5.8** /

Importing Data with Visual Basic for Applications

Visual Basic for Applications is fully capable of opening and reading text or binary files. Using Visual Basic, you can create a special program to read a data file and parse it into columns. For example, the following short procedure reads the particle physics example and stores it into columns. Note that this procedure is specific to the Particle Physics example, and would have to be changed somewhat to import a different file.

```
Option Explicit
'
'   Import the Particle Physics data
'
Sub ImportPhys()
Dim strALine As String
Dim intCtr As Integer
Open "tabular.txt" For Input As #1
Line Input #1, strALine
Sheets("PartPhys").Range("A1").Value = strALine
' Get the titles
Line Input #1, strALine
Sheets("PartPhys").Range("A2").Value = Mid$(strALine, 1, 12)
Sheets("PartPhys").Range("B2").Value = Mid$(strALine, 13, 8)
Sheets("PartPhys").Range("C2").Value = Mid$(strALine, 21, 8)
Sheets("PartPhys").Range("D2").Value = Mid$(strALine, 29, 5)
Sheets("PartPhys").Range("E2").Value = Mid$(strALine, 34, 9)
Sheets("PartPhys").Range("F2").Value = Mid$(strALine, 43, 11)
Sheets("PartPhys").Range("G2").Value = Mid$(strALine, 54, 99)
'Take everything that is left.
Line Input #1, strALine 'Skip the dashed line
'Import the body of the table.
For intCtr = 1 To 17
    Line Input #1, strALine
    Sheets("PartPhys").Cells(intCtr + 2, 1).Value
        ➡ = Mid$(strALine, 1, 12)
    Sheets("PartPhys").Cells(intCtr + 2, 2).Value
        ➡ = Mid$(strALine, 13, 8)
    Sheets("PartPhys").Cells(intCtr + 2, 3).Value
        ➡ = Mid$(strALine, 21, 8)
    Sheets("PartPhys").Cells(intCtr + 2, 4).Value
        ➡ = Mid$(strALine, 29, 5)
    Sheets("PartPhys").Cells(intCtr + 2, 5).Value
        ➡ = Mid$(strALine, 34, 9)
    Sheets("PartPhys").Cells(intCtr + 2, 6).Value
        ➡ = Mid$(strALine, 43, 11)
    'Take everything that is left.
    Sheets("PartPhys").Cells(intCtr + 2, 7).Value
        ➡ = Mid$(strALine, 54, 99)
Next intCtr
Close #1
Sheets("PartPhys").Activate
'The following was created with the recorder and then edited.
Columns("G:G").ColumnWidth = 9.57
Range("B3:B19").Select
```

```
Selection.HorizontalAlignment = xlRight
Range("A5").Select
Selection.HorizontalAlignment = xlRight
Range("A7").Select
Selection.HorizontalAlignment = xlRight
Range("C2:G2").Select
Selection.HorizontalAlignment = xlCenter
Range("F4").Select
ActiveCell.FormulaR1C1 = "-1.60E-19"
Range("D4").Select
ActiveCell.FormulaR1C1 = "0.5"
Range("A2:A19").Select
Selection.BorderAround Weight:=xlMedium, ColorIndex:=xlAutomatic
Range("B2:B19").Select
Selection.BorderAround Weight:=xlMedium, ColorIndex:=xlAutomatic
Range("C2:G19").Select
Selection.BorderAround Weight:=xlMedium, ColorIndex:=xlAutomatic
Range("A2:G2").Select
Selection.BorderAround Weight:=xlMedium, ColorIndex:=xlAutomatic
End Sub
```

The procedure uses the Line Input statement to read a line from the file into the string variable, strALine. The string is then parsed into pieces using the Mid$( ) function. The formatting of the procedure is done by turning on the recorder, formatting the sheet, and then editing out the unneeded lines.

> **NOTE**
>
> The Mid$( ) function extracts substrings from a string. The three arguments are: the string, the character position in the string to start extracting characters, and the number of characters to extract.

Importing Data from an External Database

If your data resides in an external database, Excel can access it using the Query application included with Excel. Query is a simple database front end that couples to the Microsoft Jet database engine. The Jet engine is the same as is used by Visual

Basic and Access. In addition to the dBase files (.DBF) that Excel can open directly, the Jet engine can access the following databases:

dBase   Access   FoxPro   Paradox

In addition, the Jet engine can communicate with external SQL Servers such as the Microsoft SQL server, Oracle, and Sybase. The engine sends SQL (Structured Query Language) strings to the remote database engine, and that program returns the requested information to Query.

Constructing a database and queries is another subject that can easily take a whole book. The *Microsoft Query User's Guide* that comes with Excel 5 explains how Query works, as does the online help, but you need a good database book to use it efficiently. Luckily, you don't have to write SQL statements yourself. The graphical interface in Query allows you to draw the query and the program writes the SQL statement using your selections.

To use Query, it first must be installed on your machine. It is not included in the standard installation, but must be selected separately in the custom installation. In the Microsoft Setup program for Excel or Office, select the Custom Installation option and select the Data Access Objects. The data access objects include Query and the ODBC drivers needed to access different database formats. When installation is complete, start the ODBC control panel and register your data sources. The online help will lead you through this setup.

Query can be run as a stand alone application, or attached to Excel as an add-in. Install Query in Excel by choosing the Tools ➤ Add-Ins command, and checking the Query checkbox. When Query is installed, the Get External Data command appears on the Data menu.

Once installed, you can start Query, open an external database, construct a query using the graphical interface, and execute the query. The database engine or the external database executes the query and returns the selected data. When you have the table you want, return to Excel and the data is inserted in the active worksheet.

Query the NWind Database   Open the NWind database included with Query and create a list of the products purchased by each customer.

1. Choose the Tools ➤ Add-Ins command, check the MS Query Add-In check-box and choose OK.

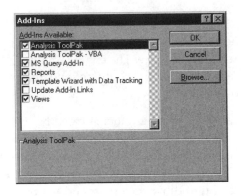

2. Switch to a blank worksheet, name it **fig. 5.10**

3. Choose the Data ➤ Get External Data command to open Query.

4. In the Select Data Source dialog box that appears, select the NWind dBase database. If the database is not listed, click the Other button and find it. It should have been installed as an example database with the Query add-in. Use the online help for assistance in registering the data source. Click Use to continue.

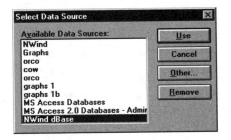

5. In the Add Tables dialog box that appears, select the **customer.dbf** table and click Add. Do the same for the **orders.dbf**, **orddtail.dbf**, and **product.dbf** tables. Click Close to continue.

The Query database should now look like Figure 5.9. Each of the tables is listed in a small window along with all of the table's field names. The lines that connect a

FIGURE 5.9:

The Query window with tables from the NWind database

field in one table with another field in a different table are known as joins. Below the tables is a subwindow where the fields to return are inserted.

> **NOTE**
>
> Joins are how relational databases connect the tables together. There are different kinds of joins, but the most common is the inner join, which specifies that the only records that are selected from the tables are those with matching values in the joined fields.

6. In the Customer table, click and drag on the COMPANY field name and drag it down to the bottom window. Do the same with the PROD_NAME field name in the product table.

7. If the autoquery button is depressed, the results of the query will already be displayed in the bottom window. If not, press the Query Now button to run the query, and the results should appear.

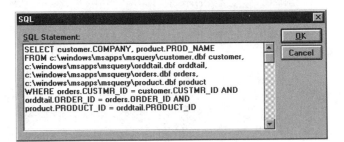

COMPANY	PROD_NAME		
Merry Grape Wine Merch	NuNuCa Nuß-Nougat-Cr		
Foodmongers, Inc.	Gorgonzola Telino		
Silver Screen Food Gem	Carnarvon Tigers		
ValuMax Food Stores	Thüringer Rostbratwurst		
Fred's Edibles, Etc.	Konbu		
Morning Star Health Foo	Queso Manchego La Pa		
Fujiwara Asian Specialtie	Tofu		

8. To see the SQL statement created by Query and executed by the database engine, press the SQL button.

> **SQL**
>
> **SQL Statement:**
>
> SELECT customer.COMPANY, product.PROD_NAME
> FROM c:\windows\msapps\msquery\customer.dbf customer,
> c:\windows\msapps\msquery\orddtail.dbf orddtail,
> c:\windows\msapps\msquery\orders.dbf orders,
> c:\windows\msapps\msquery\product.dbf product
> WHERE orders.CUSTMR_ID = customer.CUSTMR_ID AND
> orddtail.ORDER_ID = orders.ORDER_ID AND
> product.PRODUCT_ID = orddtail.PRODUCT_ID
>
> OK   Cancel

An SQL statement consists of a series of clauses, with each clause starting with a keyword. In the statement shown, the first clause is a SELECT clause, which specifies the fields to return. Next is a FROM clause that specifies the tables needed and then a WHERE clause that specifies the criteria for selecting a record.

NOTE When specifying the connectivity between two tables, you can use either a join in the FROM clause or criteria in the WHERE clause. The result is the same for inner joins.

9. Return the selected data to the worksheet by choosing the File ➤ Return Data To Microsoft Excel command. In the Get External Data dialog that appears, check Keep Query Definition and Include Field Names, and click OK.

Your worksheet should now look like Figure 5.10, with the same fields as were listed in Query. Since you saved the query definition, you can re-execute the query again, or modify it without having to completely redo it. Just click in the returned table and execute Data ➤ Get External Data again.

	A	B	C	D	E	F
1	COMPANY	PROD_NAME				
2	Merry Grape Wine Merchants	NuNuCa Nuß-Nougat-Creme				
3	Foodmongers, Inc.	Gorgonzola Telino				
4	Silver Screen Food Gems	Carnarvon Tigers				
5	ValuMax Food Stores	Thüringer Rostbratwurst				
6	Fred's Edibles, Etc.	Konbu				
7	Morning Star Health Foods	Queso Manchego La Pastora				
8	Fujiwara Asian Specialties	Tofu				
9	Seven Seas Imports	Tunnbröd				
10	Wellington Trading	Carnarvon Tigers				
11	Live Oak Hotel Gift Shop	Teatime Chocolate Biscuits				
12	Piccadilly Foods	Queso Cabrales				
13						
14						
15						
16						

fig. 5.7 / fig. 5.8 / GetFile / PartPhys \ fig. 5.10

Storing and Accessing Data in Excel

In Excel, any range of cells can be used as a database. Each column in the range is a field, and each field can contain up to 255 characters of text, a value, or a formula. Each row of the range is a record in the database. Records contain related data. For example, the parameters measured in a single experimental measurement would be stored in a single record. Each field contains the data for a different parameter, such as the pressure or voltage measured in each experiment.

The format of a database is similar to that of a data table. The difference is that Excel has special commands and methods for accessing data in a database.

Creating the Database Range

The first record in the database range contains the field names. These are like the column headings in the data table. Field names should be simple. They cannot consist of more than one row, nor be separated from the rest of the records of the database by any blank records or rows. The database records are listed below the field names.

NOTE   Field names should normally be single words or run-together words, to make using them easier. Multiple-word field names must be enclosed in quote marks to be used in formulas or Visual Basic for Applications code.

Using the Database Commands

Five commands on the Data menu are used to search and manipulate records on the database:

- The Filter ➤ AutoFilter command selects records that match a value in a column of the database.

- The Filter ➤ Show All command redisplays the whole database after it has been filtered by the Filter ➤ AutoFilter command.

- The Filter ➤ Advanced Filter command allows you to create complicated criteria on the worksheet and then use that criteria to select records from the database.

- The Form command displays a form for searching and manipulating data in the database.

- The Sort command sorts the rows in a database according to a key.

Using a Data Form

The simplest way to access an Excel database is with the Data ➤ Form command. Using the field names in the first row of the database range, Excel constructs a data form containing those fields. The data form includes command buttons to add records, delete records, create a criteria, and search for records matching that criteria. To use the form, click anywhere in the database range, and choose the Data ➤ Form command. The Data Form dialog box shown below appears. The fields displayed in the dialog box depend on the particular database you are using.

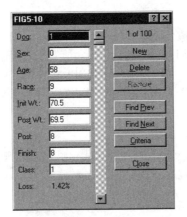

Using Data ➤ Filter ➤ AutoFilter

The Data ➤ Filter ➤ AutoFilter command inserts a dropdown list at the top of each column (field) which contains all the values found in that column. Selecting one of those values limits the visible records in the database to only those with that value in the selected column. The down-pointing arrow on the drop down list changes color for any column that is filtering the data, as do the row numbers of the selected rows. Selecting another value further limits the visible part of the database. Choosing Custom allows you to select ranges of values, and selecting All removes any filtering on that column. To turn off AutoFilter, choose Data ➤ Filter ➤ AutoFilter again.

Using Data ➤ Filter ➤ Show All

The Data ➤ Filter ➤ Show All command redisplays all of the database after it has been filtered by the AutoFilter command. The command is enabled whenever one of the other two Filter commands has reduced the visible records in the database. Use it to start over after limiting the visible database with a filter criteria.

Using Data ➤ Filter ➤ Advanced Filter

The Data ➤ Filter ➤ Advanced Filter command allows you to create more complicated filter criteria than can be created with the Data ➤ Filter ➤ AutoFilter command. The criteria is created on the worksheet in a Criteria range. You may also have a Copy To range for extracting copies of records from the database. When you use the command, a dialog box appears for you to indicate the Database (or List), Criteria and Copy To ranges.

The options are to filter the list in place, like the Data ➤ Filter ➤ AutoFilter command, or to copy the selected records to another region. If you use an extract region (the Copy To range), you can also limit the fields copied to the extract region.

Defining the Criteria Range

To use the Data ➤ Filter ➤ Advanced Filter command, you need a criteria range. The criteria range consists of a copy of the first record of the database containing the field names, plus one or more lines for inserting search criteria. Search criteria are labels or values to search for, or logical expressions for searching for ranges of values. You can put search criteria under any of the field names to further restrict the search. Criteria placed in the same row are assumed to be connected with a logical AND. Criteria placed in alternate rows are assumed to be connected with a logical OR.

Two wildcard characters are available for searching label fields: ? and *. The question mark stands for any single character. For example, C?T will match *CAT*, *COT* and *CUT*. The asterisk matches any number of characters. For example, C* matches *common*, *creation*, or *continue*.

Defining the Output Range

If you intend to extract records from the database instead of simply restricting the visible rows in place, you need an output range. An output range consists of a copy of the first record of the database containing the field names. The output range does not need to contain all the field names, only those you want to extract.

The output range can consist of one or many rows. If the output range consists of only the one row containing the field names, Excel clears all the cells below the field names before the database commands start writing records there. If there is any information in the cells below the field names, it will be lost. If you define a multiple-row output range, the database commands will write records to it until it is filled and then generate an error. Using multiple-row output ranges is a way to protect valuable data below the output range, though it is usually better to place the range in an area with nothing below it.

Sorting a List

The Data ➤ Sort command is used to sort a list according to the values in one or more columns of the list. To sort a list, select the whole range to be sorted and choose the Data ➤ Sort command. If you are sorting a database, don't select the first row containing the field names. The Sort dialog box has space for three sort keys. Select the columns you want sorted and the order in which you want them sorted. If you are sorting a database, the fields are listed by field name, otherwise they are listed by a reference to cells in the column.

NOTE When a list is actually sorted, the whole list is first sorted with the third key, then the second key, and finally the first key. The result is that all records with the same first key are together and sorted according to the second key. This places all records with the same first and second key together, sorted by the third key.

Using Database Functions

The database statistical functions (listed in Table 1.10) perform statistical calculations on the records that match the criteria. They are identical to the normal statistical functions, except that they are applied only to those records in the database range that match the criteria, rather than the whole range. Thus, for example, you can calculate averages or variances of data for only those records that have some particular characteristics.

Each of the database functions has three arguments: *database*, *criteria*, and *field*. The *database* argument is a reference to the database range. The *criteria* argument is a reference to a criteria range, and the *field* argument is the field in the database to apply the statistical function to. The *field* can be either the text of the field name from the first row of the database, or the number of the column in the database (where the first column is 1, the second is 2, and so on).

Pre-race Dehydration in Racing Greyhounds

Julie, who was proofreading some of this text, wanted to know where the biological examples were. I had lots of hard science and engineering examples, but no biology. Being a veterinarian, she is more interested in dogs and cats than in wires and computers. Not wanting to leave out any relevant science (and to keep peace in the house), I asked her to find a good problem for demonstrating database management. So she called a friend of hers, Linda Blythe, DVM, Ph.D., at the college of Veterinary Medicine at Oregon State University in Corvallis, Oregon. A week later, a box arrived containing data from 2,552 racing forms. Racing forms ??? Hmmm… bio-science is starting to look more interesting.

Dr. Blythe and her co-worker, Dr. Donald Hansen, were examining the pre-race weight loss in racing greyhounds. All the dogs are brought to the track before the racing begins and put in an air-conditioned room known as the "ginny pit." There they wait until the start of their respective races. During their interval in the ginny pit, some dogs lose up to several percent of their weight in body fluid. This is all due to drooling and panting (the dogs are trained not to urinate or defecate in their cages).

NOTE A few years after Dr. Blythe sent me the racing greyhound data, she was presented an award by Prince Edward of Great Britain for the "greatest international contribution to dog racing." This award is the first ever of this type and was made by the World Greyhound Racing Federation for her work in greyhound physiology, nutrition, diseases, reproduction, injuries, genetics, and, presumably, pre-race weight loss. (*JAVMA*, Vol. 197, No. 12, Dec. 15, 1990, p. 1563)

The dogs are weighed when they are brought into the room, and again just before their race, to ensure that the weight loss has not been excessive. If they have lost more than three pounds, they must be examined by a veterinarian before they can race. Loss of an excessive amount of fluids can cause acid/base disturbances that can leave a greyhound with a decreased capacity to handle the hydrogen ions produced during the physical activity of a race.

This weight loss is perceived to be a serious problem for some racing greyhounds, so Drs. Blythe and Hansen studied the effect of weight loss on racing performance. As data, they used the racing forms filled out for each dog at each race. The data on these forms includes the dog's age, sex, weight before and after being in the ginny pit, race number, race class, post position, and finish position.

Dr. Blythe sent me the data on 489 dogs in 2552 races, which was far more than I needed for this example. Table 5.2 contains the data for 15 dogs in 100 races. If you don't want to type in all those records, you can still try the database commands by typing only 10 or 20 records. As you would expect, the results will be different. Better yet, use the data from one of your own projects to experiment with the database commands.

Creating a Database

First, you need a database to work with. Set up and format a database, and fill it with the racing-dog data.

1. Start with a blank worksheet, name it **fig. 5.11**, and change the column widths as follows:

Cell	Contents	Cell	Contents	Cell	Contents
A	5	D	6	G	6
B	5	E	9	H	6
C	5	F	9	I	7
				J	6

2. In cell A1, enter **Pre-race weight loss in racing dogs**

   Create the criteria range, including the range names for the database. While the criteria range can be anywhere on the worksheet, it is simplest to put it directly above the database range.

3. In cell A3, enter **Criteria Range**

4. Make the following entries in cells A4:J4:

Cell	Contents	Cell	Contents	Cell	Contents
A4	**Dog**	B4	**Sex**	C4	**Age**
D4	**Race**	E4	**Init Wt.**	F4	**Post Wt.**
G4	**Post**	H4	**Finish**	I4	**Class**
J4	**Loss**				

Create the database range. First are the field names, then the actual data.

5. In cell A14, enter **Database Range**

6. Select cells A4:J4. Place the pointer on the border of the selected area, hold down Ctrl (Cmd on the Macintosh), and drag a copy of the field names to cell A15:J15 (in earlier versions of Excel, use the Copy and Paste commands.)

7. Calculate the percent weight loss in column J. In cell J16, enter **=(E16–F16)/E16**, copy it into cells J17:J115, and format them as Percent, with two decimal places.

8. In cells A16:I115, enter the data in Table 5.2.

9. Turn off the gridlines.

10. Save the workbook.

Your worksheet should look like Figure 5.11.

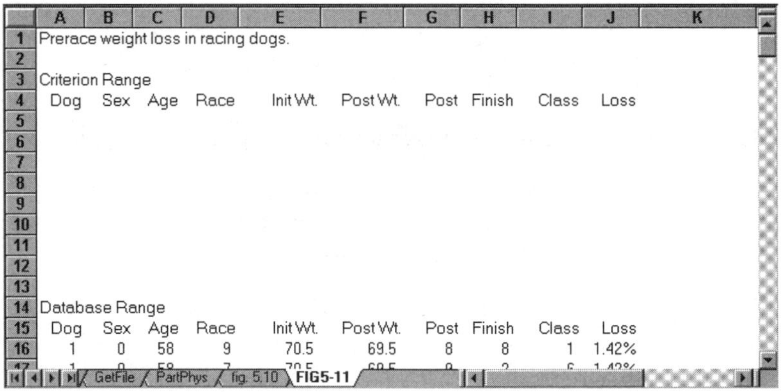

FIGURE 5.11:

Pre-race dehydration in racing dogs: initial database setup

TABLE 5.2: Pre-race Dehydration in Racing Dogs: Weight Loss/Performance Data

Dog	Sex*	Age (mon.)	Race No.	Initial Weight (lb.)	Post Weight (lb.)	Post Position	Finish Position	Race Class**	Weight Loss
1	0	58	9	70.5	69.5	8	8	1	1.42%
1	0	58	7	70.5	69.5	9	2	6	1.42%
1	0	58	6	71	70	5	4	6	1.41%
1	0	58	2	72	71.5	1	1	2	0.69%
1	0	58	6	72	71	7	2	2	1.39%
1	0	58	8	72.5	72	5	1	3	0.69%
2	0	29	12	68	67.5	2	5	1	0.74%
2	0	29	9	67	67	2	6	1	0.00%
2	0	29	9	67.5	66.5	6	1	1	1.48%
2	0	29	6	68.5	68	2	6	1	0.73%
2	0	29	6	69	68.5	7	5	1	0.72%
2	0	29	2	69	68.5	4	1	2	0.72%
2	0	29	6	68.5	68	5	5	2	0.73%
3	1	40	12	64	62.5	3	6	1	2.34%
3	1	40	2	64	63	4	9	1	1.56%
3	1	40	6	64	63.5	1	3	1	0.78%
3	1	40	4	64.5	63.5	5	6	1	1.55%
3	1	40	12	65	63	2	2	1	3.08%
3	1	40	2	65	64	5	9	1	1.54%
3	1	40	2	64.5	64	2	1	2	0.78%
4	0	23	12	76	75.5	4	8	1	0.66%
4	0	23	2	76.5	76	9	3	1	0.65%
4	0	23	6	76.5	75.5	8	1	1	1.31%
4	0	23	6	76.5	75.5	9	5	7	1.31%
4	0	23	9	77	76	8	4	1	1.30%
4	0	23	6	77	76	8	2	1	1.30%
4	0	23	9	77	76	1	6	1	1.30%
5	0	24	12	71.5	70.5	5	3	1	1.40%
5	0	24	2	71.5	71	5	2	1	0.70%
5	0	24	9	71	70.5	3	1	7	0.70%
5	0	24	6	71.5	71	6	2	7	0.70%
5	0	24	9	71	70	7	2	1	1.41%

TABLE 5.2: Pre-race Dehydration in Racing Dogs: Weight Loss/Performance Data (cont.)

Dog	Sex*	Age (mon.)	Race No.	Initial Weight (lb.)	Post Weight (lb.)	Post Position	Finish Position	Race Class**	Weight Loss
5	0	24	9	72	71.5	4	4	1	0.69%
5	0	24	9	71.5	71	8	1	1	0.70%
6	1	47	12	59	58	6	7	1	1.69%
6	1	47	6	58	57.5	2	3	1	0.86%
6	1	47	9	58.5	58	1	4	7	0.85%
6	1	47	6	59	58.5	4	4	7	0.85%
6	1	47	9	58.5	58	1	3	1	0.85%
6	1	47	9	58.5	57.5	6	2	1	1.71%
6	1	47	9	58	57	4	1	1	1.72%
7	0	34	12	72	71.5	7	2	1	0.69%
7	0	34	6	71.5	71	5	9	1	0.70%
7	0	34	9	71.5	71.5	2	3	7	0.00%
7	0	34	6	72	71.5	2	1	7	0.69%
7	0	34	9	72.5	71.5	3	1	1	1.38%
7	0	34	9	71.5	71	8	3	1	0.70%
7	0	34	9	71.5	71	2	5	1	0.70%
8	0	23	12	71.5	71	8	4	1	0.70%
8	0	23	9	72	71.5	8	2	1	0.69%
8	0	23	9	71.5	71	1	9	1	0.70%
8	0	23	11	72	71.5	1	1	2	0.69%
8	0	23	8	72	71.5	8	6	2	0.69%
8	0	23	2	72.5	72	2	4	2	0.69%
8	0	23	2	72	72	9	3	2	0.00%
8	0	23	9	72	71.5	4	6	1	0.69%
9	0	36	12	63.5	62.5	9	1	1	1.57%
9	0	36	2	63.5	63	3	1	1	0.79%
9	0	36	2	63.5	63.5	1	1	2	0.00%
9	0	36	12	64	62.5	9	2	1	2.34%
9	0	36	12	63	62.5	1	4	1	0.79%
9	0	36	9	63.5	63	5	7	1	0.79%
9	0	36	12	64	63	8	3	1	1.56%
9	0	36	9	63	63	1	9	1	0.00%

TABLE 5.2: Pre-race Dehydration in Racing Dogs: Weight Loss/Performance Data (cont.)

Dog	Sex*	Age (mon.)	Race No.	Initial Weight (lb.)	Post Weight (lb.)	Post Position	Finish Position	Race Class**	Weight Loss
10	0	26	11	66	65	1	6	3	1.52%
10	0	26	8	66	65.5	6	9	3	0.76%
10	0	26	5	66	65.5	7	9	3	0.76%
10	0	26	8	66.5	65	6	2	3	2.26%
10	0	26	6	66.5	65.5	3	6	7	1.50%
10	0	26	9	66	64	9	8	7	3.03%
10	0	26	12	67	66	6	3	2	1.49%
11	1	21	11	53.5	52.5	2	1	3	1.87%
11	1	21	5	53	52	1	6	3	1.89%
11	1	21	1	53.5	53	1	4	3	0.93%
11	1	21	1	53.5	53	5	2	3	0.93%
11	1	21	8	53.5	52.5	2	4	3	1.87%
11	1	21	10	53.5	53	2	3	3	0.93%
11	1	21	11	54	53.5	3	9	3	0.93%
11	1	21	5	54	54	2	1	4	0.00%
12	0	28	11	69	68.5	3	4	3	0.72%
12	0	28	8	68	67.5	9	2	3	0.74%
12	0	28	5	69	68.5	5	7	3	0.72%
12	0	28	8	70	69	7	9	3	1.43%
12	0	28	2	68.5	68	2	8	2	0.73%
12	0	28	6	68.5	68	3	8	2	0.73%
12	0	28	12	68	67.5	4	9	2	0.74%
13	1	51	11	62	61.5	4	2	3	0.81%
13	1	51	8	62.5	62	3	6	3	0.80%
13	1	51	7	62	61.5	8	7	6	0.81%
13	1	51	6	62.5	62	4	6	6	0.80%
13	1	51	11	62.5	62	1	4	2	0.80%
13	1	51	12	62.5	62	7	2	2	0.80%
14	1	33	11	52.5	51	5	8	3	2.86%
14	1	33	5	52.5	52	5	9	3	0.95%
14	1	33	8	52	51	7	7	3	1.92%
14	1	33	12	52	51.5	2	2	3	0.96%

TABLE 5.2:   Pre-race Dehydration in Racing Dogs: Weight Loss/Performance Data (cont.)

Dog	Sex*	Age (mon.)	Race No.	Initial Weight (lb.)	Post Weight (lb.)	Post Position	Finish Position	Race Class**	Weight Loss
14	1	33	12	52	51	4	9	3	1.92%
14	1	33	12	52	51	5	5	2	1.92%
15	0	25	11	64	63	6	5	3	1.56%
15	0	25	5	64	62.5	2	2	3	2.34%

*Sex: 0 = male, 1 = female
**Race class: 1 (fast) through 5 (slow), 6 and 7 are unclassified.
This data is courtesy of Dr. L. Blythe, Oregon State University.

Examining the Data ➤ Filter Command

Now that you have a database to work with, you can use it to locate some data of interest. Suppose you are interested in finding the records for all winning female dogs. Use the database commands to filter the records to show only those that contain winning female dogs. The sex of the dogs is coded as 0 for male and 1 for female.

1. Click anywhere in the database (say, A16).

2. Choose the Data ➤ Filter ➤ AutoFilter command (a checkmark will appear next to the command on the menu to show that it is turned on). Dropdown list buttons appear over each column.

3. Click the down-arrow button over the Finish column and select **1** from the list, to restrict the records to only those that describe winners.

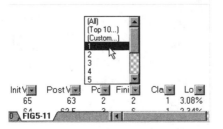

4. Click the down-arrow button over the Sex column and select **1**, to further restrict the resulting data to only females.

5. Scroll the screen up and note that the table is reduced to the four records that match the criteria you just set.

	A	B	C	D	E	F
14	Database Range					
15	D⟨▾	S▾	A⟨▾	Ra⟨▾	Init V▾	Post V▾
35	3	1	40	2	64.5	64
50	6	1	47	9	58	57
88	11	1	21	11	53.5	52.5
94	11	1	21	5	54	54

To extract these records to a separate table so you can work with them, simply select the records, choose Edit ➤ Copy, select a new location and choose Edit ➤ Paste.

Examining the Data ➤ Filter ➤ Advanced Filter Command

You can do the same type of search using the Data ➤ Filter ➤ Advanced filter command, and have the records automatically copied to the extract range. First set the criteria in the Criteria range, then let the Filter command do the rest.

1. Choose the Data ➤ Filter ➤ AutoFilter command to uncheck it, turn off the AutoFilter, and redisplay all the data.

2. In cell H5, type **1** to select only first place dogs, and in cell B5, type **1** to select only females.

3. Click somewhere in the database, and choose the Data ➤ Filter ➤ Advanced Filter command.

4. In the Advanced Filter dialog box, the List Range is filled in automatically; click in the Criteria Range, then select cells A4:J5.

5. Make sure the Filter the List In-Place option is selected, and click OK.

Again, the range of records is reduced to the four that fit the criteria.

Extracting Records to an Output Range

To extract the records into a table rather than just view them, create an output range and use the Data ➤ Filter ➤ Advanced Filter command again. Place the output range out of the way so the extraction won't overwrite any important cells. Assume you want a table of only age and weight loss for the winning female dogs.

1. Choose Data ➤ Filter ➤ Show All to redisplay the data.

2. In cell L3, type **Output Range**

3. In cell L4, type **Age**, and in cell M4, type **Loss**

4. Click in the database and choose Data ➤ Filter ➤ Advanced Filter to display the Advanced Filter dialog box. The List and Criteria ranges should still be set, but if not, set them again to **A15:I115** and **A4:J5**

5. Select the Copy to Another Location option, then click in the Copy To range, and select cells **L4:M4**.

6. Click OK, and the same set of records is copied to the output range, but including only the fields indicated in the output range.

	L	M	N
3	Output Range		
4	Age	Loss	
5	40	0.78%	
6	47	1.72%	
7	21	1.87%	
8	21	0.00%	
9			

Examining the Data ➤ Form Command

Another way to search and maintain the database is with the Data ➤ Form command.

1. Click somewhere in the database range and choose the Data ➤ Form command.

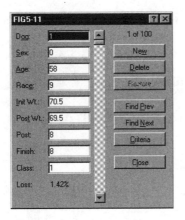

You should see the data form shown below. Each independent field in the database is represented by a text box on the form. Calculated fields are displayed with labels. The scroll bar down the center allows you to select any record in the database to be displayed. Changing any value on the form changes the corresponding value in the database, except for the last field, which is a calculated value. The New and Delete buttons allow you to add or delete records from the database without redefining the database range after making changes. When changing a record, the changes do not actually occur until you move to another record. The Restore button restores a record to the values it had before you made changes, as long as you have not moved to another record; however, Restore cannot recover a deleted record.

To set the search criteria, click the Criteria button and type the criteria on the form. The criteria used here is unrelated to any criteria ranges you might have defined on the worksheet. To set the same criteria as was set in the last example, enter a 1 in the Sex box and a 1 in the Finish box. Click the Form button to return to the form. Click the Find Next button to find the first occurrence of a matching record. The matching record is displayed in the form. The Find Next and Find Prev buttons move from one matching record to the next. If you try to go past the last matching record, or backup past the first, Excel beeps at you and remains at the current record.

2. When you are finished with the data form, click the Close button.

Suppose you want to know the fractions of male and female dogs in the races. You could search for each record and manually count them, but the database functions provide a better way. You could use the DCOUNT function to count the number of males and count the number of females, and then divide the numbers; however, since the males are marked with a 0, and the females with a 1, all you need to do is to average the Sex column of the database.

Examining the Database Functions

1. Clear the values from the criteria range in cells A5:J5.

2. In cell E10, enter the formula

   =DAVERAGE(A15:J115,2,A4:J5)

3. Format cell E10 as Percent, with two decimal places.

As soon as the worksheet recalculates, you see the number 34.00% (35.00% if you used only the first 20 records). This indicates that 34 percent of the dogs are female. Note that an empty criteria range matches the whole database.

Now see how the female dogs are doing at the finish line. Find the percentage of the dogs in the first three places that are female.

4. In cell H5, enter =H16<4

Cell E10 now contains 30.43% (33.33% for 20 records). You have limited the records being averaged to those with dogs in the first three places. You see that the percentage of winning females has decreased slightly. The reference to cell H16 establishes which field in the database to apply the criteria to, and it must be a cell in the second row of the database range.

Since this study is about weight loss, look at those dogs that win and that have a high weight loss (greater than 2.5 percent of their body weight).

5. Enter =J16>0.025 in cell J5.

Interestingly, the percentage in cell E10 changes to 100 (this value is the same for 20 records). This figure indicates that all the dogs in the first three places that have high fluid loss are females.

You could continue changing the restrictions in the criterion range and seeing what the results are. You could also count cells that match the criterion with the DCOUNT function, find the minima or maxima with DMIN and DMAX, calculate the standard deviation and variance with DSTDEV and DVAR, or add the values with the DSUM command. Additionally, you can create tables of values using these functions. Remember, the criteria range does not need to be the one you defined with the Set Criteria command, and it does not need to contain all the field names (it only need contain those that you want to search).

Examining the Data ➤ Sort Command

The Sort command on the Data menu will sort any set of data and text records. Excel can sort data in ascending or descending order, according to a primary key, a secondary key and a tertiary key. You can sort many columns of data according to the values in a single column.

As an example, sort the racing dogs database range according to finishing position and weight loss.

1. Select a cell in the database range.

2. Choose the Data ➤ Sort command.

3. Select Finish in the Sort By box, then select the Ascending option.

4. Select Loss in the first Then By box and select the Descending option.

5. Click OK.

Your worksheet database should now look like Figure 5.12. All the records are sorted according to the winning position and the weight loss.

FIGURE 5.12:

Database records sorted by Finish and Loss

	A	B	C	D	E	F	G	H	I	J	K
14	Database Range										
15	Dog	Sex	Age	Race	Init Wt.	Post Wt.	Post	Finish	Class	Loss	
16	11	1	21	11	53.5	52.5	2	1	3	1.87%	
17	6	1	47	9	58	57	4	1	1	1.72%	
18	9	0	36	12	63.5	62.5	9	1	1	1.57%	
19	2	0	29	9	67.5	66.5	6	1	1	1.48%	
20	7	0	34	9	72.5	71.5	3	1	1	1.38%	
21	4	0	23	6	76.5	75.5	8	1	1	1.31%	
22	9	0	36	2	63.5	63	3	1	1	0.79%	
23	3	1	40	2	64.5	64	2	1	2	0.78%	
24	2	0	29	2	69	68.5	4	1	2	0.72%	
25	5	0	24	9	71	70.5	3	1	7	0.70%	
26	5	0	24	9	71.5	71	8	1	1	0.70%	
27	8	0	23	11	72	71.5	1	1	2	0.69%	
28	7	0	34	6	72	71.5	4	1	7	0.69%	
29	1	0	58	2	72	71.5	1	1	2	0.69%	
30	1	0	58	2	72.5	72	5	1	3	0.69%	

GetFile / PartPhys / fig. 5.10 \ FIG5-11

Summary

Experimental data is one of the most important resources of a scientist or engineer, but managing and analyzing that data can often be difficult. Excel provides methods for importing and managing that resource. In this chapter, you investigated how to enter data into the worksheet and how to store and retrieve it after it's in Excel. You also saw how to define and use a database to analyze experimental data.

For More Information

Spark Gaps

CRC, *Handbook of Chemistry and Physics*, 51st ed. (Cleveland, Ohio: Chemical Rubber Co., 1971), p. E61.

Elementary Particles

D. Haliday and R. Resnick, *Physics* (New York: Wiley, 1967), pp. 551-552.

Prerace Dehydration in Racing Greyhounds

L.L. Blythe and D. E. Hansen, "Factors Affecting Prerace Dehydration and Performance of Racing Greyhounds," *J. Am. Vet. Med. Assoc. 189*, 12 (Dec. 15, 1986): 1572-1574.

L. L. Blythe, J. R. Gannon and A. M. Craig, "Nervous System" in *Care of the Racing Greyhound, A Guide for Trainers, Breeders and Veterinarians*, American Greyhound Council, Abilene, Kansas (Publisher), 1994, pp. 37-56.

Review Problems

1. Type the text file shown in Figure 5.3. Read it into a worksheet as text and parse it using the Data ➤ Text to Columns command.

2. Create a text file containing the following 8 rows of comma-delimited numbers:

    23.7,569.82,19.2

    1.882,27.9,26

    19.3,239,4

    95.76,9,23

    115.98,23.7,23.8

    19.220,19876.3, 2

    27.886,14.3,67.5

    23.9,14.5,14.4

    Read this file into a worksheet and parse it into separate cells using the Text Import Wizard.

3. Create a database of journal articles you are using. Store the author's name, article name, citation, and keywords in four separate fields. Create a criteria range and try extracting articles according to specific keywords and authors.

4. Using the journal article database created in problem 4, use the Data ➤ Form command to view and search the database for articles.

5. Write a Visual Basic procedure that scrolls down a database until it finds a specific string or word anywhere in a field. Each time you execute the procedure, it should scroll down to the next record containing the string. Hint: Move down one cell and test its contents for the string with InStr(). Stop when you reach the bottom of the database.

6. Use the data file from problem 3 and create a Visual Basic procedure to read this file and parse it into three columns of numbers. Do not use the Text Import Wizard this time, but write a procedure that uses OPEN to open the file, Line Input to read a line of text, InStr to locate the commas, and Mid$ to extract the characters between them.

7. Input the greyhound database (Table 5.2) and compare the average weight loss for female dogs with that for male dogs. Compare the average weight loss for dogs in the first three finish positions.

8. Using the database created in problem 7, copy the records of all female dogs into an output range. Sort the copied data first by finish position and then by weight loss.

9. Using the database created in problem 7, compare the variance in the weight loss for male and female dogs, and then for dogs in the first three finish positions.

Exercises

1. Create a database of the periodic table. Include fields for the element name, the symbol (C, O, Al, and so forth), the atomic number, the atomic weight, and the number of oxidation states. For elements with more than one oxidation state, list the states separated by commas.

2. Using the database from exercise 1, calculate the average atomic weight for elements with an atomic number less than germanium.

3. Using the database from exercise 1, select all the elements that have 4 or more oxidation states and an atomic number greater than 20. Copy the results to an output range. Use the Data ➤ Filter ➤ Advanced Filter command.

4. Using the database from exercise 1, calculate the standard deviation and variance of the oxidation states.

5. Using the Greyhound database, calculate the average finish position versus age and chart the result.

6. Using the Greyhound database, calculate the average initial weight for each finish position.

7. Using the Greyhound database, calculate the average finish position for dogs with a weight loss in the following ranges:

$$0 - 0.5\%$$
$$0.5 - 1.0\%$$
$$1.0 - 1.5\%$$
$$1.5 - 2.0\%$$
$$2.0 - 2.5\%$$
$$> 2.5\%$$

8. Use Query to open the NWind database included with Excel. Create a query to return a list of customers and their phone numbers.

9. Use Query to open the NWind database and create a query to return the sales to each customer. Use Excel to calculate the total sales to each customer. (Windows version only.)

10. Use Query to open the NWind database and create a query to return the customers and their sales region. In an Excel database, calculate the number of customers in each sales region. (Windows only.)

CHAPTER

SIX

Curve Fitting

6

Fitting an analytical equation to a set of experimental data points is a common task of scientists and engineers. For scientists, being able to fit a theoretical equation to some experimental data often vindicates (or disproves) a theory. Engineers are often required to fit instrument calibration data to an analytical equation to convert the output of the instrument to the physical parameter being measured.

There are three ways to use Excel to do curve fitting: using the built-in regression functions, transforming non-linear equations into linear equations and using the built-in functions, and using Solver or a Visual Basic program to intelligently adjust the parameters of a non-linear equation. Most data can be fit with the built-in linear and power regression functions. As long as the data is linear, or at least is linear over the range you are interested in, it can be fit with linear regression.

If your equation is non-linear, but you can linearize it by a suitable transformation of variables, you can use linear regression to fit the transformed equations. In the event that you cannot transform a nonlinear function into a linear one, you can use the Solver add-in or a Visual Basic program to intelligently adjust the coefficients of the equation until the residual error (the sum of the squares of the differences between the data and the curve) is minimized, or the correlation coefficient is maximized.

Finally, for data that cannot be fit to any reasonable curve, the curve can be represented as a table of values combined with a table lookup function that finds and interpolates the data for values not in the table.

Using the Built-In Functions

Excel has a built-in curve fitting capability known as multiple linear regression. With this capability, you can fit data to either a simple line or a complex polynomial. You can accomplish most curve-fitting tasks with Excel's linear regression capabilities.

Regression Calculations

When you fit a curve to some data points using regression, you are minimizing the residual square error between the data points and the curve (least-squares analysis). The residual square error (E) is found with the following equation.

$$E = \sum_{i=1}^{n}\left(y(x_i) - y_i\right)^2$$

where $y(x_i)$ is the curve being fit, n is the number of data points, and x_i and y_i are the data points the curve is being fit to.

Excel uses multiple linear regression, so it assumes that the curve $y(x_i)$ is of the form,

$$y\left(x_{1,i}, x_{2,i}, \ldots\right) = A + Bx_{1,i} + Cx_{2,i} + \ldots$$

where A, B and C are the coefficients of the equation that need to be adjusted to make the curve fit the data. This is done by inserting the function for $y(x_{1,i}, x_{2,i}, \ldots)$ into the equation for the residual error, and then setting the derivative of that equation with respect to each of the coefficients equal to zero. This results in one equation for each of the coefficients in terms of the other coefficients and the data points, which are then solved for the coefficients. Excel's built-in regression functions take care of all of the multiple linear regression calculations for you.

Along with the coefficients of the regression equation, Excel also calculates some statistics about the curve fit:

- Standard error of the y estimate (S_{yx})
- Correlation index (coefficient of determination) (r^2)
- Standard errors of the coefficients ($S_A, S_B, \ldots$)
- F statistic
- Number of degrees of freedom
- Sum of the squares of the regression and of the residuals

Standard Error of the y Estimate

The standard error of the y estimate is an estimate of the error in a single value of y calculated with the equation. This estimate is used, in conjunction with the Student's t test, to calculate the confidence limits of the calculated curve. The confidence limit is a band about the calculated curve that, with some level of confidence (say 95 percent), contains the true curve. The standard error of the y estimate is calculated with this equation:

$$S_{y \cdot x} = \sqrt{\frac{\sum_{i=1}^{n}\left(y_i - y(x_i)\right)^2}{p}}$$

where p is the number of degrees of freedom ($p = n - 2$ for a simple linear curve).

Correlation Index

The correlation index, or coefficient of determination, is equal to the square of the correlation coefficient (r) and is a measure of how well the curve fits the data points. It has a range of 0 to 1, with 1 indicating a perfect fit to the data points. A good curve fit has a correlation index with a value greater than 0.9. The correlation index is calculated with:

$$r^2 = 1 - \frac{\sum_{i=1}^{n}\left(y_i - y(x_i)\right)^2}{\sum_{i=1}^{n}\left(y_i - \langle y_i \rangle\right)^2}$$

where

$$\langle y_i \rangle = \frac{\sum_{i=1}^{n} y_i}{n}$$

is the average of the y data.

Standard Errors of the Coefficients

The standard errors in the coefficients are measures of the errors in each of the regression coefficients (A, B, ...) The standard error in the first coefficient (S_A) is calculated using the standard error of the y estimate:

$$S_A = \sqrt{\frac{1}{n} + \frac{\langle x \rangle^2}{\sum_{i=1}^{n}(x_i - \langle x \rangle)^2}} S_{y \cdot x}$$

where

$$x = \frac{\sum_{i=1}^{n} x_i}{n}$$

The main use of the standard errors of the coefficients is to test a coefficient to see if it is statistically zero. Since the coefficients all multiply linear x terms, if a coefficient is zero, there is no correlation between that x term and the y data. To test a coefficient, get the appropriate Student's t value for the required confidence interval $(1-\alpha)$ and degrees of freedom (p), and calculate

$$|B| > t_{\frac{\alpha}{2}, p} S_B$$

> **NOTE**
>
> The confidence interval is the probability that the true value lies within the range specified by the probability formula. For example, with the Student's t test for regression coefficients, it is common to use a 95% confidence interval (($1 - \alpha$) = 0.95), which means that you are 95% sure that the statistical test on the regression coefficient is correct.

If this equation is true, the coefficient is significant and the values of y depend on the values of x that are multiplied by the coefficient. If this equation is false, the y

values do not depend on those x values, and 0 should be used for the coefficient. The rest of the coefficients are handled in a similar manner. A good engineering statistics book will give you a lot more information about how to use these statistics. Tables of Student's t values are available in most statistics books, or can be calculated with the TINV() worksheet function. The TINV() functions returns a Student's t value given α and the number of degrees of freedom.

In general, if the absolute value of the coefficient is an order of magnitude larger than the standard error of the coefficient, you can be sure that it is significant. If you have at least four degrees of freedom (for example, six data points for a linear fit), the 95-percent confidence interval Student's t value is only about 2.1 and decreases for more degrees of freedom; therefore, a good rule of thumb is that if the absolute value of the coefficient is greater than 2.5 times the standard error of that coefficient, it is significant. If it is smaller than that, you will need to look up the correct Student's t value and insert it in the last equation to know for sure if the coefficient is significant.

NOTE

If you compare the results of the TINV( ) function with a table of cumulative Student's t values, they appear to be different. The difference, however, is due to the definition of the probability used for the tabulations. Most tables of Student's t values tabulate t versus $(1-\alpha/2)$, while TINV( ) tabulates t versus α. Keep in mind that the confidence interval is defined as $(1-\alpha)$.

F Statistic

The F statistic is used with a table of F-values to determine if the data really follows the curve, or if the apparent fit is due only to random fluctuations in the data. As with the Student's t test, to use the F statistic, you need a table of F values from a book of math tables or from the FINV( ) worksheet function. From the number of degrees of freedom and the confidence limit (say 95 percent), you get an F value from the table or function and compare it to the calculated F value. As long as the calculated F value is larger than the F value from the table, the fit is due to a real correlation, not chance.

The F table requires two degree-of-freedom values in addition to the confidence interval. The first, n_f, is equal to the number of coefficients in the regression equation minus one. The second, p, is the standard number of degrees of freedom and is equal to the number of data sets minus the number of coefficients in the equation being fit to the data. The value p is the degree-of-freedom value returned by the LINEST function and is the one used for the Student's t test.

> **NOTE** As with the TINV( ) function, the FINV( ) function returns the F value given values of α and the two degree-of-freedom values, while tables of the F statistic tabulate F versus $(1-\alpha)$.

> **WARNING** The order of the two degree-of-freedom values (n_{f1} and p) are not reversable in the function or in a table of F values. The first is the number of degrees-of-freedom of the fitting equation and the second is the number of degrees-of-freedom of the sample population of data points.

Number of Degrees of Freedom

The number of degrees of freedom, p, is equal to the number of data points minus the number of regression coefficients. The equation of a line has two coefficients: the slope, and the constant (or y-offset) term. If you have ten data points, the number of degrees of freedom would be 8 ($=10 - 2$). The number of degrees of freedom is needed with many statistical tables to calculate confidence limits.

Sum of the Squares of Regression and Residuals

The two sum-square statistics are a measure of the error still remaining in a curve fit. The regression sum-square is equal to the sum of the squared differences between the y-data values and the average of the y-data values:

$$\sum_{i=1}^{n}\left(y_i - \langle y \rangle\right)^2$$

Thus, it is a measure of the scatter of the data about the average.

The sum-square of the residuals is the sum of the squared differences between the original y-data values and the corresponding calculated y values on the curve:

$$\sum_{i=1}^{n}\left(y_i - y(x_i)\right)^2$$

Thus, it is a measure of the scatter of the y-data about the regression line. When you divide these values by the number of degrees of freedom, you get the variance of the data about the average and the variance about the regression line. Take the square root of the variance, and you get the standard deviation of the data about the average and the standard deviation of the data about the regression line. These statistics give you an indication as to whether the data follows the regression line or is actually a constant.

Linear Regression Calculations

Linear regression analysis is performed with Excel's LINEST, LOGEST, TREND, and GROWTH functions, or with the Regression Data Analysis tool. The linear regression performed by both the worksheet functions and the Data Analysis tool are nearly equivalent. The main differences are that the worksheet functions are updated whenever the data changes, while the Data Analysis tool must be executed again to update the regression values. Also, the Data Analysis tools have a lot more statistics available.

Regression with Worksheet Functions

The LINEST, LOGEST, TREND, and GROWTH functions perform regression calculations on a worksheet. All of them return arrays containing either the regression curve, or the coefficients of the regression calculation. The LINEST function performs straightforward linear regression on a set of data points and returns the offset and slope of the regression line. LOGEST is a variation of linear regression that fits the following equation to the data:

$$y = A\left(B^{x_1}\right)\left(C^{x_2}\right)\cdots$$

and returns the coefficients $(A, B, C, \ldots)$ The TREND and GROWTH functions calculate the same regression formulas as the LINEST and LOGEST functions, but return a set of points on the curve that was fit to the data. Because all four functions return arrays of data, you must insert them into blocks of cells, or use the INDEX function to extract a single element from the array.

NOTE Enter a formula into an array by selecting the cells, typing the formula into the top-left cell and pressing Ctrl+Shift+Enter (Cmd+Enter on the Macintosh) to insert it as an array. When an array function is inserted into a group of cells, you cannot change any single cell in that group. You must change the whole group, or you must delete the whole group and then insert something else.

The LINEST and LOGEST functions have the following syntax:

```
LINEST(y-array,x-array,const,statistics)
LOGEST(y-array,x-array,const,statistics)
```

where *y-array* is a reference to the *y*-data points, *x-array* is a reference to one or more sets of *x*-data points, *const* is a logical value controlling the constant term, and *statistics* is a logical value specifying whether to return the statistics of the curve fit.

If the *x-array* term is omitted, the set of ordinal numbers {1, 2, 3,…} is used. If the *const* term is True or omitted, the constant term in the curve fit (A), is calculated normally. If *const* is False, the constant term is forced to be 0 for LINEST or 1 for LOGEST. If the *statistics* term is true, a table of eight or more statistical values is returned with the coefficients of the equation.

Regression with Data Analysis Tools

The Regression Data Analysis Tool performs the same calculation as the LINEST function, but performs it at a single instant in time. If the underlying data changes, the coefficients are not recalculated unless you re-execute the tool. The Regression tool is part of the Analysis Toolpak add-in. If it has not been installed, you must install it first using the Tools ➤ Add-Ins command.

Thermal Conductivity of Gallium Arsenide

In Chapter 2, you calculated the temperature dependence of the thermal conductivity of silicon from an equation. Silicon is a well-known semiconductor, so an equation for the thermal conductivity is easy to find in the literature. Gallium arsenide (GaAs), on the other hand, is not as well known, so you must fit the experimental data to some curve.

Table 6.1 lists some experimental data for the temperature dependence of the thermal conductivity of heavily doped, p-type gallium arsenide. First try a simple linear fit of that data.

1. Start with a new worksheet, and name it **fig. 6.1**

2. Set the widths of column B to 10, D to 2 and H to 18.

TABLE 6.1: Thermal Conductivity of Heavily Doped Gallium Arsenide (GaAs) versus

T(K)	K (W/cm–K)
250	0.445
300	0.362
350	0.302
400	0.256
450	0.223
500	0.197
550	0.176
600	0.158
650	0.144
700	0.132
750	0.121
800	0.112
850	0.103

3. In cell A1, enter **Thermal conductivity of GaAs; Linear Curve Fit**

4. In cells A3:B3, enter and center the following:

   A3   **T (K)**   B3   **K (W/cm-K)**

5. In cell A4, enter **250**; in cell A5, enter **300**; select both cells, and drag the fill handle down to cell A16.

6. In cells B4:B16, enter the thermal conductivity values in Table 6.1.

Set up a formula to calculate the *y* estimates of the linear fit.

1. In cell C3, enter **K Est.** and center it.

2. Name cells F7 and G7 as **B** and **A**, respectively.

3. In cell C4, enter **=B*A4+A**; copy the formula to cells C4:C16, and format those cells as Number, with three decimal places.

Set up a location for the table of regression coefficients and statistics. The full regression table is five rows high and one column wide for each regression coefficient. For a simple linear curve fit, the table is two columns wide.

1. Make the following entries in columns E, F, G, and H:

E5 **Regression Table**	F6 **B**	H7 **Coeffs**
E9 **r^2**	F12 **Reg.**	H8 **Std Err of Coeffs**
E10 **F**	G6 **A**	H9 **Std Err of Y est.**
E11 **Sum Sq.**	G12 **Residual**	H10 **Degrees of Freedom**

2. Outline as shown in Figure 6.1

Now calculate the coefficients.

1. Select cells F7:G11 and enter this formula:

   =LINEST(B4:B16,A4:A16,TRUE,TRUE)

2. Press Ctrl+Shift+Enter (Cmd+Enter on the Macintosh) to insert the formula in all the cells as an array.

3. Turn off the gridlines.

The worksheet should now look like Figure 6.1. Use the ChartWizard to plot the data and the linear fit (Figure 6.2). Compare the linear fit with the experimental data. While you have fit the trend of the data, the individual points do not fit very well. Checking r^2, you see that it has a value of 0.875, also indicating a poor fit to the data.

The Regression Data Analysis tool can perform much the same calculation, with a lot more statistics available. Perform the same calculation, but use the Data Analysis tool instead.

FIGURE 6.1:

Thermal conductivity of GaAs: a linear curve fit

	A	B	C	D	E	F	G	H	I
1	Thermal Conductivity of GaAs; Linear Curve Fit								
2									
3	T (K)	K (W/cm-K)	K Est.						
4	250	0.445	0.362						
5	300	0.362	0.336		Regression Table				
6	350	0.302	0.311			B	A		
7	400	0.256	0.286			-0.0005	0.487797	Coeffs	
8	450	0.223	0.261			5.74E-05	0.033366	Std Err of Coeffs	
9	500	0.197	0.235		r^2	0.875417	0.038741	Std Err of Y est.	
10	550	0.176	0.210		F	77.29486	11	Degrees of Freedom	
11	600	0.158	0.185		Sum Sq.	0.116011	0.01651		
12	650	0.144	0.160			Reg.	Residual		
13	700	0.132	0.134						
14	750	0.121	0.109						
15	800	0.112	0.084						
16	850	0.103	0.059						

fig. 6.1 / fig. 6.3 / fig. 6.4 / fig. 6.6 / fig. 6.8 / fig. 6.10

FIGURE 6.2:

A comparison plot of the data and the linear fit

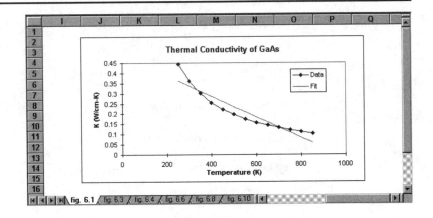

fig. 6.1 / fig. 6.3 / fig. 6.4 / fig. 6.6 / fig. 6.8 / fig. 6.10

1. Start by creating a copy of sheet fig. 6.1 (create a copy by pressing Ctrl while dragging the sheet tab). Double-click the new sheet tab and rename the copy **fig. 6.3**

2. Clear everything from column C and all columns to its right, including the chart.

3. Choose the Tools ➤ Data Analysis command (remember, you must have previously installed the Analysis Toolpak add-in), select the Regression tool from the list of Analysis Tools, and click OK.

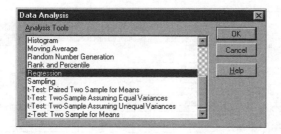

In the Regression dialog box, you'll select the input and output ranges and turn on all the Residuals options so you can see what they do. When selecting the X and Y input ranges, include the column headings along with the data and click the Labels checkbox to indicate that the labels are included. The Labels checkbox causes the column headings to be used as labels for the charts and tables.

4. In the Regression dialog box, set the options as shown in the following figure and click OK. (You can either type the ranges, or click in an edit box and then click and drag a range on the worksheet.)

5. Widen any columns necessary to make all the labels visible in the regression tables.

The Regression Data Analysis tool performs the regression, puts tables all over your worksheet as shown in Figure 6.3, and draws plots of the data, regression and

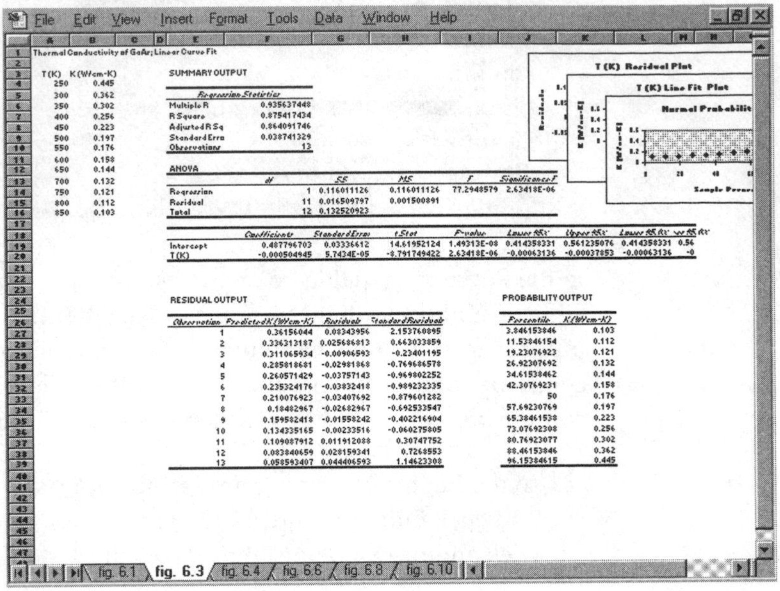

Thermal Conductivity of GaAr; Linear Curve Fit

T (K)	K (W/cm-K)
250	0.445
300	0.362
350	0.302
400	0.256
450	0.223
500	0.197
550	0.176
600	0.158
650	0.144
700	0.132
750	0.121
800	0.112
850	0.103

SUMMARY OUTPUT

Regression Statistics	
Multiple R	0.935637448
R Square	0.875417434
Adjusted R Sq	0.864091746
Standard Erro	0.038741329
Observations	13

ANOVA

	df	SS	MS	F	Significance F
Regression	1	0.116011126	0.116011126	77.2948579	2.63418E-06
Residual	11	0.016509797	0.001500891		
Total	12	0.132520923			

	Coefficients	Standard Error	t Stat	P-value	Lower 95%	Upper 95%	Lower 95.0%	per 95.0%
Intercept	0.487796703	0.03336612	14.61952124	1.49313E-08	0.414358331	0.561235076	0.414358331	0.56
T (K)	-0.000504945	5.7434E-05	-8.791749422	2.63418E-06	-0.00063136	-0.00037853	-0.00063136	-0

RESIDUAL OUTPUT

Observation	Predicted K (W/cm-K)	Residuals	Standard Residuals
1	0.36156044	0.08343956	2.153760895
2	0.336313187	0.025686813	0.663033859
3	0.311065934	-0.00906593	-0.23401195
4	0.285818681	-0.02981868	-0.769686578
5	0.260571429	-0.03757143	-0.969802252
6	0.235324176	-0.03832418	-0.989232335
7	0.210076923	-0.03407692	-0.879601282
8	0.18482967	-0.02682967	-0.692533547
9	0.159582418	-0.01558242	-0.402216904
10	0.134335165	-0.00233516	-0.060275805
11	0.109087912	0.011912088	0.30747752
12	0.083840659	0.028159341	0.7268553
13	0.058593407	0.044406593	1.14623308

PROBABILITY OUTPUT

Percentile	K (W/cm-K)
3.846153846	0.103
11.53846154	0.112
19.23076923	0.121
26.92307692	0.132
34.61538462	0.144
42.30769231	0.158
50	0.176
57.69230769	0.197
65.38461538	0.223
73.07692308	0.256
80.76923077	0.302
88.46153846	0.362
96.15384615	0.445

FIGURE 6.3:
Tables from the Regression Data Analysis Tool

probabilities. The results, though, are the same as were calculated with the worksheet functions.

Since gallium arsenide and silicon are both semiconductors, it would seem to be a good possibility that the equation used for silicon would fit the data for gallium arsenide. The thermal conductivity of silicon fits the following simple equation:

$$K = \frac{K_0}{(T - T_0)}$$

where K_0 and T_0 are constants to be determined; however, this equation is not linear, and cannot be used in a linear regression program. But solving it for the temperature:

$$T = \left(\frac{1}{K}\right)K_0 + T_0$$

yields an equation for T that is linear in the variable $1/K$, rather than a nonlinear equation for K in the variable T. You can easily rearrange the worksheet to calculate $1/K$ and use it as the x-range and T as the y-range.

1. Create a copy of worksheet fig. 6.1 to use as a starting point. Name the copy **fig. 6.4**

2. With the right mouse button, click on the column C header to select the whole column, then choose Insert on the shortcut menu to insert a new column.

3. Change the label in cell A1 to **Thermal conductivity of GaAs; Linear regression of a formula**

4. In cell C3, enter **1/K**

5. In cell C4, enter **=1/B4** and then copy it to cells C4:C16.

6. Format cells C4:C16 as Number, with three decimal places.

Put in the new estimator formula for K.

7. In cells G6 and H6, enter **K0** and **T0** respectively.

8. Select cells G6:H7, choose the Insert ➤ Name ➤ Create command, be sure Top Row is selected, and click on OK. This names cells G7 and H7 as K0 and T0.

9. In cell D4, enter **=K0/(A4–T0)** and then copy it to cells D4:D16.

Now calculate the regression.

> **NOTE** Cells G7 and H7 were previously named A and B using the name box, and are named again using the Insert ➤ Name ➤ Create command. They still retain the names A and B, as well as the names K0 and T0. Either set of names can be used in a formula. Delete a name using the Insert ➤ Name ➤ Define command.

10. Select cells G7:H11 and edit the formula to read

    =LINEST(A4:A16,C4:C16,TRUE,TRUE)

11. Press Ctrl+Shift+Enter (Cmd+Enter on the Macintosh) to enter the formula as an array.

The worksheet should now look like Figure 6.4. Note that the value of r^2 has improved tremendously; it is now 0.998, indicative of a good fit to the data points. If you plot the data as shown in Figure 6.5, you see that the regression line follows the data much better than the linear curve. Lines were turned off between the data points to make it easier to compare the curve fit (the line) to the data points (the markers.)

FIGURE 6.4:

Thermal conductivity of GaAs: fitting a nonlinear equation

	A	B	C	D	E	F	G	H	I
1	Thermal Conductivity of GaAs; Linear Regression of a formula								
2									
3	T (K)	K (W/cm-K)	1/K	K Est.					
4	250	0.445	2.247	0.484					
5	300	0.362	2.762	0.372		Regression Table			
6	350	0.302	3.311	0.302			K0	T0	
7	400	0.256	3.906	0.255			80.67975	83.17157	Coeffs
8	450	0.223	4.484	0.220			1.017655	6.342822	Std Err of Coeffs
9	500	0.197	5.076	0.194		r^2	0.998253	8.500841	Std Err of Y est.
10	550	0.176	5.682	0.173		F	6285.331	11	Degrees of Freedom
11	600	0.158	6.329	0.156		Sum Sq.	454205.1	794.9073	
12	650	0.144	6.944	0.142			Reg.	Residual	
13	700	0.132	7.576	0.131					
14	750	0.121	8.264	0.121					
15	800	0.112	8.929	0.113					
16	850	0.103	9.709	0.105					

fig. 6.1 / fig. 6.3 / **fig. 6.4** / fig. 6.6 / fig. 6.8 / fig. 6.10

FIGURE 6.5:

Comparison of the experimental data and the nonlinear curve fit

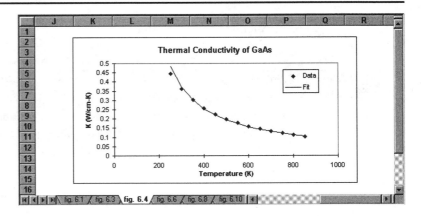

fig. 6.1 / fig. 6.3 / **fig. 6.4** / fig. 6.6 / fig. 6.8 / fig. 6.10

Something to keep in mind when you fit a nonlinear equation by transforming it is that what you calculate is the best fit to the transformed equation, not the original one. In most cases, this won't make much difference, but with exponential and logarithmic functions, you may find that the data at one end of the curve comes closer to the curve than the data at the other end.

Polynomial Regression Calculations

Although Excel's data regression functions are not explicitly set up to do polynomial regression, you can perform it easily. Polynomial regression fits data with a line of the form

$$y = A + Bx + Cx^2 + \cdots$$

You can fit this equation with a multiple linear regression program by letting

$$x_{1,i} = x_i$$
$$x_{2,i} = x_i^2$$
$$x_{3,i} = x_i^3$$
$$\vdots$$

Fit the thermal conductivity data again, but this time use a third-order (up to x^3) polynomial equation.

1. Copy the fig. 6.4 worksheet to use as a starting point. Name the sheet **fig. 6.6**

2. Change the label in cell A1 to **Thermal conductivity of GaAs; Polynomial regression**

3. Select column C and choose the Edit ➤ Delete command.

4. Select columns B and C and choose the Insert ➤ Columns command.

5. In cells B3 and C3, enter T^2 and T^3 respectively.

6. In cell B4, enter **=A4^2** and then copy it to cells B4:B16.

7. In cell C4, enter =A4^3 and then copy it to cells C4:C16.

8. Format cells B4:C16 as Scientific, with two decimal places.

Put in the new estimator equation for *K*. Note that a C with an underscore (C_) is used for the C coefficient because C is a reserved word. The cells will all show the #REF! error value because you have not defined the names for the coefficients yet.

1. In cell E4, enter =A+B*A4+C_*B4+D*C4 and then copy it into cells E4:E16.

Now move the table out of the way to make room for the regression results, and then enlarge the regression table.

2. Select A3:E16 and drag it by its outline to A14:E27.

3. Select G5:J12 and drag it to B4:E11, then select E5:E11 and drag it to G5:G11.

4. Set the widths of the columns as follows:

    A   7

    B:F 10

    G   20

5. Fix the outlined cells to match Figure 6.6.

6. In cell C5:F5, enter **D**, **C**, **B**, and **A** respectively.

7. Select cells C5:F6 and name them using the Insert ➤ Name ➤ Create command. (Note that cell D6 is named C_, not C.)

Now perform the regression.

8. Select cells C6:F10 and enter the formula

    =LINEST(D15:D27,A15:C27,TRUE,TRUE)

9. Press Ctrl+Shift+Enter (Cmd+Enter on the Macintosh) to enter the formula as an array.

The worksheet should now look like that in Figure 6.6. Again, r^2 indicates that the curve is a good fit to the data, as you can see by the chart in Figure 6.7.

FIGURE 6.6:

Thermal conductivity of GaAs:
polynomial regression curve fit

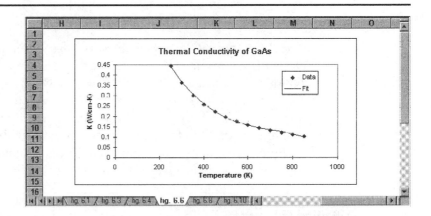

FIGURE 6.7:

Plotted curve fit to the thermal
conductivity of GaAs

WARNING

You could try using a higher-order curve to get a better fit of the data, but with polynomial regression, the curve often oscillates if the order is too high. When that happens, even though the curve hits all the data points, it is not a good predictor for points between the data points. You should always plot the results of polynomial regression, especially for curves with an order greater than 3, to make sure that the curve you have calculated is what you expect. Be sure to include points between those used to define the original curve.

Checking the Statistics

Check the statistics for the curve fit you just performed. First check the coefficients of the regression (A, B, C, and D) with a 95 percent confidence interval:

$\alpha = (1 - 0.95) = 0.05$

$\alpha/2 = 0.025$

$p = 9$ (from the worksheet)

$t_{\alpha/2,p} = t_{0.025,9} = \text{TINV}(0.05,9) = 2.262$

$S_A = 0.0303$ (from the worksheet)

$t_{0.025,9}S_A = 2.262 * 0.0303 = 0.0685$

This is much smaller than A, so A is significant. The same analysis is applied to the other coefficients.

Next check to see if the data really correlates with the curve or if the apparent correlation is the result of a random process. The F-value for $n_f = 3$, $p = 9$ and a 0.95 confidence interval is $\text{FINV}(0.05,3,9) = 3.86$, which is much smaller than the calculated F-value of 2911, so the correlation between the data and the curve is significant and not a random event. The sum-squared term for the residuals is much smaller than the term for the regression, indicating that the data fits the regression line much better than it fits the average. Thus, the data appears to follow the regression line instead of being just random scatter about some constant value.

Using Trendlines

If you want to fit a set of data and only show the regression results on a chart without making the data available on the worksheets, use the Trendline charting feature. To use it, you select a data series on a chart and choose the Insert ➤ Trendline command. The Trendline dialog box appears for you to select the options. The Trendline feature is capable of calculating linear, polynomial, power, logarithmic, exponential, and moving average curve fits to the data. The output of the Trendline command is to draw the regression line on the chart, and optionally, write the regression formula and the value of the correlation index (r^2) on the chart.

Perform polynomial regression again but this time use the trendline option on a chart.

1. Create a copy of the fig. 6.1 worksheet, and rename it **fig. 6.8**

2. Change the label in cell A1 to **Thermal Conductivity of GaAs; Trendline option**

3. Select cells C3:H16 and clear their contents.

4. Select cells A4:B16 and plot them as an XY (scatter) chart using the Chart-Wizard.

5. Activate the chart, then select the data series; choose the Format ➤ Selected Data Series command, Patterns tab and turn off lines, leaving only symbols.

6. With the series still selected, choose the Insert ➤ Trendline command.

7. In the Trendline dialog box, Type tab, select the Polynomial type, and set the order to 3. There are several functional types to choose from.

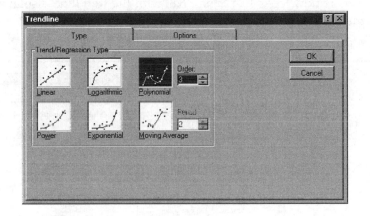

8. Select the Options tab and check the Display Equation on Chart and Display R squared Value on Chart checkboxes. Click OK to continue.

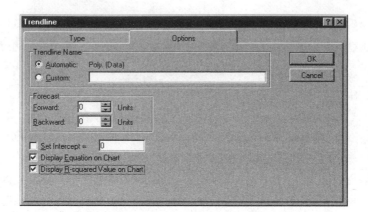

The chart now looks like Figure 6.8, with the trendline displayed along with the formula used and the value of r^2.

FIGURE 6.8:

Regression formula using the Trendline command

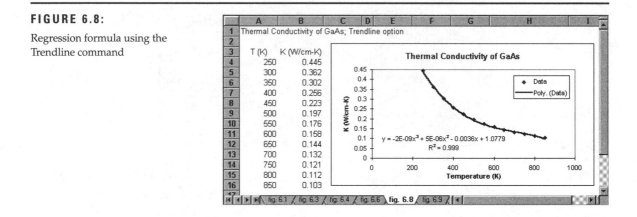

NOTE

You can format the numbers in the the formula to have more decimal places by selecting the text box that contains the formula and formatting it with a numeric format.

Working with Complex Functions

If a function cannot be linearized into the form required for linear regression, you cannot use the built-in functions to determine the best fit of an equation to the data. For example, an exponential function, $y = Ae^{Bx}$, can be linearized by taking the natural logarithm of it, $Ln(y) = Ln(A) + Bx$, and identifying $Ln(A)$ and B as the regression coefficients rather than the A and B of the original equation. On the other hand, a double exponential function such as $y = Ae^{Bx} + Ce^{Dx}$ cannot be linearized unless you know B and D.

> **WARNING**
>
> As mentioned earlier in the chapter, although the calculated coefficients for the linearized equation are the best fit (least square) for that equation, they are usually not the best fit for the original equation. For example, regression on the linearized version of the single exponential equation above calculates the best values of $Ln(A)$ and B for the logarithmic equation. The solutions do not necessarily give the best values of A and B for the exponential equation, but they will be close.

Making Manual Adjustments

To fit equations that cannot be fit with regression analysis, you must sequentially adjust the coefficients to find the maximum of r^2, which corresponds to the minimum in the residual square error. You increase or decrease a coefficient until you find the maximum of r^2. You then adjust the next coefficient to find the maximum, and so on, until you have adjusted all the coefficients. Then start with the first one again to see if changing any of the other coefficients changed the location of the maximum for this coefficient. Continue adjusting the coefficients until you find the values that simultaneously give the maximum value of the correlation coefficient, at which point you are finished.

Occasionally, instead of converging to a single solution, this algorithm oscillates between two values. Changing one coefficient changes the maximum of another, but changing the other moves the maximum of the first back again. If this happens, try adjusting the values by a smaller amount and see if that makes it converge. If that does not work, you must use your scientific judgment and knowledge of the equation being fit to determine the best values. Bear in mind that there may be two or more local maxima in the solution space, where the one you reach depends on your starting point.

Electron Ionization Cross Sections

Table 6.2 lists the total cross sections for electron impact ionization of helium versus electron energies between 150 eV and 1 KeV. A cross section is an effective area for an atom, and is used to determine the probability that a collision takes place between an electron and the atom. If you imagine atoms as a bunch of small targets that a beam of electrons is trying to hit, the cross section is the area of the target. The larger the cross section, the easier it is to hit the atom with an electron and the higher the probability that an ionization will occur.

TABLE 6.2: Experimental Total Ionization Cross Section versus Energy for Helium

Electron Energy (eV)	Cross Section (πa_0^2)*
150	0.419
175	0.408
200	0.394
250	0.365
300	0.337
350	0.313
400	0.292
450	0.272
500	0.255
550	0.240
600	0.227
650	0.216
700	0.205

From previous experience, I know that the cross section looks like a decreasing exponential in this energy range. Therefore, fit it with an equation of the following form:

$$S(E) = A(1 - e^{-B/E})$$

where S is the cross section in units $(\pi a_0{}^2)$, E is the electron energy in eV, and A and B are the coefficients to be determined by the analysis.

1. Start with a new worksheet named **fig. 6.9**

2. In cell A1, enter **Electron Ionization Cross Section in Helium**

3. Make the following entries in cells A3:E3 (enter the ¶ by holding down Alt and typing 227 on the numeric keypad):

    A3: **E (eV)**   B3: **S (¶a$_0{}^2$)**   E3: **(y-<y>)^2**

    C3: **S Est.**   D3: **(y-yx)^2**

4. In cells A4:B22, enter the data in Table 6.2.

Create a table of the coefficients to be determined.

1. Make the following entries in cells F3:G4, and right-align the labels in F3 and F4.

F3	A	G3	0.5
F4	B	G4	500

2. Name cells as follows:

G3	A	H6	AvEy
G4	B	H7	Free

Next enter the equation being fit to calculate the estimated values of y. The next two columns calculate the sum of squares about the curve and the sum of squares about the average, which are needed to calculate the standard error of the y estimate and r^2.

NOTE   Excel has built-in functions for calculating the standard error of the y estimate and r^2, but the formulas used are only valid for linear curve fits. The formulas used here are valid for any equation.

3. In cell C4, enter the formula

   =A*(1–EXP(–B/A4))

   and copy it to cells C5:C22.

4. In cell D4, enter the formula

   =(B4–C4)^2

   and copy it to cells D5:D22.

5. In cell E4, enter the formula

   =(B4–AvEy)^2

   and copy it to cells E5:E22.

Create a table of the curve-fit statistics.

1. In cell F6, enter **Average of y <y>**

2. In cell H6, enter the formula

   =AVERAGE(B4:B22)

3. In cell F7, enter **Deg. of Freedom**

4. In cell H7, enter the formula

   =COUNT(B4:B22)–2

5. Enter **Std. err of Y est** in cell F8.

6. In cell H8, enter the formula

   =SQRT(SUM(D4:D22)/Free)

7. Enter r^2 in cell F9.

8. In cell H9, enter the formula

   =1–SUM(D4:D22)/SUM(E4:E22)

9. Format cells B4:C22 as Number, with three decimal places.

10. Format cells D4:E22 as Scientific, with two decimal places.

The worksheet should now look like Figure 6.9. To use it, pick some reasonable starting values for A and B (say 0.5 and 500) and put them in the table (in cells G3

FIGURE 6.9:

Electron ionization cross section in helium: manual curve fit

	A	B	C	D	E	F	G	H	I
1	Electron Ionization Cross Section in Helium								
2									
3	E (eV)	S (πa_0^2)	S Est.	$(y - y_x)^2$	$(y - <y>)^2$	A	0.5		
4	150	0.419	0.482	3.99E-03	2.43E-02	B	500		
5	175	0.408	0.471	4.00E-03	2.10E-02				
6	200	0.394	0.459	4.22E-03	1.71E-02	Average of y <y>		0.263053	
7	250	0.365	0.432	4.53E-03	1.04E-02	Deg. of Freedom		17	
8	300	0.337	0.406	4.70E-03	5.47E-03	Std. err of Y est		0.059823	
9	350	0.313	0.380	4.51E-03	2.49E-03	r^2		0.551741	
10	400	0.292	0.357	4.19E-03	8.38E-04				
11	450	0.272	0.335	4.02E-03	8.01E-05				
12	500	0.255	0.316	3.73E-03	6.48E-05				
13	550	0.240	0.299	3.43E-03	5.31E-04				
14	600	0.227	0.283	3.10E-03	1.30E-03				
15	650	0.216	0.268	2.74E-03	2.21E-03				
16	700	0.205	0.255	2.52E-03	3.37E-03				

fig. 6.1 / fig. 6.3 / fig. 6.4 / fig. 6.6 / fig. 6.8 \ fig. 6.9

and G4). Add 0.1 to A and then subtract 0.1 from A and see which increases the value of r^2. Continue adding or subtracting 0.1 from A until you find the value that maximizes r^2. Now adjust B, adding and subtracting 100 from it until you maximize r^2 again. Go back to A and see if the maximum of r^2 has moved. Readjust A if it has changed. Continue adjusting A and B until you find the values that maximize r^2 for both of them.

Next, decrease the amount that you add to A and B by a power of ten. Add and subtract 0.01 from A and 10 from B until you maximize r^2 again. Decrease the amount that you change A and B by another power of 10 (0.001 and 1) and do it again. When you find the maximum value of r^2 this time, you will have three-place accuracy in the coefficients (A = 0.443, B = 434, r^2 = 0.999582). As you can see from Figure 6.10, the equation is a good fit to the data.

FIGURE 6.10:

Plotted curve fit to the electron ionization cross section in helium

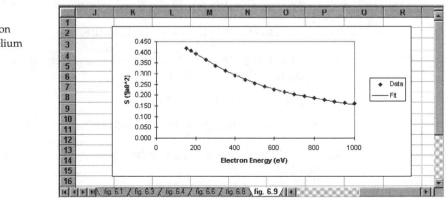

fig. 6.1 / fig. 6.3 / fig. 6.4 / fig. 6.6 / fig. 6.8 \ fig. 6.9

Making Automatic Adjustments

In the last example, you manually adjusted the coefficients of the equation being fit to the data until r^2 was maximized. Manual adjustments are sometimes necessary when the equation is extremely nonlinear or does strange things near the solution. Equations with local minima and maxima fall into this category. You need to make changes intuitively to find the true or best solution; however, in most cases, a mechanical approach can be applied to find the solution.

Excel includes the Solver add-in program, which can be used to automatically maximize r^2 and find the best fit to a data set. Solver is designed to intelligently adjust the values of a list of cells to make the value of another cell meet some criterion.

Using Solver

The worksheet setup for using Solver is identical to that for the previous example. The Solver add-in effectively takes your place, inserting the values of A and B and watching how r^2 changes. In addition, you can use array formulas to calculate the standard error of the y coefficient and r^2. You could have used these array formulas in the previous example, but they are not as easy to understand.

First, replace the formulas in the columns with array formulas.

1. Start with a copy of the worksheet from the previous example, and name it **fig. 6.11**

2. Select columns D and E and clear their contents with the Clear command on the Edit menu.

3. In cell H8, enter the formula for the standard error of the Y estimate:

    =SQRT(SUM((B4:B22–C4:C22)^2)/Free)

4. Press Ctrl+Shift+Enter (Cmd+Enter on the Macintosh) to enter it as an array formula.

5. In cell H9, enter the formula for r^2:

    =1-SUM((B4:B22–C4:C22)^2)/SUM((B4:B22–AvEy)^2)

6. Press Ctrl+Shift+Enter (Cmd+Enter on the Macintosh) to enter it as an array formula.

7. Name cell H9 as **rsq**

These two array formulas completely replace the two columns of calculations on the previous version of this worksheet. By replacing cell references in the formulas with array references and entering the formula with Ctrl-Shift pressed, you have compressed two columns of calculations into two cells.

In an array formula, Excel matches the first cell in each array reference and calculates a result. It then does this for the next set of values, and so on, until it reaches the end of the array references. For example, in cell H8, Excel subtracts the values in cells C4:C22 from the values in cells B4:B22. The result is a list of 19 numbers, which is passed to the SUM function. The SUM function adds the list, the result is divided by the value of Free, and then the square root is taken. If you had pressed Enter instead of Ctl+Shift+Enter, the formula would have been applied to only cells B8 and C8 (the array elements in the same row as the formula).

Now use Solver to find the solution.

1. Set the values of A and B in cells G3 and G4 to **0.5** and **500**

2. Choose the Tools ➤ Solver command. If Solver is not available, you must install it by choosing the Tools ➤ Add Ins command and checking the Solver add-in.

3. In the Solver dialog box, type **rsq** in the Set Target Cell box, click on the Max button for the Equal To option, and type **A,B** in the By Changing Cells box.

You have set up Solver to try to maximize the value of rsq by adjusting the values of A and B. Now run Solver to find the solution.

4. Click the Solve button and wait for Solver to find the solution.

While Solver is working, it displays the values of rsq at the bottom of the screen so you can see what is going on. When Solver finds a solution, it displays the Solver Results dialog box. You can choose to keep the solution Solver found, or restore the original values. You can also print one of the reports listed in the Reports box. If you are using the Scenario Manager, you can save the solution as a scenario with the Save Scenario button. See the *Microsoft Excel User's Guide* (in Excel 5) or online Help for more information.

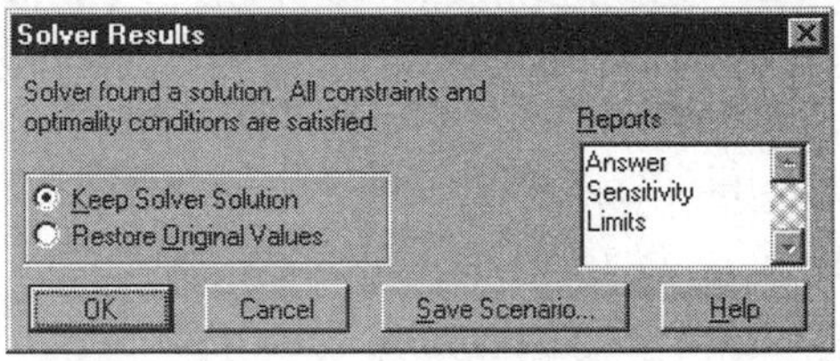

5. Click on OK in the Solver dialog box.

You see the final result, as shown in Figure 6.11. The result is slightly different from that found with the manual method, because we stopped at three places of accuracy with the manual method. Some local maxima that can fool you (and Solver) are also in the area of the solution. After Solver is finished, you might want to explore the area near the solution by changing A and B to see if there is another solution with a larger value of r^2.

FIGURE 6.11:

The worksheet after Solver adjusted the coefficients

	A	B	C	D	E	F	G	H	I
1	Electron Ionization Cross Section in Helium								
2									
3	E (eV)	S (¶a_0^2)	S Est.			A	0.443651		
4	150	0.419	0.419			B	432.7025		
5	175	0.408	0.406						
6	200	0.394	0.393			Average of y <y>		0.263	
7	250	0.365	0.365			Deg. of Freedom		17	
8	300	0.337	0.339			Std. err of Y est		0.001817	
9	350	0.313	0.315			r^2		0.999587	
10	400	0.292	0.293						
11	450	0.272	0.274						
12	500	0.255	0.257						
13	550	0.240	0.242						
14	600	0.227	0.228						
15	650	0.216	0.216						
16	700	0.205	0.205						

Using a Visual Basic Procedure for Automatic Adjustments

If, for some reason, Solver does not work as you want it to, or if you want more control over how the solution is obtained, you can write a Visual Basic procedure to adjust the coefficients and find the solution. The following procedure, named AdjustIt, adjusts A and B up and down looking for an increase in the value of r^2.

```
Option Explicit
'
' Adjuster Macro
' Curve fitting procedure.
'
'
Sub AdjustIt
Dim dblA As Double
Dim dblB As Double
Dim dblDA As Double 'Delta A
Dim dblDB As Double 'Delta B
Dim dblStop As Double 'Stop value
Dim fTest As Boolean 'Change flag
Dim dblRsq As Double 'The value or r squared
Dim dblRsqMax As Double 'The largest value of r squared found
'Initialize the variables.
dblA = ActiveSheet.Range("A").Value
dblB = ActiveSheet.Range("B").Value
dblDA = dblA / 10
dblDB = dblB / 10
dblStop = dblDA / 10000
dblRsqMax = ActiveSheet.Range("rsq").Value
'Loop until you reach the stopping value.
Do While (dblDA > dblStop)
    'fTest is True if A or B have changed in an iteration.
    fTest = True
    Do While (fTest = True)
        fTest = False
        'Increase A and update the worksheet, see if r^2 increases.
        dblA = dblA + dblDA
        ActiveSheet.Range("A").Value = dblA
        Calculate
        dblRsq = ActiveSheet.Range("rsq").Value
        If (dblRsq > dblRsqMax) Then
            'If r^2 increases, update r^2max and set the flag.
            dblRsqMax = dblRsq
```

```
            fTest = True
        Else
            'If r^2 decreases, try decreasing A and check again.
            dblA = dblA - 2 * dblDA
            ActiveSheet.Range("A").Value = dblA
            Calculate
            dblRsq = ActiveSheet.Range("rsq").Value
            If (dblRsq > dblRsqMax) Then
                'If r^2 increases, update r^2max and set the flag.
                dblRsqMax = dblRsq
                fTest = True
            Else
                'If r^2 decreases, reset A to its original value.
                dblA = dblA + dblDA
                ActiveSheet.Range("A").Value = dblA
                Calculate
            End If
        End If
        'Now do exactly the same for B.
        'Increase B and update the worksheet, see if r^2 increases.
        dblB = dblB + dblDB
        ActiveSheet.Range("B").Value = dblB
        Calculate
        dblRsq = ActiveSheet.Range("rsq").Value
        If (dblRsq > dblRsqMax) Then
            'If r^2 increases, update r^2max and set the flag.
            dblRsqMax = dblRsq
            fTest = True
        Else
            'If r^2 decreases, try decreasing B and check again.
            dblB = dblB - 2 * dblDB
            ActiveSheet.Range("B").Value = dblB
            Calculate
            dblRsq = ActiveSheet.Range("rsq").Value
            If (dblRsq > dblRsqMax) Then
                'If r^2 increases, update r^2max and set the flag.
                dblRsqMax = dblRsq
                fTest = True
            Else
                'If r^2 decreases, reset B to its original value.
                dblB = dblB + dblDB
                ActiveSheet.Range("B").Value = dblB
                Calculate
            End If
        End If
```

```
    Loop
    'Get here if neither A or B are changed during an iteration.
    'Decrease both Delta A and Delta B by a factor of 10.
    dblDA = dblDA / 10
    dblDB = dblDB / 10
Loop
End Sub
```

The procedure first copies the starting values of A and B from the worksheet and initializes some values. Next is a loop that continues until the value of delta A (dblDA) is less than the stop value. This loop determines the number of decimals in the solution. Next, the flag (fTest) is cleared and a loop started that continues until fTest is True. The flag (fTest) is set to False at the beginning of each iteration of the loop, and is changed to True if any of the coefficients are changed. If none of the coefficients are changed, the maximum of r^2 has been found and the loop terminates. Inside the loop, the first block of code increases the value of A by DA, updates the worksheet, and checks to see if r^2 increased. If it did, the macro saves the value of r^2, sets the flag fTest, otherwise, it reduces A by 2*dblDA and r^2 is checked again. If it increased, r^2 is saved, and the fTest flag is set. If it didn't increase r^2, A is restored to its previous value. The next block of code does the same for B.

This loop continues until r^2 can't be increased by changing A and B. Delta A and Delta B (dblDA, dblDB) are then reduced by a factor of 10, Delta A is checked to see if it has reached the stopping criterion, and if not, the loop starts again. If the stopping value has been reached, the procedure ends.

Use the procedure to calculate the Electron Ionization Cross Section again.

1. Start with a copy of worksheet fig. 6.11 and name it **fig. 6.12**

2. Choose the Insert ➤ Macro ➤ Module command to create a new module sheet.

3. Name the module sheet **Adjusters**

4. Enter the AdjustIt procedure into the module sheet.

5. Switch to the fig. 6.12 worksheet, click the Drawing button, select the Create Button button on the Drawing toolbar and draw a button on the worksheet. In the Assign Macro dialog box that appears, select the AdjustIt macro and click OK.

6. Change the name on the button to **Fit Data**

7. Close the Drawing toolbox.
8. Change the values of A in cell G3 to **0.5** and B in cell G4 to **500**
9. Click the Fit Data button.

The values of A and B are continuously adjusted until the solution is reached, as shown in Figure 6.12.

FIGURE 6.12:

Nonlinear curve fitting using a Visual Basic procedure.

	A	B	C	D	E	F	G	H	I
1	Electron Ionization Cross Section in Helium								
2								Fit Data	
3	E (eV)	S (¶a_0^2)	S Est.			A	0.4437		
4	150	0.419	0.419			B	432.6		
5	175	0.408	0.406						
6	200	0.394	0.393			Average of y <y>		0.263	
7	250	0.365	0.365			Deg. of Freedom		17	
8	300	0.337	0.339			Std. err of Y est		0.001817	
9	350	0.313	0.315			r^2		0.999586	
10	400	0.292	0.293						
11	450	0.272	0.274						
12	500	0.255	0.257						
13	550	0.240	0.242						
14	600	0.227	0.228						
15	650	0.216	0.216						
16	700	0.205	0.205						

fig. 6.9 / fig. 6.11 / **fig. 6.12** / Adjusters / fig. 6.13 / fig

Table Lookup and Interpolation

Often, you will have data that cannot be fit with any simple or moderately complex equation. In this case, the best method is to use a data table and a table lookup function. A table lookup function finds and interpolates values in the table for a particular value of *x*. Essentially, you are fitting a simple curve to a few of the data points in the neighborhood of the point that you are interested in rather than fitting a complicated curve to the whole data set.

Table lookup is accomplished with Excel's HLOOKUP, VLOOKUP, and MATCH functions. The HLOOKUP and VLOOKUP functions search for a value in one column of a table and return the value from another column on the same row. The MATCH function searches for a value in a table and returns the position of the cell that contains that value.

The interpolation method can be coded as a procedure or with worksheet formulas. The differences in the various interpolation methods are in the equation used to estimate the value of the function between two known data points. The simplest, and most common, is linear interpolation. Actually, the simplest method is to use the table lookup functions and accept the value returned rather than interpolating between values in the table. In many cases, this may be sufficient and saves you a lot of work. Also common are quadratic and cubic curves, which are fit to three or four data points. More complicated functions are splines and Chebyshev polynomials. Consult an applied numerical analysis text for more information about these functions.

Using Linear Interpolation

Linear interpolation consists of simply connecting the two data points on either side of the value being interpolated with a straight line. If the data points are not far apart, linear interpolation works very well. It is also simple to implement compared with higher-order interpolations.

The interpolation formula in Lagrangian form for linear interpolation is

$$y = \frac{(x - x_2)}{(x_1 - x_2)} y_1 + \frac{(x - x_1)}{(x_2 - x_1)} y_2$$

where x_1, x_2, y_1, and y_2 are the data points from the table and x, the value being interpolated, is between x_1 and x_2.

Steam Tables

Steam tables are tables of temperature; pressure; density; enthalpy; and entropy of saturated steam and water, superheated steam, and compressed water. Saturated steam and water is a mixture of steam and water at a temperature and pressure where they both coexist in equilibrium. The saturation line on a graph of temperature and pressure divides the graph into all water and all steam regions, as shown in Figure 6.13. Superheated steam data points are those pressure and temperature points above the saturation line in the direction of increasing temperature. Compressed water data points are those pressure and temperature points above the saturation line in the direction of increasing pressure.

FIGURE 6.13:

Pressure/temperature saturation line of a steam-water mixture (above the line is all water, below is all steam; only on the saturation line can steam and water coexist)

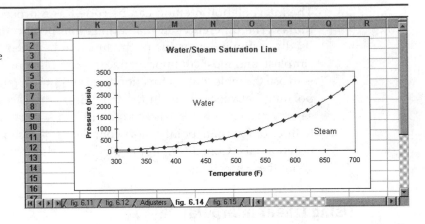

Steam tables are used by engineers who design and operate energy transportation and conversion equipment that employs steam as the working fluid. This equipment includes steam engines, steam turbines, steam and hot water heating systems, and nuclear reactors. Steam tables are also used by scientists who need to know the properties of hot, pressurized water and steam.

For example, in a pressurized water reactor (PWR), if the pressure decreases to the saturation line, the water flashes into steam. The temperature and pressure in the reactor then move along the saturation line until either the pressure is increased to the point that the water stops boiling into steam, or all the water is boiled away (not a good thing). Luckily, this is a self-quenching process. As the pressure decreases, the enthalpy (the heat-carrying capacity) also decreases which, in a reactor (or any boiler for that matter), causes the water temperature to increase, because the heat flow from the heat-generation region has been decreased. Increasing the temperature increases the pressure and quenches the process.

In any event, it is not a good idea to let your cooling water boil away inside a reactor, so reactor engineers and operators need to know where this saturation line is so that they can design and operate the reactor with an adequate safety margin. A representative PWR operates at around 600°F and 2250 psi, well away from the saturation line.

In the next example, build a worksheet that calculates the saturated pressure for a given temperature. The worksheet uses a table lookup function and linear interpolation to calculate the pressure. Table 6.3 contains the data for the steam table.

TABLE 6.3: Pressure and Temperature Saturation Line for a Water and Steam Mixture

Temperature (F)	Pressure (psia)*
300	67
320	90
340	118
360	153
380	196
400	247
420	309
440	382
460	467
480	566
500	681
520	812
540	963
560	1133
580	1326
600	1543
620	1787
640	2060
660	2366
680	2709
700	3094

*psia = pounds per square inch absolute

1. Start with a new worksheet named **fig. 6.14**

2. In cell A1, enter **Steam table: Saturated steam/water: Linear Interpolation**

3. Change the width of column B to 10.

4. Enter the following in cells A3 and B3:

     A3   **Temp. (F)**   B3   **Press (psia)**

Now enter the temperature and pressure data.

5. In cells A4:A24, enter **300** to **700** in steps of 20.

6. In cells B4:B24, enter the pressure data in Table 6.3.

7. Name the range A4:A24 as **Temperature** and range B4:B24 as **Pressure**

Next create a table to do the linear interpolation.

8. Enter the following in the indicated cells:

D4	**Temperature**	F4	**Output Pressure**
D5	**Input**	F5	**Calc.**
E3	**Linear Interpolation**	G5	**'True**
E5	**Index**	H5	**Error**

Use some random temperature values for input to the linear interpolation. Put the true values of the pressure in column G so that you can compare them with the interpolated values.

9. Make the following entries in cells D6:D11:

D6	**510**	D9	**622**
D7	**520**	D10	**538**
D8	**302**	D11	**456**

The table lookup and interpolation equations are too large to fit in one cell, so put the table lookup function in one cell and the interpolation function in the next. For each temperature value, the MATCH function returns the index of the row that contains the largest temperature that is less than or equal to the lookup value. Note that the temperature values must be sorted for MATCH to work. You can set the third argument in MATCH to 0, in which case it finds an exact match and the data can be in random order, but we need the data to be ordered for the interpolation algorithms to work. Use this index with the INDEX function to access the pressure and temperature values needed for the linear interpolation function in column F.

10. In cell E6, enter the formula

=MATCH(D6,Temperature)

and copy it into cells E7:E11.

11. In cell F6, enter the formula

    =(D6–INDEX(Temperature,E6+1))*INDEX(Pressure,E6)
    ➥/(INDEX(Temperature,E6)–INDEX(Temperature,E6+1))
    ➥+(D6–INDEX(Temperature,E6))*INDEX(Pressure,E6+1)
    ➥/(INDEX(Temperature,E6+1)–INDEX(Temperature,E6))

    and copy it into cells F7:F11.

12. In cells G6:G11, make the following entries:

G6	**744**	G9	**1812.8**
G7	**812**	G10	**946.9**
G8	**69**	G11	**448.7**

Calculate the error in the interpolated values.

13. In cells H6:H11, enter the formula

    =(G6–F6)/G6

14. Format cells H6:H11 as Percent, with three decimal places.

Your worksheet should now look like Figure 6.14. Note that for the six random test values, the maximum error is only about one half of a percent.

FIGURE 6.14:

Steam table, steam/water saturation line: using the table lookup function and linear interpolation

	A	B	C	D	E	F	G	H	I
1	Steam table: Saturated steam/water. Linear Interpolation								
2									
3	Temp. (F)	Press (psia)			Linear Interpolation				
4	300	67		Temperture		Output Pressure			
5	320	90		Input	Index	Calc.	True	Error	
6	340	118		510	11	746.5	744	-0.336%	
7	360	153		520	12	812	812	0.000%	
8	380	196		302	1	69.3	69	-0.435%	
9	400	247		622	17	1814.3	1812.8	-0.083%	
10	420	309		538	12	947.9	946.9	-0.106%	
11	440	382		456	8	450	448.7	-0.290%	
12	460	467							
13	480	566							
14	500	681							
15	520	812							
16	540	963							
17	560	1133							

fig. 6.11 / fig. 6.12 / Adjusters / **fig. 6.14** / fig 6.15

WARNING	For a smooth function like this, linear interpolation works quite well. But be aware that the derivative of linearly interpolated functions is not continuous; it has sharp changes at each data point in the table. In most cases, this is not a problem; however, I have encountered a case where the discontinuity caused obvious structure in the output of a simulation code that used a table lookup function to create the input. Until I tracked it down, we thought that we had found some new physical process. If you need something with a continuous derivative, a spline curve would be more appropriate (and harder to implement, of course).

Cubic Interpolation

After linear interpolation comes quadratic, then cubic interpolation. Cubic interpolation is more accurate than quadratic interpolation, not only because it uses a higher-order curve, but more important, because it is more symmetric about the range being interpolated. Cubic interpolation fits a third-order curve to four data points in a row, with the point being interpolated between the center two points. The interpolation equation, in Lagrangian form, is

$$y = \frac{(x-x_2)(x-x_3)(x-x_4)}{(x_1-x_2)(x_1-x_3)(x_1-x_4)}y_1 + \frac{(x-x_1)(x-x_3)(x-x_4)}{(x_2-x_1)(x_2-x_3)(x_2-x_4)}y_2$$

$$+ \frac{(x-x_1)(x-x_2)(x-x_4)}{(x_3-x_1)(x_3-x_2)(x_3-x_4)}y_3 + \frac{(x-x_1)(x-x_2)(x-x_3)}{(x_4-x_1)(x_4-x_2)(x_4-x_3)}y$$

where x_1, x_2, x_3, x_4, y_1, y_2, y_3, and y_4 are consecutive x and y values from the table. The value being interpolated, x, should lie between x_2 and x_3 to get the best value for y.

So that you can compare cubic interpolation to linear interpolation, put a cubic interpolation table on the same worksheet as the linear interpolation. Since the cubic interpolation formula is somewhat more complicated than the linear formula, create a function to calculate it instead of placing it on the worksheet. First, make an interpolation table with the same test values as the linear interpolation table.

1. Start with a copy of the worksheet fig. 6.14, and name it **fig. 6.15.**

2. Change the label in cell A1 to, **Steam table: Saturated steam/water: Linear &
   Cubic Interpolation**

3. In cell E12, enter **Cubic Interpolation**

4. Select cells D6:D11 and copy them to cells D13:D18.

5. Select cells G6:H11 and copy them to cells G13:H18.

6. In cell F13, enter the formula

   =CubicInterpolation(Temperature,Pressure,D13)

   and copy it to cells F13:F18.

7. Choose the Insert Macro Module command and name the macro sheet
   Interpolator

8. Enter the following two procedures into the module sheet:

```
Option Explicit
Option Base 1 'Make arrays start at 1
'
'Cubic interpolation function
'
Function CubicInterpolation(rngXArray As Variant,
    ↪rngYArray As Variant, rngX As Variant) As Double
Dim intIndex As Integer
Dim intI As Integer
Dim intJ As Integer
Dim dblProd As Double
'Find the location of the value to be interpolated.
For intIndex = 1 To UBound(rngXArray.Value)
    If (rngX.Value < rngXArray(intIndex)) Then
        Exit For
    End If
Next intIndex
'If it is less than 2 data points from either end of the table,
'reset the index to two points from the end.
If intIndex < 2 Then intIndex = 2
If intIndex > UBound(rngXArray.Value) - 2 Then
    intIndex = UBound(rngXArray.Value) - 2
End If
'Zero the summation variable.
CubicInterpolation = 0
'These loops calculate the terms in the Lagrangian form of
```

```
'the interpolation formula.
For intI = intIndex - 1 To intIndex + 2
   dblProd = 1
   For intJ = intIndex - 1 To intIndex + 2
      If (intI <> intJ) Then
         dblProd = dblProd * (rngX.Value - rngXArray(intJ))
            ➥ /(rngXArray(intI) - rngXArray(intJ))
      End If
   Next intJ
   CubicInterpolation = CubicInterpolation
         ➥ + dblProd * rngYArray(intI)
Next intI
End Function
'
'Use this procedure to run CubicInterpolation
'within the Module to test it.
'
Sub testit()
Dim scratch As Double
scratch = CubicInterpolation("a1", "a1", "a1")
End Sub
```

The worksheet should now look like Figure 6.15. If the worksheet did not recalculate, press F9 (Cmd+= on the Macintosh) to force a recalculation.

Note that the error has decreased by an order of magnitude over the linear interpolation value. This decrease may not seem so important, since the linear

FIGURE 6.15:

Linear and cubic interpolation of the steam-water saturation line

	A	B	C	D	E	F	G	H	I
1	Steam table: Saturated steam/water: Linear & Cubic Interpolation								
2									
3	Temp. (F)	Press (psia)			Linear Interpolation				
4	300	67		Temperture		Output Pressure			
5	320	90		Input	Index	Calc.	True	Error	
6	340	118		510	11	746.5	744	-0.336%	
7	360	153		520	12	812	812	0.000%	
8	380	196		302	1	69.3	69	-0.435%	
9	400	247		622	17	1814.3	1812.8	-0.083%	
10	420	309		538	12	947.9	946.9	-0.106%	
11	440	382		456	8	450	448.7	-0.290%	
12	460	467			Cubic Interpolation				
13	480	566		510		743.9375	744	0.008%	
14	500	681		520		812	812	0.000%	
15	520	812		302		69.132	69	-0.191%	
16	540	963		622		1812.929	1812.8	-0.007%	
17	560	1133		538		947.111	946.9	-0.022%	
18	580	1326		456		448.944	448.7	-0.054%	
19	600	1543							
20	620	1787							

Adjusters / fig. 6.14 / **fig. 6.15** / Interpolator / Sheet4 /

interpolation did well on this curve. On more nonlinear curves, however, the increase in accuracy may be needed. Also, the discontinuity in the derivative at the data points is much less severe with this type of interpolation.

Weighting

Weighting is a simple process that is often very confusing if you look at it strictly in terms of its implementation equations. Weighting is simply a way to indicate that some data points are more accurate than others. When fitting a curve to a weighted data set, you want to fit the heavily weighted points more closely than the less heavily weighted points.

When you weight a data point, you are effectively adding more points with the same value to the data set to be fit. In most algorithms, you multiply each data point by a weighting function and then multiply the number of points by the same factor. Weighting of this type must be a part of the solution algorithm, which we do not have access to in Excel. To weight a data point on a worksheet, simply duplicate the weighted points in proportion to the accuracy or importance of that point. The scale you use is not important as long as the relative weighting of the different data points is correct. For example, if you have two data points, and one is twice as accurate as the other, you can weight them by doubling the more accurate point, or you can double the less accurate point and quadruple the more accurate point (the result is the same).

Summary

In this chapter, you saw how to fit curves to data points. Simple linear curve fitting is accomplished with the built-in linear regression functions LINEST and LOGEST, or with the Regression Data Analysis add-in program. In many cases, even nonlinear equations can be fit by suitably transforming the variables to convert them into linear equations that can then be fit with the linear regression commands. In addition, the LINEST function can be used to perform polynomial regression to fit a data set with a polynomial.

If you are not planning to use the data in the worksheet, the Trendline feature for charts is available. The Trendline feature fits several different curves to a data set and displays the function fit to the data and its regression coefficients on the chart along with the curve.

For more complicated non-linear equations, you must use a steepest-descents algorithm to find the coefficients that make the equation best fit the data. While the steepest-descents algorithm can be done by hand, it can be automated with the Solver add-in or with a Visual Basic program.

When it is difficult or unreasonable to fit experimental data with a known function, you can use table lookup and interpolation functions. Table lookup and interpolation functions can be implemented either with worksheet functions or as a Visual Basic function.

Weighting is the process of stating that some data points are more accurate than others, and thus, a curve fit should fit them closer than other data points that have less weight. Weighting is implemented in the worksheet by duplicating the more accurate data points.

For More Information

Statistical Methods and t Tests

C. Lipson and N. J. Sheth, *Statistical Design and Analysis of Engineering Experiments* (New York: McGraw-Hill, 1973).

R. M. Bethea, B. S. Duran, and T. L. Boullion, *Statistical Methods for Scientists and Engineers* (New York: Marcel Dekker, 1975).

Thermal Conductivity in Gallium Arsenide

Maycock, "Thermal Conductivity of Silicon, Germanium, III-V Compounds and III-V Alloys," *Solid State Electronics 10* (1967): 161-168.

Electron Ionization Cross Sections

D. Rapp and P. Englander-Golden, "Total Cross Sections for Ionization and Attachment in Gases by Electron Impact: I. Positive Ionization," *J. Chem. Physics 43*, 5 (Sept. 1, 1965): 1464-1479.

Curve-Fitting Functions and Methods

C. Gerald, *Applied Numerical Analysis* (Reading, Mass: Addison-Wesley, 1978).

W. H. Press, et al., *Numerical Recipes: The Art of Scientific Computing* (Cambridge, Eng.: Cambridge University Press, 1986).

Steam Tables

C. A. Meyer, *Thermodynamic and Transport Properties of Steam* (New York: American Society of Mechanical Engineers, 1967).

Review Problems

1. The temperature dependence of the band gap in silicon is shown in the following table:

Temperature (K)	Band Gap (eV)	Temperature (K)	Band Gap (eV)
0	1.16	400	1.09
50	1.16	450	1.07
100	1.15	500	1.05
150	1.15	550	1.03
200	1.14	600	1.01
250	1.13	650	0.99
300	1.12	700	0.97
350	1.10	750	0.95
		800	0.92

Using linear regression, find the line that best fits this data and plot the data and the regression results.

2. Fit the data in problem 1 using a second-order polynomial regression and plot the results.

3. The temperature dependence of the band gap of silicon follows the equation

$$E_g = E_{g0} - \frac{AT^2}{(T+B)}$$

Where E_g is the energy gap; T is the temperature in Kelvin; and E_{g0}, A, and B are constants to be determined. This equation can be rewritten as a polynomial

$$\left[\frac{1}{E_{g0} - E_g}\right] = \frac{A}{B}\left[\frac{T}{E_{g0} - E_g}\right]^2 - \frac{1}{B}\left[\frac{T}{E_{g0} - E_g}\right]$$

E_{g0} is equal to the value of E_g at $T = 0$. Solve for the coefficients of this equation using polynomial regression. The solution will yield A/B and $1/B$, from which you can easily determine A and B. Plot the results.

4. Use the manual and automatic methods of coefficient adjusting to fit the data in problem 1 to the first equation in problem 3. Plot the results.

5. Do the manual adjustments example in the book (Figure 6.9). For integer values of B from 430 to 438, maximize the value of r^2 by adjusting only the value of A. Plot the values of r^2 versus the values of B. The three local maxima in that chart confuse the automatic search routines, which will find one, but not necessarily the largest, of them.

6. Use the data in problem 1 as a lookup table. Write a linear lookup function to interpolate the values of E_g for given values of T.

7. Complete problem 6 using cubic interpolation.

8. Fit a line to the steam table values of pressure versus temperature in Table 6.3. Calculate and plot the residual error (the difference between the regression curve and the data value) at each point.

9. Fit the steam table values of pressure versus temperature in Table 6.3 using polynomial regression. Try different orders of the regression and plot the results. Calculate and plot the residual error.

10. Use linear interpolation to calculate the value of the electron ionization cross section given in Table 6.2 for electrons with an energy of 524 eV.

11. Complete problem 10 using cubic interpolation.

Exercises

1. Plot the data in review problem 1, and fit it using the Trendline feature on the chart. Try different trendline curve types to see which one fits the best.

2. The following table shows the measured deflection versus position along the beam for a cantilever beam with a weight on the free end. Fit the data using linear regression formulas.

Location (in)	Deflection (in)	Location (in)	Deflection (in)
0	0.0000	84	0.9938
12	0.0245	96	1.2533
24	0.0951	108	1.5295
36	0.2077	120	1.8184
48	0.3581	132	2.1156
60	0.5420	144	2.4170
72	0.7553		

3. Fit the data in exercise 2 using polynomial regression. Be sure to check the coefficients of the fit to see if they are significant.

4. Using the data in exercise 2 and the beam description shown in Figure 2.15, fit the data to the equation for bending of the beam using Solver, and determine the magnitude of the weight on the end from the calculated coefficients.

5. The intrinsic carrier density versus temperature is given in the following table. Fit the data using the LOGEST function. How does this compare to the equations given in Chapter 2? Fit the data using polynomial regression. How does this compare to the equation?

Temperature (K)	Intrinsic carrier density (cm^{-3})	Temperature (K)	Intrinsic carrier density (cm^{-3})
300	6.21E+09	600	2.26E+15
350	2.18E+11	650	6.44E+15
400	3.28E+12	700	1.60E+16
450	2.79E+13	750	3.54E+16
500	1.58E+14	800	7.18E+16
550	6.70E+14		

6. Using the data in exercise 5, fit the data to the curve given in Chapter 2. How do the calculated coefficients compare to those given in Chapter 2?

7. Table 3.1 lists the temperature versus position in an overstressed silicon diode. Write a linear interpolation function that interpolates the temperature given a value of z and one of the fixed values of y (that is, interpolate along one of the columns in the table).

8. Do exercise 7 again but use cubic interpolation.

9. Using Table 3.1 again, write a two-dimensional linear interpolation function that returns the temperature for any arbitrary value of y and z. (Hint: Interpolate along two columns of the table using the value of z, then use those two results to interpolate for the value of y.)

10. Lookup the linear least squares algorithm with weighting, and implement it as a Visual Basic function. Input the data and the arbitrary weighting function as separate cell ranges and return the coefficients of the line and the value of r^2.

CHAPTER
SEVEN

Summing Series

- Extracting recursion relations

- Summing a series in cells

- Iterating a solution

- Calculating a solution with a procedure

7

Many important functions of science and engineering are available only as series formulas. Especially in areas where differential equations are involved, the solutions to those equations are often not available as closed-form equations, but only as series formulas. Bessel functions, Legendre polynomials, and Laguerre polynomials are examples of series solutions of differential equations.

With Excel, you can calculate the value of a series formula in three ways: the first way is to calculate the series term by term in the cells of the worksheet and then add them up; the second way is to write an iteration formula that calculates one term with each iteration of the worksheet and adds that term to the solution; the third, and most powerful, method is to write a Visual Basic function to calculate the series for any number of terms.

Summing a Series in the Worksheet

The simplest method you can use to sum a series is to calculate the terms in consecutive cells, and then add them up. While this method can use a lot of worksheet real estate if many terms are required, it is also the most intuitive as you can see the values of all the terms. Seeing these values gives you a better feel for how the series is calculating its result, and for when the series has converged.

Excel's built-in series-summing function, SERIESSUM, is limited to a series of the following form:

$$ssum = a_1 x^n + a_2 x^{(n+m)} + a_3 x^{(n+2m)} + \cdots$$

To use this function, you must supply an array that contains all the coefficients (a_i). If you need to create an array with all the coefficients, you might as well include the powers of x there as well, and not use the SERIESSUM function at all.

For most series, you can find a recursion relation for calculating a term using the previous term. A recursion relation is a multiplicative factor that, when multiplied times the value of a term in the series, gives the value of the next term. Using a recursion relation significantly reduces the number of calculations that Excel must perform to calculate the series. This is especially true when a series involves powers and factorials.

Bessel Functions

A Bessel function ($J_n(x)$) is the solution to Bessel's differential equation:

$$x^2 \frac{d^2 y}{dx^2} + x \frac{dy}{dx} + \left(x^2 - n^2\right)y = 0$$

with $y = J_n(x)$. Bessel's equation is encountered in many physical problems. For example, the solution of the wave equation in cylindrical coordinates results in Bessel's equation. Bessel functions are also solutions of a class of definite integrals with the following form:

$$J_n(x) = \frac{1}{\pi} \int_0^\pi \cos(nv - x\sin(v))dv$$

Although Bessel functions are defined for any value of n, the most commonly encountered values of n are integers. A series solution exists for Bessel functions with integer values of n:

$$J_n(x) = \sum_{s=0}^{\infty} \frac{(-1)^s}{s!(n+s)!}\left(\frac{x}{2}\right)^{n+2s} = \sum_{s=0}^{\infty} G_s(n,x)$$

For noninteger values of n, the gamma function, $\Gamma(n + s + 1)$ is substituted for the factorial, $(n + s)!$.

For the Bessel function, you can find the recursion relation for the terms ($G_s(n,x)$) of the series by inspection:

$$G_s(n,x) = G_{s-1}(n,x)\frac{(-1)}{s(n+s)}\left(\frac{x}{2}\right)^2$$

$$G_0 = \frac{x^n}{2^n n!}$$

Using this recursion relation, you need only calculate a factorial in the first term (G_0). The rest of the terms in the series are calculated without calculating another factorial. Each term is created from the previous term by multiplying by the recursion factor above.

In the next example, calculate values of the Bessel function with integral values of n. You need only sum the first ten terms to get less than one percent error for values of x up to about seven or eight. Additionally, Excel has an add-in function, BESSELJ, which also calculates the value of Bessel functions. Use it to check the accuracy of your calculations.

1. Start with a new worksheet, and name it **fig. 7.1**

2. Set the width of column A to 14.

3. In cell A1, enter **Bessel Function; Worksheet summation method**

Now put in n, $n!$, and x.

4. In cells A4, B2, and B3, enter the labels **x**, **n**, and **n!**, respectively, and right-align them.

5. Name cell C2 as **N**, C3 as **NF**, and B4 as **X**

6. Enter **=FACT(N)** in cell C3.

Insert the BESSELJ add-in function. Note that you can use only discrete values or cell references with the add-in function; you cannot use named ranges. Enter a summation formula to add up all the terms.

7. In cell A5, enter **BESSELJ(X,N)** and right-align it.

8. In cell B5, enter the formula

      =BESSELJ(X,N)

9. In cell A6, enter **Jn(x)** and right-align it.

10. In cell B6, enter **=SUM(B8:B18)**

Calculate the first ten terms of the series for the values of the summation variable s. In cell B8, insert the value of the zero-order term. In cells B9:B18, use the recursion relation to calculate the different terms.

11. In cell A7, enter **s** and right-justify it.

12. In cell B7, enter **Terms** and right-justify it.

13. In cell B8, enter **=B4^N/(2^N*NF)**

14. In cell B9, enter **=B8*(–1)*X^2/(4*$A9*(N+$A9))** and copy it to cells B10:B18.

15. In cell A8, enter **0**, and in cell A9, enter **1**

16. Select cells A8:A9, and drag the fill handle down to cell A18 to create the ten *s* values.

17. Format cells B8:B18 as Scientific, with two decimal places.

18. Turn off the gridlines.

To use the worksheet, put the value of *x* (0.5, for example), up to a maximum of 8, in cell B5, and the value for *n* (1, for example) in cell C2. When the worksheet is updated, the value of the Bessel function is in cells B5 and B6. Note that the size of the terms in cells B8:B18 decreases rapidly, indicating rapid convergence of the series. Your worksheet should now look like Figure 7.1.

FIGURE 7.1:

Bessel function using the worksheet summation method

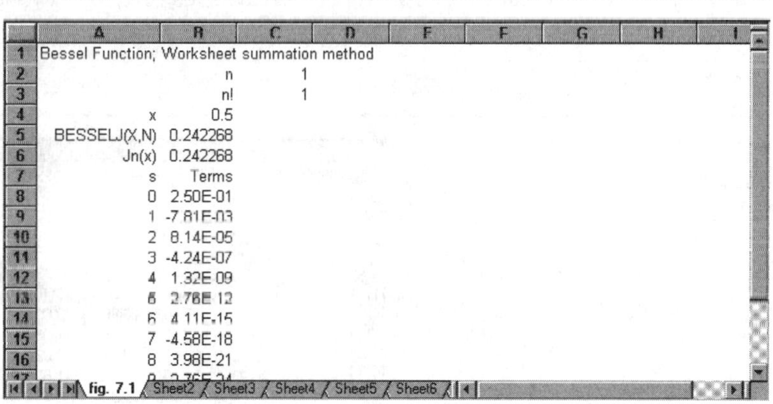

Using this format, you can calculate the Bessel function for a whole set of *x* values. Note that the appropriate parts of the cell references have been made absolute, so that the formulas in cells B8:B18 can be copied into the cells to their right and still reference the correct cells.

1. Make a copy worksheet fig. 7.1 and name it **fig. 7.2**

2. Copy cells B4:B18 into C4:AB18.

3. In cell B4, enter **0**, and in cell C4, enter **0.3**

4. Select cells B4:C4, and drag the fill handle to cell AB4.

5. Name cells B4:AB4 as **x**

6. Change the formula in cell B5 to **=BESSELJ(B4,N)** and copy it to cells B5:AB5.

> **NOTE**
>
> You have to change the argument here because the add-in function does not correctly select a value from the array of values named X. If you pass it the array, it accepts the whole array instead of only the value in the same column as the formula, generating an error.

Your worksheet should now look like Figure 7.2. If the worksheet didn't recalculate, press F9 (Cmd+= on the Macintosh.) Here you have calculated the Bessel function for *n* = 1 and for a series of *x* values up to 7.8. Figure 7.3 is a chart of those values. If you want to calculate the Bessel function for larger values of *x* or increase the accuracy for the current values of *x*, you must increase the number of terms in the series.

FIGURE 7.2:

Bessel function for multiple values of *x*

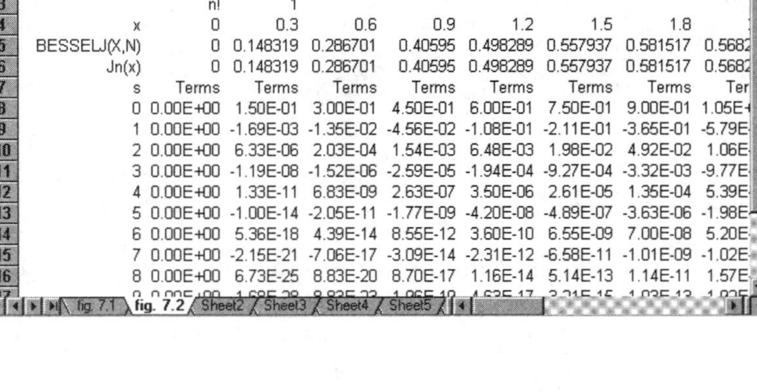

FIGURE 7.3:

A line chart of Bessel function $J_1(x)$

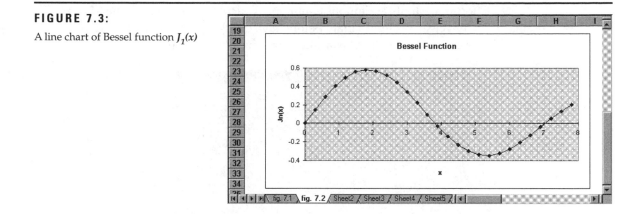

Iterating a Series in the Worksheet

The second method of calculating a series in a worksheet is to use the worksheet's iteration capabilities. The formulas in the worksheet are written such that each time the worksheet is recalculated, the next term in the series is calculated and added to the total. To do this, you must turn off automatic recalculation and switch to worksheet iteration. You must also add a reset capability to set the initial values for the summation and the terms.

Perform the Bessel function calculation again, but use worksheet iteration to calculate the terms instead of listing the terms in separate cells.

1. Start with a copy of worksheet fig. 7.1 and name it **fig. 7.4**

2. Select and delete the contents of cells A10:B18.

3. Select cells A7:B9 and move them to cells A9:B11.

4. In cell A7, enter **First Term** and right-align it.

5. In cell A8, enter **Initialize** and right-align it.

6. In cell B7, enter **=B4^N/(2^N*NF)**

7. In cell B8, enter **True**

8. Name cells B7 and B8 as **Term0** and **INIT**

9. Choose the Tools ➤ Options command, Calculation tab; select the Manual option, clear the Recalculate Before Save checkbox, check the Iteration checkbox, and set the Maximum Iterations to 1; then click OK.

10. In cell A10, enter **=A11**

11. In cell A11, enter **=IF(INIT,0,A10+1)**

12. In cell B10, enter **=B11**

13. In cell B11, enter the formula

    =IF(INIT,Term0,B10*(−1)*X^2/(4*$A11*(N+$A11)))

14. In cell C9, enter **Summation**

15. In cell C10, enter **=C11**

16. In cell C11, enter **=IF(INIT,B7,C10+B11)**

17. In cell B6, enter **=C11**

18. Format cells B5:B6 and C10:C11 as Number, with four decimal places.

To use this worksheet: insert values for x and n, and press F9 (Crtl+= on the Macintosh) to intitialize the worksheet; then change B8 to False and press F9 again, once for each term you want to add to the series. The term number is in cell A10, the value

FIGURE 7.4:

Calculating the Bessel function series by iterating the worksheet

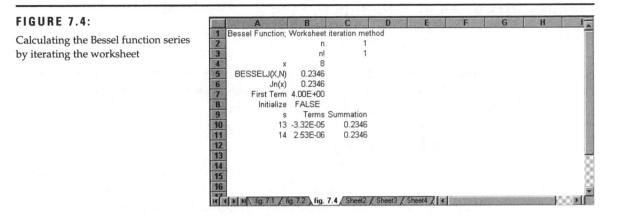

of the next term to be added to the series is in cell B11, and the current value of the series is in cell C11 and duplicated in cell B6. Figure 7.4 shows the result of using 8 for x, 1 for n and iterating the worksheet 14 times.

The worksheet operates by creating three circular references: between cells A10 and A11, B10 and B11, and C10 and C11. The formulas in cells A10:C10 store the current value of the formula while the formulas in cells A11:C11 use that value to calculate the next iterate number, term, and summation. The IF functions in cells A11:C11 initialize the calculation whenever INIT (B8) is True.

To calculate a new value with this setup: change x and n, change B8 to True, press F9, change B8 to False, and repeatedly press F9 until the summation converges.

> **NOTE**
>
> You can iterate the worksheet multiple times with each press of F9, by changing the value of Maximum Iterations in the Calculation dialog box to a value larger than 1. The worksheet will be iterated that number of times, or until all changes in values on the worksheet are less than the value in the Maximum Change box. Be careful, though   the value in the Maximum Change box is a value, not a fraction. If the value you are calculating is small, the value of Maximum change must be smaller by the number of decimal places you want in your result.

Using a Visual Basic Function to Sum a Series

You can also write a Visual Basic procedure to calculate the value of a series summation. The algorithm is the same as you would use to calculate the series summation in any high-level language such as Fortran.

Legendre Polynomials

Legendre polynomials ($Pn(x)$) are often encountered in central-force problems (such as electromagnetics) defined in spherical coordinates. For example, an electric dipole consists of two charges of magnitude $+q$ and $-q$, located at $+a$ and $-a$ in a spherical coordinate system. The potential (ϕ) due to this dipole at large distances ($r > a$) from the dipole is described with a Legendre polynomial:

$$\Phi = \frac{2aq}{4\pi\varepsilon} \frac{P_1(\cos(\theta))}{r^2}$$

where ε is the free space dielectric constant, and r and θ are the coordinates in a spherical polar coordinate system.

Legendre polynomials are solutions of the differential equation:

$$\left(1 - x^2\right)\frac{d^2 y}{dx^2} - 2x\frac{d^2 y}{dx^2} + n(n+1)y = 0$$

with $y = Pn(x)$. The series representation of the Legendre polynomials is:

$$P_n(x) = \sum_{s=0}^{n/2} \frac{(-1)^s (2n - 2s)!}{2^n\, s!(n-s)!(n-2s)!} x^{n-2s}$$

which has a finite number of terms in the summation.

In the following example, create a Visual Basic function to calculate the series formula above. Explicitly calculate the factorials for each term, rather than using a term recursion relation.

1. Insert a new module sheet, and name it **Functions**

2. Type the following procedures into the module:

```
Option Explicit
'
' Function to calculate Legendre Polynomials.
'
Function Legendre(dblX As Double, intN As Integer) As Variant
Dim intS As Integer 'The summation counter.
'Zero the summation variable.
Legendre = 0
'Loop over the number of terms needed to calculate the sum.
For intS = 0 To intN \ 2
    Legendre = Legendre + (((-1) ^ intS) * Fact(2 * intN - 2
    ➥* intS)* dblX ^ (intN - 2 * intS)) / (2 ^ intN * Fact(intS)
    ➥* Fact(intN - intS) * Fact(intN - 2 * intS))
Next intS
End Function
'
' Function to calculate the factorial of the argument.
'
Function Fact(intM As Integer) As Double
Dim intCtr As Integer
'Initialize the product.
Fact = 1
'Loop over the terms, multiplying out each.
For intCtr = 1 To intM
    Fact = Fact * intCtr
Next intCtr
End Function
'
' A short Sub to use while testing
'
Sub test1
Dim intN As Integer
Dim dblX As Double
'Pick some test values
intN = 3
dblX = 0.3
'Print the values and the results in the debug window.
Debug.Print dblX, intN, Legendre(dblX, intN),
    ➥0.5 * (5 * dblX ^ 3 - 3 * dblX)
Stop
End Sub
```

There are three procedures here: one to calculate the Legendre polynomial, one to calculate the factorial, and a short test procedure to use during debugging. The debugging procedure is needed because syntax errors are not announced on the worksheet when they occur in a called function; they just cause error values to be returned. By testing within the same module as the function, you will see any syntax errors that occur. The test procedure writes the values of x, n, Legendre(x,n), and the analytical value for $n = 2$.

In this case, the series has a finite number of terms, with a fixed upper limit of $n/2$. Thus, you know how many terms to calculate to get the correct value. For a series with an infinite number of terms, you must decide when to stop adding terms. You can pick some fixed number of terms that produces accurate results over the range of arguments you are interested in, such as you did with the Bessel function. Alternatively, you can put some logic in the function to watch the size of each term as it is added and to stop calculating when it becomes insignificant.

Now create a worksheet to call the function for several values of n and x. As a comparison, here are the analytical solutions for the first six Legendre polynomials:

$$P_0(x) = 1$$
$$P_1(x) = x$$
$$P_2(x) = (1/2)(3x^2 - 1)$$
$$P_3(x) = (1/2)(5x^3 - 3x)$$
$$P_4(x) = (1/8)(35x^4 - 30x^2 + 3)$$
$$P_5(x) = (1/8)(63x^5 - 70x^3 + 15x)$$

Calculate these solutions as well and compare them with the results from the function.

First, put in some values of x and n to calculate.

1. Select a new worksheet and name it **fig. 7.5**

2. In cell A1, enter **Legendre Polynomials; Visual Basic Function**

3. In cells A3 and A4, type **n** and **x** respectively, and right-align them.

NOTE   You could name cells A3 and A4 as n and x here, but doing so in the normal manner would replace the ones already defined on other sheets. You must create a local name, valid only on this sheet. To make the name local, choose the Insert ➤ Name ➤ Define command and enter the sheet name followed by a ! followed by the name in the Names in Workbook box. Insert the definition and click OK. The name is then only valid in that sheet.

4. In cells B3:G3, enter the integers **0** through **5**

5. In cell B4, enter **0.3** and copy it to cells C4:G4.

Next, put in the calls to the Visual Basic function. The simplest way to ensure that you do it correctly is to use the Function Wizard and select the function from the User Defined section of the dialog box. Following the Visual Basic function solution, put in the analytic solutions shown earlier.

6. In cell A5, enter **Pn(x)** and right-align it.

7. In cell B5, enter (or insert with the Function Wizard) =**Legendre(B4,B3)** and copy it to cells C5:G5.

8. In cell A6, enter **Analytic** and right-align it.

9. Make the following entries in cells B6:G6:

B6	=1	E6 =0.5*(5*E4^3–3*E4)
C6	=C4	F6 =0.125*(35*F4^4–30*F4^2+3)
D6	=0.5"(3"D4^2–1)	G6 =0.125"(63"G4^5–70"G4^3+15"G4)

As you can see in Figure 7.5, the analytic values and Visual Basic function values match. Now create a table of values as shown at the bottom of the figure and plot the results. First, put in a range of x values.

1. In cell A8, enter **0** and in cell A9, enter **0.3**

2. Select cells A8:A9, and drag the fill handle to cell A30.

FIGURE 7.5:

Legendre polynomials calculated with a Visual Basic function

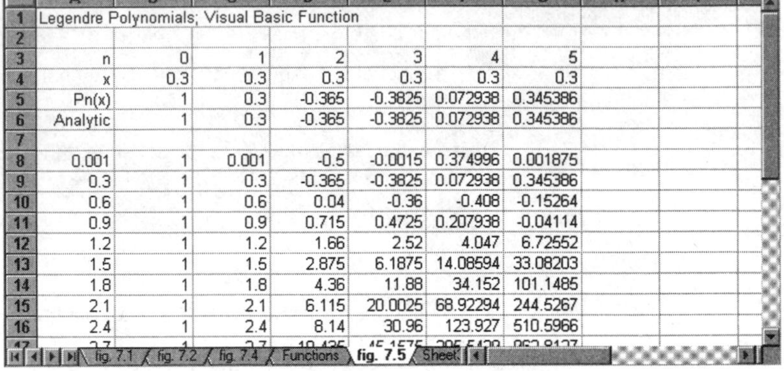

	A	B	C	D	E	F	G	H	I
1	Legendre Polynomials; Visual Basic Function								
2									
3	n	0	1	2	3	4	5		
4	x	0.3	0.3	0.3	0.3	0.3	0.3		
5	Pn(x)	1	0.3	-0.365	-0.3825	0.072938	0.345386		
6	Analytic	1	0.3	-0.365	-0.3825	0.072938	0.345386		
7									
8	0.001	1	0.001	-0.5	-0.0015	0.374996	0.001875		
9	0.3	1	0.3	-0.365	-0.3825	0.072938	0.345386		
10	0.6	1	0.6	0.04	-0.36	-0.408	-0.15264		
11	0.9	1	0.9	0.715	0.4725	0.207938	-0.04114		
12	1.2	1	1.2	1.66	2.52	4.047	6.72552		
13	1.5	1	1.5	2.875	6.1875	14.08594	33.08203		
14	1.8	1	1.8	4.36	11.88	34.152	101.1485		
15	2.1	1	2.1	6.115	20.0025	68.92294	244.5267		
16	2.4	1	2.4	8.14	30.96	123.927	510.5966		

fig. 7.1 / fig. 7.2 / fig. 7.4 / Functions \ **fig. 7.5** / Sheet

Next, change the first *x* value to a small number other than 0, because the function is not defined at *x*=0, and copy the function reference to the Visual Basic function into the body of the table.

3. Change cell A8 to **0.001**

4. In cell B8, enter **=Legendre($A8,B$3)**

5. Copy cell B8 into cells B8:G30 by first copying it down column B to B30, then copying across to column G.

6. Calculation is still set to manual, so press F9 (Cmd+= on the Macintosh) to recalculate the worksheet.

The worksheet should now look like Figure 7.5. If you plot the values in the table, you get the chart shown in Figure 7.6.

SHORTCUT

The series on the bottom of the chart overlap each other, making it hard to select a single series so that you can add a legend. To quickly move from one data series on the chart to another, select a series by clicking on it and use the arrow keys to move from series to series.

FIGURE 7.6:

The first six orders of the Legendre polynomials

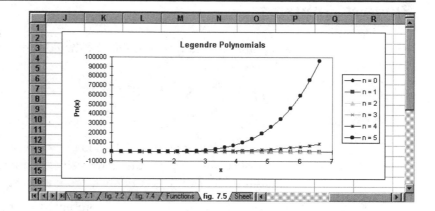

Summary

In this chapter, we looked at three methods for summing a series with a worksheet. The simplest is to calculate the series term by term in the cells of the worksheet and then add the terms together. The second method is to create an iterative worksheet function in which each time you iterate the worksheet, a new term is added to the series. The most conventional method is to write a Visual Basic function to calculate the series for any number of terms. A Visual Basic function doesn't use much worksheet area, and you can increase the number of terms calculated by simply changing a number. Unfortunately, it is not as intuitive since you can not see all of the terms on the worksheet.

For More Information

Bessel Functions and Legendre Polynomials

G. Arfken, *Mathematical Methods for Physicists* Orlando, Fla.: Academic Press, 1970, pp. 438, 537.

Review Problems

1. A square wave can be described by the Fourier series

$$f(x) = \frac{4}{\pi} \sum_{n=1,3,5,\ldots} \frac{1}{n} \sin\left(\frac{n\pi x}{L}\right)$$

   where L is the half period of the square wave. Sum the series using the spreadsheet method and plot it for values of x where $0 \leq x \leq 2L$ and $L = 1$. Use enough values of x to accurately represent the square wave.

2. A saw-toothed function can be represented by the Fourier series

$$f(x) = \frac{2}{\pi} \sum_{n=1}^{\infty} \frac{(-1)^{n+1}}{n} \sin\left(\frac{n\pi x}{L}\right)$$

   Create a Visual Basic function and a worksheet to calculate $f(x)$ for a range of values of x where $0 \leq x \leq 2L$ and $L = 3$. Plot the function.

3. The natural logarithm can be calculated using the series representation for values of x between 0 and 2

$$\ln(1 + x) = \sum_{n=1}^{\infty} \frac{(-1)^{n+1} x^n}{n}$$

   Use the worksheet iteration method to sum this series and calculate the value of $\ln(1.7)$.

4. Calculate the cosine of 2.85 radians using this series formula and the worksheet method:

$$\cos(x) = \sum_{n=0}^{\infty} \frac{x^{2n}(-1)^n}{(2n)!}$$

   Compare the result to the value of =COS(2.85) found with the cosine function.

5. The arccosine is calculated by the series

$$\arccos(x) = \frac{\pi}{2} - \left(x + \frac{1}{2 \cdot 3} x^3 + \frac{1 \cdot 3}{2 \cdot 4 \cdot 5} x^5 + \frac{1 \cdot 3 \cdot 5}{2 \cdot 4 \cdot 6 \cdot 7} x^7 + \ldots \right)$$

Write a Visual Basic function to calculate the arccosine, and then use it to calculate the arccosine of 0.85.

6. The following Fourier series produces a positive square pulse at $x = L/4$ of width c, and a negative square pulse at $x = 7L/4$ of width c:

$$f(x) = \frac{4}{\pi} \sum_{n=1}^{\infty} \frac{1}{n} \sin\left(\frac{n\pi}{4} \right) \sin\left(\frac{n\pi c}{2L} \right) \sin\left(\frac{n\pi x}{L} \right)$$

Let $L = 2$ and $c = 0.25$. Calculate and plot $f(x)$ for $0 \le x \le 2L$.

7. The Chebyshev polynomials $T_n(x)$ and $U_n(x)$ are defined by the series

$$T_n(x) = x^n - \binom{n}{2} x^{n-2} \left(1 - x^2 \right) + \binom{n}{4} x^{n-4} \left(1 - x^2 \right)^2 - \binom{n}{6} x^{n-6} \left(1 - x^2 \right)^6 + \ldots$$

$$U_n(x) = \binom{n+1}{1} x^n - \binom{n+1}{3} x^{n-2} \left(1 - x^2 \right) + \binom{n+1}{5} x^{n-4} \left(1 - x^2 \right)^2 + \ldots$$

where

$$\binom{p}{n} = \frac{p(p-1)(p-2)\ldots(p-n+1)}{1 \cdot 2 \cdot 3 \cdots n} = \frac{p!}{(p-n)!n!}, \quad p > n-1$$

$$\binom{p}{n} = 0, \quad n < n$$

Calculate $T_3(5)$ and $U_3(5)$ and compare the results to the exact results calculated by

$$T_3(x) = 4x^3 - 3x, \qquad U_3(x) = 8x^3 - 4x$$

8. The Hermite polynomials $H_n(x)$ are defined by

$$H_n(x) = 2^n x^n - 2^{n-1}\binom{n}{2}x^{n-2} + 2^{n-2}1\cdot3\binom{n}{4}x^{n-4} - 2^{n-3}1\cdot3\cdot5\binom{n}{6}x^{n-6} + \ldots$$

Calculate $H_4(7)$ and compare the result to the exact results calculated by

$$H_4(x) = 16x^4 - 48x^2 + 12$$

9. The Laguerre polynomials $L^a_n(x)$ are defined by

$$L^a_n(x) = \sum_{m=0}^{n}(-1)^m\binom{n+a}{n-m}\frac{x^m}{m!}$$

Calculate $L^0_2(2.3)$.

10. The Bernoulli polynomials $B_n(x)$ for $0 \le x \le 1$ are defined by

$$B_{2n}(x) = \frac{(-1)^{n-1}2(2n)!}{(2\pi)^{2n}}\sum_{k=1}^{\infty}\frac{\cos(2k\pi x)}{k^{2n}}$$

Calculate $B_4(13)$ and compare the result with the exact result calculated by

$$B_4(x) = x^4 - 2x^3 + x^2 - 1/30$$

Exercises

1. Write a Visual Basic procedure to calculate the square wave series in Review Problem 1. Calculate a list of values and plot them.

2. Redo Review problem 2 using worksheet iteration.

3. The exponential is given with the following equation:

$$Exp(x) = 1 + x + \frac{x^2}{2!} + \frac{x^3}{3!} + \cdots$$

   Calculate the exponential of 3.7 using the worksheet method. Compare the result to that given by EXP(3.7).

4. Recalculate exercise 3 using the iterated worksheet method.

5. Jacobi's polynomials are given by the following equation:

$$P_n^{(\alpha,\beta)}(x) = \frac{1}{2^n} \sum_{m=0}^{n} \binom{n+\alpha}{m}\binom{n+\beta}{n-m}(x-1)^{n-m}(x+1)^m$$

   Calculate and plot a set of curves for x = 0 to 6, n = 0, 1, 2, 3, and 4, and for α = 2 and β = 3. Use the worksheet method.

6. Redo exercise 5 using a Visual Basic function to calculate the value of Jacobi's polynomials.

7. For $z^2 < 1$, the following relation holds.

$$\frac{1}{1-z} = \sum_{n=0}^{\infty} z^n$$

   Verify that the relation holds by calculating both sides of the equation for several values of x between –1 and 1, and comparing the results. Use the worksheet method to calculate the series.

8. The following relation holds for any value of a:

$$a^x = 1 + x\ln(a) + \frac{(xLn(a))^2}{2!} + \frac{(xLn(a))^3}{3!} + \cdots$$

Verify that the relation holds by calculating both sides of the equation for several values of a and comparing the results. Use the iterated worksheet method to calculate the series.

9. The Tangent of x for $x^2 < \pi^2/4$ is given by the following series formula:

$$Tan(x) = x + \frac{x^3}{3} + \frac{2x^5}{15} + \frac{17x^7}{315} + \frac{62x^9}{2835} + \cdots + \frac{2^{2n}\left(2^{2n}-1\right)|B_{2n}|x^{2n-1}}{(2n)!} + \cdots$$

where B_n are the Bernoulli numbers. Bernoulli numbers are calculated from Bernoulli polynomials with $x = 0$ (see Review Problem 10). Use the worksheet method to calculate the tangent of 0.8 radians.

10. Calculate the last exercise again using a Visual Basic function.

CHAPTER

EIGHT

Performing Differentiation and Integration

- Differencing formulas for calculating the derivative

- Rectangle rule integration

- Trapezoid rule integration

- Romberg integration

- Simpson's rule integration

- Gaussian quadrature integration

8

Differentiation and integration are usually performed on analytical equations; however, if a function exists only as a set of discrete data points, or if the integral of a function does not exist or is difficult to determine, you must use numerical differencing and integration techniques to calculate derivatives and integrals.

You can use Excel to calculate numerical derivatives and to numerically integrate data and functions. The techniques shown here are usually applied with short computer programs, but they can easily be applied in a worksheet format. In a worksheet, you can also see the intermediate results, which can often be enlightening (or scary).

Calculating Numerical Derivatives

Differentiation of discrete data (or functions that are troublesome to work out) can be done with difference formulas. Central difference formulas are the most accurate and the most popular. Forward and backward differences are used in special situations.

Types of Difference Formulas

Forward, backward, and central differences predict the derivative at a point based on different sets of data. Forward differences predict the derivative at a point using data points that come after the point in question. Backward differences are the same, except that they use the points that come before the point in question. Central differences use an equal number of data points before and after the point in question; thus, they give a more balanced prediction of the derivative for relatively continuous data.

Forward and backward differences are useful at the boundaries of a data set where a central difference cannot be calculated. A central difference requires an equal number of data points on each side of the point in question. At a boundary, data points exist only within the boundary and not outside of it, making it impossible to implement a central difference formula there. Forward and backward differences are also often more accurate representations of the true derivative in data that has sharp changes, because they reduce the effect of the change on the derivative for points at the change. You would use backward differences as you approach a sharp change and forward differences after you have passed it.

The equation for the first derivative is the same for forward, backward, and central differences. The difference between them is the value of x at which they are predicting the derivative. For example, the basic approximation formula for the first derivative is:

$$\frac{dy}{dx} = \frac{y_2 - y_1}{h}$$

where $h = x_1 - x_0 = x_0 - x_{-1}$ is the separation between the data points, and (x_{-1}, y_{-1}), (x_0, y_0) and (x_1, y_1) are consecutive pairs of x-y data. The type of difference calculated depends on where the derivative is being approximated:

- If this equation is an approximation for the derivative at x_1, it is a backward difference.

- If it is an approximation for the derivative at x_1, it is a forward difference.

- If it is an approximation for the derivative at x_0, it is a central difference.

The following are the difference formulas for the first few derivatives and the order ($O(h^n)$) of the error associated with them. The formulas all calculate the derivative at the point x_0. The order of the error is the power (n) of the separation between the data points (h) to which the error is proportional. Use this order to check the relative accuracy of the formulas. The higher the power of h, the more accurate the formula.

Derivative at x_0	Error	Difference Type
$\dfrac{dy}{dx} = \dfrac{y_1 - y_0}{h}$	$O(h)$	Forward
$\dfrac{dy}{dx} = \dfrac{y_0 - y_{-1}}{h}$	$O(h)$	Backward
$\dfrac{dy}{dx} = \dfrac{y_1 - y_{-1}}{2h}$	$O(h^2)$	Central
$\dfrac{d^2y}{dx^2} = \dfrac{y_2 - 2y_1 + y_0}{h^2}$	$O(h)$	Forward
$\dfrac{d^2y}{dx^2} = \dfrac{y_0 - 2y_{-1} + y_{-2}}{h^2}$	$O(h)$	Backward
$\dfrac{d^2y}{dx^2} = \dfrac{y_1 - 2y_0 + y_{-1}}{h^2}$	$O(h^2)$	Central
$\dfrac{d^3y}{dx^3} = \dfrac{y_3 - 3y_2 + 3y_1 - y_0}{h^3}$	$O(h)$	Forward
$\dfrac{d^3y}{dx^3} = \dfrac{y_0 - 3y_{-1} + 3y_{-2} - y_{-3}}{h^3}$	$O(h)$	Backward
$\dfrac{d^3y}{dx^3} = \dfrac{y_2 - 2y_1 + 2y_{-1} - y_{-2}}{2h^3}$	$O(h^2)$	Central

Errors in Difference Formulas

Difference formulas can have truncation and round-off errors. The order of the error shown with the equations above is for truncation error. Truncation error results from predicting the derivative with a few discrete data points rather than a continuous function. Since truncation error is proportional to the separation of the data points (h), it would seem that if you decreased h you would decrease the error; however, this is true only to the point where round-off error becomes significant.

Round-off error results from the fact that a computer stores numbers with a fixed number of digits. When two nearly equal numbers are subtracted, the difference can be quite small, and you need to test the result to see if it is significant. Divide this difference into one of the original numbers and see how many digits are to the left of the decimal. If the number of digits is comparable to or more than the number of digits in the computer's numbers, the difference is meaningless, and will produce meaningless results if used. For example, if two numbers with values near 1 are subtracted, and the difference is on the order of 1×10^{-14} on a machine with 14 digits of accuracy, the difference is meaningless. Thus, round-off error increases with decreasing h *at the same time that truncation error is decreasing*. This means that you need to consider the trade-off between decreasing h to reduce truncation error and increasing h to reduce round-off error. Some optimum, nonzero value of h will minimize the total error.

Using Difference Formulas in a Worksheet

The difference formulas shown above are relatively simple, so the best way to apply them to a data set is in the worksheet, rather than by writing a Visual Basic function. In the worksheet, you can keep an eye on the scatter in the differences to see if the truncation error is growing.

Free Fall

A classic experiment in college freshman physics is on uniformly accelerated motion in free fall. It is performed by dropping a metal weight along a strip of waxed paper. High-voltage alternating current is applied across the weight and a wire behind the paper. At every half-cycle of the power supply, a spark is generated between the weight and the wire. The spark burns a small hole in the paper, marking the position of the weight as it falls. By knowing the frequency of the power supply and the distance between the holes in the paper, you can calculate the velocity and acceleration of the weight.

The following data is from such a free-fall experiment. The sparks were generated at a rate of 60 per second, making the holes in the paper 1/60 of a second apart. To calculate the velocity, you need the first derivative of this data. To calculate the acceleration due to gravity, you need the second derivative, which should be a constant.

The values represent distance of the holes from an arbitrary starting point (in centimeters):

0.00	7.55	19.50	35.75
1.55	10.20	23.15	40.55
3.25	13.05	27.05	45.55
5.30	16.15	31.30	50.80

Enter some titles and the time between sparks that generated the holes in the paper.

1. Start with a new worksheet, and name it **fig. 8.1**

2. In cell A1, enter **Free Fall**

3. In cell C1, enter ΔT = and right-align it.

> **NOTE** The Δ symbol is created using a capital D in the Symbol font.

4. In cell D1, enter **=1/60** and name the cell **DT**

5. In cell E1, enter **sec.**

Label the column headings.

6. In cells A3:D3, enter the labels **t**, **x**, **dx/dt**, and $\mathbf{d^2x/dt^2}$ and right-align them.

7. In cells A4:D4, enter the labels **(s)**, **(cm)**, **(cm/s)**, and $\mathbf{(cm/s^2)}$ and right-align them.

Calculate the time in column A. Note that zero time in this table does not imply zero velocity at the first data point. In the experiment, I skipped the first few data points because they were not clear enough to read accurately. Put the free-fall data in column B.

8. Enter **0** in cell A5.

9. In cell A6, enter =A5+DT and copy it to cells A7:A20.

10. In cells B5:B20, enter the free-fall data listed above.

In column C, calculate the first derivative of the data using a central difference centered on the interval between two points. In column D, calculate the second derivative using a central difference centered on each point. Average the acceleration found in column D.

> **NOTE** Instead of using a second derivative central difference formula to calculate the acceleration, you could also use a first derivative formula applied to the velocity data. The result will be identical.

11. In cell C5, enter =(B6–B5)/DT and copy it to cells C6:C19.

12. In cell D6, enter =(B7–2*B6+B5)/(DT^2) and copy it to cells D6:D19.

13. In cell C2, enter **Ave. =** and right-align it.

14. In cell D2, enter **=AVERAGE(D5:D19)**

15. In cell E2, enter **cm/s^2**

16. Format cells B5:D20 and D2 as Number, with two decimal places, and cells A5:A20 as Number, with four decimal places.

17. Turn off the worksheet gridlines.

Your worksheet should now look like Figure 8.1, without the regression output in cells F5:G15 (which will be added in a moment). Column C contains the velocity of the weight, which is plotted in Figure 8.2. As expected, this appears to be uniformly accelerated motion, with a relatively smooth curve.

Since the object is freely falling, the acceleration in column D should be a constant and equal to the acceleration due to gravity (980 cm/s^2). As you can see in the worksheet and in the chart in Figure 8.3, there is a tremendous amount of scatter in the data, although the average gives a reasonable value (951.43 cm/s^2).

FIGURE 8.1:

Uniformly accelerated motion:
numerical differentiation

	A	B	C	D	E	F	G	I	J
1	Free Fall			ΔT =	0.016667 sec.				
2				Ave. =	951.4286 cm/s²				
3	t	x	dx/dt	d²x/dt²					
4	(s)	(cm)	(cm/s)	(cm/s²)		Regression Output			
5	0.0000	0.00	93.00			Regression Output			
6	0.0167	1.55	102.00	540.00		Offset	89.65		
7	0.0333	3.25	123.00	1260.00		Std. Err.	1.326619		
8	0.0500	5.30	135.00	720.00		Slope	973.2857		
9	0.0667	7.55	159.00	1440.00		StdErr.	9.676316		
10	0.0833	10.20	171.00	720.00		r²	0.998717		
11	0.1000	13.05	186.00	900.00		F	10117.21		
12	0.1167	16.15	201.00	900.00		SS-Reg	73677.73		
13	0.1333	19.50	219.00	1080.00		SS-Resid	94.67143		
14	0.1500	23.15	234.00	900.00		Std. Err. y	2.698595		
15	0.1667	27.05	255.00	1260.00		DOF	13		
16	0.1833	31.30	267.00	720.00					

Graphics / **fig. 8.1** / Gamma / fig. 8.5 / fig. 8.6 / Gamma

FIGURE 8.2:

Uniformly accelerated motion:
velocity of the free-falling object

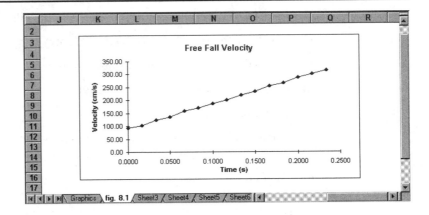

Graphics \ **fig. 8.1** / Sheet3 / Sheet4 / Sheet5 / Sheet6

FIGURE 8.3:

Uniformly accelerated motion:
acceleration of the free-falling object

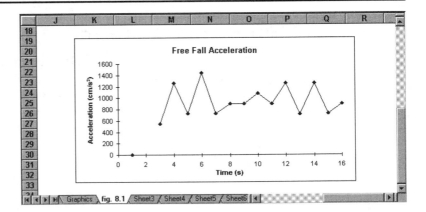

Graphics \ **fig. 8.1** / Sheet3 / Sheet4 / Sheet5 / Sheet6

Taking the average of differences may not give you what you expect. If you insert the difference formulas into the formula for an average, you will find that the average of a series of difference formulas is based on only the first two and last two data points, and completely ignores those in the middle.

In the acceleration calculation, the random experimental error is magnified each time you take the difference. This happens because you are taking the difference of data that contains random error. When you subtract two numbers of similar size, the result is smaller than the original numbers; however, the magnitude of the error is unchanged by the subtraction because it is random. For example, if x_1 contains Δx error and x_2 is a similarly sized number with no error, the difference between the two is:

$$(x_1 + \Delta x) - x_2 = (x_1 - x_2) + \Delta x$$

The result contains the small difference $x_2 - x_1$, plus the same amount of error as was in the original number. You might wonder about the situations when both numbers have the same amount of error—wouldn't the error in the difference cancel completely? Yes it would, but for random error, there are an equal number of possibilities where the errors are equal but opposite in sign, in which case the error in the difference doubles. The result is that you have the same average magnitude of error in smaller numbers, which makes the percent error increase with each subtraction. To find the second derivative, you subtract the differences, and this increases the relative magnitude of the error even more.

If you know that the error in a data set is all of the same magnitude and sign, it is systematic error instead of random error. Systematic error is reduced significantly by taking the difference.

Experimental data is usually smoothed before a reasonable approximation of the derivative can be calculated. A good way to smooth the data is to fit a known curve to the data and to take the derivative of that curve. But be careful not to smooth out any important details. You know that this should be uniformly accelerated motion, and the velocity data shows that, so fit a line to the velocity data. The slope of that line is equal to the derivative of the velocity, or the acceleration.

1. In cell F5, enter **Regression Output**

2. Select cells G8:H12 and enter the formula

   =LINEST(C5:C19,A5:A19,TRUE,TRUE)

   Enter the formula into the whole range as an array formula by pressing Ctrl+Shift+Enter (Cmd+Enter on the Macintosh).

Add some labels on the regression output and put in range references to move parts of the regression output to a more readable position. You cannot simply move the values, because they are part of an array, and you cannot change or move a part of an array. Hide column H after you have displayed the regression output in column G.

3. Enter the following values in the indicated cells:

F6	**Offset**	F11	**F**	G6	**=H8**
F7	**Std. Err.**	F12	**SS-Reg**	G7	**=H9**
F8	**Slope**	F13	**SS-Resid**	G13	**=H12**
F9	StdErr.	F14	**Std. Err. y Est.**	G14	**=H10**
F10	r^2	F15	**DOF**	G15	**=H11**

4. Select column H and choose Format ➤ Column ➤ Hide to hide it.

The slope of the line through the velocity data (973 cm/s^2) is in cell G8, and is quite close to the expected value of 980 cm/s^2.

Integrating Data

Integrating discrete data involves fitting a function with a known integral to the discrete data and then using that known integral as the result. In most cases, you don't know a function that fits the whole data set, so break the data into a large number of subintervals and fit simple functions such as lines or second- or third-order curves to the points in those subintervals. Then just add each of these subintervals to get the total integral of the curve.

Types of Integration Formulas

The most common integral formulas for discrete data are the rectangle rule, the trapezoid rule, Romberg integration, Simpson's rules, and Gaussian quadrature. Each of these formulas is more accurate than the last, because it puts a more complicated curve through the data to approximate the function between the data points.

Rectangle Rule

The rectangle rule fills the space between two data points with a rectangle whose height is equal to the value of the function at one of the data points, and whose width is equal to the width of the interval. This rule is stated as follows, where I is the value of the integral:

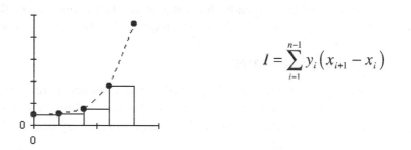

$$I = \sum_{i=1}^{n-1} y_i \left(x_{i+1} - x_i \right)$$

This would seem like a terrible approximation, and in the figure above, it underestimates the integral of the curve by a significant amount, but it works quite well as long as the functions are smooth and the width of the intervals are small. It is also very simple to implement, because you only need to multiply each data value by the width of the interval and then add the products together.

Trapezoid Rule

The trapezoid rule puts a line between each pair of data points, creating a series of trapezoids.

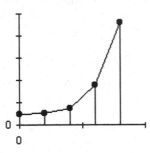

$$I_1 = \sum_{i=1}^{n-1} \frac{(y_i + y_{i+1})}{2}(x_{i+1} - x_i)$$

The area of the trapezoid formed is equal to the average of the two data values times their separation. The total integral is just the sum of these trapezoids.

Romberg Integration

The trapezoid rule can be improved by using Romberg integration, which uses two estimates of the integral to extrapolate the true value of the integral. The first integral uses every data value, and the second uses every other value.

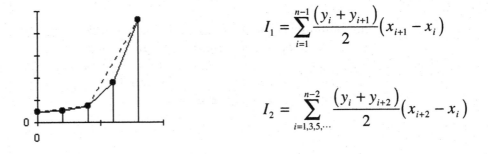

$$I_1 = \sum_{i=1}^{n-1} \frac{(y_i + y_{i+1})}{2}(x_{i+1} - x_i)$$

$$I_2 = \sum_{i=1,3,5,\cdots}^{n-2} \frac{(y_i + y_{i+2})}{2}(x_{i+2} - x_i)$$

The two solutions give two estimates of the integral for two different grid spacings. Romberg integration assumes the error is proportional to the square of the spacing.

$$I = I_1 + Ch^2$$

$$I = I_2 + C(2h)^2$$

where C is a constant. These two equations are solved to eliminate the error term and give the following formula for the true value of the integral:

$$I = I_1 + \tfrac{1}{3}\left(I_1 - I_2\right)$$

Simpson's Rules

Simpson's 1/3 rule puts a quadratic (piece of a parabola) equation through three data values and then calculates the area.

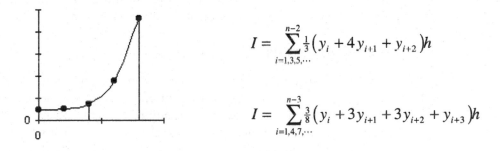

$$I = \sum_{i=1,3,5,\cdots}^{n-2} \tfrac{1}{3}\left(y_i + 4y_{i+1} + y_{i+2}\right)h$$

$$I = \sum_{i=1,4,7,\cdots}^{n-3} \tfrac{3}{8}\left(y_i + 3y_{i+1} + 3y_{i+2} + y_{i+3}\right)h$$

Simpson's 3/8 rule puts a cubic equation through four data values. Note that Simpson's rules require that h, the separation between data points, is constant.

Gaussian Quadrature

If you are integrating a formula rather than a set of data points, you can use Gaussian quadrature. This is an integration formula where the value of an integral is found by adding the value of the function at a few specific points. The number of points needed is determined by the order of the curve that you want to be fit between the limits. A third-order curve can be calculated with only two values of the function:

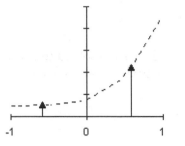

$$\int_{-1}^{+1} f(t)dt = f(-0.5773) + f(0.5773)$$

While this may seem like magic, there is a mathematical basis for it (see the references if you are interested). To use the formula, with a specific function and specific limits of integration, you must change variables to put your function into the form above (see the references for higher order formulas). You then simply read off the values at the two indicated points to get the value of the integral.

Improper Integrals

Often, you must integrate functions where one or both of the limits of integration are infinite, or functions that become infinite or undefined somewhere between the limits of integration. For example, many of the special functions of physics and engineering (gamma function, error function, and so on) are defined with integrals that have infinity as one of the limits. You can handle these problems in several ways.

The simplest method is to transform the variables of the function so that the function no longer has an infinite upper limit. For example, consider the following function:

$$I = \int_0^\infty x^2\, e^{-x}\, dx$$

Break it into two integrals:

$$I = \int_0^1 x^2\, e^{-x}\, dx + \int_1^\infty x^2\, e^{-x}\, dx$$

Then transform the variables in the second integral with $y = 1/x$:

$$I = \int_0^1 x^2 \, e^{-x} \, dx + \int_0^1 \frac{e^{-1/y}}{y^4} \, dy$$

Now you have two integrals with rational limits. The value of the function at the lower limit is indeterminate (0/0), but the limit is zero, so this will not be a problem.

Many calculations with infinite limits converge rapidly to zero as the argument of the function increases towards infinity. Actually, they must converge rapidly for the value of the function to be finite. In this case, you can continue integrating the function until the value of the term to be added is much smaller than the value of the integral, and then truncate the integration at that point.

The function in the second integral in the equation above is indeterminate at the lower limit. You may happen to know that the limit of the function at this value is zero, so you could use that fact to evaluate the integral. If you did not know the value of the function at the limit, or if it is infinite, as in

$$I = \int_0^1 \frac{dx}{\sqrt{x}}$$

you need to add a small number ε to the lower limit and then perform the integral. You then reduce the size of ε until the value of the integral converges (assuming it does converge). Note that this is exactly how you would solve the integral analytically.

Using Integration Methods in a Worksheet

Worksheet integration methods are relatively straightforward. Each cell calculates the value of the integral between two of the data points. A final cell then adds them up.

Gamma Function

A gamma function is one of the so-called special functions of science and engineering. It arises occasionally in physical problems, such as the normalization of the

Coulomb wave functions and the computation of probabilities in statistical mechanics. You encountered it in the last chapter as part of the series representation of the Bessel function ($J_n(x)$) for cases when n is not an integer. When n is an integer, the gamma function reduces to the factorial function:

$$\Gamma(n+1) = n!$$

The gamma function is defined with the following integral:

$$\Gamma(x) = \int_0^\infty e^{-t}\, t^{x-1} dt$$

which has no analytic solution. The gamma function is generally listed in a table for various values of x. Figure 8.4 is a chart of the integrand of the gamma function integral for $x = 1.5$. Note that it goes to zero rapidly, so you can truncate the integral at a value of t of about 10, and have better than three-place accuracy.

FIGURE 8.4:

A chart of the integrand of the gamma function integral for $x = 1.5$

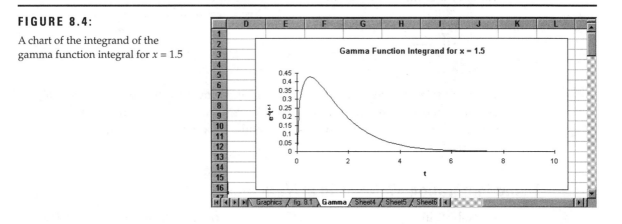

In the next example, calculate the gamma function by numerically integrating the integrand above. Use all the integration methods discussed so far and compare the results. The value of the gamma function at $x = 1.5$ is equal to

$$\sqrt{\pi}\,/\,2$$

Use that value of x so that you can compare the integration results with the correct result.

1. Start with a new worksheet, and name it **fig. 8.5**

2. Change the width of column A to 11.

3. In cell A1, enter **Gamma Function**

Insert and name the value to calculate for (x) and the grid spacing (dt).

4. In cell C1, enter **x =** and right-align it.

5. In cell D1, enter **1.5** and name the cell **X**

6. In cell E1, enter **dt =** and right-align it.

7. In cell F1, enter **0.1** and name the cell **DelT**

8. In cells B3:G3, enter the labels **'True, Rect., Trap.,Trap.2, Romberg**, and **Sim.1/3** and center them.

> **NOTE** The single quote (') is needed before the label True to make Excel treat it as a label instead of a logical value.

Write formulas to add the contents of each column to get the total integral for each method. Calculate the error in each method by comparing the calculated integral to the correct value in cell B4. Cell F4 contains the Romberg formula to combine the two trapezoid rule integrals.

9. Enter the following values in the indicated cells:

Cell	Contents	Special
A4	**Integral =**	right-align
A5	**Error =**	right-align
B4	**=SQRT(PI( ))/2**	
C4	**=SUM(C8:C102)**	copy to D4:E4
C5	**=(C4–$B$4)/$B$4**	copy to D5:G5

F4	**=D4+(D4-E4)/3**
G4	**=SUM(G8:G102)**

In columns A and B, insert the 96 values of t and the integrand.

10. Enter the following values in the indicated cells:

Cell	Contents	Special
A7	**t**	right-align
A8	**0**	
A9	**=A8+DelT**	copy to A10:A103
B7	**f(x,t)**	right-align

11. Format A8:A103 as Number, with four decimal places.

12. In cell B8, enter **=EXP(–A8)*A8^(X–1)** and copy it to cells B9:B103.

Now calculate the rectangle rule.

13. In cell C8, enter **=B8*DelT** and copy it to cells C9:C102.

Calculate the trapezoid rule twice, once with single spacing and once with double. The second evaluation of the trapezoid rule is needed to calculate the Romberg formula in cell F4. Note that the second evaluation of the trapezoid rule uses every other data point, so you zero every other formula in column E so that you do not count them twice.

14. In cell D8, enter **=DelT*(B8+B9)/2** and copy it to cells D9:D102.

15. In cell E8, enter **=DelT*(B8+B10)** and copy it to cells E9:E101.

16. In alternate rows in column E (E9, E11, E13, …, E101), replace the formula with **0**

TIP   Use the down arrow and the 0 keys to quickly insert zeroes in every other formula.

Calculate Simpson's 1/3 rule. As before, zero out every other value of the formula in column G.

17. In cell G8, enter **=DelT*(B8+4*B9+B10)/3** and copy it to cells G9:G101.

18. In alternate rows in column G (G9, G11, G13, …, G101), replace the formula with **0**

19. Turn off the gridlines.

Your worksheet should now look like Figure 8.5. The value calculated with the rectangle rule and the trapezoid rule are about the same. The Romberg integration decreased the error in the trapezoid rule by about 50 percent, to a value near that calculated with Simpson's rule. In each of these calculations, the range was covered by 96 equally spaced grid points.

FIGURE 8.5:

Gamma function: calculation of an integral using the rectangle rule, trapezoid rule, Romberg integration, and Simpson's 1/3 rule

	A	B	C	D	E	F	G	H	I
1	Gamma Function		x =	1.5	dt=	0.1			
2									
3		True	Rect.	Trap.	Trap. 2	Romberg	Sim. 1/3		
4	Integral =	0.886227	0.879481	0.879492	0.867036	0.883370	0.883346		
5	Error =		-0.00761	-0.0076	-0.02075	-0.00321	-0.00325		
6									
7		t	f(x,t)						
8	0.0000	0	0	0.014307	0.036615		0.050356		
9	0.1000	0.286135	0.028613	0.032614	0		0		
10	0.2000	0.366148	0.036615	0.038596	0.07901		0.080438		
11	0.3000	0.405763	0.040576	0.041486	0		0		
12	0.4000	0.423948	0.042395	0.042641	0.084906		0.085486		
13	0.5000	0.428882	0.042888	0.042699	0		0		
14	0.6000	0.425108	0.042511	0.042029	0.0827		0.082963		
15	0.7000	0.415473	0.041547	0.040868	0		0		
16	0.8000	0.401892	0.040189	0.03938	0.076977		0.077086		

Graphics / fig. 8.1 / Gamma \ **fig. 8.5** / fig. 8.6 / Sheet5

The Gaussian quadrature formula has not been used yet in this worksheet because it is more accurate and needs fewer grid points. Calculate it using only 15 grid points instead of 96. Actually, you will be using 43 grid points, because third-order Gaussian quadrature calculates two more grid points in each interval. The layout of this worksheet is the same as the previous one. As a comparison, calculate the trapezoid rule using the same grid points.

To use Gaussian quadrature, you first must change variables to make the limits of integration –1 to 1. Do this with the following substitution:

$$t = \frac{(b-a)y+b+a}{2}$$

where a is the lower limit and b is the upper limit. Inserting this into the integral for the gamma function above gives:

$$\Gamma(x) = \int_0^\infty e^{-t} \, t^{x-1} dt$$

$$= \frac{(b-a)}{2} \int_{-1}^{+1} e^{-((b-a)y+b+a)/2} \left(\frac{(b-a)y+b+a}{2} \right)^{x-1} dy$$

In this case, you are calculating an integral between each pair of grid points, so the upper and lower limits of integration are equal to the values of t at those grid points. Note that this method can only be used for cases where an explicit function is known, not for experimental data, unless, of course, you have the value of the integral available.

1. Start with a copy of the previous example, and name it **fig. 8.6**

2. Change the width of column A to 11.

Enter the grid to use for the integration. Use a nonlinear grid to put a few more grid points at the beginning where the function changes rapidly and fewer later where it does not.

3. Enter the following values in cells A8:A22:

A8 **0**	A11 **0.6**	A14 **2**	A17 **5**	A20 **8**
A9 **0.2**	A12 **0.8**	A15 **3**	A18 **6**	A21 **9**
A10 **0.4**	A13 **1**	A16 **4**	A19 **7**	A22 **10**

4. Clear the contents of cells A23:D103, E1:G103, and C22:D22.

Calculate the Gaussian quadrature formula for each pair of data points and then add these cells together in cell C4. Cells C8:C21 calculate the quadrature formula developed for the gamma function.

5. In cell C3, enter **Gaussian** and center it.

6. Change the contents of cell C4 to =SUM(C8:C21)

7. In cell C8, enter the formula

$$=((A9–A8)/2)*(EXP(–((A9–A8)*(–1/SQRT(3))+A9+A8)/2)$$

➡ $$*(((A9–A8)*(–1/SQRT(3))+A9+A8)/2)^(X–1)$$

➡ $$+EXP(–((A9–A8)*(1/SQRT(3))+A9+A8)/2)$$

➡ $$*(((A9–A8)*(1/SQRT(3))+A9+A8)/2)^(X–1))$$

and copy it to cells C9:C21.

Keep the trapezoid rule integration in column D for comparison.

8. Change the contents of D4 to =SUM(D8:D21)

Your worksheet should now look like Figure 8.6. Note that the Gaussian quadrature integration has only about one-fifth the error of the trapezoid rule integration.

FIGURE 8.6:

Gamma function: integral formula solved with Gaussian quadrature

	A	B	C	D	E	F	G	H	I
1	Gamma Function		x =	1.5					
2									
3		True	Gaussian	Trap.					
4	Integral =	0.886227	0.886862	0.883346					
5	Error =		0.000716	-0.00325					
6									
7	t	f(x,t)							
8	0.0000	0	0.053628	0.036615					
9	0.2000	0.366148	0.000454	0.07901					
10	0.4000	0.423948	0.085489	0.084906					
11	0.6000	0.425108	0.082964	0.0827					
12	0.8000	0.401892	0.077087	0.076977					
13	1.0000	0.367879	0.275676	0.279636					
14	2.0000	0.191393	0.13281	0.138813					
15	3.0000	0.086234	0.050132	0.061433					
16	4.0000	0.036631	0.02432	0.025849					

Implementing Integration Formulas as Visual Basic Functions

As you might expect, all the integration formulas can be implemented as Visual Basic functions. The equations are the same. You just use a FOR loop to calculate the parts of the integral and add them together, rather than calculating them in separate cells and then combining them with the SUM function.

A Visual Basic program is much more flexible than the worksheet for integration of functions. You can change the limits or the step width by simply changing a variable or constant, instead of adding or deleting cells. On the other hand, if you are integrating experimental data, the limits and the step width are fixed, and the data is already in cells, so the worksheet methods are just as easy to use as a function.

> **NOTE**
> While a Visual Basic for Applications program is much more flexible for calculating integrals, a worksheet formula lets you see all the values in the calculation, making it easier to assure yourself that you are not calculating with garbage.

A Visual Basic Function to Calculate the Gamma Function

The Visual Basic program in the next example calculates the gamma function using the trapezoid rule.

1. Start with a new module sheet, and name it **GammaF**

2. Type the following procedures into the module sheet:

```
Option Explicit
'
' Gamma function using the
' trapezoid rule
'
Function Gamma(dblX As Double) As Double
Dim dblT As Double 'The integration variable.
Dim dblTerm As Double 'A term of the summation.
Dim dblTerm1 As Double 'The two parts of a term.
Dim dblTerm2 As Double
Const tStart = 0      'Lower limit for the integral.
```

```
Const tEnd = 20  'Upper limit for the integral.
Const DelT = 0.01    'Step size for the integral.
Const CutOff = 0.000000001 'A cutoff value for the size of a term
'Zero the summation variable.
Gamma = 0
'Loop to integrate the integrand, one term per loop.
For dblT = tStart To tEnd Step DelT
    'Calculate a single term using the trapezoid rule.
    dblTerm1 = Exp(-dblT) * dblT ^ (dblX - 1)
    dblTerm2 = Exp(-dblT - DelT) * (dblT + DelT) ^ (dblX - 1)
    dblTerm = DelT * (dblTerm1 + dblTerm2) / 2
    'Add the term to the total.
    Gamma = Gamma + dblTerm
    'Quit if the last term is 1e-9 smaller than the total.
    If dblTerm / Gamma < CutOff Then
        Exit For
    End If
Next dblT
End Function
'
' A short Sub to use while testing
'
Sub test1()
Dim dblX As Double
Const Pi = 3.14159265358979
'Pick a test value
dblX = 1.5
'Print the value and the result and the correct value
' in the debug window.
Debug.Print dblX, Gamma(dblX), Sqr(Pi) / 2
Stop
End Sub
```

The procedure first declares some variables and then defines three constants to mark the starting, ending and step size for the integration. Using the constants makes it much easier to make modifications to the integration loop while testing. The next step is to initialize the summing variable Gamma and start the loop that performs the integration. Within the loop, two values of the integrand are calculated, averaged, and multiplied by the step width to get the area of the trapezoid. The area is then added to the summation variable. At the bottom of the loop is an If statement to compare the size of the last term to the size of the summation variable. If the term is less than 1×10^{-9} of the summation, the Exit For statement is called to end the loop.

Following the function is a short test procedure. The procedure is used to execute the function for finding syntax errors and for testing the integrator to see that it calculates the correct values. The procedure sets the variables, invokes the function and prints the results on the debug window. The stop statement then halts execution and displays the Debug window for you to see the values. Debugging commands can be used at this point to examine other variables if there is a problem.

To use the new function in a worksheet, open a new worksheet and call the function with a value. Use 1.5 again for the argument so that you can check the accuracy of the result.

1. Start with a copy of worksheet fig. 8.6 and name it **fig. 8.7**

2. Make the following entries in cells E3:E5:

      E3   **Gamma**

      E4   **=Gamma(X)**

      E5   **=(E4–$B$4)/$B$4**

After a few seconds, the worksheet should look like Figure 8.7. The error using this function is only 0.02 percent. The accuracy can be increased even more by making the step size and the cutoff value smaller, and the ending value of the loop larger. The trade-off is a slower calculation time, but that may be acceptable, depending on your situation.

FIGURE 8.7:

Using the gamma function as a Visual Basic function in a worksheet

	A	B	C	D	E	F	G	H	I
1	Gamma Function		x =	1.5	dt=	0.2			
2									
3		True	Gaussian	Trap.	Gamma				
4	Integral =	0.886227	0.886216	0.867413	0.886019				
5	Error =		-1.2E-05	-0.02123	-0.00023				
6									
7	t	f(x,t)							
8	0.0000	0	0.053628	0.036615					
9	0.2000	0.366148	0.080454	0.07901					
10	0.4000	0.423948	0.085489	0.084906					
11	0.6000	0.425108	0.082964	0.0827					
12	0.8000	0.401892	0.077087	0.076977					
13	1.0000	0.367879	0.06981	0.069782					
14	1.2000	0.329942	0.062155	0.062172					
15	1.4000	0.291777	0.054676	0.054716					
16	1.6000	0.255381	0.047664	0.047715					
17	1.8000	0.221772	0.041261	0.041315					

Gamma / fig. 8.5 / fig. 8.6 / GammaF / **fig. 8.7** / Sheet5

Summary

In this chapter, you calculated numerical derivatives of data and functions. In particular, you looked at worksheet methods to calculate forward, backward, and central differences of worksheet data. You encountered some of the problems in calculating numerical derivatives, namely: truncation, round-off, and error growth due to differencing.

You also numerically integrated functions and data, both on the worksheet and with Visual Basic functions. You implemented several of the standard numerical integration methods that are normally applied with a high-level computer language. These methods include the rectangle rule, the trapezoid rule, Romberg integration, Simpson's rules, and Gaussian quadrature.

If you are interested in the mathematical background of these methods, or in other methods and examples, refer to a book on numerical methods. Most differentiation and integration methods can be adapted to the worksheet format with little difficulty.

For More Information

Science and Engineering Special Functions

G. Arfken, *Mathematical Methods for Physicists* (Orlando, Fla: Academic Press, 1970).

Numerical Differentiation and Integration

C. Gerald, *Applied Numerical Analysis*, 2nd ed. (Reading, Mass.: Addison-Wesley, 1978).

W. H. Press, et al., *Numerical Recipes: The Art of Scientific Computing* (Cambridge, Eng.: Cambridge University Press, 1986).

Review Problems

1. A simulation of free fall on the moon created the following list of numbers describing the position of an object every 1/60 of a second. The object is dropped from rest. Using central differences, calculate the velocity and acceleration of the object at each time point. What is the acceleration due to gravity on the moon?

Point	Position (cm)	Point	Position (cm)
1	0	6	0.578
2	0.023	7	0.833
3	0.093	8	1.134
4	0.208	9	1.481
5	0.370	10	1.874
		11	2.314

2. Using the following table of x and y data points, calculate and plot the first and second derivatives of y with respect to x. Compare the numerically integrated values with the analytic solutions $y' = 6x + 12x^2$ and $y'' = 6 + 24x$. (The difference is caused by approximating a continuous curve with a discrete set of points.)

x	y	x	y	x	y
0.0	2.00	3.5	210.25	7.0	1521.00
0.5	3.25	4.0	306.00	7.5	1858.25
1.0	9.00	4.5	427.25	8.0	2242.00
1.5	22.25	5.0	577.00	8.5	2675.25
2.0	46.00	5.5	758.25	9.0	3161.00
2.5	83.25	6.0	974.00	9.5	3702.25 3.0
3.0	137.00	6.5	1227.25	10.0	4302.00

3. Ampère's law is used to calculate the current (I) in a wire by integrating the magnetic field (B) over a closed loop that surrounds the wire. A wire carrying current has its magnetic field measured at several points along the edge of a square centered on the wire. The following are the magnetic field values from the center of one edge to the corner. Because the problem is symmetric,

integrals along the eight other half-sides of the square are identical, and the total current is eight times the integral along the one half-edge. Calculate the current in the wire by integrating Ampère's law using the spreadsheet form of the rectangle rule, trapezoid rule, Romberg integration, and Simpson's 1/3 rule. Ampère's law is

$$I = \frac{8}{\mu_0} \int_0^5 B(y)\,dy$$

$$\mu_0 = 1.26 \times 10^{-6} \quad H/m$$

y m	$B(y)$ web/m^2	y m	$B(y)$ web/m^2
0.0	$1.20*10^{-5}$	2.5	$9.63*10^{-6}$
0.5	$1.19*10^{-5}$	3.0	$8.85*10^{-6}$
1.0	$1.16*10^{-5}$	3.5	$8.08*10^{-6}$
1.5	$1.10*10^{-5}$	4.0	$7.34*10^{-6}$
2.0	$1.04*10^{-5}$	4.5	$6.65*10^{-6}$
		5.0	$6.02*10^{-6}$

4. The sine integral is a special function defined by

$$Si(x) = -\int_x^\infty \frac{\sin(t)}{t}\,dt = -\frac{\pi}{2} + \int_0^x \frac{\sin(t)}{t}\,dt$$

For $x - 0.5$, calculate $Si(x)$ using the rectangle and trapezoid rules on a spreadsheet.

5. The exponential integral is a special function defined by

$$Ei(x) = -\int_{-x}^\infty \frac{e^{-t}}{t}\,dt \qquad x < 0$$

$$= -\lim_{\varepsilon \to 0}\left[\int_{-x}^{-\varepsilon} \frac{e^{-t}}{t}\,dt + \int_\varepsilon^\infty \frac{e^{-t}}{t}\,dt\right] \quad x > 0$$

For $x = -3$, calculate $Ei(x)$ using the trapezoid rule in a Visual Basic function.

6. Complete problem 4 using Gaussian quadrature.

7. Complete problem 5 using Simpson's rule in a Visual Basic function.

8. An integral formula for a Bessel function with integer values of n is

$$J_n(z) = \frac{1}{\pi} \int_0^\pi \cos\left(n\theta - z\sin(\theta)\right) d\theta$$

Calculate $J_n(z)$ for $n = 1$ and $z = 0.5$ using the spreadsheet method and the trapezoid rule.

9. Complete problem 8 using Simpson's rule in a Visual Basic function.

10. Complete problem 8 using Gaussian quadrature in a Visual Basic function. Compare the result to that in Figure 7.2.

Exercises

1. Using the following pairs of x and y data values, calculate and plot the first and second derivatives of y with respect to x. Compare the numerical results to the analytic results $y' = 6x^2 + 15x^4$ and $y'' = 12x + 60x^3$.

x	y	x	y	x	y
0	7.00	1.4	28.62	2.8	567.22
0.2	7.02	1.6	46.65	3.0	790.00
0.4	7.16	1.8	75.35	3.2	1079.17
0.6	7.67	2.0	119.00	3.4	1448.67
0.8	9.01	2.2	182.90	3.6	1914.30
1.0	12.00	2.4	273.53	3.8	2493.80
1.2	17.92	2.6	398.59	4.0	3207.00

2. The following table lists the position above the ground of a small rocket during takeoff. Calculate and plot the velocity and acceleration versus time. Can you tell when the engine burns out?

Time	Position (m)	Time	Position (m)
0.0	0	5.0	1335
0.2	4	5.2	1398
0.4	18	5.4	1460
0.6	41	5.6	1522
0.8	71	5.8	1584
1.0	108	6.0	1645
1.2	151	6.2	1706
1.4	199	6.4	1766
1.6	251	6.6	1826
1.8	308	6.8	1885
2.0	367	7.0	1945
2.2	428	7.2	2003
2.4	490	7.4	2062
2.6	552	7.6	2120
2.8	620	7.8	2177
3.0	687	8.0	2235
3.2	753	8.2	2291
3.4	820	8.4	2348
3.6	885	8.6	2404
3.8	951	8.8	2459
4.0	1016	9.0	2515
4.2	1080	9.2	2570
4.4	1145	9.4	2624
4.6	1209	9.6	2678
4.8	1272	9.8	2732
		10.0	2785

3. A reservoir has a depth (d) that goes as

   $d = 80 - x \times 0.04$ **feet**

   and a width (w) that goes as

   $w = 1000 + x/2$ **feet**

   where x is measured out into the lake from the dam. Using the rectangle rule and trapeziod rule, calculate the volume of water in the lake in acre-feet (one acre one foot deep).

4. The logarithm integral is a special function represented as follows:

   $$Li(x) = \int_0^x \frac{dt}{\ln(t)} \qquad\qquad x < 1$$

   $$Li(x) = x \int_1^\infty \frac{dt}{t^2(\ln(x) - \ln(t))} \qquad\qquad x > 1$$

   Use Romberg integration to calculate a table of values of Li(x) for x between 0 and 1.

5. Assume you are on a chunk of comet Schoemaker-Levy, on your way to make a big splat on Jupiter. Estimate the collision velocity by numerically integrating the acceleration times the time ($a \times \Delta t$)of the comet from rest at relative infinity (a is very small) to the surface of Jupiter (r_J). You must also track the position ($v \times \Delta t$) to see when to stop integrating. The accelertion is given by:

   $$a = G\frac{m_J}{r^2}$$

   $G = 6.67 \times 10^{-11}$ nt-m^2/kg^2

   $m_J = 1.90 \times 10^{27}$ kg

   $r_J = 7.0 \times 10^7$ m

   Compare to the analytical result:

   $$v = \sqrt{2G\frac{m_J}{r_J}}$$

6. When excavating for a road, the quantity of dirt to be removed from a cut is estimated using numerical integration. The cross section of the cut is assumed to be as shown in the figure below. The roadway width (w) is always a fixed width (20 feet in this example) and the slope of the sidewalls is 1 to 1-1/2 (rise to run). The planned cut is surveyed and sliced into a series of slabs. The survey results for a cut through a hill are shown in the right figure and in the table of values. The cut is marked with a series of stations (a, b, c, d, ...), with the depth listed for each station. The volume of dirt is estimated by calculating the volume of each slab, and then summing them up. To calculate the volume of a slab, average the areas of the two trapezoidal ends and multiply by the thickness, this is known as the Average End Area method. Calculate the total volume of dirt to be excavated.

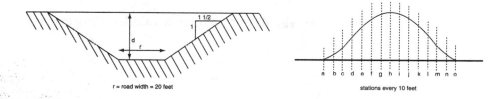

r = road width = 20 feet   stations every 10 feet

Station	Depth of Cut (ft)	Station	Depth of Cut (ft)
a	0	i	13
b	2	j	12
c	4	k	10
d	7.5	l	7
e	12	m	4
f	13.5	n	2
g	14	o	0
h	14		

7. Redo exercise 4 using Simpson's rule.

8. Redo exercise 4 using Gaussian quadratures.

9. Write a Visual Basic procedure to calculate the logarithm integral for any value of x.

10. The three Fresnel integrals are defined as follows:

$$\Phi(x) = \frac{2}{\sqrt{\pi}} \int_0^x e^{-t^2} dt$$

$$S(x) = \frac{2}{\sqrt{2\pi}} \int_0^x \sin(t^2) dt$$

$$C(x) = \frac{2}{\sqrt{2\pi}} \int_0^x \cos(t^2) dt$$

Write three Visual Basic functions to calculate these integrals for any value of x.

CHAPTER

NINE

Solving Nonlinear Equations

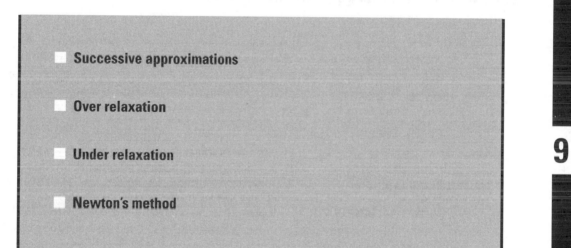

- Successive approximations

- Over relaxation

- Under relaxation

- Newton's method

9

Solving a nonlinear equation is often a frustrating experience. An equation that looks simple can defy solution by any analytical means. Except for polynomials up to order 4, and the simplest transcendental equations (those involving trigonometric or exponential functions), most nonlinear equations cannot be solved analytically. In fact, the analytic solutions of polynomials of order 3 and 4 are so unwieldy that they are seldom used.

The numerical methods for solving nonlinear equations are all based on guessing a solution and systematically refining that guess. You insert a guess into the equation, and use the result to try to improve the guess. You then repeat this process until you find a root of sufficient accuracy. Or the method diverges, and you give up and go home for the night, to try again the next morning.

Using the Successive Approximations Method

Although there are several simple methods for finding the roots of nonlinear equations, the one most adaptable to a worksheet is known as *successive approximations*. To perform successive approximations, you first rewrite the equation in the following form:

$x = f(x)$

Any of the several ways to rewrite your original equation are valid for this method, although some may not converge to a solution.

Once you have rewritten the equation, make an initial guess of the value of x. While any value of x may do, the closer your initial guess is to the solution, the faster the problem will converge. Note that for problems with multiple solutions, the initial guess of the value of x determines which solution you get. To get the other solutions, use different initial guesses.

Insert the initial value of x into $f(x)$ and calculate a new value of x. This is the new guess of the value of x, which you reinsert into $f(x)$. Continue calculating new values of x in this manner, until the value of x converges.

$$x_0 = \text{initial guess}$$
$$x_1 = f(x_0)$$
$$x_2 = f(x_1)$$
$$\vdots$$
$$x_n = f(x_{n-1})$$

Figure 9.1 shows the progress of a solution using this method. In the figure, you are searching for the solution of $x = \text{Cos}(x)$, which is the point at the intersection of the lines $y = x$ and $y = \text{Cos}(x)$. The solution method works its way in a circle, surrounding the solution, and getting closer and closer to it. The calculation is stopped when the calculated solution is sufficiently close to the actual solution.

NOTE
Graphical methods are a time-honored method for solving nonlinear equations. While they are not very accurate, they are useful for locating the neighborhood of a solution to provide a starting point for numerical methods. To find a rough solution to a nonlinear equation, plot $y = x$ and $y = f(x)$ as shown in Figure 9.1, and the solution is at the intersection.

FIGURE 9.1:

Progress of the solution using successive approximations

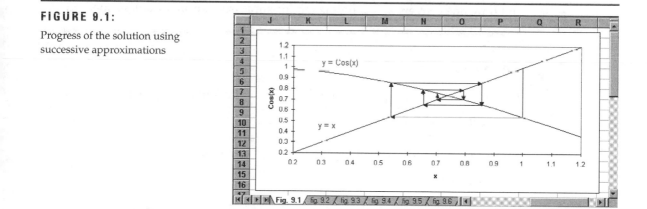

387

When Will Successive Approximations Converge?

Not all functions converge to a root when solved with the successive approximations method. In order for the function to converge to a root of the original equation, the absolute value of the slope of $f(x)$ must be less than 1:

$$|f'(x)| < 1$$

In general, there is more than one way to rewrite a function to put it into the converted form, $x = f(x)$; for some, the slope is less than one and for others, it is greater than one. You could write the derivatives of your functions and test them with the condition above, but it is usually faster to rewrite your equation in the simplest way and try it. If it does not converge, then rewrite it a different way, and try it again. For example,

$$x = Cos(x)$$

and

$$x = ArcCos(x)$$

are both manipulations of

$$Cos(x) - x = 0$$

but only one converges to a root using the successive approximations method.

Cos(x) = x

Consider the following simple, nonlinear, transcendental equation:

$$Cos(x) - x = 0$$

which can quickly be rewritten into the required form:

$$x = Cos(x)$$

Use the worksheet's iteration capability to solve this equation by successive approximations. You could write the formulas in the worksheet in the same manner as the equations defining this method, but the worksheet's iteration capability lets you do it in a few cells instead of a page full. To implement this method, turn off the worksheet's automatic recalculation and enter formulas with circular references.

Normally, the worksheet calculates cells in natural recalculation order. In natural recalculation order, a cell's precedents (those cells that a cell depends on) are calculated before a cell is calculated. This order is applied to all cells in a worksheet, until all the cells have been calculated. If you change the value of a cell, all cells that depend on that cell, both directly and indirectly, are recalculated. A circular reference occurs when a cell depends on itself, either directly or indirectly through the formulas in other cells. The natural recalculation order cannot calculate a circular reference, because a cell's precedents can never be calculated (it must calculate itself before it can calculate itself).

When you turn on iteration, the worksheet calculates every cell that does not contain a circular reference. It then calculates all the cells that contain circular references one or more times, depending on the settings in the Tools ➤ Options, Calculation tab dialog box. The cells containing circular references are simply calculated, using the current values of the arguments, without trying to calculate all precedents first. After the cells are recalculated the number of times specified in the Calculation dialog box, the recalculation stops. When you press the Calc key (F9 or Ctrl+=; Cmd+= on the Macintosh), all the cells are recalculated again. This capability is used to successively calculate a formula, and then insert the value of that calculation back into the formula.

In this example, set the number of iterations to 1, so that you can watch the values change as the worksheet recalculates. In your own work, you will probably use a higher number to find a solution more quickly.

1. Start with a new worksheet, and name it **fig. 9.2**

2. Choose the Tools ➤ Options command, Calculation tab; check the Manual checkbox, set the Maximum iterations to 1, and clear the Recalculate Before Save checkbox. Click OK to continue.

3. Change the width of column A to 16.

4. In cell A1, enter **x = Cos(x); Successive approximations**

Create a table with the initialization value and the initialization flag. The initialization flag forces the worksheet into a predetermined initial state.

5. In cells A3:B4, enter the indicated values. Right-align the contents of cells A3:A4.

Cell	Contents	Cell	Contents
A3	**Initial Value**	B3	**0**
A4	**Init Flag**	B4	**True**

6. Name cells B3 and B4 as **INIT_VALUE** and **INIT**

In cell B6, test the value of INIT to see if it is True. If INIT is True, set x equal to the initialization value; otherwise, set it equal to the cosine of x in cell B7. In cell B7, calculate the cosine of the value in cell B6, creating a circular reference.

7. In cells A6:B7, enter the indicated values. Right-align the contents of cells A6:A7.

Cell	Contents	Cell	Contents
A6	**x**	B6	**=IF(INIT,INIT_VALUE,B7)**
A7	**Cos(x)**	B7	**=COS(B6)**

Calculate the difference between x and $\cos(x)$, to help to determine when the calculation is sufficiently converged.

8. In cell A9, enter **Difference** and right-align it.

9. In cell B9, enter =B7–B6

10. Format cell B9 as Scientific with two decimal places.

Set up a second circular reference to count the number of iterations.

11. In cell A11, enter **Iteration** and right-align it.

12. In cell B11, enter =IF(INIT,0,B12+1)

13. In cell B12, enter =B11

14. Turn off the gridlines.

15. To perform the calculation, set the value of the initialization flag in cell B4 to **True** and press F9, the Calc key, to initialize the problem.

16. Change the value of the initialization flag to **False** and press F9 again.

Each time you press F9, the calculation is iterated one time, calculating the next value of x.

17. Continue pressing F9 until the value of x converges to sufficient accuracy.

You can test the accuracy by comparing the value of x with the value of the difference between x and $f(x)$ in cell B9. The worksheet should now look like Figure 9.2, with the converged value of x in cells B6 and B7.

If this calculation diverged instead of converged, you would rewrite the equation in the equivalent form (arccosine),

$$x = \cos^{-1}(x)$$

and try again.

Excel can watch the change in your values for you and stop automatically when values of sufficient accuracy are achieved. To see how this works, change the current example to use Excel's stopping criteria, instead of watching the change in the last term. Begin by clearing cells A9:B12, since these values are different every iteration, and would prevent Excel's stopping criteria from ever activating. Next

FIGURE 9.2:

Successive approximations method to find the root of the equation $\text{Cos}(x) = x$

	A	B	C
1	x = Cos(x); Successive approximations		
2			
3	Initial Value	0	
4	Init Flag	FALSE	
5			
6	x	0.739085	
7	Cos(x)	0.739085	
8			
9	Difference	-6.15E-08	
10			
11	Iteration	41	
12		41	
13			
14			
15			
16			

Heading / Fig. 9.1 \ **fig. 9.2** / fig. 9.3

set the iteration and stopping criteria in the Tools ➤ Options, Calculation tab dialog box.

1. Start with a copy of sheet fig. 9.2 and name it **fig. 9.3**

2. Delete the contents of cells A9:B12.

3. Choose the Tools ➤ Options command, Calculation tab; change Maximum Iterations to **100**, Maximum Change to **1.0E–7**, and Calculation to Automatic. Then click OK.

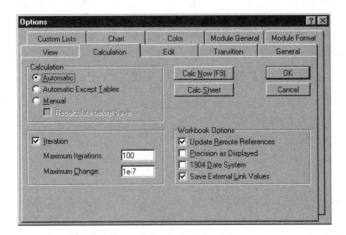

Initialize the calculation by entering True in cell B4, and letting the worksheet recalculate. Start the calculation by entering False in cell B4. The worksheet recalculates until the maximum change in any cell is less than 1.0×10^{-7} as shown in Figure 9.3.

FIGURE 9.3:

Successive approximations, letting the worksheet control when the calculation is complete.

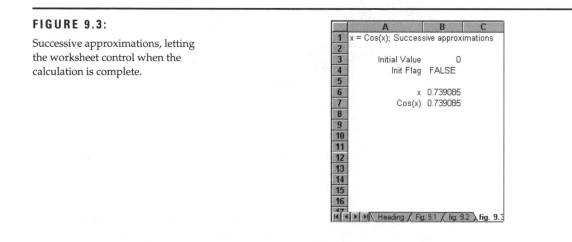

	A	B	C
1	x = Cos(x); Successive approximations		
2			
3	Initial Value	0	
4	Init Flag	FALSE	
5			
6	x	0.739085	
7	Cos(x)	0.739085	

Heading / Fig. 9.1 / fig. 9.2 \ fig. 9.3

NOTE If a calculation is slow to converge, you might reach the maximum iterations (100) set in the Tools ➤ Options Calculation tab dialog box. If this is the case, press F9 (Cmd+= on the Macintosh) to calculate for up to another 100 iterations. Press it again if necessary.

Using the Under Relaxation Method

In some situations, a function is so nonlinear that the successive approximations method will not converge. Extreme nonlinearity is often caused by inflection points in the curve near the root. These points cause the value of x_i to change too much at each iteration and prevent the calculation from converging.

NOTE An inflection point is a point on a curve where the curvature (second derivative) changes sign.

You can correct for this problem by decreasing the change in x_i between steps by a fractional amount c. This is known as under relaxation. Using under relaxation, the iteration of successive values of x proceeds as

$$x_0 = \text{Initial guess}$$
$$x_1 = x_0 + c\,\Delta x_0$$
$$x_2 = x_1 + c\,\Delta x_1$$
$$\vdots$$
$$x_n = x_{n-1} + c\,\Delta x_{n-1}$$

where $\Delta x_n = f(x_n) - x_n$ is the change in x in an iteration, and c is the relaxation factor $(0 < c < 1)$. Using a value of $c = 1$ is equivalent to using the successive approximations method. Using values of c that are greater than 1 is known as over relaxation. Over relaxation is used to speed the convergence of slowly converging problems. Inserting the value for Δx_n into the equation for x_n gives

$$x_n = c\,f(x_{n-1}) + (1 - c)x_{n-1}$$

which is the iteration equation to use in the calculation.

Over Relaxation

When the relaxation factor, c, is greater than one, the method is known as over relaxation. Over relaxation will occasionally increase the convergence speed of slowly converging problems. If a problem is converging slowly using successive approximations, try using the layout for under relaxation, but with a value of c between 1 and 2. It is unlikely that any problem will be stable for values of c greater than 2.

Try a few iterations and see if the values are converging or diverging. If they are diverging, reduce the value of c until they start to converge.

The most efficient value for c is the largest value that still converges. The value of c does not need to remain a constant throughout a solution calculation, because the ultimate solution does not depend on it. The value of the relaxation factor does not change the solution, only the speed with which the method approaches the solution. When the solution is reached, $f(x_{n-1}) = x_{n-1}$ and the iteration equation reduces to: $x_n = x_{n-1} = f(x_{n-1})$, which does not depend on c. You can change c as often as is necessary throughout the calculation to speed the convergence.

Electron Temperature in GaAs

The electron temperature in gallium arsenide (GaAs) due to acceleration by an electric field has been calculated by solving the conservation equations for energy and momentum. This solution is complicated by the fact that GaAs has two conduction bands with different mobilities (that is, electrons move faster in one band than in the other). The result is

$$Te = T + \left(\frac{2}{3}\right)\frac{\tau q E^2 \mu}{k}\left(1 + R\,e^{-\varepsilon/(kTe)}\right)^{-1}$$

where

Te Electron temperature

T Ambient temperature (300 K)

τ Lifetime for relaxation of energy from the electrons to the crystal lattice (10^{-12} s)

q Electron charge (1.6×10^{-19} coulomb)

E Electric field

k Planck's constant (1.38×10^{-23} J/K)

μ Electron mobility in the lower electron conduction band (0.85 m^2/V–s)

ε Energy difference between the upper and lower conduction bands (0.31 eV)

R Splitting factor for splitting of electrons between the upper and lower conduction bands (94.1)

This equation is already in the form for the successive approximations method, so try that method for values of the electric field between 10^2 and 10^8 V/m.

1. Start with a new worksheet named **fig. 9.4**

2. Choose the Tools ➤ Options command, Calculation tab; check Iteration, set the Maximum Iterations to **1**, and select Manual Calculation. Click OK to continue.

3. Set the width of column C to 10.

4. In cell A1, enter **Electron temperature in GaAs; Successive approximations**

Create a table of the coefficients of the equation.

5. Enter the following in cells A3:F5:

Cell	Contents	Cell	Contents	Cell	Contents
A3	**Delt_E**	B3	**=0.31*Q**	C3	**J**
A4	**Tau**	B4	**1.0E–12**	C4	**s**
A5	**U**	B5	**0.85**	C5	**m^2/V–s**
D3	**K**	E3	**1.38E–23**	F3	**J/K**
D4	**Q**	E4	**1.6E–19**	F4	**Coul**
D5	**T**	E5	**300**	F5	**K**
D6	**R**	E6	**94.1**		

6. Right-align cells A3:A5 and D3:D6.

7. Select cells A3:B5, choose Insert ➤ Name ➤ Create, make sure the Left Column checkbox is checked, and click OK.

8. Select cells D3:D6, choose Insert ➤ Name ➤ Create, make sure the Left Column checkbox is checked, and click OK. Note that cell E6 is named R_.

Next, create a table of the initial value and the initialization flag.

9. In cell A7, enter **Initial value**

10. In cell C7, enter **300**

11. In cell A8, enter **Init Flag**

12. In cell C8, enter **True**

13. Name cells C7 and C8 as **INIT_VALUE2** and **INIT2**

Now enter the list of electric field values to solve the equation for.

14. Make the following entries in cells E8:E16:

Cell	Contents	Cell	Contents	Cell	Contents
E8	E	E11	1E3	E14	1E6
E9	(V/m)	E12	1E4	E15	1E7
E10	1E2	E13	1E5	E16	1E8

15. Center the contents of cells E8 and E9.

In column F, test the initialization flag. If the worksheet is initializing, use the initial value; otherwise, set it equal to the function in column E. In column G, calculate the function.

16. Make the following entries in cells F8:G9 and center them:

Cell	Contents	Cell	Contents
F8	Te	G8	f(Te)
F9	(K)	G9	(K)

17. In cell F10, enter the formula =IF(INIT2,INIT_VALUE2,G10) and copy it to cells F11:F16.

18. In cell G10, enter the formula

$$=T+(2/3)*Tau*Q*E10^2*U/(K*(1+R*EXP(-Delt\_E/(K*F10))))$$

and copy it to cells G11:G16.

19. Format cells E10:E16 as Scientific, with one decimal place.

20. Format cells F10:G16 as Scientific, with two decimal places.

21. Turn off the gridlines.

To use this worksheet, set the initialization flag in cell C8 to **TRUE** and press F9 (the Calc key, Cmd+= on the Macintosh). Set the initialization flag to **FALSE** and press F9 again. The worksheet is calculated each time you press the F9 key. The worksheet will now look like Figure 9.4.

After about five iterations, all the formulas except the fifth one have converged. At a field of 10^6 V/m, the temperature is alternating between a value of 6.76×10^3 and 4.17×10^2 K. The plot of $f(Te)$ versus Te, in Figure 9.5, shows the cause of the problem. The function has two plateaus separated by an inflection point that the calculation is alternating between. Notice that the magnitude of the slope of the function is greater than 1 to the left of the intersection, which violates our convergence condition.

To correct this problem, you need to get the calculation down into the region near the solution, so change to the under relaxation method, which will decrease the length of the arrows in Figure 9.5 and pull the calculation down where you want it.

1. Start with a copy of sheet fig. 9.4, and name it **fig. 9.6**

2. Change cell A1 to **Electron temperature in GaAs; Under relaxation**

   Now enter a relaxation factor of 0.5 and calculate the new values of Te using the under relaxation equation.

3. In cell A9, enter **Relaxation Factor**

FIGURE 9.4:

Electron temperature in GaAs;
Successive approximations

	A	B	C	D	E	F	G	H	I
1	Electron temperature in GaAs; Successive approximations								
2									
3	Delt_E	4.96E-20 J			K	1.38E-23 J/K			
4	Tau	1.00E-12 s			Q	1.60E-19 Coul			
5	U	0.85 m²/V-s			T	300 K			
6					R	94.1			
7	Initial Value		300						
8	Init Flag		FALSE		E	Te	f(Te)		
9					(V/m)	(K)	(K)		
10					1.0E+02	3.00E+02	3.00E+02		
11					1.0E+03	3.00E+02	3.00E+02		
12					1.0E+04	3.01E+02	3.01E+02		
13					1.0E+05	3.65E+02	3.65E+02		
14					1.0E+06	6.76E+03	4.17E+02		
15					1.0E+07	1.01E+04	1.01E+04		
16					1.0E+08	6.95E+05	6.95E+05		

Fig. 9.1 / fig. 9.2 / fig. 9.3 / **fig. 9.4** / fig. 9.5 / fig. 9.6

Using the Under Relaxation Method

FIGURE 9.5:

Electron temperature in GaAs: plotting $f(Te)$ versus Te at a field of 10^6 V/m to determine the cause of nonconvergence

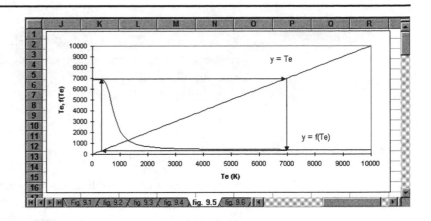

4. In cell C9, enter **0.5**

5. Name cell C9 as **C_**

6. Change cell G8 to **C*f(Te)+(1–C)*Te**

7. Change cells G10:G16 to

$$=C\_*(T+(2/3)*Tau*Q*E10^2*U/(K*(1+R\_*EXP(-Delt\_E/(K*F10)))))$$
$$\rightarrow+(1-C\_)*F10$$

Now when you iterate the calculation, it quickly converges for all the values of the electric field, as shown in Figure 9.6. The under relaxation factor has decreased the amount of change applied in each step of the solution, allowing it to converge.

FIGURE 9.6:

Electron temperature in GaAs; Under relaxation method

Electron temperature in GaAs; Under relaxation

Delt_E	4.96E-20 J			K	1.38E-23 J/K			
Tau	1.00E-12 s			Q	1.60E-19 Coul			
U	0.85 m²/V-s			T	300 K			
				R	94.1			
Initial Value		300						
Init Flag		FALSE			E	Te	f(Te)+(1-C)*Te	
Relaxation Factor		0.5			(V/m)	(K)	(K)	
					1.0E+02	3.00E+02	3.00E+02	
					1.0E+03	3.00E+02	3.00E+02	
					1.0E+04	3.01E+02	3.01E+02	
					1.0E+05	3.65E+02	3.65E+02	
					1.0E+06	1.28E+03	1.28E+03	
					1.0E+07	1.01E+04	1.01E+04	
					1.0E+08	6.95E+05	6.95E+05	

399

Using Newton's Method

No discussion of the solution of nonlinear equations would be complete without Newton's method. The methods discussed previously in this chapter all converge linearly to the roots of the equations. Newton's method, on the other hand, converges quadratically, giving a large amount of precision in the solution with fewer iterations of the worksheet; however, to implement Newton's method, you must calculate the derivative of the function, either analytically or numerically.

To use Newton's method, first write your equation as a function equal to 0:

$$g(x) = 0$$

Second, calculate the derivative of the function:

$$g'(x) = \frac{dg(x)}{dx}$$

Finally, iterate the approximations to x as follows:

$$x_0 = \text{initial guess}$$

$$x_1 = x_0 - \frac{g(x_0)}{g'(x_0)}$$

$$x_2 = x_1 - \frac{g(x_1)}{g'(x_1)}$$

$$\vdots$$

$$x_n = x_{n-1} - \frac{g(x_{n-1})}{g'(x_{n-1})}$$

The main drawback of Newton's method is that you must determine the derivative of your function. Taking the derivative of a function is usually straightforward, but it is not always simple. If the derivative is difficult to derive analytically, you can calculate it numerically using the central difference formulas discussed in Chapter 8.

Modify the previous example to use Newton's method instead of the under relaxation method. For the electron temperature in GaAs, the function and its derivative are as follows:

$$g(Te) = T - Te + \left(\frac{2}{3}\right)\frac{\tau q E^2 \mu}{k}\left(1 + Re^{-\varepsilon/(kTe)}\right)^{-1}$$

$$g'(Te) = -1 - \left(\frac{2}{3}\right)\frac{\tau q E^2 \mu \varepsilon R e^{-\varepsilon/(kTe)}}{k^2 Te^2}\left(1 + Re^{-\varepsilon/(kTe)}\right)^{-2}$$

1. Start with a copy of the previous worksheet, and name it **fig. 9.7**
2. Change cell A1 to **Electron temperature in GaAs; Newton's method**
3. Clear cells A9:C9.

Now insert Newton's iteration equation, replacing the under relaxation iteration equation.

4. In cell G8, enter

   Te–g(Te)/g'(Te)

5. In cell G10, enter the formula

   =F10–(T–F10+(2/3)*Tau*Q*E10^2*U/(K*(1+R_
      ➨***EXP(–Delt_E/(K*F10)))))/(–1–(2/3)*Tau*Q*E10^2**
      ➨***U*Delt_E*R_*EXP(–Delt_E/(K*F10))/((K*F10)^2**
      ➨***(1+R_*EXP(–Delt_E/(K*F10)))^2))**

   and copy it to cells G11:G16.

FIGURE 9.7:

Electron temperature in GaAs:
Newton's method

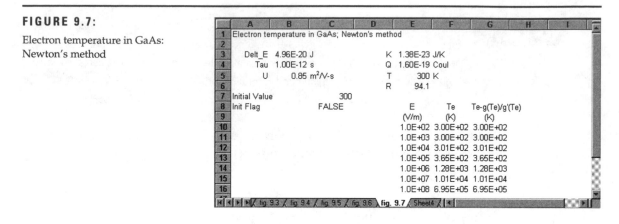

Your worksheet will now look like Figure 9.7. This worksheet operates in the same way as the earlier examples. Set the value of the initialization flag to **TRUE** and press F9. Reset the initialization flag to **FALSE** and press F9 again. Each time that you press F9, the worksheet is iterated once.

This method is much faster than the other methods. Under relaxation required 16 iterations of the worksheet to converge the calculations to three-place accuracy. Newton's method required only 4 iterations. The successive approximations method needed 5 iterations to converge all but one equation, and that equation would not converge at all.

Using Solver

You can use Excel's Solver to control the solution of nonlinear equations. Solver operates by guessing a trial solution, trying it, and using the result to intelligently select a new trial solution. Since Solver requires a goal, begin by moving everything to the right side of an equation so that the expected result, or goal, is 0.

1. Start with a copy of sheet fig. 9.4, and name it **fig. 9.8**

2. Select cells A7:C8 and clear them with the Edit ➤ Clear command.

3. Choose the Tools ➤ Options command, Calculation tab. Change the calculation method to Automatic, and turn iteration off by clearing the Iteration checkbox.

4. Change cell A1 to **Electron temperature in GaAs; Solver**

5. In cells F10:F16, enter **300**

6. Change cell G10 to this formula:

    =T+(2/3)*Tau*Q*E10^2*U/(K*(1+R_*EXP(–Delt_E/(K*F10))))–F10

    and copy it to cells G11:G16.

Since you have seven separate solutions, apply Solver to each separately.

OTE

You may be able to combine the solutions into a single cell and use that as the goal for Solver, but it does not always work. To combine the solutions, take the absolute value of the separate solutions so that positive and negative values don't cancel each other out, then sum them together. This is the goal, and if it is a zero, the results of all the formulas are also zero, and you have a solution.

7. Choose the Tools ➤ Solver command. In the dialog box, set Target Cell to **$G$10**, select Equal to Value of **0**, and set By Changing Cells to **$F$10**. Click on Solve and wait for the solution.

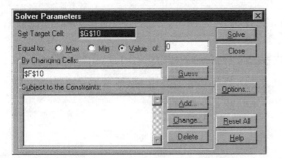

OTE

Because Solver might reach its maximum number of trials before the calculations converge, you may need to run Solver more than once to get a good solution.

8. Calculate solutions for the six other formulas using Solver, by changing the Target Cell and the By Changing Cells boxes as appropriate.

FIGURE 9.8:

Electron temperature in GaAs: the
Solver method

	A	B	C	D	E	F	G	H	I
1	Electron temperature in GaAs; Solver								
2									
3	Delt_E	4.96E-20 J			K	1.38E-23 J/K			
4	Tau	1.00E-12 s			Q	1.60E-19 Coul			
5	U	0.85 m²/V-s			T	300 K			
6					R	94.1			
7									
8					E	Te	f(Te)		
9					(V/m)	(K)	(K)		
10					1.0E+02	3.00E+02	-1.14E-13		
11					1.0E+03	3.00E+02	0.00E+00		
12					1.0E+04	3.01E+02	-1.14E-13		
13					1.0E+05	3.65E+02	8.75E-07		
14					1.0E+06	1.28E+03	-5.54E-04		
15					1.0E+07	1.01E+04	-1.07E-08		
16					1.0E+08	6.95E+05	1.16E-10		

fig. 9.3 / fig. 9.4 / fig. 9.5 / fig. 9.6 / fig. 9.7 \ **fig. 9.8** /

Your worksheet should look like Figure 9.8. Using Solver for a set of formulas tends to be a little slow, because you generally must apply it to each formula separately. You can occasionally combine the outputs of several formulas to apply Solver to several equations at once, but that does not always work. For a single formula it is very fast and easy to setup. To use the method again, place the initial guesses in cells F10:F16 and apply the Solver command.

NOTE   If Solver is having a problem finding a solution, you can apply constraints to the values in the cells being adjusted to keep them in the vicinity of the solution. This is also useful if there are multiple possible solutions and you are looking for one in a particular range of input values.

Summary

In this chapter, you examined four different methods for solving nonlinear equations with a worksheet: successive approximations, over and under relaxation, Newton's method, and Solver. The first two methods will probably solve most of your problems, especially those with large numbers of equations to be solved simultaneously. Newton's method is useful when you need to more quickly solve many formulas and Solver is useful to quickly solve small numbers of equations. There are other methods described in books of numerical methods, but the ones covered here are the easiest to implement on a worksheet.

For More Information

Numerical Methods for Solving Nonlinear Equations

C. Gerald, *Applied Numerical Analysis*, 2nd. ed. (Reading, Mass.: Addison-Wesley, 1978).

W. H. Press, B. P. Flannery, S. A. Teukolsky, W. T. Vetterling, *Numerical Recipes; The Art of Scientific Computing* (Cambridge, UK: Cambridge University Press, 1986).

Electron Temperature in GaAs

S. M. Sze, *Physics of Semiconductor Devices*, 2nd. ed. (New York: John Wiley & Sons, 1981), p. 647.

Review Problems

1. Using the method of successive approximations, solve the following equation for the nontrivial solution for x (that is, a solution other than $x = 0$):

$$x = \tan(0.805x) \qquad x \neq 0$$

2. Complete problem 1 using over relaxation and compare the number of iterations of the worksheet needed to achieve the solution with the same degree of accuracy.

3. The forward current density in a Schottky barrier diode is temperature dependent:

$$J = AT^2 e^{\left(\frac{B}{T}\right)}$$

where

$A = 3.8 \times 10^{-10} \, A/cm^2\text{-}K^2$

$B = 1.7 \times 10^3 \, K$

Find the temperature that gives a current density of $J = 10^{-2} \, A/cm^2$, using successive approximations or under relaxation if necessary.

4. The operational equation for a simple RC circuit with a resistance (R) and capacitance (C) in series with a battery (V) is:

$$q = CV\left(1 - e^{-\left(\frac{t}{RC}\right)}\right)$$

where q is the charge on the capacitor and t is the time. If $V = 10$ volts and R = 2000 ohms, what capacitance is needed to have a charge of $q = 10^{-5}$ coulombs in $t = 4 \times 10^{-3}$ seconds? Use successive approximations and under relaxation to find the answer.

5. The Fermi energy E_f in an n-type semiconductor is calculated by solving this equation:

$$N_c \, e^{-\left(\frac{E_c - E_f}{KT}\right)} = \frac{N_d}{1 + 2e^{\left(\frac{E_f - E_d}{KT}\right)}} + N_v \, e^{\left(\frac{E_v - E_f}{KT}\right)}$$

if

N_c = Density of states in the conduction band = $10^{19} \, cm^{-3}$

N_v = Density of states in the valance band = $10^{19} \, cm^{-3}$

N_d = Number of donor states = $10^{16} \, cm^{-3}$

E_c = Conduction band energy = 1.1 eV

E_d = Donor energy level = 1.05 eV

E_v = Valance band energy = 0 eV

KT = 0.0259 eV

Find the value of the Fermi energy using successive approximations and under or over relaxation.

6. When designing a photovoltaic energy converter (solar cell) to operate in a maximum power configuration, you must solve the following equation for the optimum operating voltage (V):

$$\left(1 + \frac{eV}{KT}\right)e^{\left(\frac{eV}{KT}\right)} = 1 + \frac{J_s}{J_0}$$

at T = 300 K (KT/e = 0.0259 volts) and $J_s/J_0 = 2 \times 10^{10}$ (the ratio of the short circuit to the saturation current density). Find the value of the optimum voltage using Solver.

7. Use Newton's method to find the value of x that is a solution of this equation:

$$3.54 = 2 + 0.3x + 0.07x^2 + 0.004x^3$$

8. Use Newton's method to find the three values of x that are solutions of this equation:

$$27.6 = 14.7x^2 e^{-0.386x}$$

9. Complete problem 4 using Newton's method.

10. Complete problem 6 using Newton's method.

Exercises

1. Perform the successive approximations example in Figure 9.2 without itera-
    tion. Explicitly write out the formulas in successive cells to calculate each
    value of x as follows:

    x_0 = initial guess

    $x_1 = \text{Cos}(x_0)$

    $x_2 = \text{Cos}(x_1)$

    $\vdots$

    $x_n = \text{Cos}(x_{n-1})$

    Include enough terms to see the result converge. Plot the x_n terms versus n
    and the difference between x_n and the converged value of x.

    Do the problem again, but this time use the alternate formulation of the
    equation.

    x_0 = initial guess

    $x_1 = \text{Arccos}(x_0)$

    $x_2 = \text{Arccos}(x_1)$

    $\vdots$

    $x_n = \text{Arccos}(x_{n-1})$

    See if the result diverges. Plot the result versus n.

2. Add a Visual Basic procedure and a button to the Successive Approximations
    example in Figure 9.2 that initializes the problem and calculates the first
    iteration. Add a second button and procedure that displays a dialog box that
    requests the number of iterations and then iterates the problem.

3. Calculate successive approximations solutions to the biological growth
    equation:

    $$P_{n+1} = kP_n(1 - P_n)$$

    which describes a population at generation $n+1$ in terms of the population at
    generation n and the factor k. The factor k describes such things as availabil-
    ity of food, shelter, and fertility. Calculate solutions for values of k between

0.5 and 4.0 with an initial value of P of 0.5. For some values of k, the value of P is a constant, while for others, the solutions appear totally random. Calculations of this type form the basis of the study of Chaos and chaotic dynamics.

4. The resistance (R_T) of a platinum resistance thermometer operating at a temperature below 660°C follows this equation:

$$R_T = R_{20}(1 + \alpha(T - 20) + \beta(T - 20)^2)$$

where $\alpha = 3.6 \times 10^{-3}$ K^{-1}, $\beta = -16.0 \times 10^{-7}$ K^{-2}, R_{20} is the resistance at room temperature (20C) and T is the temperature in centigrade. If $R_{20} = 21.3\ \Omega$ and $R_T = 28.2\ \Omega$, calculate the temperature using successive approximations with over or under relaxation if necessary.

5. Redo Exercise 4 using Newton's method.

6. Redo Review Problem 5 using Newton's method.

7. Use successive approximations to find the solution of:

$$0 - Sin(ax) + Cos(bx) - x$$

where $a = \pi/4$ and $b = \pi/8$.

8. Use Newton's method to find the solution of:

$$7721 = 245 + 718x + 29x^2 + 3x^3$$

9. Solve Review Problem 5 again, but use Newton's method and calculate the derivative numerically, using a central difference formula.

10. Write a Visual Basic program to automatically apply Solver to a set of equations, such as that in Figure 9.8.

CHAPTER

TEN

Solving Sets of Equations

- Matrix solution methods for linear equations

- Gauss-Seidel iteration for linear and nonlinear equations

- Over/Under relaxation methods for linear and nonlinear equations

- Using Solver to solve simultaneous equations

The process of solving many problems in science and engineering often results in sets of simultaneous equations. Numerical solution of partial differential equations; steady-state potentials in electrical networks; and concentration equations for multiple, coupled, chemical reactions are examples of problems whose solutions involve sets of simultaneous equations. Most of these problems result in sets of linear equations, for which there are several good solution methods. If the equations are nonlinear, relaxation methods will usually work, although they are often difficult to get to converge.

NOTE A set of simultaneous equations are only solved when all the equations in the set are satisfied at the same time. If all the equations in the set were independent, solving them would not be difficult. In general, sets of simultaneous equations are heavily coupled, which makes solving them much more difficult.

Solving Linear Equations

Most problems that involve simultaneous equations result in sets of linear equations. This is fortunate, in that linear equations are the easiest to solve. You can solve most of them with Excel's built-in matrix functions, which can handle inversion and multiplication of up to about 60-by-60-element matrices.

NOTE The fact that most physical problems result in sets of linear equations is often by design rather than because of some physical principle. When you approximate a physical system with a formula, the common method is to chop up the domain of the solution into many small pieces and to then approximate the system with a line within each of those pieces. The result is a set of simple linear equations, one for each piece.

Gauss-Seidel iteration and over/under relaxation methods also work well on a worksheet, and can be used for both linear and nonlinear equations. Gauss-Seidel iteration is the multi-equation form of the successive approximations method used on single equations in the previous chapter. As you might expect, the over/under relaxation method is the multi-equation analog of the single-equation over/under relaxation method.

Using Matrix Methods

Matrix solutions of sets of linear equations are the simplest to implement with Excel. First you must write your set of simultaneous equations in matrix format:

$$\mathbf{Ax} = \mathbf{b}$$

where $\mathbf{A}$ is the coefficient matrix, $\mathbf{x}$ is the vector of unknowns, and $\mathbf{b}$ is the result vector. To solve this matrix equation, multiply both sides from the left by the inverse of $\mathbf{A}$:

$$\mathbf{A}^{-1}\mathbf{Ax} = \mathbf{A}^{-1}\mathbf{b}$$

By definition, a matrix times its inverse gives the identity matrix, and the identity matrix times any vector gives the vector back, so the equation above reduces to the following:

$$\mathbf{x} = \mathbf{A}^{-1}\mathbf{b}$$

and you have the solution. Although this seems simple as an abstract equation, calculating the inverse of a matrix is usually not a trivial matter. Fortunately, Excel has that capability built in, in the MINVERSE function.

A Brief Review of Matrix Algebra

In case you have forgotten the rules of matrix algebra, they are reviewed here briefly.

When multiplying a square matrix times a square matrix, you proceed across a row of the matrix on the left and down a column of the matrix on the right. Each element on a row is multiplied by the corresponding term on the column. The sum of these terms forms the result term. The location of the result in the result matrix has the row of the matrix on the left and the column of the matrix on the right.

$$\begin{vmatrix} a & b & c \\ d & e & f \\ g & h & i \end{vmatrix}\begin{vmatrix} j & k & l \\ m & n & o \\ p & q & r \end{vmatrix} = \begin{vmatrix} aj+bm+cp & ak+bn+cq & al+bo+cr \\ dj+em+fp & dk+en+fq & dl+eo+fr \\ gj+hm+ip & gk+hn+iq & gl+ho+ir \end{vmatrix}$$

Multiplication of a matrix times a vector proceeds the same as for a single column in the matrix above.

$$\begin{vmatrix} a & b & c \\ d & e & f \\ g & h & i \end{vmatrix}\begin{vmatrix} j \\ k \\ l \end{vmatrix} = \begin{vmatrix} aj+bk+cl \\ dj+ek+fl \\ gj+hk+il \end{vmatrix}$$

An inverse matrix is defined as the matrix that when multiplied times the matrix gives the identity matrix as a result. The identity matrix is a square matrix with ones on the diagonal and zeroes everywhere else.

$$\mathbf{A}^{-1}\mathbf{A} = \mathbf{I} = \begin{vmatrix} 1 & 0 & 0 & \cdots \\ 0 & 1 & 0 & \cdots \\ 0 & 0 & 1 & \cdots \\ \vdots & \vdots & \vdots & \ddots \end{vmatrix}$$

The identity matrix, when multiplied times any other matrix or vector, returns the original matrix or vector. This is the same as multiplying any number by one:

$$\mathbf{Ix} = \mathbf{x}$$

A matrix is singular if any row is a simple multiple of any other row. A singular matrix does not contain enough information to be solved. If a matrix is singular, its determinant is zero.

Three Equations with Three Variables

As an example, consider this set of linear equations:

$$-8\,x_1 + x_2 + 2\,x_3 = 0$$
$$5\,x_1 + 7\,x_2 - 3\,x_3 = 10$$
$$2\,x_1 + x_2 - 2\,x_3 = -2$$

The solution is $x_1 = 1$, $x_2 = 2$, and $x_3 = 3$. These three equations can be written in matrix format as follows:

$$\begin{vmatrix} -8 & 1 & 2 \\ 5 & 7 & -3 \\ 2 & 1 & -2 \end{vmatrix} \begin{vmatrix} x_1 \\ x_2 \\ x_3 \end{vmatrix} = \begin{vmatrix} 0 \\ 10 \\ -2 \end{vmatrix}$$

You can solve this problem easily in a worksheet.

1. Start with a new worksheet, and name it **fig. 10.1**
2. In cell A1, enter **Solving sets of equations; Matrix inversion**
3. In cell B3, enter **Ax = b**

Enter the coefficient matrix A and the result vector b.

4. In cell A5, enter **Input Matrix (A)**
5. In cells A6:C8, enter the contents of matrix A:

Cell	Contents	Cell	Contents	Cell	Contents
A6	–8	B6	1	C6	2
A7	5	B7	7	C7	–3
A8	2	B8	1	C8	–2

6. In cell E5, enter **Result Vector (b)**
7. In cells E6:E8, enter the contents of the result vector:

Cell	Contents	Cell	Contents	Cell	Contents
E6	0	E7	10	E8	–2

Invert matrix **A** and then multiply vector **b** by the inverse of **A**. The MINVERSE function returns an array of values, so the function must be inserted into the whole range as an array.

8. In cell A10, enter **Inverse matrix (1/A)**

9. Select cells A11:C13, then type

    =MINVERSE(A6:C8)

    and press Ctrl+Shift+Enter (Cmd+Enter on the Macintosh) to insert this formula into the whole selection.

10. In cell E10, enter **Solution Vector x = (1/A)b**

11. Select cells E11:E13, then type

    =MMULT(A11:C13,E6:E8)

    and press Ctrl+Shift+Enter (Cmd+Enter on the Macintosh) to insert the formula into the whole selection.

12. Turn off the gridlines, and outline the worksheet cells as shown in Figure 10.1.

The worksheet should now look like Figure 10.1, with the solution values 1, 2, and 3, for x_1, x_2 and x_3, in cells E11:E13.

FIGURE 10.1:

Solving simultaneous linear equations with the Excel matrix functions

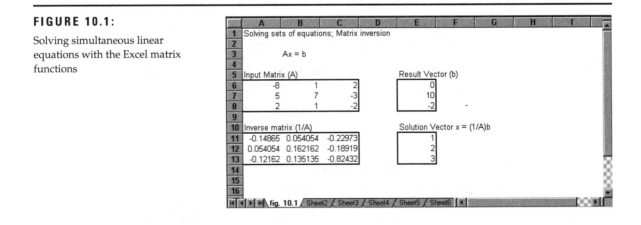

Using Gauss-Seidel Iteration

Gauss-Seidel iteration is a form of the Jacobi method for solving sets of equations. It is a two-dimensional version of the successive approximations method described in the previous chapter. To use it, first solve each of the simultaneous equations for each of the variables, one variable per equation. To decrease the size of the round-off error, try to solve for the variables with the largest coefficients. Pick a set of initial guesses of the values of the variables. Insert them into the equations and calculate a new set of values. Put these values back into the equations and calculate another set. Continue this process until the values converge.

Calculating all the new values of the variables using only the old values in the equations is Jacobi iteration; however, since the cells are calculated one at a time, some of the new values are available before you finish calculating each of the equations. Using these new values as soon as they are available rather than waiting for the next iteration is known as Gauss-Seidel iteration.

To apply Gauss-Seidel iteration to the example problem, first solve the equations for each of the variables:

$$x_1 = \left(\tfrac{1}{8}\right)\left(x_2 + 2x_3\right)$$
$$x_2 = \left(\tfrac{1}{7}\right)\left(10 - 5x_1 + 3x_3\right)$$
$$x_3 = \left(\tfrac{1}{2}\right)\left(2 + 2x_1 + x_2\right)$$

Create a worksheet to solve these equations using Gauss-Seidel iteration.

1. Start with a new worksheet named **fig. 10.2**

2. Choose the Tools ➤ Options command, Calculation tab, and change Calculation to Manual. Check the Iteration check box, set Maximum Iterations to **1**, clear the Recalculate Before Save checkbox, and click OK.

3. In cell A1, enter **Solving sets of equations: Gauss-Seidel iteration**

Add an initialization flag to reset the calculation to a known state. Entering True in cell B3 causes the IF functions in cells C8:C10 to return the initial values in cells A8:A10.

4. In cell A3, enter **Init Flag**

5. In cell B3, enter **True**

6. Name cell B3 as **Init**

Put in an initial guess of 0 for the solution.

7. In cell A6, enter **Initial**

8. In cell A7, enter **Values**

9. In cells A8:A10, enter **0**

Enter the three equations. When a worksheet is iterated, cells with circular references are calculated left to right, top down. If you place formulas in column C that use values stored in column B, the values in column B are equated to the value of the formulas before the formulas are calculated, so column B contains the old values. When the formulas in column C are calculated, they will use only the old values in column B for calculating new values. This is Jacobi iteration.

If you reverse that order and put the formulas in column B and store the values in column C, a formula is calculated in column B, and its new value is stored in column C. The next formula in column B can then use that new value, thus the new values are used in the iteration as soon as they are calculated. This is Gauss-Seidel iteration, which is what you want to use.

10. In cell B6, enter **Equations**

11. In cell B8, enter **=(C9+2*C10)/8**

12. In cell B9, enter **=(10–5*C8+3*C10)/7**

13. In cell B10, enter **=(46–5*C8–7*C9)/9**

Reference the equations, creating a circular reference, and do the initialization test.

14. In cell C6, enter **Solutions**

15. In cell C8, enter the formula **=IF(INIT,A8,B8)** and copy it to cells C9:C10.

16. Format cells B8:C10 as Number, with three decimal places.

17. Turn off the gridlines and outline the cells as shown in Figure 10.2.

To use this worksheet, set the initialization flag to **True** in cell B3, then press F9 (Cmd+= on the Macintosh) and let it recalculate. Once the worksheet has initialized, change the initialization flag to **False** and press F9 again to iterate the worksheet. Continue iterating the worksheet by pressing F9 until the values converge. Your worksheet should look like Figure 10.2.

FIGURE 10.2:

Solving simultaneous linear
equations: Gauss-Seidel iteration

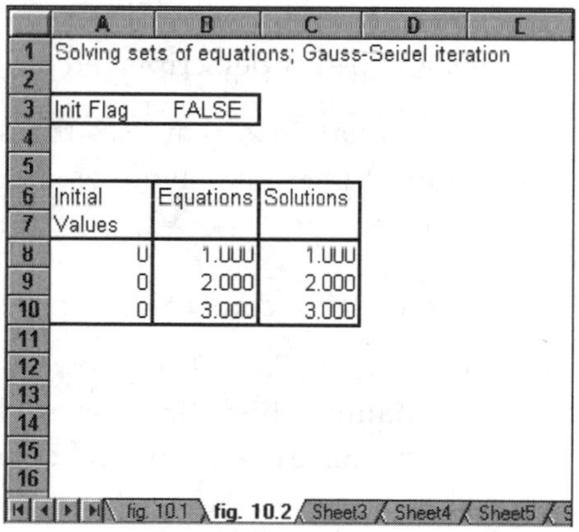

If you are solving a set of equations that are slow to converge, you do not need to press F9 many times to iterate your equations. Instead, choose the Tools ➤ Options command, Calculation tab and change the Maximum Iterations setting to the number of iterations you want executed each time you press F9 (Cmd+= on the Macintosh).

Using the Over/Under Relaxation Method

As with single equations, you can often cause a problem to converge more quickly or more stably by adjusting the amount of the correction applied to the values during each iteration. The over/under relaxation method adds only the fraction C_f of the calculated correction to the values during each step. The fraction C_f can be either greater than or less than 1. If C_f equals 1, this method is equivalent to the Jacobi or Gauss-Seidel method.

First, calculate a new value for each of the unknowns as you did in the Gauss-Seidel method example. Second, instead of using this value in the next iteration, subtract the old value of each unknown to find the change in the unknown. Third, multiply the change in the unknown by C_f and then add it to the old value of the unknown. This is the value to use in the next iteration.

$$x_1^{n+1} = x_1^n + Cf\left[\left(\tfrac{1}{8}\right)\left(x_2^n + 2x_3^n\right) - x_1^n\right]$$

$$x_2^{n+1} = x_2^n + Cf\left[\left(\tfrac{1}{7}\right)\left(10 - 5x_1^n + 3x_3^n\right) - x_2^n\right]$$

$$x_3^{n+1} = x_3^n + Cf\left[\left(\tfrac{1}{2}\right)\left(2 + 2x_1^n + x_2^n\right) - x_3^n\right]$$

The n and $n+1$ superscripts refer to iteration n and $n+1$.

Create a worksheet that uses the over/under relaxation method. This worksheet has almost the same layout as the previous example, so start with a copy of that worksheet.

1. Start with a copy of sheet fig. 10.2, and name it **fig. 10.3**

2. Choose the Tools ➤ Options command, Calculation tab; change Calculation to Manual, check Iteration, set Maximum Iterations to **1**, clear the Recalculate Before Save checkbox, and click OK.

3. Change the width of columns B and C to 11.

4. Change cell A1 to **Solving sets of equations: Over/Under Relaxation**

This worksheet has both an initialization flag and a relaxation factor. The initialization flag sets the worksheet to a predefined initial state. The relaxation factor is multiplied by the change in the values to increase or decrease the amount of correction applied at each iteration.

5. Select cell B3 and drag it to cell C3.

6. In cell A4, enter **Relaxation factor**

7. In cell C4, enter **0.5**

8. Name cell C4 as **Cf**.

NOTE While you can use any reasonable values for the initial values, the closer they are to the solution, the quicker all the formulas will converge.

Put in the relaxation equations. You will recognize the equations from the Gauss-Seidel method, with the added complication of the relaxation factor controlling the amount of the change in each value. Do this by subtracting the old value from the equation, multiplying by C_f, and then adding the old value to the result.

9. Enter the following formulas in cells B8:B10:

Cell	Contents
B8	=C8+Cf*(((C9+2*C10)/8)–C8)
B9	=C9+Cf*(((10–5*C8+3*C10)/7)–C9)
B10	=C10+Cf*(((46–5*C8–7*C9)/9)–C10)

The circular references are already in place in cells C8:C10, using the formulas from the previous problem.

10. Draw borders around the blocks on the table as shown in Figure 10.3.

To use this worksheet, set the value of the relaxation factor in C4. A value of 0.5 seems to work well for this problem. Different problems will respond differently to the value of the relaxation factor. Although you can use any value, it is doubtful that you could get the worksheet to converge with a value greater than about 2. Smaller values are generally more stable but do not converge as fast. Usually, you would start with a value of 1 or 1.5 and see if the worksheet is converging. If it is converging, increase the value; otherwise, decrease it. You do not need to reinitialize the worksheet when you change the value of the relaxation factor as long as the calculated solution values are still reasonable. If the solution values have started to diverge, you should reinitialize the problem.

Set the value of the initialization flag in cell C3 to **True** and press F9 (Cmd+= on the Macintosh.) Change the initialization flag to **False** and press F9 again. Continue pressing F9 until the values converge.

When the worksheet converges, it should look like Figure 10.3. Remember, you do not need to sit at your computer and press F9 many times to iterate your equations. You can increase the number of times the problem is iterated by changing the Maximum Iterations setting in the Options Calculation dialog box.

FIGURE 10.3:

Solving simultaneous linear equations: over/under relaxation method

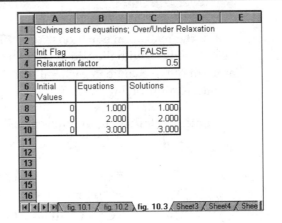

Using Solver with Sets of Equations

If you lay out the worksheet carefully, you can use Solver with simultaneous linear equations. Solver optimizes the value of a single cell, so to use it to solve several simultaneous equations, you must combine the results of all the equations into a single value and then optimize that value. One way to combine the results is to rewrite all the equations to equal zero when a solution is reached, and then add the absolute values of these solutions. When that sum is zero, you have solved all the equations. The absolute value ensures that the results from two equations don't cancel each other by having equal results of the opposite sign instead of zero. Solver can adjust several values to optimize the result, so the input cells do not require special handling.

WARNING Be sure you take the absolute value of the result of each formula before you sum them, or one negative result may cancel a positive result, making the sum zero when the individual equations are not zero.

WARNING Solver can solve multiple equations as long as the results that are added together are roughly the same size. If not, then one result dominates the calculation, making it difficult or impossible for Solver to find a solution. If the results are of different orders of magnitude, multiply the results by some factor to make their magnitudes roughly equal. Multiplying by some value won't change the results, because the wanted result is 0.

1. Start with a new worksheet, and name it **fig. 10.4**

2. Change the width of column A to 4.

3. In cell A1, enter **Solving sets of equations; Solver method**

Now put in the formulas. These formulas are the same as in the last problem, except that the value on the left side of the equation is subtracted from the right to make the result 0. When all these formulas evaluate to 0, the problem is solved.

4. In cells B8:B10, enter

Cell	Contents
B8	=((C9+2*C10)/8)−C8
B9	=((10−5*C8+3*C10)/7)−C9
B10	=((46-5*C8-7*C9)/9)-C10

Next, insert the initial guess as to the solutions.

5. In cell C8, enter **1** and copy it to cells C9:C10.

Sum the absolute values of these solutions in a cell to create a single value for Solver to optimize. The cell calculates an array formula, so enter it with Ctrl+Shift+Enter(Cmd+Enter on the Macintosh).

6. In cell C12, type

   =SUM(ABS(B8:B10))

   and press Ctrl+Shift+Enter (Cmd+Enter on the Macintosh.)

7. Outline the cells as shown in Figure 10.4.

FIGURE 10.4:

Solving simultaneous equations using Solver

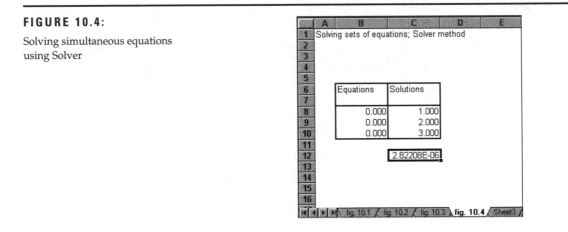

Now solve the formulas with Solver.

8. Choose Tools ➤ Solver.

9. Select cell $C$12 for the Set Cell option (the cell to optimize) and cells $C$8:$C$10 as the cells to change. Select the Value Of option and enter **0** in the Value Of box. Click Solve to search for a solution.

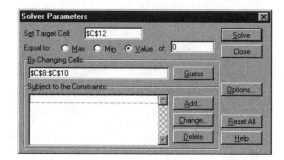

When Solver locates a solution to the problem, it displays the Solver Results dialog shown below.

If Solver can't find a solution, it will tell you. If this happens, try running Solver again. It may have reached its maximum number of trial solutions and just needs to try a few more. You may also need to try different starting values if you are having trouble getting the solutions to converge. The results are shown in Figure 10.4.

Solving Simultaneous Nonlinear Equations

In some cases, you can use the Gauss-Seidel or Jacobi method to solve multiple, simultaneous, nonlinear equations; however, you will usually need the extra control of the over/under relaxation method to get the equations to converge. Solver is also useful if the equations can be put into a form where only a single cell needs to be optimized, and the results of the formulas are all of about the same size. If the results vary widely, the formula with the largest value dominates the solution. You apply these methods to non-linear equations in the same way you applied them to linear equations.

Nonlinear equations may have multiple solutions, so the starting value can be important. If the equations are extremely nonlinear, they may not converge if the initial values are too far from the solution. Try changing those values as well as the relaxation factor if you are having trouble getting a solution.

Accuracy and Scaling

An unfortunate consequence of using matrix and iteration methods to solve simultaneous equations is that the accuracy of the solution can depend on the order in which you solve the equations. When you are preparing the equations for numerical solution, you must solve one equation for each variable. For the best results, try to solve each equation for the variable with the largest coefficient (ignore the sign of the coefficient). Ideally, you would end up with one equation solved for each variable, but that is not usually the case. Use your judgment to decide which equation to solve for which variable.

NOTE

When deciding what variables to solve for, a factor of two difference between two coefficients is not important, while a factor of ten is.

When you are using the matrix methods, the relative size of the values in the coefficient matrix that you are solving is also important. All the values in the coefficient matrix should be about the same order of magnitude. If one equation has coefficients that are several orders of magnitude larger or smaller than any of the others, the accuracy of the solution will be poor. To correct this situation, scale each equation (a row in the matrix) by dividing each of the coefficients by the magnitude of the largest coefficient in that equation. When you are scaling an equation, do not forget to scale the result (the **b** values on the right sides of the equations) also.

If your matrix is singular (it has a zero on the diagonal), you will never get a solution. To test for singularity, calculate the determinant of the **A** matrix using the MDETERM function. If the determinant is zero, the matrix is singular. If the determinant is very small, but not zero, it may have a solution, but that solution might be very hard to find. Round-off error may make a matrix appear singular even though it has a small but real determinant. If the determinant is small, check the result very carefully to be sure it is real. If you are having trouble getting a good solution, consult a numerical methods book for more information about matrix methods.

Summary

This chapter reviewed five methods for solving linear and nonlinear sets of simultaneous equations with a worksheet. Excel has the built-in capability to invert and multiply matrices, which can be used to solve most sets of linear equations. The Gauss-Seidel, Jacobi, and over/under relaxation methods are all implemented with the iteration capability of the worksheet. These three methods are applicable to the solution of nonlinear as well as linear equations. Also, the Solver add-in program can often be adapted to solve both linear and nonlinear equations.

For More Information

Numerical Methods for Solving Nonlinear Equations

C. Gerald, *Applied Numerical Analysis*, 2nd. ed. (Reading, Mass.: Addison-Wesley, 1978).

W. H. Press, B. P. Flannery, S. A. Teukolsky, W. T. Vetterling, *Numerical Recipes; The Art of Scientific Computing* (Cambridge, UK: Cambridge University Press, 1986)

Review Problems

1. Solve the following set of equations for x, y, and z using the matrix functions.

$$4x + 3.9y + 0.27z = 39.6$$
$$22x + 14y + 5z = 233.12$$
$$5.6x + 4.8y + 2.1z = 69.91$$

2. Solve these circuit equations (for the circuit in the illustration below) for I_1 and I_2 using Gauss-Seidel iteration.

$$V = I_1(R_1 + R_2) + I_2 R_1$$
$$0 = I_2 R_3 - I_1 R_2$$

$R_1 = 10$ ohms, $R_2 = 5$ ohms, $R_3 = 10$ ohms, $V = 10$ volts

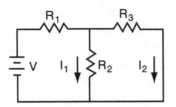

3. Solve the following set of equations for x, y, and z using the matrix functions.

$$x + y - 2z = 10$$
$$1.5x + 2y + 2z = 1$$
$$2.5x + 4y + 3z = 4$$

4. Solve the following set of equations for x, y, z, w, and v using the matrix functions.

$$3x + 7y + 5z + 20w + 4v = 96$$
$$x + 2y + 3z + 9w + 10v = 67$$
$$5x + y + 16z - 4w + 6v = 124$$
$$2x + 2y + z + w + 18v = 73$$
$$x + 3y - z + 5w + 2v = 19$$

5. Solve the following set of equations for x, y, and z using the over/under relaxation method.

$$x + 3y + z = 17$$
$$4x + 2y + z = 27$$
$$5x + 6y - z = 25$$

6. Balanced bridge circuits (illustrated below) are commonly used in pressure transducers. Resistors R_5 and R_6 are strain gauges that are such that when pressure is applied to the transducer, they change in opposite directions (one

increases and one decreases), creating an imbalance in the bridge. This produces an output V_0 at the terminals.

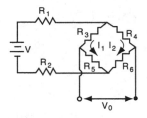

Given that:

$$R_1 = R_2 = 1 \text{ ohm}$$
$$R_3 = R_4 = 100 \text{ ohms}$$
$$R_5 = 1002 \text{ ohms}$$
$$R_6 = 998 \text{ ohms}$$
$$V = 10 \text{ volts}$$

solve the following circuit equations for I_1, I_2, and V_0 using the over/under relaxation method.

$$V = (I_1 + I_2)(R_1 + R_2) + I_1(R_3 + R_5)$$
$$V_0 = I_2R_4 - I_1R_3 \quad V_0 = I_1R_5 - I_2R_6$$

Solve the equations again, letting $R_5 = R_6 = 1000$ ohms (this is the balanced situation). Try different values of R_5 and R_6, always increasing one while decreasing the other.

7. When one particle scatters elastically off of a stationary particle (illustrated below), the initial and final velocities and directions can be calculated using the equations for conservation of momentum and energy.

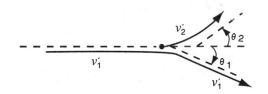

Here, unprimed velocities (v) occur before the collision and primed ones occur after.

$$m_1 v_1 = m_1 v_1' \cos(\theta_1) + m_2 v_2' \cos(\theta_2)$$
$$m_1 v_1' \sin(\theta_1) = m_2 v_2' \sin(\theta_2)$$
$$\tfrac{1}{2} m_1 v_1^2 = \tfrac{1}{2} m_1 v_1'^2 + \tfrac{1}{2} m_2 v_2'^2$$

If particle 1 is a proton ($m_1 = m_p = 1.67 \times 10^{-27}$ Kg) moving at 250 m/s, particle 2 is a helium nucleus ($m_2 = 4m_p$), and particle 1 flies off at an angle (θ_1) of 25 degrees, calculate θ_2, v_1', and v_2' using over/under relaxation.

8. Four different springs are attached end-to-end and stretched between two walls (illustrated below). The force (F) applied by each spring to the adjacent springs is of the form

$$F = k(x - x_0)$$

k is the spring constant and x_0 is the unstretched length of the spring.

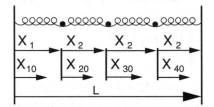

At equilibrium, all the forces are equal, and the system can be described by the following equations.

$$k_1(x_1 - x_{10}) = k_2(x_2 - x_{20})$$
$$k_2(x_2 - x_{20}) = k_3(x_3 - x_{30})$$
$$k_3(x_3 - x_{30}) = k_4(x_4 - x_{40})$$
$$x_1 + x_2 + x_3 + x_4 = L$$

Given that:

$$k_1 = 10 \text{ Nt/m}$$

$$k_2 = 20 \text{ Nt/m}$$
$$k_3 = 30 \text{ Nt/m}$$
$$k_4 = 40 \text{ Nt/m}$$
$$x_{10} = x_{20} = x_{30} = x_{40} = 10 \text{ cm}$$
$$L = 80 \text{ cm}$$

find x_1, x_2, x_3, and x_4 using over/under relaxation.

9. Solve the following nonlinear equations for x and t using over/under relaxation.

$$x = ae^{-\alpha t}$$
$$x = b \, \text{Sin}(\theta t)$$
$$a = b = 2, \ \theta = 4, \ \alpha = 0.5$$

10. Solve the following nonlinear equations for ϖ, α, and β using over/under relaxation.

$$2 \, \text{Sin}(\theta) + 3 \cos(\alpha) + 9 \cos(\beta) = 7.548$$
$$4 \, \text{Cos}(\theta) + 4 \, \text{Cos}(\alpha) + 2 \, \text{Sin}(\beta) = 6.390$$
$$5 \, \text{Sin}(\theta) + \text{Sin}(\alpha) + 2 \, \text{Sin}(\beta) - 3.587$$

Exercises

1. Solve the following set of equations for x, y, and z using the matrix functions.

$$18x + 3y + 2.2z = 493.1$$
$$67x + 5.9y + 7z = 1745.78$$
$$14x + 6y + 15.6z = 609.2$$

2. Solve the following set of equations for x, y, and z using Gauss-Seidel iteration. Beware of scaling problems.

$$100x + 120y + 220z = 3840$$
$$1x + 2y + 1z = 36$$
$$0.1x + 0.2y + 0.3z = 5.2$$

3. The balanced bridge circuit shown in Review Problem 6 is also used to measure small displacements by inserting a strain gauge in one of the arms and attaching the gauge to a bar that is bent when the displacement occurs. The displacement bends the bar, which stresses the strain gauge, changing its resistance. Solve the balanced bridge problem using Solver and the values from Review Problem 6, except let $R_5 = 1000$ ohms and $R_6 = 1200$ ohms.

4. Solve the following set of equations for a, b, c, d, e, f, and g using the matrix functions.

$$57a + 77b + 72c + 45d + 54e + 63f + 99g = 20643$$
$$4a + 100b + 16c + 23d + 44e + 11f + 67g = 11902$$
$$1a + 79b + 94c + 27d + 62e + 55f + 88g = 19526$$
$$53a + 25b + 62c + 33d + 73e + 2f + 8g = 9898$$
$$48a + 73b + 58c + 46d + 43e + 56f + 14g = 11492$$
$$38a + 71b + 94c + 86d + 72e + 78f + 25g = 17226$$
$$17a + 70b + 10c + 6d + 59e + 69f + 59g = 16303$$

5. Redo exercise 4 using Gauss/Seidel iteration.

6. Redo exercise 4 using over/under relaxation.

7. Redo exercise 4 using Solver.

8. Solve the following two equations for x and t using over/under relaxation.

$$x = ae^{bt} + ce^{dt} + e$$
$$x = a\mathrm{Sin}(bt) + c\mathrm{Cos}(dt)$$

where

$a = 23$

$b = -2$

$c = 19$

$d = 2$

$e = -158.38$

9. Solve the following three equations for a, b, and c.

$$3\text{Sin}(a)+4\text{Cos}(b)+5\text{Tan}(c) = 5.69$$
$$3\text{Sin}(2a)+4\text{Cos}(2b)+5\text{Tan}(2c) = 4.01$$
$$3\text{Sin}(3a)+4\text{Cos}(3b)+5\text{Tan}(3c) = 5.91$$

10. Refer to the spring arrangement in Review Problem 8; solve for the situation where the spring constants are the same but the unstretched lengths are different.

$$k_1 = k_2 = k_3 = k_4 = 20 \text{ Nt/m}$$
$$x_{10} = 10 \text{ cm}$$
$$x_{20} = 20 \text{ cm}$$
$$x_{30} = 30 \text{ cm}$$
$$x_{40} = 40 \text{ cm}$$
$$L = 200 \text{ cm}$$

CHAPTER

ELEVEN

Solving Ordinary
Differential Equations

- Solving initial-value problems

- Solving boundary-value problems

- Using the Taylor Series method

- Using the Euler method

- Using the modified Euler method

- Using the Runge-Kutta method

- Using the shooting method

- Using the finite difference method

Most people don't think of using a worksheet to solve differential equations; however, with a worksheet's dynamically linked cells and iterative capability, you can calculate solutions for many different types of differential equations. Two kinds of ordinary differential equations are readily solved on a worksheet: initial-value problems and boundary-value problems. The differential equations for these types of problems can be the same; the difference is in the location of the boundary conditions.

Solving Initial-Value Problems

Initial-value problems are those in which the known boundary conditions are all at one boundary of the problem. The goal is to integrate the differential equation from the known boundary to the unknown one. Differential equations with time derivatives are often of this type, where you know the value of the solution now (the known boundary) and need to integrate the differential equation for some time into the future (the unknown boundary). In this section, you will examine four of the most popular methods for solving these types of equations: Taylor series, Euler, modified Euler, and Runge-Kutta.

An Initial-Value, Ordinary Differential Equation

Consider the following first-order ordinary differential equation:

$$(1 + x^2)^{1/2} \frac{du(x)}{dx} + u(x) = x \qquad x>0$$

with the boundary condition:

$$u(0) = 0$$

This is an initial-value problem because the boundary condition is known only at one location. Actually, first-order, ordinary differential equations with one variable should have only one boundary condition. If there were more than one boundary condition, the problem would be over-specified and possibly unsolvable.

Second- and higher-order differential equations require more boundary conditions in order to be solved.

Understanding Boundary Conditions

To understand why some differential equations need one boundary condition and others need more, consider a simple function:

$$y = f(x)$$

With this equation, you can plot the value of y for every value of the independent variable x. This equation is fully specified and needs no boundary conditions to determine the correct values of y. Next consider the following equation:

$$y' = f(x)$$

This equation is a first-order differential equation, with the derivative of y specified for every value of x. The derivative is the slope of the plot of y, and knowing the slope, you can draw the shape of the plot of y; however, while you know the shape of the plot, you don't know where the plot belongs. All of the plots in the following graphic are valid solutions to a differential equation—you need to know the value of the function somewhere (for example, the black dot at the left boundary) to determine which is the correct solution. That single point is a boundary condition.

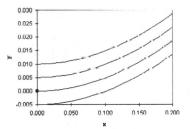

Next, consider a second-order differential equation such as the following:

$$y'' = f(x)$$

Here, you know the curvature of the function for every value of x. If you know the initial slope and value of the function, or the value of the function at two points, you can use the curvature to figure out the rest. The initial value and slope are the two boundary conditions needed to solve the problem. Thus, for each order of the differential equation, you need a boundary condition to get a complete solution. If the equation involves more than one independent variable, such as a two-dimensional differential equation, you need a set of boundary conditions for each of those variables.

The problem is to calculate the value of u over the range $x = 0$ to 0.2. For this problem, I know that the analytical solution is

$$u(x) = \frac{1}{2}\left[x - \frac{\ln\left(x + \sqrt{1+x^2}\right)}{\left(x + \sqrt{1+x^2}\right)} \right]$$

which we will use to evaluate the effectiveness of the different solution methods. Figure 11.1 shows this solution over the range $x = 0$ to 0.2.

FIGURE 11.1:

Analytic solution to an initial-value problem

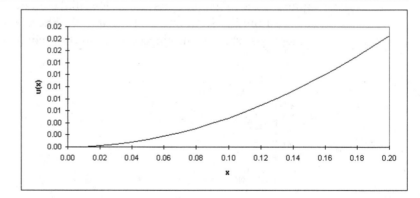

Using the Taylor Series Method

One of the more popular methods of solving an initial-value problem is the Taylor series method. Consider the Taylor series expansion of some function $u(x)$ about the value x_0.

$$u(x) = u(x_0) + \frac{(x - x_0)}{1!}u'(x_0) + \frac{(x - x_0)^2}{2!}u''(x_0)$$
$$+ \frac{(x - x_0)^3}{3!}u'''(x_0) + \frac{(x - x_0)^4}{4!}u''''(x_0) + \cdots$$

using the notation

$$u'(x) = \frac{du}{dx}, \quad u''(x) = \frac{d^2u(x)}{dx^2}, \cdots$$

Let $h = (x - x_0)$, and the equation becomes

$$u(x) = u(x_0) + \frac{h}{1!}u'(x_0) + \frac{h^2}{2!}u''(x_0)$$
$$+ \frac{h^3}{3!}u'''(x_0) + \frac{h^4}{4!}u''''(x_0) + \cdots$$

For $x_0 = 0$, the values of the first two terms of the Taylor series are known. You know the first from the boundary condition and the second from the differential equation. These values are

$$u(0) = 0$$

$$u'(x) = \frac{(x - u(x))}{(1 + x^2)^{1/2}}$$

By successively taking derivatives of the equation for the first derivative, you get equations for the higher-order derivatives:

$$u''(x) = \frac{(x - u'(x))}{(1 + x^2)^{1/2}} - \frac{x(x - u(x))}{(1 + x^2)^{3/2}}$$

$$u''' = -\frac{u''(x)}{(1+x^2)^{1/2}} - \frac{2x\,(1-u'(x))+x-u(x)}{(1+x^2)^{3/2}} + \frac{3x^2\,(x-u(x))}{(1+x^2)^{5/2}}$$

$$u''''(x) = -\frac{u'''(x)}{(1+x^2)^{1/2}} - \frac{3xu''(x)-3(1-u'(x))}{(1+x^2)^{3/2}} + \frac{9x^2\,(1-u'(x))+9x\,(x-u(x))}{(1+x^2)^{5/2}}$$

$$+ \frac{15x^2\,(x-u(x))}{(1+x^2)^{7/2}}$$

from which you get:

$u(0) = 0$

$u'(0) = 0$

$u''(0) = 1$

$u'''(0) = -1$

$u''''(0) = -2$

Insert these into the first five terms of the Taylor expansion, and then truncate the expansion after the fifth term. This creates the approximation function:

$$u(h) = \frac{h^2}{2} - \frac{h^3}{6} - \frac{h^4}{12}$$

which is used to calculate values of the differential equation for different values of h.

WARNING	Truncating the Taylor series is only valid if the truncated terms are small, which is only true if h is small. Thus, the Taylor series method is only valid for small values of h.

In this next example, use the Taylor series method to calculate the values of $u(x)$ for $x = 0$ to 0.2.

1. Start with a new worksheet, and name it **fig. 11.2**

2. Change the widths of columns A through D as follows.

Cell	Width	Cell	Width
A	7	C	11
B	12	D	11

3. In cell A1, enter **Ordinary Differential Equations; Taylor series method**

Enter the *x* range data and calculate the value of the analytic solution to the problem to use as a comparison. Next, use the Taylor series expansion to calculate the solution of the partial differential equation. Compare the values calculated with the Taylor series expansion with the correct values in column B.

4. In cells A3:D3, enter and center the indicated labels:

Cell	Contents	Cell	Contents	Cell	Contents	Cell	Contents
A3	x	B3	**u(x)**	C3	**u(x)**	D3	**Error**
		B4	**Analytical**	C4	**Taylor**	D4	**%**

5. In cell A5, enter **0**, and in cell A6, enter **0.01**; select cells A5:A6 and drag the fill handle to cell A25.

6. Format cells A5:A25 as Number, with two decimal places.

7. In cell B5, enter

   =0.5*(A5–LN(A5+SQRT(1+A5^2))/(A5+SQRT(1+A5^2)))

   and copy it to cells B6:B25.

8. In cell C5, enter

   =A5^2/2–A5^3/6–A5^4/12

   and copy it to cells C6:C25.

9. Format cells B5:C25 as Scientific, with two decimal places.

10. In cell D6, enter **=(B6–C6)/B6** and copy it to cells D7:D25.

11. Format cells D6:D25 as Percent, with five decimal places.

FIGURE 11.2:

Solution of an initial-value problem using the Taylor series method

	A	B	C	D	E	F	G	H
1	Ordinary Differential Equations; Taylor series method							
2								
3	x	u(x)	u(x)	Error				
4		Analytical	Taylor	%				
5	0.00	0.00E+00	0.00E+00					
6	0.01	4.98E-05	4.98E-05	0.00001%				
7	0.02	1.99E-04	1.99E-04	0.00011%				
8	0.03	4.45E-04	4.45E-04	0.00037%				
9	0.04	7.89E-04	7.89E-04	0.00088%				
10	0.05	1.23E-03	1.23E-03	0.00174%				
11	0.06	1.76E-03	1.76E-03	0.00303%				
12	0.07	2.39E-03	2.39E-03	0.00486%				
13	0.08	3.11E-03	3.11E-03	0.00731%				
14	0.09	3.92E-03	3.92E-03	0.01049%				
15	0.10	4.83E-03	4.83E-03	0.01451%				
16	0.11	5.82E-03	5.82E-03	0.01946%				

fig. 11.1 / fig. 11.2 / Sheet3 / Sheet4 / Sheet5 / Sheet6

The worksheet should now look like Figure 11.2. Note that the solution is extremely accurate for these small values of x. If you try larger values of x (say 0 to 2) the error will be quite large. You must use values of h (x in this case, since $x_0 = 0$) that are less than 1 for this method to be accurate.

Note that for the Taylor series method, h is measured from x_0 and is not the step size that will be used in the rest of these problems. To calculate values of u over longer distances, you must recalculate the values of the derivatives at the end of the current step so that you can take another step beyond that point.

Using the Euler and Modified Euler Methods

One of the major difficulties with the Taylor series method is that you must analytically calculate several derivatives of your equation. Some equations may have simple derivatives, but others, such as the one used in the example, do not. The Euler method eliminates calculating these derivatives by truncating the Taylor series at the first derivative term. To make it work, you must use small steps (h) and recalculate the value of the first derivative at each step:

$$u(x+h) = u(x) + hu'(x)$$

Create a worksheet to calculate the differential equation using the Euler method. Start with the worksheet for the Taylor series example, because the layouts are similar.

1. Start with a copy of sheet fig. 11.2, and name it **fig. 11.3**

2. Change the widths of column E to 11 and F to 9.

3. Change cell A1 to **Ordinary Differential Equations; Euler and modified Euler methods**

4. Clear cells C3:C25.

Calculate the solution of the equation using the Euler method.

5. In cell C4, enter **Euler**

6. In cell C5, enter **0**

7. In cell C6, enter

    =C5+(A6–A5)*(A5–C5)/SQRT(1+A5^2)

    and copy it to cells C7:C25.

Your worksheet should now look like Figure 11.3. As you can see, this method is not very accurate.

Since you are using the slope (the derivative) at the beginning of a step to determine the value at the end of the step, the method is in error every time, and the error is additive and grows as you integrate farther. A better way to estimate the value of the next point is to use the average slope over a step:

$$u(x+h) = u(x) + h\frac{(u'(x)+u'(x+h))}{2}$$

FIGURE 11.3:

Solution to the initial-value problem using the Euler method

	A	B	C	D	E	F	G	H
1	Ordinary Differential Equations; Euler and modified Euler methods							
2								
3	x	u(x)		Error				
4		Analytical	Euler	%				
5	0.00	0.00E+00	0.00E+00					
6	0.01	4.98E-05	0.00E+00	100.00000%				
7	0.02	1.99E-04	1.00E-04	49.66362%				
8	0.03	4.45E-04	2.99E-04	32.88452%				
9	0.04	7.89E-04	5.96E-04	24.49477%				
10	0.05	1.23E-03	9.90E-04	19.46078%				
11	0.06	1.76E-03	1.48E-03	16.10470%				
12	0.07	2.39E-03	2.06E-03	13.70744%				
13	0.08	3.11E-03	2.74E-03	11.90946%				
14	0.09	3.92E-03	3.51E-03	10.51101%				
15	0.10	4.83E-03	4.37E-03	9.39225%				
16	0.11	5.82E-03	5.32E-03	8.47691%				

fig. 11.1 / fig. 11.2 / **fig. 11.3** / fig. 11.4 / Sheet3 / She

The difficulty with this approach is that you do not know the value of the slope at the end of the step. The modified Euler method uses the Euler method to make an initial estimate of the solution. This initial estimate is then used to calculate the value of the slope at the end of the step. Using the average of the slope at the beginning of the step and the estimate of the slope at the end, you calculate a better value for the solution. You could apply this method again to try to improve the solution, but when you use more than one or two iterations, the error in the method is as large as any increase in accuracy gained by iteration.

Now recalculate the worksheet using the modified Euler method. First, calculate the initial prediction of the solution using the Euler method.

1. Start with a copy of sheet fig. 11.3, and name it **fig. 11.4**

2. In cell E3, enter **Modified Euler**

3. Select cells E3:F3 and click on the Center Across Columns button on the toolbar.

4. In cell E4, enter **Predicted** and center it.

5. In cell E5, enter

$$=F5+(A6-A5)*(A5-F5)/SQRT(1+A5\text{^}2)$$

and copy it to cells E6:E25.

Use that initial prediction to calculate the average slope and to calculate a corrected value of the solution. Compare that value to the analytic solution.

6. In cell F4, enter **Corrected** and center it.

7. In cell F5, enter **0**

8. In cell F6, enter

$$=F5+((A6-A5)/2)*((A5-F5)/SQRT(1+A5\text{^}2)+(A6-C6)/SQRT(1+A6\text{^}2))$$

and copy it to cells F7:F25.

9. Format cells E5:F25 as Scientific, with two decimal places.

10. In cell G3, enter **Error** and center it.

11. In cell G4, enter **%** and center it.

12. In cell G6, enter **=(B6–F6)/B6** and copy it to cells G6:G25.

13. Format cells G6:G25 as Percent, with two decimal places.

FIGURE 11.4:

Solution to an initial-value problem using the Euler and modified Euler methods

	A	B	C	D	E	F	G	H
1	Ordinary Differential Equations; Euler and modified Euler methods							
2								
3	x	u(x)	u(x)	Error	Modified Euler		Error	
4		Analytical	Euler	%	Predicted	Corrected	%	
5	0.00	0.00E+00	0.00E+00		0.00E+00	0.00E+00		
6	0.01	4.98E-05	0.00E+00	100.00000%	1.49E-04	5.00E-05	-0.33%	
7	0.02	1.99E-04	1.00E-04	49.66362%	3.97E-04	1.99E-04	-0.29%	
8	0.03	4.45E-04	2.99E-04	32.88452%	7.42E-04	4.47E-04	-0.27%	
9	0.04	7.89E-04	5.96E-04	24.49477%	1.18E-03	7.91E-04	-0.26%	
10	0.05	1.23E-03	9.90E-04	19.46078%	1.72E-03	1.23E-03	-0.26%	
11	0.06	1.76E-03	1.48E-03	16.10470%	2.35E-03	1.77E-03	-0.25%	
12	0.07	2.39E-03	2.06E-03	13.70744%	3.07E-03	2.40E-03	-0.25%	
13	0.08	3.11E-03	2.74E-03	11.90946%	3.89E-03	3.12E-03	-0.25%	
14	0.09	3.92E-03	3.51E-03	10.51101%	4.79E-03	3.93E-03	-0.25%	
15	0.10	4.83E-03	4.37E-03	9.39225%	5.78E-03	4.84E-03	-0.24%	
16	0.11	5.82E-03	5.32E-03	8.47691%	6.87E-03	5.83E-03	-0.24%	

fig. 11.1 / fig. 11.2 / fig. 11.3 / **fig. 11.4** / Sheet3 / She

Your worksheet should now look like Figure 11.4. Note that the solution has improved tremendously, with the error staying around ¼ percent. You can use this method to calculate the value of the solution to large values of x, as long as you take small steps to get there.

Using the Runge-Kutta Method

The current method of choice for most initial-value problems is the fourth-order Runge-Kutta method. This method uses a combination of four estimators to calculate an accurate value of the solution. Refer to a book on numerical methods if you are interested in the background of this method.

The development of a step with the Runge-Kutta method goes as follows:

$$u(x+h) = u(x) + \frac{1}{6}\left(k_1 + 2k_2 + 2k_3 + k_4\right)$$

where

$$k_1 = hu'(x, u(x))$$

$$k_2 = hu'(x + \frac{h}{2}, u(x) + \frac{k_1}{2})$$

$$k_3 = hu'(x + \frac{h}{2}, u(x) + \frac{k_2}{2})$$

$$k_4 = hu'(x + h, u(x) + k_3)$$

445

Here $u'(x,u(x))$ is the first derivative of $u(x)$ with respect to x, which is a function of x and $u(x)$.

Now recalculate the worksheet using the Runge-Kutta method. This problem uses the same differential equation and set up as the two previous examples.

1. Start with a copy of sheet fig 11.4, and name it fig. **11.5**

2. Clear cells C3:G25.

3. Change the widths of columns A through H as follows:

Column	Width	Column	Width
A	7	B	11
C	10	D	10
E	10	F	10
G	10	H	11

4. Change cell A1 to **Ordinary Differential Equations; Runge-Kutta method**

Calculate the values of the four estimators. These estimators are used to advance to the next step.

5. In cells C3:G3, enter and center: **k1, k2, k3, k4,** and **u(x).**

6. In cell C5, enter **0**

7. In cell C6, enter

$$=(A6–A5)*(A5–G5)/SQRT(1+A5\text{^}2)$$

and copy it to cells C7:C25.

8. In cell D6, enter

$$=(A6–A5)*((A5+(A6–A5)/2)–(G5+C6/2))/SQRT(1+(A5+(A6–A5)/2)\text{^}2)$$

and copy it to cells D7:D25.

9. In cell E6, enter

$$=(A6–A5)*((A5+(A6–A5)/2)–(G5+D6/2))/SQRT(1+(A5+(A6–A5)/2)\text{^}2)$$

and copy it to cells E7:E24.

10. In cell F6, enter

    =(A6–A5)*(A6–(G5+E6))/SQRT(1+A6^2)

    and copy it to cells F7:F25.

Calculate the solution of the problem by combining the values of the estimators. Compare the solution to the analytic result.

11. In cell G5, enter 0

12. In cell G6, enter

    =G5+(1/6)*(C6+2*D6+2*E6+F6)

    and copy it to cells G7:G25.

13. Format cells B5:G25 as Scientific, with two decimal places.

14. In cell H3, enter **Error** and center it.

15. In cell H4, enter % and center it.

16. In cell H6, enter **=100*(B6-G6)/B6** and copy it to cells H7:H25.

17. Format cells H6:H25 as Scientific, with two decimal places.

Your worksheet should look like Figure 11.5. Now you see some real improvement in the accuracy of the solution. Although this method takes up five columns of the worksheet, the largest error is -1.26×10^{-6} percent. This is several orders of magnitude better than any of the other methods.

FIGURE 11.5:

Solving an initial-value problem using the Runge-Kutta method

	A	B	C	D	E	F	G	H
1	Ordinary Differential Equations; Runge-Kutta method							
2								
3	x	u(x)	k1	k2	k3	k4	u(x)	Error
4		Analytical						%
5	0.00	0.00E+00	0.00E+00				0.00E+00	
6	0.01	4.98E-05	0.00E+00	5.00E-05	4.97E-05	9.95E-05	4.98E-05	-1.26E-06
7	0.02	1.99E-04	9.95E-05	1.49E-04	1.49E-04	1.98E-04	1.99E-04	-6.27E-07
8	0.03	4.45E-04	1.98E-04	2.47E-04	2.47E-04	2.95E-04	4.45E-04	-4.17E-07
9	0.04	7.89E-04	2.95E-04	3.44E-04	3.44E-04	3.92E-04	7.89E-04	-3.12E-07
10	0.05	1.23E-03	3.92E-04	4.40E-04	4.39E-04	4.87E-04	1.23E-03	-2.49E-07
11	0.06	1.76E-03	4.87E-04	5.34E-04	5.34E-04	5.81E-04	1.76E-03	-2.07E-07
12	0.07	2.39E-03	5.81E-04	6.28E-04	6.28E-04	6.74E-04	2.39E-03	-1.77E-07
13	0.08	3.11E-03	6.74E-04	7.21E-04	7.20E-04	7.66E-04	3.11E-03	-1.54E-07
14	0.09	3.92E-03	7.66E-04	8.12E-04	8.12E-04	8.57E-04	3.92E-03	-1.37E-07
15	0.10	4.83E-03	8.57E-04	9.02E-04	9.02E-04	9.47E-04	4.83E-03	-1.23E-07
16	0.11	5.82E-03	9.47E-04	9.92E-04	9.91E-04	1.04E-03	5.82E-03	-1.11E-07

fig. 11.2 / fig. 11.3 / fig. 11.4 / **fig. 11.5** / Sheet3 / She

Solving Higher-Order Equations

Boundary-value problems are not always first-order differential equations; often they are second- or third-order equations. To solve these higher-order equations, divide them into two or more simultaneous differential equations by substituting new variables for the derivatives. For example, consider this equation:

$$au'' + bu' + cu + d = 0$$

Make the substitution $y = u'$, and you have two coupled simultaneous first-order differential equations:

$$u' - y = 0$$
$$ay' + by + cu + d = 0$$

To solve these equations, use the methods described earlier for solving a single equation. For each step, calculate the solutions for both equations independently using the single-equation methods. At the end of each step, you have solutions for both equations. Use those solutions to calculate the solutions at the end of the next step.

Solving Boundary-Value Problems

Boundary-value problems make up a second class of ordinary differential equations. While initial-value problems have all the boundary conditions located at one side of the solution space, boundary-value problems have part of the boundary conditions on one side and the rest on the other. Thus, they must satisfy boundary conditions at both boundaries of the problem rather than just one.

Two well-known methods for solving boundary-value problems are the shooting method and the finite-difference method.

Using the Shooting Method

The shooting method solves boundary-value problems using the methods used to solve initial-value problems. You guess values for the unknown boundary conditions at one of the boundaries (side 1) to change the problem into an initial-value problem. Then you integrate the equations from side 1 to the other side (side 2) with, for example, the modified Euler method. When you have completed the solution, compare the boundary values you calculated at side 2 with those specified by the boundary conditions. If they are the same, you have solved the problem; otherwise, you need to change your guess at the unknown boundary values on side 1 and integrate the problem again. Thus, you are shooting at the boundary values on side 2 of the solution space by guessing values of the boundary conditions on side 1.

For example, to solve a second-order differential equation, you need two boundary conditions. If this were an initial-value problem, you would be given the value of the solution and its derivative at one of the boundaries. For a typical boundary-value problem, you would be given only the value of the solution at both sides of the solution space. To integrate this solution to the other side of the solution space using the initial-value problem methods, you need an estimate of the derivative of the solution at one boundary as well. Given that value, you could integrate the solution to the other boundary, and then compare the value of your solution with the required value from the boundary condition. If they are the same, you are finished; otherwise, try a different estimate of the value of the derivative of the solution. Continue this process until you find the value on the boundary.

Bending of a Uniformly Loaded Beam

If you simply support a beam at both ends, as shown in Figure 11.6, it will sag slightly under its own weight. The amount of that sag can be calculated using this differential equation:

$$\frac{d^2 y}{dx^2} = -\frac{m}{EI}$$

NOTE A simply supported beam is one that is resting on its supports and is not solidly attached to them.

FIGURE 11.6

A simply supported beam bending
under its own weight

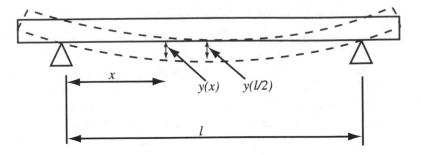

FIGURE 11.6

A simply supported beam bending
under its own weight

Here, y is the displacement or sag at the point x, I is the moment of inertia, E is the modulus of elasticity (30×10^6 psi for steel), and m is the bending moment. For a beam with a constant cross-section, m is equal to

$$m = \frac{w}{2}x(l-x)$$

where w is the weight per unit length and l is the length. Calculate the sag in a 50-foot piece of an 8-WF-67 steel beam—an 8-inch wide-flange section (a wide I-beam) that weighs 67 pounds per foot. For the orientation with the flange horizontal, the moment of inertia is $I = 271.8$ in^4. For small displacements, the analytic solution of this differential equation is

$$y = \frac{wx}{24\,EI}\left(l^3 - 2lx^2 + x^3\right)$$

with the maximum displacement at the center:

$$y(l/2) = \frac{5wl^4}{384\,EI}$$

This differential equation has two boundary conditions, one at each end of the beam where it is supported:

$y(0) = 0$

$y(l) = 0$

To solve it using initial-value problem methods, you need the value and the derivative at one side. You have the value, so you must estimate the value of the derivative at $x = 0$, solve the problem, and then see if $y(l) = 0$. If it does not, pick another value for the derivative at $x = 0$. Note that you could also integrate this problem from $x = l$ to $x = 0$ and get the same results.

Solve this problem using the modified Euler method. First, split the second-order equation into two first-order differential equations by substituting a variable u for one of the derivatives:

$$y'(x) = u(x)$$

$$u'(x) = -\frac{m}{EI}$$

Normally, using the modified Euler method, you would first calculate the solutions using the standard Euler method with

$$u(x+h) = u(x) + hu'(x)$$
$$y(x+h) = y(x) + hy'(x)$$

and then refine the values using

$$u(x+h) = u(x) + h\frac{(u'(x) + u'(x+h))}{2}$$

$$y(x+h) = y(x) + h\frac{(y'(x) + y'(x+h))}{2}$$

But in this case you can go directly to the final step since you know the exact value of $u'(x + h)$ from the differential equation. Create a worksheet to solve these equations, given an initial estimate of the value of $u(0)$.

1. Start with a new worksheet, and name it **fig. 11.7**

2. Change the width of column F to 13.

3. In cell A1, enter **Deflection of a Beam; Boundary-value problem; Shooting method**

Create a table containing the beam parameters. The weight of the bar in cell B5 is 67 pounds per foot. Convert this to pounds per inch by dividing by 12. Include the length in cell B8, converting it to inches by multiplying by 12.

4. In cell A4, enter **8-WF-67 Beam parameters**

5. Enter the following values in the indicated cells:

Cell	Contents	Cell	Contents	Cell	Contents
A5	w	B5	=67/12	C5	lb/in
A6	I	B6	271.8	C6	in^4
A7	E	B7	3.0E7	C7	psi
A8	l	B8	=50*12	C8	in

6. Right-align cells A5:A8. Select cells A5:B8 and choose the Insert ➤ Names ➤ Create command. Make sure Left Column is selected and click OK.

Since you know the analytic solution of this equation, create a second table to show the analytic solution for some value of x (say 72 inches) and for the maximum deflection at $x = \frac{1}{2}$.

7. Enter the following values in the indicated cells:

Cell	Contents	Cell	Contents	Cell	Contents
E3	Analytic solution				
E4	x	F4	72	G4	in
E5	y			G5	in
E6	y(l/2)			G6	in

8. Name cell F4 as **X**

9. In cell F5, enter

    =(W*X/(24*E*I))*(L^3–2*L*X^2+X^3)

10. In cell F6, enter

    =5*W*L^4/(384*E*I)

11. Format cells F5 and F6 as Number, with five decimal places.

Span the solution space, from 0 to 600 inches, with a grid of x values spaced every 12 inches, and calculate the derivative of u for all values of x. You get this directly from the differential equation.

12. Enter and center the following values in the indicated cells:

Cell	Contents	Cell	Contents	Cell	Contents	Cell	Contents
A10	x	B10	u'(x)	C10	u(x)	D10	y(x)
A11	(in)	B11	(1/in)	C11	(in/in)	D11	(in)

13. In cell A12, enter **0**, and in cell A13, enter **12**; select cells A12:A13 and drag the fill handle down to cell A62.

14. In cell B12, enter

   =–W*A12*(L–A12)/(2*E*I)

   and copy it to cells B13:B62.

15. Format cells B12:B62 as Scientific, with one decimal place.

Calculate the value of $u(x)$ at each step, using the average value of its derivative in the step interval between the values of x. The first value of u is the missing boundary condition. It references cell F9, where you will input your guesses.

16. In cell C12, enter **=F9**

17. In cell C13, enter

   =C12+(A13–A12)*(B12+B13)/2

   and copy it to cells C14:C62.

Calculate the value of y at each step, using the average value of $u(x)$ in the interval between the values of x. Set the first value of y to 0, which is the known boundary condition at this side of the solution space.

18. In cell D12, enter **0**

19. In cell D13, enter

   =D12+(A13–A12)*(C12+C13)/2

   and copy it to cells D14:D62.

Create a table to summarize the numerical results, with the value of y at $x = l$ and $x = \frac{1}{2}$. This is also the place where you input your guesses for the value of u(0).

20. In cell E8, enter **Numerical solution**

21. Enter the following values in the indicated cells:

Cell	Contents	Cell	Contents	Cell	Contents
E9	**u(0)**	F9	**0.01**	G9	**in/in**
E10	**y(l/2)**	F10	**=D37**	G10	**in**
E11	**y(l)**	F11	**=D62**	G11	**in**

22. Right-align cells E9:E11. Format cells F10 and F11 as Number, with five decimal places.

To use this worksheet, put a guess for the value of $u(0)$ into cell F9. After the worksheet recalculates, check the value of $y(l)$ that is repeated in cell F11 to see if it is 0. If it is not 0, try a different value for $u(0)$. Continue changing the value of $u(0)$ until you get $y(l)$ equal to 0 to as many decimal places as you need.

You could do this by hand, and it only takes about five minutes to find a solution, but this is an excellent place to use Solver. There is a single input cell and a single result cell, which works well with Solver.

23. Choose the Tools ➤ Solver command. Set the Target Cell to **F11**, select Value Of **0**, and set By Changing Cells to **F9**.

24. Click Solve to calculate the result.

When Solver completes, the worksheet should look like Figure 11.7.

FIGURE 11.7:

Bending of a simply supported beam under its own weight: boundary-value problem solved using the shooting method

	A	B	C	D	E	F	G	H	I
1	Deflection of a Beam; Boundary-value problem; Shooting method								
2									
3					Analytic solution				
4	8-WF-67 Beam parameters				x	72	in		
5	w	5.583333	lb/in		y	0.43170	in		
6	I	271.8	in⁴		y(l/2)	1.15549	in		
7	E	3.00E+07	psi						
8	l	600	in		Numerical solution				
9					u(0)	0.006160155	in/in		
10	x	u'(x)	u(x)	y(x)	y(l/2)	1.15475	in		
11	(in)	(1/in)	(in/in)	(in)	y(l)	0.00000	in		
12	0	0.0E+00	0.00616	0					
13	12	-2.4E-06	0.006146	0.073835					
14	24	-4.7E-06	0.006103	0.147325					
15	36	-7.0E-06	0.006033	0.220138					
16	48	-9.1E-06	0.005937	0.291953					

fig. 11.2 / fig. 11.3 / fig. 11.4 / fig. 11.5 \ fig. 11.7 / Sh

Compare the analytic values of the solution in cells F5 and F6 with the numerical solutions in cells D18 and F10, respectively. Note that even though you have hit the boundary value to four places of accuracy, the rest of the solution values have only about three places of accuracy. This loss of accuracy is due to the inherent accuracy of the method. Since the accuracy is proportional to the spacing between the grid points, decreasing this spacing increases the accuracy, until round-off error becomes significant.

Using the Finite-Difference Method

Another way to solve this problem is to write the derivatives in the differential equation as central differences. You used this method in Chapter 8 to calculate derivatives. By centering each of these differences on the grid points, you get a set of coupled equations that must be solved simultaneously. Use the following substitutions for the first and second derivatives:

$$\frac{du}{dx} = \frac{u(x+h) - u(x-h)}{2h}$$

$$\frac{d^2u}{dx^2} = \frac{u(x+h) - 2u(x) + u(x-h)}{h^2}$$

For example, for the bending beam problem, if you rewrite the second derivative in the differential equation using the central difference substitutions, it becomes:

$$\frac{y(x+h) - 2y(x) + y(x-h)}{h^2} = -\frac{m}{EI}$$

You will have one of these equations for each of the grid points except for the two at the boundaries, where the values of y are fixed by the boundary conditions.

Three methods that work well in a worksheet to solve a problem in this form are iterative, iterative with acceleration, and matrix.

Iterated Finite Differences

The iterative method is a form of the successive approximations method, which was discussed in Chapters 9 and 10. Solve the difference equation for the differential equation problem for $y(x)$:

$$y(x) = \frac{1}{2}\left[y(x+h) + y(x-h) + h^2\,\frac{m}{EI} \right]$$

Use this equation for all the interior points of the problem, and use

$y(0) = 0$

$y(l) = 0$

at the endpoints. Create a worksheet to solve this problem using the iterative method. The first part of this worksheet is the same as the one you used for the shooting method example, so reuse part of that worksheet.

1. Start with a copy of sheet fig. 11.7, and name it **fig. 11.8**

Turn on iteration and set it to continue iterating until the changes in the values on the worksheet get smaller than 10^{-6}.

2. Switch to manual recalculation and iteration with the Tools ➤ Options command, Calculation tab. Set Maximum Iterations to **1000** and Maximum Change to **1E–6**.

3. Change cell A1 to **Deflection of a Beam; Boundary-value problem; Finite Difference**

4. Clear cells B10:D62.

Put in the initialization flag so that you can reset the values in the worksheet to a known value.

5. In cell A3, enter **Init Flag**

6. In cell B3, enter **True**, and in cell C3, enter **0**

7. Name cells B3 and C3 as **Init** and **Init_Val**, respectively.

Put in the difference equation, and then enter the boundary values in the first and last cells of the range (B12 and B62). Test the initialization flag to see if the problem needs to be reset.

8. In cell B10, enter **y(x)** and center it.

9. In cell B11, enter **(in)** and center it.

10. In cell B12, enter **0**

11. In cell B13, enter

$$\texttt{=IF(Init,Init\_Val,0.5*(B14+B12+((A14–A12)/2)^2}$$
$$\texttt{➥*W*A13*(L–A13)/(2*E*I)))}$$

and copy it to cells B14:B61.

12. In cell B62, enter **0**

13. Format cells B12:B62 as Number, with five decimal places.

14. Clear cells E9:G9, and E11:G11.

15. In cell F10, enter **=B37**

To use this worksheet, set the value of the initialization flag (in cell B3) to **True** and press F9 or Ctrl+= (Cmd+= on the Macintosh). After the sheet has been reset, change the initialization flag to **False**, and press F9 again to start the iteration process.

The worksheet continues recalculating until the values change less than 10^{-6}, at which point you have the solution. This worksheet takes about 6-1/2 minutes to converge on a 386SX-20 computer or only a few seconds on a 486 DX2-80. Press F9 again if it does not completely converge on the first set of iterations. The worksheet should look like Figure 11.8 after it has converged.

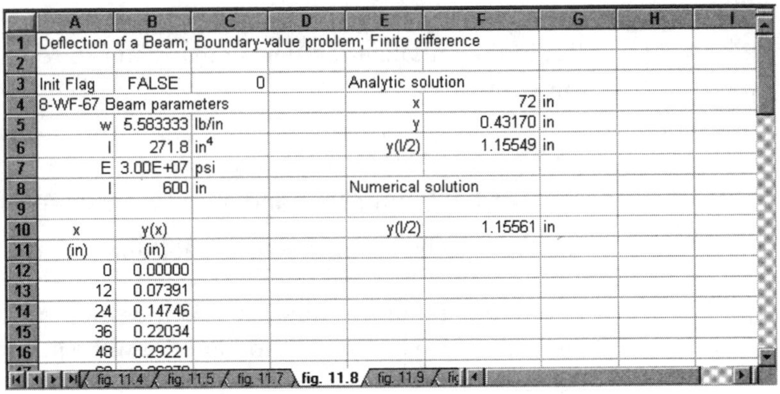

FIGURE 11.8:

Bending of a beam; a boundary-value problem solved with iterated finite differences

	A	B	C	D	E	F	G	H	I
1	Deflection of a Beam; Boundary-value problem; Finite difference								
2									
3	Init Flag	FALSE	0		Analytic solution				
4	8-WF-67	Beam parameters			x	72	in		
5	w	5.583333	lb/in		y	0.43170	in		
6	I	271.8	in⁴		y(l/2)	1.15549	in		
7	E	3.00E+07	psi						
8	I	600	in		Numerical solution				
9									
10	x	y(x)			y(l/2)	1.15561	in		
11	(in)	(in)							
12	0	0.00000							
13	12	0.07391							
14	24	0.14746							
15	36	0.22034							
16	48	0.29221							

fig. 11.4 / fig. 11.5 / fig. 11.7 \ **fig. 11.8** / fig. 11.9 / fig

Accelerated Finite Differences

A worksheet that converges as slowly as this one is just begging for some acceleration. You can use the over/under relaxation method here, just as you did in the previous chapter to speed the solution of systems of equations. Rewrite the difference equation so that you can control the amount of change in the solution at each iteration. Use the constant multiplier, Cf, to control the amount of that change:

$$y(x) = y(x) + Cf\left[\frac{1}{2}\left(y(x+h) + y(x-h) + h^2 \frac{m}{EI}\right) - y(x)\right]$$

Make this change to a copy of the existing worksheet. First, enter the relaxation factor.

1. Start with a copy of sheet fig. 11.8, and name it **fig. 11.9**

2. In cell A2, enter **With relaxation**

3. In cell A9, enter **Relax Fac**

4. In cell B9, enter **1.9**

5. Name cell B9 as **Cf**

Change the difference formula to incorporate the relaxation factor, to control the amount of change in the solution during each iteration. The value of the solution in the formula refers to the cell that contains the formula, creating a circular reference. You could also store the solution in a separate column and get the same effect.

6. In cell B13, enter

   =IF(Init,Init_Val,(0.5*(B14+B12+((A14−A12)/2)^2)
   ➥*W*A13*(L−A13)/(2*E*I))−B13)*Cf+B13)

   and copy it to cells B14:B61.

This worksheet operates in the same manner as the previous one. First, set the value of the initialization flag (B3) to **True** and press F9 or Ctrl+= (Cmd+= on the Macintosh). After the problem has initialized, change the value of the initialization flag to a **False** and press F9 again to start the worksheet calculating. This version of the worksheet converges in 26 seconds on a 386SX-20, nearly 1500 percent faster than with the other methods! The resulting worksheet is shown in Figure 11.9.

FIGURE 11.9:

Bending of a beam; a
boundary-value problem solved
with accelerated finite differences

	A	B	C	D	E	F	G	H	I
1	Deflection of a Beam; Boundary-value problem; Finite difference								
2									
3	Init Flag	FALSE	0		Analytic solution				
4	8-WF-67 Beam parameters				x	72	in		
5	w	5.583333	lb/in		y	0.43170	in		
6	I	271.8	in^4		y(I/2)	1.15549	in		
7	E	3.00E+07	psi						
8	l	600	in		Numerical solution				
9	Relax Fac	1.9							
10	x	y(x)			y(I/2)	1.15586	in		
11	(in)	(in)							
12	0	0.00000							
13	12	0.07392							
14	24	0.14750							
15	36	0.22039							
16	48	0.29228							

fig. 11.4 fig. 11.5 fig. 11.7 fig. 11.8 **fig. 11.9** fig

NOTE

If you try to make the worksheet converge faster by using larger values of the relaxation factor, *Cf*, the worksheet diverges. With a relaxation factor of 2, the solution values get very large after a few iterations. If you have a solution that diverges, use a smaller acceleration factor. For problems that diverge with iterated finite differences, use an acceleration factor that is less than one (deceleration factor) to slow down the changes.

Matrix Solution of Finite Differences

You can also use Excel's built-in matrix functions to solve a set of linear simultaneous equations. The only restriction is that there must be less than about 60 equations. Excel has no specified limit for matrix inversion, but the actual limit is around 60×60, depending on the amount of memory available and the contents of the matrix. If Excel can't solve the matrix because it is too large, the MINVERSE function returns #VALUE!.

For larger matrices, you need to use a Visual Basic procedure or an external application to do the inversions. You could write a matrix solver in FORTRAN and store it in a Dynamic Link Library (a CODE resource on the Macintosh). That matrix inverter could then be registered with Excel and called with the Call function.

To use the matrix solver, rewrite the difference equations as matrix equations. Rewrite the example differential equation

$$\frac{y(x+h) - 2y(x) + y(x-h)}{h^2} = -\frac{m}{EI}$$

as

$$y(x+h) - 2y(x) + y(x-h) = -h^2 \frac{m}{EI}$$

with the boundary conditions

$y(0) = y(l) = 0$

These can be easily rewritten into a matrix equation

Ax = b

$$
\begin{vmatrix}
1 & 0 & 0 & 0 & 0 & & \cdot & \cdot & \cdot \\
1 & -2 & 1 & 0 & 0 & & \cdot & \cdot & \cdot \\
0 & 1 & -2 & 1 & 0 & & \cdot & \cdot & \cdot \\
0 & 0 & 1 & -2 & 1 & & & & \\
 & & & & \cdot & & & & \\
 & & & & & \cdot & & & \\
 & & & & \cdot & & & & \\
 & & \cdot & \cdot & \cdot & 1 & -2 & 1 & 0 \\
 & & \cdot & \cdot & \cdot & 0 & 1 & -2 & 1 \\
 & & \cdot & \cdot & \cdot & 0 & 0 & 0 & 1
\end{vmatrix}
\begin{vmatrix}
x_0 \\
x_1 \\
x_2 \\
x_3 \\
\cdot \\
\cdot \\
\cdot \\
x_{n-2} \\
x_{n-1} \\
x_n
\end{vmatrix}
=
\begin{vmatrix}
b_0 \\
b_1 \\
b_2 \\
b_3 \\
\cdot \\
\cdot \\
\cdot \\
b_{n-2} \\
b_{n-1} \\
b_n
\end{vmatrix}
$$

where

$$b_0 = b_n = 0$$

$$b_i = -h^2 \frac{m_i}{EI} \quad i = 1, 2, 3, \cdots n - 1$$

$$m_i = \frac{wx_i}{2}(l - x_i)$$

Once the equations are in this form, the solution is straightforward. Invert the matrix **A** and multiply that inverse by the vector **b** to get the solution vector **x**. Create a worksheet to solve this problem. The top part of this worksheet is the same as for the last example, so reuse that part.

1. Start with a copy of sheet fig. 11.9, and name it **fig. 11.10**

2. Switch to manual recalculation with the Tools ➤ Option command, Calculation tab.

3. In cell A2, enter **Matrix method**

4. Clear cells B12:B62.

Mark a space for the solution vector.

5. In cell C10, enter **b** and center it.

Enter **b**, the right side of the matrix equation, including the boundary conditions.

6. In cell C12, enter **0**

7. In cell C13, enter

    =−((A13−A12)^2*W*A13*(L−A13)/(2*E*I))

    and copy it to cells C14:C61.

8. In cell C62, enter **0**

9. Name cells C12:C62 as **B**

Mark and name the locations of the matrix **A** and its inverse **A**$^{-1}$.

10. In cell D11, enter **A** and center it.

11. Select cells D12:BB62, name the range **A**, and outline the cells.

12. In cell D65, enter **AINV** and center it.

13. Select cells D66:BB116, name them **AINV**, and outline them.

The matrix contains mostly zeros, with ones and twos along the diagonal. Since you probably don't feel like typing in 2601 values, create a Visual Basic program to fill the matrix.

14. Open a new module sheet and name it **MakeMat**

15. Enter the following program into the module.

```
'
'   Make a Matrix
'   Program to fill in the finite difference matrix.
'
Sub MakeMatrix()
Dim intI As Integer
Const numRows = 51
'Fill the whole matrix with zeroes.
Range("A").Select
Selection.Formula = "0"
'Insert the boundary condition
'in the upper-left corner.
Range("A").Cells(1, 1).Select
ActiveCell.Formula = "1"
'Handle the interior cells with a loop.
For intI = 2 To numRows - 1
    Range("A").Cells(intI, intI).Select
    ActiveCell.Formula = "-2"
    Range("A").Cells(intI, intI + 1).Select
    ActiveCell.Formula = "1"
    Range("A").Cells(intI, intI - 1).Select
    ActiveCell.Formula = "1"
Next intI
'Insert the boundary condition in the
'lower-right corner.
Range("A").Cells(numRows, numRows).Select
ActiveCell.Formula = "1"
End Sub
```

The procedure first selects the whole matrix and fills it with zeroes.

```
Range("A").Select
Selection.Formula = "0"
```

Next the program sets the boundary condition at the upper-left corner. The Range("A") method returns the cells named A on the worksheet, then the Cells(1, 1) method returns the cell in the first row, first column. The Select method selects that cell, making it the active cell. The ActiveCell.Formula statement inserts the value one into the selected cell.

```
Range("A").Cells(1, 1).Select
ActiveCell.Formula = "1"
```

The next block of cells starts a loop over the rows (or columns) and inserts three values along the diagonal of the matrix each iteration of the loop.

```
For intI = 2 To numRows - 1
    Range("A").Cells(intI, intI).Select
    ActiveCell.Formula = "-2"
    Range("A").Cells(intI, intI + 1).Select
    ActiveCell.Formula = "1"
    Range("A").Cells(intI, intI - 1).Select
    ActiveCell.Formula = "1"
Next intI
```

The last block inserts the boundary condition at the lower-right corner of the matrix, in the same manner as at the other corner of the matrix.

```
Range("A").Cells(numRows, numRows).Select
ActiveCell.Formula = "1"
```

Insert a button on the worksheet and attach it to the MakeMatrix procedure.

16. Switch to sheet fig. 11.10.

17. Open the Drawing toolbar by clicking the Drawing button on the Standard toolbar, then click the Create Button button and draw a button on the worksheet.

18. When the Assign Macro dialog box appears, select the MakeMatrix procedure and click OK.

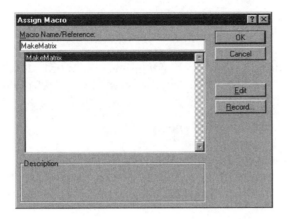

19. Select the caption on the button and change it to **Fill Matrix**

20. Close the Drawing toolbar.

21. Click anywhere on the worksheet to deselect the button, then click the button to run the procedure.

Invert the matrix in AINV.

22. Select **AINV** from the Name box, or choose the Edit ➤ GoTo command and select AINV.

23. In the top-left cell of the selection, type =MINVERSE(A) and press Ctrl+Shift+Enter (Cmd+Enter on the Macintosh) to insert it as an array into the whole selection.

You may need to wait several minutes for the inverse matrix to be calculated if you have an older, slower computer. Faster models calculate it in a few seconds. If the calculation returns #VALUE! instead of numbers, you have typed something wrong, or you may have hit Excel's limit on matrix size. If the matrix is too large, your only choice is to reduce the size of the matrix until it can be solved. You can do this by making the spacing between grid points wider, which reduces the total number of grid points.

WARNING   Reducing the number of grid points also reduces the accuracy.

Now multiply the inverse matrix by the vector **b**, in cells C12:C62, and store the result in cells B12:B62. This is the solution of the problem.

24. Select cells B12:B62. In the top cell of the selection, type **=MMULT(AINV,B)** and press Ctrl+Shift+Enter (Cmd+Enter on the Macintosh) to insert it as an array.

25. Press F9 to recalculate the worksheet.

The worksheet should now look like Figure 11.10. To use the worksheet, make any changes in the input values and press F9 or Ctrl+= (Cmd+= on the Macintosh) to recalculate the matrix. When the calculation is complete, the result will be in column B.

FIGURE 11.10:

Bending of a beam: a boundary-value problem solved with finite differences

	A	B	C	D	E	F	G	H	I
1	Deflection of a Beam; Boundary-value problem; Finite difference								
2	Matrix method								
3	Init Flag	FALSE	0		Analytic solution			Fill Matrix	
4	8-WF-67 Beam parameters					x	72	in	
5	w	5.583333	lb/in			y	0.43170	in	
6	I	271.8	in⁴			y(l/2)	1.15549	in	
7	E	3.00E+07	psi						
8	l	600	in		Numerical solution				
9	Relax Fac	1.9							
10	x	y(x)	b			y(l/2)	1.15586	in	
11	(in)	(in)		A					
12	0	0.00000	0	1	0	0	0	0	
13	12	0.07392	-0.00035	1	-2	1	0	0	
14	24	0.14750	-0.00068	0	1	-2	1	0	
15	36	0.22039	-0.001	0	0	1	-2	1	
16	48	0.29228	-0.00131	0	0	0	1	-2	

fig. 11.5 / fig. 11.7 / fig. 11.8 / fig. 11.9 \ **fig. 11.10** /

NOTE   You can turn Automatic Recalculation back on at this point, and you will get error dialog boxes indicating that there are circular references that can not be calculated. These are not on this sheet, but are on other worksheets saved previously in this workbook, so don't worry about them now.

Handling Higher-Order Boundary Conditions

The problem you just solved had Dirichlet boundary conditions. The problem could just as easily have had Neumann boundary conditions, or it could have had a mix of Dirichlet and Neumann boundary conditions.

> **NOTE**
>
> **Dirichlet boundary conditions** have the value specified at the boundary.
> **Neumann boundary conditions** have the derivative of the function specified at the boundary.
> **Mixed boundary conditions** have the value specified at one boundary and the derivative specified at the other.

To handle these higher-order boundary conditions, put an extra grid point into the problem, just outside the boundary with the derivative boundary condition. Construct a central difference at the boundary using that extra point to set the value of the derivative. For example, in the previous problem, if the boundary condition at $x = 0$ was

$$y'(0) = 0.00616015$$

instead of

$$y(0) = 0$$

you would add another grid point at $x = -h$. Then write a first-order central difference at $x = 0$ and set it equal to 0.00616015.

$$\frac{y(h) - y(-h)}{2h} = 0.00616015$$

Solve this equation for $y(-h)$ and use it to define the value of the function at the extra grid point, $y(-h)$. At the actual boundary point, use the same difference equation that you used in the interior of the problem. Higher-order derivative boundary conditions are handled in the same manner—just insert the difference equation for the higher-order derivative. Alternatively, you could algebraically combine the equation above with the equation at the boundary, and achieve the same results without actually adding another grid point to the problem.

Neumann Boundary Conditions

Bear in mind that problems with Neumann boundary conditions on all sides may not have unique solutions. If you can add an arbitrary constant to the function in the differential equation and not change the differential equation, a unique solution might not exist. This happens when the function ($u(x)$) appears only in the derivatives of a differential equation.

The bending beam problem is just such an equation. If you were to add some value y_0 to the function $y(x)$, the differential equation would not change, because the derivative of a constant is zero. If there were no Dirichlet boundary conditions to fix the value of $y(x)$ at some point, the result would not be unique, and you could add any arbitrary amount to $y(x)$ and it would still be correct. Note that physically this amounts to raising or lowering the beam as a complete unit, which has no effect on the amount of bending. The beam bends the same amount whether it is in the basement or on the roof.

Summary

In this chapter, you have seen how a worksheet can be a medium for performing numerical solutions of ordinary differential equations. Initial-value problems can be solved on a worksheet using the Taylor series, the Euler or modified Euler, and the Runge-Kutta methods. Each of these methods has varying degrees of accuracy and difficulty to implement.

Boundary-value problems can be solved using the shooting method, where you pick values of the boundary condition on one side of the problem until you get the correct result on the other side. Boundary-value problems can also be rewritten using finite differences, and the resulting difference equations can be solved using iterative or matrix techniques.

Excel's Solver was not really designed to solve tens of simultaneous equations at one time, but with careful planning, you could probably solve these equations as you did the simultaneous equations in the previous chapter. The iterative methods are faster than Solver when many equations are involved.

As you might expect, all of these methods can be implemented as Visual Basic programs, using well-known programming algorithms; however, as with any program, you only see the results of the calculation and not the intermediate values that you see on the worksheet. Calculations are also not as intuitive when performed in code as when they are performed on a worksheet.

For More Information

Bending and Stretching of Structural Materials

S. Timoshenko, D. H. Young, *Elements of Strength of Materials*, 5th. ed. (New York: D. Van Nostrand Co., 1968).

Numerical Methods for Solving Differential Equations

C. Gerald, *Applied Numerical Analysis*, 2nd. ed. (Reading, Mass: Addison-Wesley, 1978).

W. H. Press, B. P. Flannery, S. A. Teukolsky, W. T. Vetterling, *Numerical Recipes; The Art of Scientific Computing* (Cambridge, Eng.: Cambridge University Press, 1986).

Review Problems

1. The charge (q) in a capacitor (C) being charged by a battery (V) in series with a resistor (R) follows the equation

$$\frac{dq}{dt} = \frac{V}{R} - \frac{q}{RC}$$

Given that $R = 1000$ ohms, $C = 10^{-5}$ f, $V = 10$ volts, and that at $t = 0$, $q = 0$, solve this equation using the Taylor series, Euler, and modified Euler methods for the interval $0 \le t \le 5 \times 10^{-2}$ s. Compare the result to the analytic solution:

$$q = CV\left(1 - e^{-\left(\frac{t}{RC}\right)}\right)$$

2. Complete problem 1 using the Runge-Kutta method for the discharging capacitor. Here, $V = 0$ and at $t = 0$, $q = 10^{-4}$ coul ($=CV$). Compare the result to the analytic solution:

$$q = CV e^{-\left(\frac{t}{RC}\right)}$$

3. An LCR oscillator circuit is described by the differential equation

$$L\frac{d^2q}{dt^2} + R\frac{dq}{dt} + \frac{q}{C} = 0$$

$L = 10^{-2}$ Henry, $C = 3 \times 10^{-6}$ farad, $R = 20$ ohms, and at $t = 0$, $q = 10^{-5}$ coul and $dq/dt = -0.01$ coul/s. Solve this equation for the interval $0 \le t \le 4 \times 10^{-3}$ s using the modified Euler method.

4. The motion of a simple harmonic oscillator is described by the equation

$$\frac{d^2x}{dt^2} = -\omega^2 x$$

At $t = 0$, $x = 0$ and $dx/dt = 1$. If $\omega = 6$, solve this equation over the interval $0 \le t \le 3$ using the modified Euler method.

5. The differential equation of the elastic line of a uniformly loaded cantilever beam is

$$\frac{d^2y}{dx^2} = \frac{wx^2}{2EI}$$

L is the length of the beam and x is measured from the free end of the beam. At $x = L$, $y = 0$ and $dy/dx = 0$. $E = 30 \times 10^6$ psi, $I = 271.8$ in^4, $w = 100$ lb/in, and $L = 10$ feet. Using the Euler method, solve for y for $0 \leq x \leq L$. Compare the result to the analytic solution:

$$y = \frac{w}{EI}\left(\frac{x^4}{24} - \frac{L^3 x}{6} + \frac{L^4}{8}\right)$$

6. The growth rate of a colony of bacteria is described by the equation

$$\frac{dn}{dt} = kn$$

n is the number of bacteria and k is the growth rate. If at $t = 0$ there are 10^4 bacteria and at $t = 10$ hours there are 4×10^4 bacteria, calculate k using the shooting method.

7. Given that $y(0) = 3$ and $y(1) = 7.49$, solve the following differential equation using the shooting method on the range $0 \leq x \leq 1$

$$\frac{d^2 y}{dx^2} + \frac{dy}{dx} - 6y = 0$$

8. Given that $y(0) = 2$ and $y(1) = 5.288$, solve the following differential equation using the finite-difference method on the range $0 \leq x \leq 1$.

$$x\frac{d^2 y}{dx^2} - \frac{dy}{dx} + 4x^3 y = 0$$

Compare the result with the analytic solution:

$$y = 5\sin(x^2) + 2\cos(x^2)$$

9. Given that $y(-0.5) = 60.703$ and $y(0.5) = 9.1$, solve the following differential equation using the finite-difference method on the range $-0.5 \leq x \leq 0.5$.

$$\frac{d^2 y}{dx^2} + 2\frac{dy}{dx} - 18y = 0$$

10. The differential equation of the elastic line of a beam fixed at both ends and loaded at the center is

$$\frac{d^2 y}{dx^2} = \frac{wL}{2EI}\left(\frac{x}{L} - \frac{1}{4}\right) \qquad 0 < x < L/2$$

$$\frac{d^2 y}{dx^2} = \frac{wL}{2EI}\left(\frac{x}{L} - \frac{3}{4}\right) \qquad L/2 < x < L$$

L is the length of the beam, $y = 0$ at $x = 0$ and $x = L$, $E = 30 \times 10^6$ psi, $I = 271.8$ in^4, $w = 100$ lb, and $L = 200$ feet. Solve for y for $0 \leq x \leq L$ using the finite-difference method. Compare the result to the analytic solution:

$$y = \frac{wL}{2EI}\left(\frac{x^2}{8} - \frac{x^3}{6L}\right) \qquad 0 < x < L/2$$

Exercises

1. An inductor in series with a charged capacitor is described with the following equation:

$$V + LC\frac{d^2 V}{dt^2} = 0$$

If $C = 1$ microfarad, $L = 10$ microhenries and $V_0 = 50$ volts, calculate the voltage across the capacitor for the first 10 microseconds using the Taylor series method.

2. Redo problem 1 using the Euler and Modified Euler methods.

3. A projectile fired from a gun with initial velocity v_0 at an angle with the ground of α has the following equation of motion:

$$\frac{d\mathbf{v}}{dt} = -g\mathbf{k}$$

where k is the vertical unit vector. If there is negligable air resistance, this two-dimensional equation can be separated into two one-dimensional equations, one in the vertical direction and one in the horizontal.

Vertical

$$\frac{dv_v}{dt} = -g$$

Horizontal

$$\frac{dv_h}{dt} = 0$$

The horizontal motion is a constant $v_h = v_0 \text{Cos}(\alpha)$. The vertical motion goes up, stops, and comes back down again under the force of gravity. Using the shooting method, find α and calculate the time the projectile is in the air given that $v_0 = 500$ m/s, $g = 9.8$ m/s^2, and the range is 22,300 meters. Compare to the analytic solution of

$$t = \frac{2V_0 \sin(\alpha)}{g}$$

$$Range = \frac{V_0^2 \sin(2\alpha)}{g}$$

4. Redo Exercise 2 using finite differences.

5. A block sliding down a ramp with an angle α with the horizontal, with friction is described with the following equation.

$$\frac{d^2 x}{dt^2} = g(\sin(\alpha) - \mu\cos(\alpha))$$

where υ is the coefficient of friction and g is the force of gravity. Calculate and plot the position versus time for 10 seconds, given that:

$g = 9.8$ m/s²

$\mu = 0.6$

$\alpha = 55$ degrees

$x_0 = 0$

$x_0' = 0$

Split the problem into two first-order equations and use the Runge-Kutta method.

6. Calculate $y(x)$ from the following differential equation using iterated finite differences, for $x = 0$ to $x = 1$, given that $y(0) = 5$ and $y(1) = 8$.

$$\frac{d^2 y}{dx^2} - 3\frac{dy}{dx} + 2y = e^x$$

7. Redo exercise 6 using finite differences and a matrix solver.

8. Solve exercise 6 again, but with the boundary conditions $y(0) = 0$, $y'(1) = 0$.

9. Solve exercise 6 again, but with the boundary conditions $y'(0) = 5$, $y'(1) = -5$. Note how with Neumann boundary conditions, the solution continues to grow as you iterate and never converges. Fix the lower boundary at zero while still maintaining the slope and get a converged solution.

10. Solve the following equation using finite differences over the range $x = 0$ to 6. Where $y(0)=0$ and $y'(6)=25$.

$$\frac{d^2 y}{dx^2} - 2\frac{dy}{dx} = \sin(x)$$

CHAPTER

TWELVE

Solving Partial Differential Equations

- Differentiating the types of partial differential equations

- Solving elliptical partial differential equations

- Solving parabolic partial differential equations

- Solving hyperbolic partial differential equations

- Solving Poisson's and Laplace's equations

- Solving the wave equation

12

Partial differential equations are probably the most heavily used type of equation for modeling physical processes. Except for those simple processes, such as a block sliding down a plane, that are describable with a simple analytic equation, most processes require a differential equation to be adequately described. For example, simply adding friction and air resistance to the block problem complicates the motion by adding differential terms to the equations describing the motion. In many cases, partial differential equations, instead of ordinary differential equations, are used because of the independent nature of the variables in partial differential equations.

Like ordinary differential equations, partial differential equations usually don't have analytic solutions, or if they do have an analytic solution, it is very difficult to find. Also like ordinary differential equations, numerical methods are the most commonly used methods for obtaining solutions to partial differential equations.

Many important science and engineering problems are only described with partial differential equations. In fact, any problem involving a differential process that has more than one independent variable must be described with partial differential equations rather than ordinary differential equations.

For a second-order function (u) involving two independent variables (x,y), there are five possible differentials:

$$\frac{\partial u}{\partial x}, \frac{\partial^2 u}{\partial x^2}, \frac{\partial u}{\partial y}, \frac{\partial^2 u}{\partial y^2}, \frac{\partial^2 u}{\partial x \partial y}$$

These can be combined into a general partial differential equation of two independent variables:

$$A\frac{\partial^2 u}{\partial x^2} + B\frac{\partial^2 u}{\partial x \partial y} + C\frac{\partial^2 u}{\partial y^2} + D\frac{\partial u}{\partial x} + E\frac{\partial u}{\partial y} + F = 0$$

Each of the coefficients ($A - F$) can be functions of either of the two variables (x, y).

Ordinary and Partial Differential Equations

The difference between ordinary and partial differential equations is more than simply using a d or ∂ to write the differential terms. An ordinary differential equation involves a single independent variable, functions of the independent variable, and derivatives with respect to that variable. For example,

$$\frac{\partial^2 u}{\partial x^2} + 4\frac{\partial u}{\partial x} + 2u + 3x = 0$$

contains a single independent variable (x), functions of the independent variable ($u(x)$ and $3x$), and first- and second-order derivatives with respect to the independent variable.

A partial differential equation involves one or more independent variables, functions of those variables, and partial derivatives with respect to the independent variables. For example,

$$\frac{\partial u(x,y)}{\partial x} + 3\frac{\partial^2 u(x,y)}{\partial x \partial y} + \frac{\partial^2 u(x,y)}{\partial y^2} + u(x,y) + 3x + 5y = 0$$

contains two independent variables (x and y), functions of the independent variables ($u(x, y)$ and $3x + 5y$), and partial derivatives with respect to one or both of the independent variables.

Types of Partial Differential Equations

The three categories of partial differential equations are elliptic, parabolic, and hyperbolic. The equations in these categories are distinguished by the relationships of the coefficients of the second-order terms. For example, for the second-order equation with two variables, the category is determined as follows:

- Elliptic: $B^2 - 4AC < 0$
- Parabolic: $B^2 - 4AC = 0$
- Hyperbolic: $B^2 - 4AC > 0$

The coefficients are functions of the independent variables, so a differential equation can move from one category to another as the variables change.

Solving Elliptic Partial Differential Equations

Elliptic partial differential equations usually arise from equilibrium problems. That is, the steady state value of some field variable, such as density or potential, is usually a solution of an elliptical partial differential equation. For example, the Poisson and Laplace equations are well-known examples of elliptic partial differential equations. Both arise in numerous branches of science, especially in electrostatics and heat flow problems. In both of these equations, the coefficient of the cross term (B) is zero, which makes $B^2 - 4AC$ less than zero (assuming A and C are both positive or both negative).

Elliptic partial differential equations are solved in much the same manner as ordinary differential equations are solved with iterated finite differences, except that you must deal with at least a two-dimensional domain.

Poisson and Laplace Equations

Poisson and Laplace equations are generally used for scalar-field problems. For example, you can describe a steady-state electrostatic potential with the Poisson equation, written as

$$\nabla^2 \Phi = -q\frac{\rho}{\varepsilon}$$

where q is the electron charge, ρ is the charge density, and ε is the permittivity. Note that this equation uses the differential operator

$$\nabla \equiv \mathbf{i}\frac{\partial}{\partial x} + \mathbf{j}\frac{\partial}{\partial y} + \mathbf{k}\frac{\partial}{\partial z}$$

where **i**, **j**, and **k** are unit vectors in the x, y, and z directions. This is the definition of the differential operator in three-dimensional Cartesian coordinates. The definition differs for other coordinate systems. The square of the ∇DT operator is the vector dot product of the operator on itself.

$$\nabla^2 = \nabla \cdot \nabla = \frac{\partial^2}{\partial x^2} + \frac{\partial^2}{\partial y^2} + \frac{\partial^2}{\partial z^2}$$

If no charges are present ($\rho = 0$), the Poisson equation reduces to the Laplace equation:

$$\nabla^2 \Phi = 0$$

Potential between Two Concentric Cylinders

Consider two long concentric cylinder conductors of radii a and b in a vacuum, as illustrated in Figure 12.1. If you apply a voltage across the conductors, the potential in the space between them is described with a two-dimensional Laplace equation.

The outer conductor is grounded (0 volt) and the inner conductor is held at 20 volts. The inner diameter, a, is 5 cm, and the outer diameter, b, is 15 cm. To calculate the potential in the volume between them, use a two-dimensional Laplace

FIGURE 12.1

Concentric cylinders in a vacuum

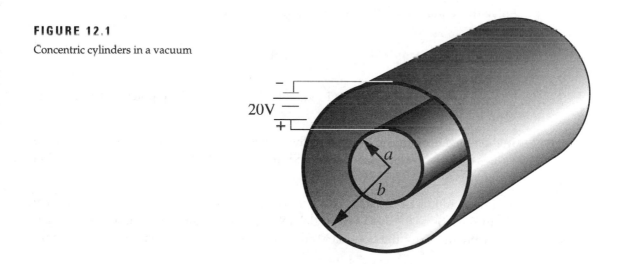

equation. The two-dimensional domain is valid because the cylinders are infinitely long, which makes variations of the potential in the direction parallel to the axes of the cylinders negligible:

$$\nabla^2 \Phi = \frac{\partial^2 \Phi}{\partial x^2} + \frac{\partial^2 \Phi}{\partial y^2} = 0$$

I solved this problem analytically, so that you can compare the analytical results to those that you calculate. The analytical solution for the potential at some distance r from the center of the cylinders is

$$\Phi(r) = \frac{\Phi_b \ln(r/a) - \Phi_a \ln(r/b)}{\ln(b/a)}$$

To solve the differential equation on a worksheet, replace the derivatives in the equation with central differences, centered on grid point (i,j). Assume that the grid spacing (h) is constant in both directions.

$$\frac{\Phi_{i+1,j} - 2\Phi_{i,j} + \Phi_{i-1,j}}{h^2} + \frac{\Phi_{i,j+1} - 2\Phi_{i,j} + \Phi_{i,j-1}}{h^2} = 0$$

Solve this equation for the term at the grid point $\Phi_{i,j}$:

$$\Phi_{i,j} = \left(\tfrac{1}{4}\right)\left(\Phi_{i+1,j} + \Phi_{i-1,j} + \Phi_{i,j+1} + \Phi_{i,j-1}\right)$$

The potential at any grid point is equal to the average of the potentials of the surrounding four grid points.

In the worksheet, the boundaries of the problem are set with the fixed or derivative values of the boundary conditions, and the interior points are set with the equation shown here.

You need model only a slice of the cylinder, because the solution is symmetrical about the axis of the cylinder. Model a 90-degree, pie-shaped slice of the cylinder; it is difficult to fix the boundary conditions for anything smaller. The boundary condition on the outer cylinder is fixed at 0 and that on the inner cylinder at 20. The boundary condition along the cut edges of the pie-shaped slice is that the derivative of the potential, perpendicular to the boundary, is zero.

1. Start with a new worksheet, and name it **fig. 12.2**

2. Change the widths of columns A through R to **2.43**, and columns S and T to **9**

SHORTCUT   To change the widths of several columns to the same value, select the columns by shift-clicking the column headers, then change the width of one of the selected columns. All of the selected columns will be changed to the same width. The same method can be used to change the height of several rows to the same value.

3. Change the heights of rows 3 through 20 to **11.25**

4. Select cells A1:T20 and reduce the font size to 8 points using the Format ➤ Cells command, Font tab.

5. Choose the Tools ➤ Options command, Calculation tab; change Calculation to Manual, check Iteration, and set Maximum Iterations to **100**. Then click OK.

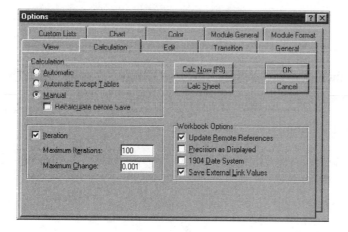

6. In cell A1, enter **Laplace equation between concentric cylinders; Elliptical PDE**

Enter some labels to locate the x- and y-axes, and the rows and columns that will contain the boundary conditions.

7. Insert the following labels in the indicated cells, and center the contents of cells A6, A7, and B6.

Cell	Contents	Cell	Contents
A6	**B.**	B3	**Analytic**
A7	**C.**	C4	**B.C.**
B6	**y**	C5	**x**

Create a table to contain the values of the potentials on the inner and outer cylinders.

8. In cell S9, enter **Applied Potentials**

9. Select cells S9 and T9 and click the Center Across Columns button.

10. Insert the following values in the indicated cells. Center the contents of cells S10:S11.

Cell	Contents	Cell	Contents
S10	**Inner**	T10	**20**
S11	**Outer**	T11	**0**

11. Name cells T10 and T11 as **Inner** and **Outer**, respectively.

Enter the outer and inner boundary conditions, along the edges of the outer and inner conductors. I drew two concentric circles on grid paper to see which cells to include as part of the boundary. I assumed that any cell that the circle touched was part of the boundary.

12. Enter and copy the formula **=Outer** into the following cells: Q4:Q8, P9:P12, O13, N14:N15, M16, L17, J18:K18, G19:I19, and A20:F20.

13. Enter and copy the formula **=Inner** into the following cells: G4:G7, F8, E9, and A10:D10.

Along the edges of the pie slice, the boundary condition is that the derivative is zero. To insert this boundary condition, add an extra row of cells just outside the boundary and set their values equal to those in the first row of cells, just inside the boundary. This makes the derivative zero at the cells on the boundary (H5:P5 and B11:B19). Mark those extra rows with arrows.

14. In cell H4, enter **=H6** and copy it to cells I4:P4.

15. In cell A11, enter **=C11** and copy it to cells A12:A19.

Fill the interior of the region between the cylinders with the finite-difference form of the differential equation. Enter the equation into cell H5 and then copy it into row H5:P5. Next copy the row from H5:P5 into cells H6:P7. Continue copying the equation in blocks until it completely fills the region within the boundary condition cells.

16. In cell H5, enter **=0.25*(G5+H4+I5+H6)**

17. Copy the contents of cell H5 into the following ranges:

H5:P5	E10:O10	B15:M15
H6:P6	B11:O11	B16:L16
H7:P7	B12:O12	B17:K17
G8:P8	B13:N13	B18:I18
F9:O9	B14:M14	B19:F19

Insert the analytic solution along the upper boundary as a comparison. The analytic solution needs the value of the radius at each cell, so enter them in a row just below the bottom of the table.

18. In cells G22 and H22, enter **5** and **6**, respectively; select cells G22:H22, and drag the fill handle to cell Q22.

19. In cell G3, enter the formula:

$$=(\text{Outer*LN(G22/5)}-\text{Inner*LN(G22/15)})/\text{LN(15/5)}$$

and copy it to cells H3:Q3.

20. Display the Drawing toolbar by clicking the Drawing button on the Standard toolbar. Draw arrows using the Arrow button as shown in Figure 12.2.

21. Shift-select all the arrows and choose the Format ➤ Object command, Patterns tab; make the arrow heads smaller by reducing both the width and length.

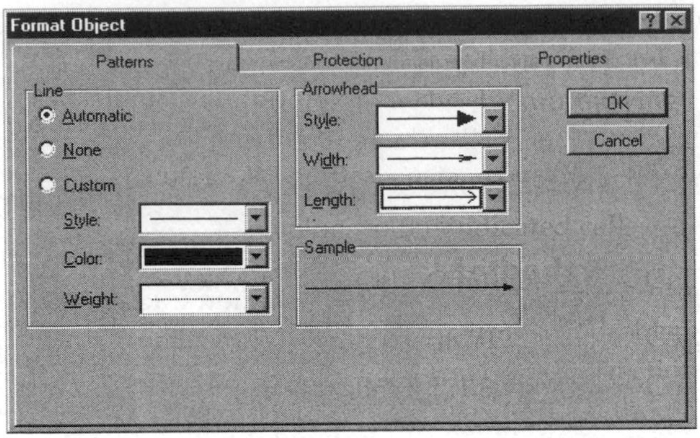

22. Calculate the worksheet by pressing F9 or Ctrl+= (Cmd+= on the Macintosh).

After a few minutes, Excel will stop calculating, and your worksheet should look like Figure 12.2. You may need to press F9 more than once to get the values to converge. Figure 12.3 shows a comparison of the analytic equation in cells G3:Q3 with the values of the numerical solution on the boundary in cells G4:Q4. The curves in the figure are nearly identical. The slight differences can be ascribed to the error induced by the difference formula. Using a smaller value of h would reduce the error in the calculated values.

FIGURE 12.2:

Potential between two concentric cylinders: solving a two-dimensional, elliptical partial differential equation

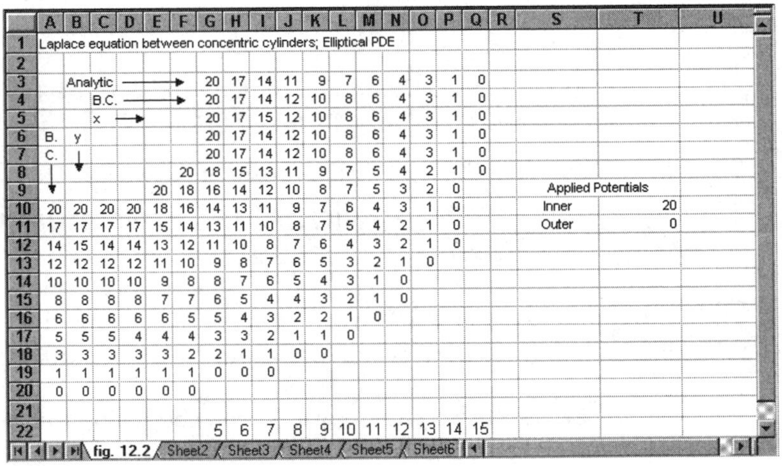

	A	B	C	D	E	F	G	H	I	J	K	L	M	N	O	P	Q	R	S	T	U
1	Laplace equation between concentric cylinders; Elliptical PDE																				
2																					
3		Analytic	→				20	17	14	11	9	7	6	4	3	1	0				
4			B.C.	→			20	17	14	12	10	8	6	4	3	1	0				
5			x	→			20	17	15	12	10	8	6	4	3	1	0				
6	B.	y					20	17	14	12	10	8	6	4	3	1	0				
7	C.	↓					20	17	14	12	10	8	6	4	3	1	0				
8						20	18	15	13	11	9	7	5	4	2	1	0				
9	↓				20	18	16	14	12	10	8	7	5	3	2	0			Applied Potentials		
10	20	20	20	20	18	16	14	13	11	9	7	6	4	3	1	0			Inner		20
11	17	17	17	17	15	14	13	11	10	8	7	5	4	2	1	0			Outer		0
12	14	15	14	14	13	12	11	10	8	7	6	4	3	2	1	0					
13	12	12	12	12	11	10	9	8	7	6	5	3	2	1	0						
14	10	10	10	10	9	8	8	7	6	5	4	3	1	0							
15	8	8	8	8	7	7	6	5	4	4	3	2	1	0							
16	6	6	6	6	6	5	5	4	3	2	2	1	0								
17	5	5	5	4	4	4	3	3	2	1	1	0									
18	3	3	3	3	3	2	2	1	1	0	0										
19	1	1	1	1	1	1	0	0	0												
20	0	0	0	0	0	0															
21																					
22							5	6	7	8	9	10	11	12	13	14	15				

fig. 12.2 / Sheet2 / Sheet3 / Sheet4 / Sheet5 / Sheet6

FIGURE 12.3:

The finite-difference and the analytic solutions to the concentric cylinders problem

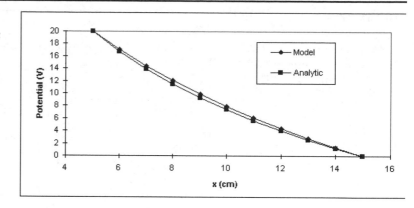

Once this problem is set up, you can quickly modify it for different potentials on the cylinders by simply changing the value in cells T10:T11. You can also add other conductors to the problem. For example, if you want to put a wire charged to 25 volts halfway between the two cylinders, just replace the difference equation in cell L5 with the value 25 and recalculate the worksheet. The result is shown in Figure 12.4 and graphed in Figure 12.5. The graph shows the situation calculated with the wire and the analytic solution without the wire.

FIGURE 12.4:

Potential between two concentric cylinders, with a wire charged to 25 volts inserted halfway between them in cell L5

	A	B	C	D	E	F	G	H	I	J	K	L	M	N	O	P	Q	R	S	T	U
1	Laplace equation between concentric cylinders; Elliptical PDE																				
2																					
3		Analytic ——▶					20	17	14	11	9	7	6	4	3	1	0				
4		B.C. ——▶					20	18	17	17	17	17	13	9	6	3	0				
5		λ ——▶					20	19	10	10	19	25	15	10	6	3	0				
6	B.	y					20	18	17	17	17	17	13	9	6	3	0				
7	C.	↓					20	18	16	15	15	13	11	8	5	2	0				
8	↓					20	18	17	15	14	13	11	9	6	4	2	0				
9					20	18	17	15	14	12	11	9	7	5	3	0			Applied Potentials		
10	20	20	20	20	18	16	15	13	12	11	9	8	6	4	2	0			Inner		20
11	17	17	17	17	15	14	13	12	10	9	8	6	5	3	2	0			Outer		0
12	14	14	14	14	13	12	11	10	9	8	6	5	4	2	1	0					
13	12	12	12	12	11	10	9	8	7	6	5	4	3	1	0						
14	10	10	10	9	9	8	8	7	6	5	4	3	2	0							
15	8	8	8	8	7	7	6	5	5	4	3	2	1	0							
16	6	6	6	6	6	5	5	4	3	2	2	1	0								
17	4	4	4	4	4	3	3	2	1	1	0										
18	3	3	3	3	2	2	2	1	1	0	0										
19	1	1	1	1	1	1	0	0	0												
20	0	0	0	0	0	0															
21																					
22							5	6	7	8	9	10	11	12	13	14	15				

fig. 12.2   **fig. 12.4**   Sheet2   Sheet3   Sheet4   Sheet5

FIGURE 12.5:

Graph of the concentric cylinder problem with a wire charged to 25 volts inserted halfway between the cylinders (the analytic solution is for the case without the conductor)

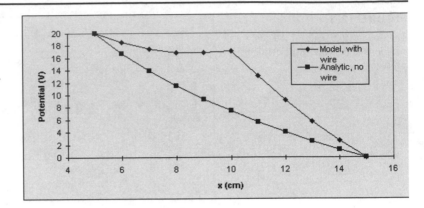

Solving Parabolic Partial Differential Equations

When the relationship between the coefficients, $B^2 - 4AC$, of the general partial differential equation equals zero, the equation is parabolic. Parabolic partial differential equations show up in problems involving diffusion and fluid flow. In general, these problems use the first derivative with respect to time and the second derivative with respect to the position of the concentration of some physical quantity (electron density, temperature, chemical concentration, and so on). The most important of these equations is the continuity equation.

Continuity Equations

A general continuity equation states that the time rate of change in concentration of a physical quantity in some volume is equal to the amount of that quantity flowing into the volume, minus the amount that flows out, plus the amount that is created in the volume, minus the amount that is absorbed in the volume. If the physical quantity moves at some velocity, v, the partial differential equation can be written as

$$\frac{\partial u}{\partial t} = -\nabla \cdot (u\mathbf{v}) + G - A$$

where the divergence term (the first term on the right) calculates the flow out of (or into) some volume, G is the generation term, and A is the absorption term.

The continuity equation is very general and quite common in all branches of science and engineering. Any substance or physical quantity that can flow from one point to another can have that flow described with a continuity equation. It does not matter whether it is heat in a solid or tuna cans moving down a conveyor belt, the basic continuity equation is the same.

Transient Heat Flow in a Copper Bar

Consider the flow of heat Q in a solid. The velocity at which heat flows through a solid is proportional to the negative gradient of the temperature. Substituting the negative gradient of the temperature for the velocity in the continuity equation and using the chain rule on the time derivative results in this equation:

$$\frac{\partial Q}{\partial T}\frac{\partial T}{\partial t} = \nabla \cdot (K\nabla T) + G - A$$

The derivative of the heat with respect to the temperature is just the specific heat, ρC, where ρ is the density and C is the heat capacity. Inserting these, the equation becomes

$$\rho C \frac{\partial T}{\partial t} = \nabla \cdot (K\nabla T) + G - A$$

If you have simple transient heat flow in a metal bar, with no heat generation or absorption mechanisms, the equation above reduces to a one-dimensional, time-dependent partial differential equation:

$$\frac{\partial T}{\partial t} = \frac{K}{\rho C}\frac{\partial^2 T}{\partial x^2}$$

To solve this equation, first rewrite the spatial derivative as a central difference and the time derivative as a forward difference:

$$\frac{T_i^{n+1} - T_i^n}{\Delta t} = \frac{K}{\rho C} \frac{T_{i+1}^n - 2T_i^n + T_{i-1}^n}{\Delta x^2}$$

where Δx and Δt are the spatial and temporal step sizes. The superscript (n, $n+1$) indicates the time step. Solve this equation for the temperature at the future time (T_i^{n+1}):

$$T_i^{n+1} = T_i^n + \frac{K\Delta t}{\rho C \Delta x^2}\left(T_{i+1}^n - 2T_i^n + T_{i-1}^n\right)$$

The coefficient of the temperatures must be less than or equal to 1/2 for the equation to be stable:

$$\frac{K\Delta t}{\rho C \Delta x^2} \leq \frac{1}{2}$$

If you use 1/2, the equation reduces to

$$T_i^{n+1} = \tfrac{1}{2}\left(T_{i+1}^n + T_{i-1}^n\right)$$

For a copper bar:

$$\frac{K}{\rho C} = 1.15 \text{ cm}^2 \text{ / s}$$

This equation fixes the relationship between the time step (Δt) and the spatial grid step (Δx).

$$\Delta x^2 = 2.31\Delta t$$

Origin of the Stability Criteria

The following is a simplified explanation of the stability criteria. See a good numerical methods book for a more rigorous technical explanation. The stability criteria, that the coefficient of the second-order term must be less than 1/2, comes from the following argument.

Using a variation of the heat flow difference formula, with T being the calculated numerical solution, U the exact solution and $e = U - T$ being the error in the solution.

$$T_i^{n+1} = T_i^n + \frac{K\Delta t}{\rho C \Delta x^2}\left(T_{i+1}^n - 2T_i^n + T_{i-1}^n\right)$$

Inserting $T = U - e$ and solving for the error at the future time, gives the following equation:

$$e_i^{n+1} = e_i^n(1-2r) + (e_{i+1}^n + e_{i-1}^n)r$$

where

$$r = \frac{K\Delta t}{\rho C \Delta x^2}$$

For the numerical solution to be stable, the errors must smoothly go to zero as Δx or Δt go to zero (ignoring roundoff errors). To do this, the coefficients of each of the error terms must be positive. If the coefficient of one of the terms is negative then the errors could oscillate and the solution would be unstable. By examination, you see that the coefficients are positive for $0 < r \leq 1/2$.

If the spatial grid step equals 1 cm, the time step must be 0.433 s.

Consider the problem with a 10 cm copper bar, initially at 0°C, with one end held at 0°C and the other at 20°C. Create a worksheet to calculate the change in temperature of this bar over time.

1. Start with a new worksheet, and name it **fig. 12.6**

2. If automatic recalculation is still off from the previous example, turn it back on using the Tools ➤ Options command, Calculation tab.

3. Select columns A through L and change the column widths to 6.

4. In cell A1, enter **Heat flow in a copper bar; Parabolic partial differential equation**

5. In cell C3, enter **Temperature versus position and time**

Enter the time step as multiples of 0.433 second.

6. In cell A5, enter **Time** and center it.

7. In cell A6, enter **(s)** and center it.

8. In cell A7 enter **0**, and in cell A8, enter **0.433**; select cells A7:A8 and drag the fill handle to cell A20.

Enter the spatial grid, with a grid point every centimeter.

9. In cell E5, enter **Position (cm)**

10. In cell B6, enter **0**, and in cell C6 enter **1**; select cells B6:C6, and drag the fill handle to cell L6.

Enter the first boundary condition, a fixed value of 20°C. The formula in cells B8:B20 makes it simple to change the value of that boundary condition.

11. In cell B7, enter **20**

12. In cell B8, enter **=B7** and copy it to cells B9:B20.

Enter the second boundary condition with a fixed value of 0°C.

13. In cell L7, enter **0**

14. In cell L8, enter **=L7** and copy it to cells L9:L20.

Enter the initial condition of 0°C at t = 0.

15. In cell C7, enter **0** and copy it to cells D7:K7.

Enter the difference equation into the first cell of the range, and then copy it to the rest of the range.

16. In cell C8, enter **=0.5*(B7+D7)** and copy it to cells C8:K20.

17. Format cells A7:L20 as Number, with two decimal places.

18. Add borders as shown in Figure 12.6.

The worksheet should now look like Figure 12.6, with the resulting temperatures versus position and time. You can see the flow of heat down the bar by observing the changes in the temperature.

FIGURE 12.6:

Heat flow in a copper bar: solution of a parabolic partial differential equation

	A	B	C	D	E	F	G	H	I	J	K	L
1	Heat flow in a copper bar; Parabolic partial differential equation											
2												
3				Temperature versus position and time								
4												
5	Time				Position (cm)							
6	(s)	0	1	2	3	4	5	6	7	8	9	10
7	0.00	20.00	0.00	0.00	0.00	0.00	0.00	0.00	0.00	0.00	0.00	0.00
8	0.43	20.00	10.00	0.00	0.00	0.00	0.00	0.00	0.00	0.00	0.00	0.00
9	0.87	20.00	10.00	5.00	0.00	0.00	0.00	0.00	0.00	0.00	0.00	0.00
10	1.30	20.00	12.50	5.00	2.50	0.00	0.00	0.00	0.00	0.00	0.00	0.00
11	1.73	20.00	12.50	7.50	2.50	1.25	0.00	0.00	0.00	0.00	0.00	0.00
12	2.17	20.00	13.75	7.50	4.38	1.25	0.63	0.00	0.00	0.00	0.00	0.00
13	2.60	20.00	13.75	9.06	4.38	2.50	0.63	0.31	0.00	0.00	0.00	0.00
14	3.03	20.00	14.53	9.06	5.78	2.50	1.41	0.31	0.16	0.00	0.00	0.00
15	3.46	20.00	14.53	10.16	5.78	3.59	1.41	0.78	0.16	0.08	0.00	0.00
16	3.90	20.00	15.08	10.16	6.88	3.59	2.19	0.78	0.43	0.08	0.04	0.00
17	4.33	20.00	15.08	10.98	6.88	4.53	2.19	1.31	0.43	0.23	0.04	0.00
18	4.76	20.00	15.49	10.90	7.75	4.53	2.92	1.31	0.77	0.23	0.12	0.00
19	5.20	20.00	15.49	11.62	7.75	5.34	2.92	1.85	0.77	0.44	0.12	0.00
20	5.63	20.00	15.81	11.62	8.48	5.34	3.59	1.85	1.15	0.44	0.22	0.00

fig. 12.2 / fig. 12.4 / fig. 12.6 / Sheet3 / Sheet4 / Shee

Using Iterated Time Steps

Another way to calculate a time step is by iterating the worksheet, rather than proceeding down the worksheet as time increases. The solution method uses two rows of cells, creating a circular reference. One row of cells saves the values of the function from the last step, and the other row calculates the value of the function at a new time step.

Now recreate the heat flow problem, this time iterating the time steps.

1. Start with a new worksheet, and name it **fig. 12.7**

2. Choose the Tools ➤ Options command, Calculation tab; change Calculation to Manual, check Iteration, and set Maximum Iterations to 1. Then click OK.

3. Select columns B through L and change the column widths to 6. Change the width of column A to 7.

4. In cell A1, enter **Heat flow in a copper bar; Parabolic partial differential equation**

Enter the initialization flag. Entering a True in cell B4 will cause the problem to be initialized.

5. In cell A4, enter **Init Flag**

6. Enter **True** in cell B4.

7. Name cell B4 as **Init_Flag**

Set up a circular reference to calculate the time of the current iteration. The formula in cell F3 checks for an initialization iteration and then adds the time step to the current time. Cell G3 stores the time for the next step.

8. In cell E3, enter **Time**

9. In cell F3, enter **=IF(Init_Flag,0,G3+0.433)**

10. In cell G3, enter **=F3**

Enter the *x* positions across the top of the table.

11. In cell E5, enter **Position (cm)**

12. In cell B6, enter **0**, and in cell C6, enter **1**; select cells B6:C6, and drag the fill handle to cell L6.

Enter the initial conditions of 0 and the boundary conditions of 20 at $x = 0$ and 0 at $x = 10$.

13. In cell A7, enter **I.C.**

14. In cell C7, enter **0** and copy it to cells D7:K7.

15. In cell B7, enter **20** and copy it to cells B8:B9.

16. In cell L7, enter **0** and copy it to cells L8:L9.

Enter the finite difference equation in row 8. The formula also checks for an initialization iteration. If the initialization flag equals 0, the value of the function is set equal to the initial conditions in row 7.

17. In cell C8, enter **=IF(Init_Flag,C7,0.5*(B9+D9))** and copy it to cells D8:K8.

18. In cell C9, enter **=C8** and copy it to cells D9:K9.

19. Format cells B7:L9, F3, and G3 as Number, with two decimal places.

To use the worksheet, set the initialization flag in cell C4 to **True** and press F9 or Ctrl+= (Cmd+= on the Macintosh). Change the value of the initialization flag to **False** and press F9 again.

The worksheet now shows the results after the first time step. Each time you press F9, the worksheet increments the time step by 0.433 seconds. Press F9 ten more times and the worksheet will look like Figure 12.7, at a problem time of 4.76 seconds. These results are identical to those in row 18 of Figure 12.6.

One of the benefits of iterated time steps is that you can calculate the results for any number of time steps without using a lot of worksheet area. For example, if you wanted to know the results after 1,000 time steps, the noniterated method (Figure 12.6) would use 1,000 rows in the worksheet. The iterated method would use no more than it does now.

FIGURE 12.7:

Heat flow in a bar: iterated time steps

	A	B	C	D	E	F	G	H	I	J	K	L
1	Heat flow in a copper bar; Parabolic partial differential equation											
2												
3					Time	4.76	4.76					
4	Init Flag	FALSE										
5					Position (cm)							
6		0	1	2	3	4	5	6	7	8	9	10
7	I.C.	20.00	0.00	0.00	0.00	0.00	0.00	0.00	0.00	0.00	0.00	0.00
8		20.00	15.49	10.98	7.75	4.53	2.92	1.31	0.77	0.23	0.12	0.00
9		20.00	15.49	10.98	7.75	4.53	2.92	1.31	0.77	0.23	0.12	0.00
10												
11												
12												
13												
14												
15												
16												

fig. 12.2 / fig. 12.4 / fig. 12.6 \ **fig. 12.7** / fig. 12.8 / Sf

NOTE

To do 1,000 iterations without pressing F9 1,000 times, choose the Tools ➤ Options command, Calculation tab and set Maximum Iterations to 1000. Click OK, then press F9, and the worksheet is iterated 1,000 times, or until it reaches a steady-state condition (nothing is changing).

Another benefit of the iteration method is that it lends itself to two-dimensional, time-dependent calculations. Represent the two spatial dimensions in the rows and columns of the worksheet and iterate the time dimension. The set up is similar to the worksheet in Figure 12.7, except that you need three rectangular ranges of cells corresponding to the three rows of cells in the figure. The first range holds the initial conditions, the second contains the two-dimensional, finite-difference equation, and the third holds the values for the next step.

Solving Hyperbolic Partial Differential Equations

In hyperbolic differential equations, the relationship between the coefficients in the general equation ($B^2 - 4AC$) is greater than zero. These equations have second derivatives of both variables. Hyperbolic partial differential equations arise from wave mechanics and vibration, transport (of radiation, for example), diffusion, and gas dynamics problems.

The Wave Equation

Probably the most important hyperbolic partial differential equation to modern physics and engineering is the wave equation. The wave equation is used to model everything from electromagnetic waves in space to the electronic properties of solid semiconductors. It consists of second-order derivatives of space and time, related with speed:

$$\frac{\partial^2 y}{\partial t^2} = c^2 \nabla^2 y$$

where c is the speed of the traveling wave. An electromagnetic wave in space and a wave in a vibrating string are both described with the wave equation.

You solve the wave equation in the same manner as you solved the previous examples. Consider a one-dimensional form of the wave equation:

$$\frac{\partial^2 y}{\partial t^2} = c^2 \frac{\partial^2 y}{\partial x^2}$$

First substitute central differences for the derivatives:

$$\frac{y_i^{n+1} - 2y_i^n + y_i^{n-1}}{\Delta t^2} = c^2 \frac{y_{i+1}^n - 2y_i^n + y_{i-1}^n}{\Delta x^2}$$

Then solve the equation for the value of the function at the future time:

$$y_i^{n+1} = 2y_i^n + y_i^{n-1} + \frac{c^2 \Delta t^2}{\Delta x^2}\left(y_{i+1}^n - 2y_i^n + y_{i-1}^n\right)$$

This equation requires data from two time steps to calculate the value at the future time. This is a problem only during the first time step, where there is no history from which to get the value for y_i^{n-1}. To start the problem, you must somehow estimate the value of this term. If you are given the value of y and its derivative as your initial conditions, use them in a simple extrapolation to get the value of the function at the time $-\Delta t$:

$$y_i^{n-1} = y_i^n - \Delta t \frac{\partial y}{\partial t}$$

If you have other information, use it to get an estimate of the value of the function at $-\Delta t$.

Vibrating String

The oscillations of a vibrating string are described with a one-dimensional form of the wave equation. The boundary conditions are that the ends of the string are held fixed at zero. If the string is plucked, the extent and location that the string was pulled determine the initial conditions. Assume that you have a 70-cm string that is pulled off center by 0.1 cm at a point 20 cm from one end. The initial conditions are then:

$$y = 0.1\frac{x}{20} \qquad\qquad x < 20$$

$$y = 0.1\frac{70 - x}{50} \qquad\qquad x > 20$$

For stability, the coefficient in the finite difference equation needs to be equal to 1:

$$\frac{c^2 \Delta t^2}{\Delta x^2} = 1$$

Setting the coefficient equal to 1 also simplifies the difference equation:

$$y_i^{n+1} = y_{i+1}^n + y_{i-1}^n - y_i^{n-1}$$

Stretching the string sets the wave velocity, which then fixes the relationship between the time step and spatial step. For example, if you stretch the string until the wave velocity is 5×10^4 cm/s, the relationship between the spatial and temporal steps is:

$$\Delta x = 5 \times 10^4 \, \Delta t$$

If Δx is 10 cm, then Δt must be 2×10^{-4} s.

You know from the initial conditions that the string is plucked. Therefore, it is at the maximum extent of an oscillation at the time $t = 0$, which makes the value of the function at the $-\Delta t$ step equal to the value of the function at the first step ($t + \Delta t$):

$$y_i^{n-1} = y_i^{n+1}$$

Enter this value into the difference equation for the first step only:

$$y_i^{n+1} = \left(\tfrac{1}{2}\right)\left(y_{i+1}^n + y_{i-1}^n\right)$$

Create a worksheet to calculate the oscillations of the string described here.

1. Start with a new worksheet, and name it **fig. 12.8**

2. Turn automatic recalculation back on if it is still off from the previous example.

3. Select columns B through M and change the column widths to 6. Change the width of column A to 9.

4. In cell A1, enter **Vibrating String; Hyperbolic equation**

5. In cell C2, enter **Displacement of a Plucked String**

Enter the time values with steps of 2×10^{-4} s, and the spatial values with a step of 10 cm.

6. In cell A3, enter **Time** and center it.

7. In cell A4, enter **(s)** and center it.

8. In cell A5, enter **0**, and in cell A6 enter **0.0002**; select cells A5:A6, and drag the fill handle to cell A35.

9. Format cells A5:A35 as Scientific, with one decimal place.

10. In cell B3, enter **B.C.** and center it.

11. In cell E3, enter **Length (cm)**

12. In cell I3, enter **B.C.** and center it.

13. Enter **0** in cell B4, **10** in cell C4, select cells B4:C4, and drag the fill handle to cell I4.

Enter the initial condition of the string being plucked by 0.1 cm at a point 20 cm from the end. The extension numbers are linear from the point the string is plucked to each end.

14. Make the following entries in cells B5:J5:

     B5: **0**   C5: **0.05**   D5: **0.1**

     E5: **0.08**   F5: **0.06**   G5: **0.04**

     H5: **0.02**   I5: **0**   J5: **I.C.**

Enter the boundary conditions down both sides.

15. In cell B6, enter **=B5** and copy it to cells B7:B35.

16. In cell I6, enter **=I5** and copy it to cells I7:I35.

Put in the special difference equation for the first step with the estimate for the back step contained in it.

17. In cell C6, enter **=0.5 * (B5+D5)** and copy it to cells D6:H6.

Complete the problem with the normal difference equation.

18. In cell C7, enter **=B6+D6–C5** and copy it to cells C8:H35.

19. Format cells B5:H35 as Numeric, with two decimal places.

The worksheet should look like Figure 12.8. If you follow the changes in the position of the string, you will note that it is oscillating with a period of 2.8×10^{-3} s, or

FIGURE 12.8:

A vibrating string: solution of a hyperbolic partial differential equation

	A	B	C	D	E	F	G	H	I	J	K	L
1	Vibrating String:Hyperbolic equation											
2			Displacement of a Plucked String									
3	Time	B.C.			Length (cm)				B.C.			
4	(s)	0	10	20	30	40	50	60	70			
5	0.0E+00	0.00	0.05	0.10	0.08	0.06	0.04	0.02	0	I.C.		
6	2.0E-04	0.00	0.05	0.07	0.08	0.06	0.04	0.02	0			
7	4.0E-04	0.00	0.02	0.03	0.05	0.06	0.04	0.02	0			
8	6.0E-04	0.00	-0.02	-0.01	0.01	0.03	0.04	0.02	0			
9	8.0E-04	0.00	-0.02	-0.04	-0.03	-0.01	0.01	0.02	0			
10	1.0E-03	0.00	-0.02	-0.04	-0.06	-0.05	-0.03	-0.02	0			
11	1.2E-03	0.00	-0.02	-0.04	-0.06	-0.08	-0.07	-0.05	0			
12	1.4E-03	0.00	-0.02	-0.04	-0.06	-0.08	-0.10	-0.05	0			
13	1.6E-03	0.00	-0.02	-0.04	-0.06	-0.08	-0.07	-0.05	0			
14	1.8E-03	0.00	-0.02	-0.04	-0.06	-0.05	-0.03	-0.02	0			
15	2.0E-03	0.00	-0.02	-0.04	-0.03	-0.01	0.01	0.02	0			
16	2.2E-03	0.00	-0.02	0.00	0.01	0.03	0.04	0.02	0			
17	2.4E-03	0.00	0.02	0.03	0.05	0.06	0.04	0.02	0			
18	2.6E-03	0.00	0.05	0.07	0.08	0.06	0.04	0.02	0			
19	2.8E-03	0.00	0.05	0.10	0.08	0.06	0.04	0.02	0			
20	3.0E-03	0.00	0.05	0.07	0.08	0.06	0.04	0.02	0			
21	3.2E-03	0.00	0.02	0.03	0.05	0.06	0.04	0.02	0			
22	3.4E-03	0.00	-0.02	0.00	0.01	0.03	0.04	0.02	0			
23	3.6E-03	0.00	-0.02	-0.04	-0.03	-0.01	0.01	0.02	0			
24	3.8E-03	0.00	-0.02	-0.04	-0.06	-0.05	-0.03	-0.02	0			
25	4.0E-03	0.00	-0.02	-0.04	-0.06	-0.08	-0.07	-0.05	0			

fig. 12.2 / fig. 12.4 / fig. 12.6 / fig. 12.7 \ **fig. 12.8** / S

a frequency of 357 Hz. The analytical equation for the oscillation frequency gives the same result:

$$f = \frac{c}{2l} = \frac{5 \times 10^4 \text{ cm / s}}{2 \cdot 70 \text{ cm}} = 357 \text{ Hz}$$

where f is the frequency and l is the length of the string.

Summary

In this last chapter, you looked at solving multidimensional, time-dependent, partial differential equations with a worksheet. Surprisingly, solving partial differential equations on the spreadsheet is easier than most of the other problems in this book. The methods described here all use explicit finite differences. In explicit finite differences, the value of the function in the future time is explicitly determined by the known values of the function in the past.

The finite-difference equations can also be written as implicit finite differences, where the value of the function at the future time is a function of the value of the function in the past and in the future. The equations thus formed are sets of coupled simultaneous equations that must be solved in a matrix format, a much more complicated calculation than that required by the explicit method.

Now that you have worked through the examples in this book, you should have a good idea of what you can do with Excel, or any worksheet that can be iterated. Now, use the techniques with your own scientific or engineering problems.

For More Information

Numerical Methods for Partial Differential Equations

C. Gerald, *Applied Numerical Analysis*, 2nd. ed. (Reading, Mass.: Addison-Wesley, 1978).

W. H. Press, B. P. Flannery, S. A. Teukolsky, W. T. Vetterling, *Numerical Recipes; The Art of Scientific Computing* (Cambridge, Eng.: Cambridge University Press, 1986).

General Partial Differential Equations

H. F. Weinberger, *A First Course in Partial Differential Equations* (New York: Blaisdell Publishing Co., 1965).

Review Problems

1. Classify the following partial differential equations as elliptic, parabolic, or hyperbolic.

   a. $$\frac{\partial^2 u}{\partial t^2} + 2t \frac{\partial^2 u}{\partial x^2} + x^2 \frac{\partial u}{\partial x} = 0$$

   b. $$\frac{\partial^2 u}{\partial t^2} + \frac{\partial^2 u}{\partial x^2} + xt \frac{\partial u}{\partial x} = 0$$

   c. $$x \frac{\partial^2 u}{\partial t^2} + \frac{\partial^2 u}{\partial x^2} + u = 0$$

   d. $$t \frac{\partial^2 u}{\partial t^2} + 5 \frac{\partial^2 u}{\partial x \partial t} + x^2 \frac{\partial^2 u}{\partial x^2} + \frac{\partial u}{\partial x} = 0$$

   e. $$xt \frac{\partial^2 u}{\partial t^2} + \frac{\partial^2 u}{\partial x \partial t} + u = 0$$

2. Solve the Laplace equation between two infinite parallel plates spaced 10 cm apart. The upper plate at $x = 10$ cm is held at 200 volts, and the lower one at $x = 0$ is set at 0 volts.

3. Complete problem 2, inserting a wire, parallel to the plates, charged to 50 volts at $x = 6$ cm.

4. The Poisson equation is used to calculate the potential in a volume due to applied voltages and charges:

   $$\nabla^2 \varphi = -q \frac{\rho}{\varepsilon}$$

   q is the charge on an electron (1.6×10^{-19} coul), ρ is the charge density, and ε is the permittivity (8.85×10^{-14} F/cm). Solve the Poisson equation φ between two infinite parallel plates spaced 10 cm apart, as in problem 2. Fill the lower half of the volume between the plates with fixed negative charges at a density of $\rho = -10^7$ cm^{-3}. Fill the upper half of the volume with fixed positive charges at a density of $\rho = +10^5$ cm^{-3}.

5. The decay of charge carriers (n) generated in silicon by light is described by the equation

$$\frac{\partial n}{\partial t} = -\frac{(n - n_0)}{\tau_n} + D\frac{\partial^2 n}{\partial x^2}$$

n_0 is the equilibrium carrier density (10^{15} cm^{-3}), τ_n is the lifetime (10^{-6} s), and D is the diffusion coefficient (100 cm^3/s). The initial carrier density in a 10 cm bar of silicon illuminated at one end is

$$n = 10^{17} \text{ cm}^{-3} \qquad 0 < x < 0.03 \text{ cm}$$
$$n = 10^{15} \text{cm}^{-3} \qquad 0.03 \text{ cm} < x < 0.1 \text{ cm}$$

The derivative of the carrier density is 0 at the ends of the bar. Calculate the decay of the pulse of charge carriers for the first 5 microseconds after the light is turned off.

6. The Fick equation describes the thermal diffusion of dopants into silicon.

$$\frac{\partial C}{\partial t} = D\frac{\partial^2 C}{\partial x^2}$$

C is the concentration of the dopant. At a temperature of 1200 K, boron diffuses into silicon at a rate of $D = 8 \times 1 0^{-11}$ cm^2/s. If the surface is held at a concentration of $C_s = 10^{19}$ cm^{-3} for 1 hour, what is the doping density in the first 10 microns of the silicon? Compare the result to the analytic solution. (efrc is the complementary error function.)

$$C(x,t) = C_s erfc\left(\frac{x}{2\sqrt{Dt}}\right)$$

7. Complete the vibrating string example, inserting a pulse at the beginning of the string with the following initial condition:

$$y(x) = 0.5 \quad 0 < x \leq 20 \text{ cm}$$
$$y(x) = 0 \quad\;\; x > 20 \text{ cm}$$

The pulse will move along the string and reflect at the ends.

8. Solve Burger's equation for $T = 5$ and $n = 0.1$ using explicit finite differences. Try solving it again for values of n between 10^{-2} and 10^{-4}. You will need a predictor-corrector (modified Euler) method to achieve stability in this region.

$$\frac{\partial u}{\partial t} + u\frac{\partial u}{\partial x} = v\frac{\partial^2 u}{\partial x^2} \qquad 0 < x < 1 \qquad 0 < t < T$$

$u(0,t) = u(1,t) = 0$

$u(x,0) = \sin(\pi x)$

9. Where γ is the ratio of specific heats ($\frac{7}{5}$ for air), ρ is the density, and u is the velocity. Propagation of a pressure wave in a gas is described by the equation

$$\frac{\partial u}{\partial t} + u\frac{\partial u}{\partial x} + \rho^{\gamma-2}\frac{\partial \rho}{\partial x} = 0$$

$$\frac{\partial \rho}{\partial t} + \rho\frac{\partial u}{\partial x} + u\frac{\partial \rho}{\partial x} = 0$$

A 10-cm tube contains compressed air ($\rho = 0.0012$ gm/cm^3) in the first 2 cm and vacuum ($\rho = 0$) in the rest. At $t = 0$, the valve is suddenly opened and the air is allowed to flow from the pressurized side into the rest of the tube. Calculate the density of the air in the tube as it begins to flow into the rest of the tube. You will need to calculate alternating solutions for both equations at each time step.

10. Calculate the solution of the following equation for $t = 0$ to 2.

$$\frac{\partial^2 u}{\partial t^2} - \frac{\partial^2 u}{\partial x^2} = e^x$$

$u(x,0) = u'(x,0) = u'(0,t) = u'(1,t) = 0$

11. Calculate the solution of the following equation within the square $x = \pm1$, $y = \pm1$. The solution is 0 on the boundary.

$$\frac{\partial^2 u}{\partial x^2} + \frac{\partial^2 u}{\partial y^2} = x^2 + y^2 \quad -1 < x < 1 \qquad -1 < y < 1$$

Exercises

1. Over what ranges of x and y is the following equation elliptic, parabolic and hyperbolic?

$$(2x - y)\frac{\partial^2 u}{\partial x^2} + (x + y)\frac{\partial^2 u}{\partial x \partial y} + (2y - 3x)\frac{\partial^2 u}{\partial y^2} = 0$$

2. Solve the Laplace equation in cylindrical coordinates for the voltage in a 10-cm diameter metal sphere, where a one centimeter diameter sphere at the center is at 25 volts and the surface is at 0 volts. The Laplace equation is cylindrical coordinates is as follows:

$$\nabla^2 \phi = \frac{1}{r^2}\frac{\partial}{\partial r}\left(r^2\frac{\partial \phi}{\partial r}\right) + \frac{1}{r^2 \sin^2(\theta)}\frac{\partial}{\partial \theta}\left(\sin(\theta)\frac{\partial \phi}{\partial \theta}\right) + \frac{1}{r^2 \sin^2(\theta)}\frac{\partial^2 \phi}{\partial \varphi^2} = 0$$

Note that both angular terms are 0 and only the radial term (the first term) is nonzero.

3. Calculate the potential in a semiconductor junction. The junction is modeled with four layers of silicon with different charge densities. The following table lists the thickness and charge densities in each layer.

Layer	Thickness, microns	Charge density, cm^{-3}
1	2	0
2	0.1	-10^{18}
3	1	10^{15}
4	2	0

Exercises

The junction is 5 microns long and has a built-in voltage of 0.85 volts from the outside of slab 1 to the outside of slab 4. Calculate the potential everywhere in the device using the Poisson equation. The dielectric constant for silicon is $\varepsilon = 1.04 \times 10^{-10}$ farad/meter.

4. Calculate the electric field strength and direction in exercise 3. The electric field strength is a vector quantity, that is, it has a magnitude and direction.

$$\mathbf{E} = -\nabla\phi$$

5. Solve the following equation over the range $0 < x \le 1$ and $0 < y \le 1$, with the boundary conditions $z = 0$ at $x = 0$ and $z = 0$ at $y = 0$.

$$2\frac{\partial z}{\partial x} + 3\frac{\partial z}{\partial y} = 1$$

6. A chemical reaction,

$$A + B + D \rightarrow E$$

actually proceeds in two steps:

$$A + B \rightarrow C$$
$$C + D \rightarrow E$$

The reaction rates for each of the reactions are proportional to the concentrations (n_x) of the chemicals, and proceed in both directions.

$$\frac{\partial n_C}{\partial t} = k_{AB}n_A n_B \qquad\qquad A + B \rightarrow C$$

$$\frac{\partial n_A}{\partial t} = \frac{\partial n_B}{\partial t} = k_C n_C \qquad\qquad C \rightarrow A + B$$

$$\frac{\partial n_E}{\partial t} = k_{CD}n_C n_D \qquad\qquad C + D \rightarrow E$$

$$\frac{\partial n_C}{\partial t} = \frac{\partial n_D}{\partial t} = k_E n_E \qquad\qquad E \rightarrow C + D$$

505

Given the following reaction rates and initial concentrations, calculate the concentrations of all the chemicals versus time until the reaction reaches equilibrium.

$$k_{AB} = 4 \qquad n_A = 2$$
$$k_C = 2 \qquad n_B = 1$$
$$k_{CD} = 1 \qquad n_C = 0 \qquad n_D = 1$$
$$k_E = 2 \qquad n_E = 0$$

7. The Telegrapher's equation arises when calculating the transmission of electrical pulses along a wire with distributed resistance, capacitance and inductance.

$$\frac{\partial^2 u}{\partial t^2} + 2a\frac{\partial u}{\partial t} + bu - c^2\frac{\partial^2 u}{\partial x^2} = 0, \qquad 0 \le x \le \pi, \qquad t > 0$$
$$u(0,t) = u(\pi,t) = 0$$
$$u(x,0) = 0$$
$$\frac{\partial u(x,0)}{\partial t} = g(x)$$

If $g(x) = \sin(x)$, $a = 2$, $b = 1$, and $c = 2$, calculate u for $t = 0$ to 4.

8. Solve the equation,

$$\frac{\partial^2 z}{\partial x^2} + 2\frac{\partial^2 z}{\partial x \partial y} - 8\frac{\partial^2 z}{\partial y^2} = \sqrt{2x + 3y}$$

on a 5 by 5 cm rectangular domain, with the boundary conditions as follows.

$$z(0, y) = -\frac{1}{210}(3y)^{5/2}$$

$$z(5, y) = -\frac{1}{210}(10 + 3y)^{5/2}$$

$$z(x, 0) = -\frac{1}{210}(2x)^{5/2}$$

$$z(x, 5) = -\frac{1}{210}(2x + 15)^{5/2}$$

9. The wave equation in two dimensions describes the motion of a vibrating membrane, such as a drum head. The wave equation in two dimensions in cylindrical coordinates is:

$$\frac{\partial^2 u}{\partial t^2} = c^2 \left[\frac{1}{r}\frac{\partial}{\partial r}\left(r\frac{\partial u}{\partial r} \right) + \frac{1}{r^2}\frac{\partial^2 u}{\partial \theta^2} \right]$$

where $u(r,\theta,t)$ is the vertical displacement of the drum head at some time t.

For a circular drum head, the θ term on the right is ignorable for cylindrically symmetric vibrations, which leaves only the radial term.

$$\frac{\partial^2 u}{\partial t^2} = c^2 \left[\frac{1}{r}\frac{\partial}{\partial r}\left(r\frac{\partial u}{\partial r} \right) \right]$$

Solve the wave equation for a 10 cm diameter drum head for the first few oscillations of the drum. Set the wave velocity (c) to 5×10^4 cm/s. The boundary condition is that the position of the drum head is fixed at the edge.

$u(5,t) = 0$

The initial condition is that the center of the drum is raised 3 mm.

$u(0,0) = 0.3$ cm

To get the initial conditions for the rest of the points, set the time derivative equal to 0 in the wave equation and solve the remaining equation using the initial condition and boundary condition as the boundary conditions.

$$\frac{\partial}{\partial r}\left(r\frac{\partial u}{\partial r} \right) = 0$$

Save the result as the initial condition for the solution of the wave equation.

10. When applying the wave equation to the rectangular side of a metal box, a two-dimensional Cartesian solution must be calculated. The two-dimensional wave equation in two-dimensions is

$$\frac{\partial^2 u}{\partial t^2} = c^2\left(\frac{\partial^2 u}{\partial x^2} + \frac{\partial^2 u}{\partial y^2} \right)$$

where $u(x,y,t)$ is the displacement of the side. The boundary conditions are that the edges of the side of the box are fixed.

$0 \le x \le 10$

$0 \le y \le 5$

$u(0,y,0) = u(10,y,0) = u(x,0,0) = u(x,5,0) = 0$

The initial condition is that the point (2.5,2.5) is pressed down 0.1 cm. To calculate the rest of the initial conditions, set the time derivative to zero and solve the remaining equation for the boundary conditions and the one fixed point.

$$\frac{\partial^2 u}{\partial x^2} + \frac{\partial^2 u}{\partial y^2} = 0$$

With this as an initial condition, solve the wave equation. The speed of sound in steel is 5×10^5 cm/s.

APPENDIX

A

Science and Engineering Programs That Complement Excel

There are several excellent programs available for scientists and engineers that complement Excel. Actually, there are many programs that complement Excel, but I have found that the following programs are especially useful in science and engineering situations.

DeltaGraph Pro 3.5

While Excel's graphs are more than sufficient in most research situations, the science and engineering type graphs are not suitable for publications. To remedy this sutuation, use the DeltaGraph Pro program. DeltaGraph Pro is a graphing utility designed to complement an Excel worksheet. For example, Figure A.1 shows Figure 7 from Chapter 3. You could paste this figure in your lab notebook without any problems, but if you planned to submit a paper containing that graph to a journal, you would have to redraw it. You can copy the graph into a drawing program and fix the image there, or you can use a program like DeltaGraph Pro.

FIGURE A.1:

The resistivity of silicon, an Excel graph (fig. 3.7)

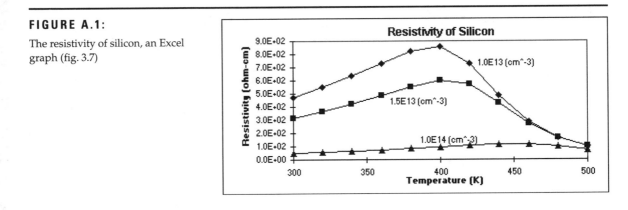

To use DeltaGraph Pro to plot your data, simply copy the data from the Excel worksheet, paste it into a DeltaGraph Pro data sheet, select the appropriate graph type and plot it. After adding some labels and setting the format of the axis labels, you get a graph like Figure A.2.

FIGURE A.2:

The resistivity of silicon in DeltaGraph Pro

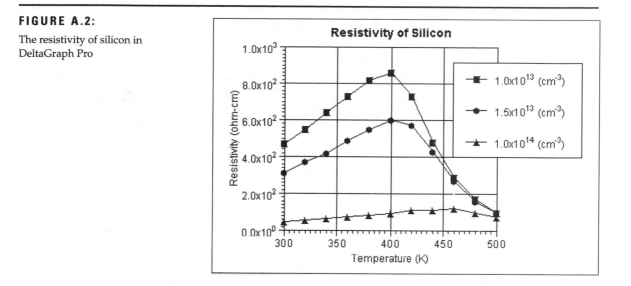

Clearly, the graph in Figure A.2 is much superior to that in Figure A.1, and is acceptable to most journals. Note that the numbers are in scientific notation instead of the computer's E format, the labels contain superscripts, and the whole graph is much cleaner-looking.

DeltaGraph Pro does more than publication-quality graphics. It has about 60 different chart types, and a complete slide show preparation and presentation creation capability. The plot types include polar plots, radar plots, bubble charts, contour plots, colored contour plots, vector plots, 3-D wireframe, surface fill and surface line plots. Some examples are shown in Figure A.3.

DeltaGraph Pro is created by DeltaPoint, Inc, of Monterey, CA, (408) 648-4000. It is available for both Mac and Windows machines for under $150 (I've seen it in special sales for less than $50) from most software retailers.

IMSL Mathematical Routines

Anyone who has programmed scientific and engineering calculations on a mainframe computer is familiar with the IMSL mathematical library. Whenever you need a procedure to calculate the value of a special function, or to perform a

FIGURE A.3:

Examples of
some of the
technical
graphs in
DeltaGraph Pro

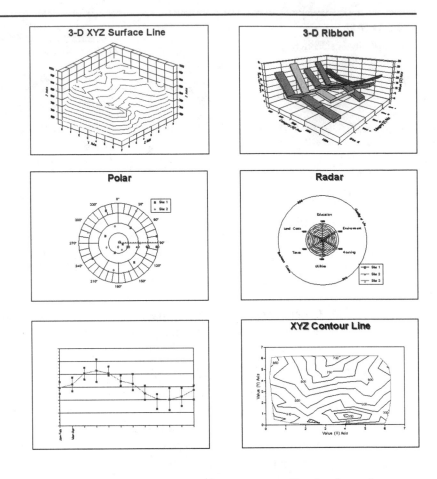

standard mathematical algorithm, the IMSL library is usually the first place you look. IMSL is a large, well-established and tested, commercial computer subroutine library developed by the Visual Numerics company.

The Visual Numerics company has recently adapted the IMSL library functions to run as Excel worksheet functions. Similar to the Analysis Toolpak add-in program, the IMSL functions are attached to Excel. After that, they are accessible with the Function Wizard, like any of the built-in functions. Figure A.4 shows the Visual Basic Object Browser displaying the contents of the IMSL library file. The list of function categories shows the breadth of functions stored in the library.

FIGURE A.4:

Object Browser window showing the categories of functions available in the IMSL library

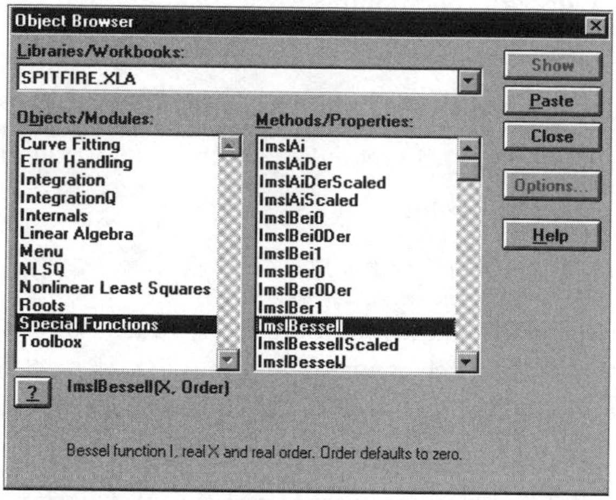

The library contains about one hundred special functions, including:

- Airy functions
- Kelvin functions
- Bessel functions
- beta functions
- Binomial functions
- Carlson functions
- Jacobi functions
- sine and cosine integrals

- hyperbolic function integrals
- Dawson functions
- elliptic and exponential integrals
- error functions
- Fresnel integrals
- Gamma functions
- Mathieu functions
- many more

If you are using special functions in your work, and don't want to code them yourself, this function library has just about everything you would ever need.

In addition to the special functions, the library has a set of add-in numerical analysis functions and programs. These add-in programs calculate several specific numerical analysis algorithms that are useful in science and engineering.

- Linear algebra (matrix solutions)
- Eigensystems
- Fast Fourier transforms

- Roots of polynomials
- Interpolation using cubic splines
- Functional integration in one and two dimensions
- Ordinary differential equation initial-value problems
- Nonlinear least squares
- Nonlinear regression

Many of these add-in programs are called with a special dialog box tool (to simplify data entry) such as that in Figure A.5, which shows the integration dialog box tool. Note that the tool mimics the equation being calculated.

FIGURE A.5:

The integration tool being used to integrate a formula

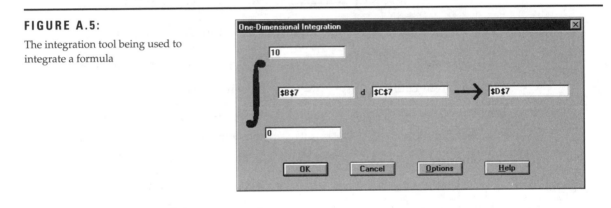

In this figure, cell B7 contains a formula that depends on cell C7. When the integral is complete, the result is placed in cell D7. With a tool like this, it is much easier to insure that you are placing the right value in the right location.

The IMSL library for Excel for Windows is expected to be available in fourth quarter of 1995. A Macintosh version is expected to be available within a year, as are other modules (statistics, graphing, and so forth.) The IMSL library was created by Visual Numerics of Houston, TX, 713-784-3131. It will be available from most computer software dealers for between one and two hundred dollars. There will also be a discounted student edition.

IMSL and Visual Numerics are registered US trademarks of Visual Numerics, Inc.

MathType

The MathType program is not really an attachment for Excel, but is a good way to create drawings of equations. These drawings can then be pasted on a worksheet to illustrate the calculation being performed. Note that all of the equations shown in this book were created with MathType.

Equations are formatted in MathType using a palette of symbols and templates. The templates, for such things as parentheses and fractions, automatically grow to encompass the symbols they contain.

Mathtype was created by Design Science of Long Beach, California, (213) 433-0685. It is available in both Windows and Macintosh versions for about one hundred dollars.

Microsoft Access

While Visual Basic for Applications and the Query utility program can both manipulate a database, a dedicated database program like Access is much easier to use. Using a visual interface, you draw your database structure and queries, instead of having to create them with commands or SQL statements.

Access is created by Microsoft Corporation of Redmond, Washington. If you purchased the Pro version of Microsoft Office, you already have Access. Otherwise, you can get it from the same places you get Excel. Access in not available on the Macintosh.

Visual Basic

Visual Basic, Enterprise Edition is the parent programming language of Visual Basic for Applications. Visual Basic is a complete, separate programming language that can also access the Visual Basic for Applications objects. Visual Basic has a lot more flexibility and capability than Visual Basic for Applications, including a compiler, fully separate windows instead of dialog boxes, and many more buttons and controls.

Visual Basic is created by Microsoft Corporation of Redmond, Washington, and is available from most software vendors. Visual Basic does not run on the Macintosh.

Using the Included Disk

The disk included with this book contains all the examples developed in the text and solutions to all of the review problems at the end of each chapter. The examples and review problem solutions are arranged in workbooks by chapter. The workbook files are compressed into two self-extracting .LZH archives, created with LHA version 2.13 (LHA is ©Haruyasu Yoshizaki, 1988-91). The two archive files are EXAMPLES.EXE and REVPROB.EXE.

EXAMPLES.EXE contains all the examples developed in the chapters, one workbook per chapter, plus any support files needed to work the examples. It also contains the files from Visual C++ needed to work the examples in Appendix D.

The EXAMPLES.EXE archive expands to:

File	Size (Bytes)	File	Size (Bytes)
CH1.XLS	18,432	MYLIB.VCW	90
CH2.XLS	60,416	MYLIB.MAK	1,879
CH3.XLS	349,696	MYLIB.C	234
CH4.XLS	78,336	MYLIB.DEF	220
CH5.XLS	57,344	MYLIB.PDB	64
CH6.XLS	88,064	MYLIB.SBR	0
CH7.XLS	51,712	MYLIB.WSP	468
CH8.XLS	88,064	MYLIB.MAP	17,803
CH9.XLS	51,880	MYLIB.OBJ	420
CH10.XLS	20,480	MYLIB.BSC	433
CH11.XLS	182,272	MYLIB.PCH	45,804
CH12.XLS	74,240	MYLIB.LIB	1,536
COLUMNS.TXT	594	MYLIB.XLS	35,328
TABULAR.TXT	1,246	MYLIB.DLL	10,112
TABDELIM.TXT	486	FIG2-5.XLS	16,384
PROG.FOR	499	CHA.XLS	15,360

32 files   1,276,896 bytes

The archive file REVPROB.EXE contains all the workbooks for the review problems, one workbook per chapter.

The REVPROB.EXE archive expands to:

File	Size (Bytes)	File	Size (Bytes)
CH1PROB.XLS	19,968	CH8PROB.XLS	430,592
CH2PROB.XLS	60,928	CH9PROB.XLS	77,824
CH3PROB.XLS	557,056	CH10PROB.XLS	67,072
CH4PROB.XLS	186,880	CH11PROB.XLS	218,624
CH5PROB.XLS	106,496	CH12PROB.XLS	441,856
CH6PROB.XLS	138,752	FIG5-3.TXT	594
CH7PROB.XLS	396,288	PROB5-2.TXT	127

14 files   2,703,057 bytes

To extract the workbooks from the archive files, create a directory on your hard drive, copy one of the archive files to that directory, and run the file. The archive automatically expands all the files it contains into that directory. The two archives can be expanded into separate directories, or they can be expanded into the same directory.

The examples are readable by Excel versions 5 and later on Windows 3.1, Windows 95, Windows NT, and Macintosh computers. Macintosh users can open this format directly after the workbooks have been expanded from the archives and copied onto a Macintosh disk. Macintosh users with SoftPC or SoftWindows can expand the archive files directly on the Macintosh. Others must first expand the files on a PC and then transfer them to the Macintosh. If you have PC Exchange or DOS Mounter, you can insert and mount PC format disks containing the workbook files directly on the Macintosh desktop. If your Macintosh displays the "This is not a Macintosh disk, Do you want to initialize it?" alert box, eject the disk and use Apple File Exchange (included with the Macintosh operating system) to transfer the files from the DOS format disk onto the Macintosh hard drive.

Users of Excel version 4 can use the files, but they must first be converted to Excel 4 format. To convert the files, open them with Excel version 5 or later, and then save them with the Excel 4 workbook file type (.XLW). Note that saving the workbooks in the earlier file type will cause them to lose all of the Visual Basic for Applications modules.

For some worksheets, the Calculation properties of the application must be changed (depending on which example is being run). The Calculation properties apply to the workbook as a whole and not to the individual worksheets within it. In most cases, the needed changes are switching between Automatic and Manual calculation, turning iteration on or off, and setting the iteration count. All of these properties are changed using the Tools ➤ Options command, Calculation tab.

Science and Engineering
Functions Included in Excel

The Excel package includes many useful science and engineering functions. Some of those functions are built-in and some are included as part of the Analysis Toolpak. Also included in the Analysis Toolpak are Visual Basic versions of the worksheet functions and several special add-in analysis programs. All of the functions and add-in programs included with Excel were listed in Chapter 1. In this appendix is more detail on the functionality and uses of the science and engineering add-ins and functions.

Excel's Analysis Toolpak Add-In Programs

The Analysis Toolpak add-in package contains 19 programs for advanced mathematical analysis. These are all statistical analysis programs.

ANOVA—Analysis of Variance

There are three analysis of variance (ANOVA) programs: single-factor, two-factor, and two-factor with replication. Technically, analysis of variance is a statistical test to determine if two or more data samples have the same mean, and thus are taken from the same population.

> **NOTE** In statistics, the population is all possible values for some process or measurement. Whenever you make measurements of some value or process, you are extracting a sample of the population.

What ANOVA is primarily used for is to test multiple data samples to see if they were taken from the same population, and thus can be considered measurements of the same thing. For example, imagine you have a field contaminated with some chemical, and you want to make sure the contamination level is not changing. Since you can't drag the whole field (the population) into the lab every month to measure the total quantity of contaminant, you take a few samples from random locations around the field, analyze and average them. After a few months, you would like to know if the differences in the average you calculate each month signify a change or are simply caused by the statistical nature of sampling. To answer this question, you perform an ANOVA analysis. If the analysis indicates that the samples come from the same population, the contamination level is not changing. If the analysis shows that they come from different populations, the indication is that the contamination level is changing.

Another use of ANOVA is to see how well an average or curve fit (the first data sample) fits a data set (the second data sample.) If the analysis indicates that the data from the curve fit appears to come from the same population as the data the curve was fit to, you have an indication that you have a good curve fit.

The testing is done by calculating several statistics for the data.

Single-factor ANOVA performs the analysis on multiple columns or rows of data on the worksheet. Two-factor ANOVA performs the analysis on both the columns and the rows. Replication indicates that each sample point was sampled more than one time (that is, you have more than one measurement for each sample point). In terms of the example, use replication if you are taking several samples at each random location each month.

Correlation

Correlation analysis compares two data sets to see if their curves have the same shape. In other words, do their values go up and down at the same time (positive correlation), or does one curve go down whenever the other goes up (negative correlation), or are they uncorrelated. Correlation analysis is used to determine if there is some relationship between two data sets.

Covariance

The covariance is also used to determine if two data sets are related. In fact, the Correlation coefficient is just the covariance divided by the product of the standard deviations for the two data sets.

Descriptive Statistics

The descriptive statistics add-in program calculates several different statistics for the data in a sample. Statistics include the mean, mode, standard deviation, variance, and so forth.

Exponential Smoothing

Exponential smoothing is a curve-fitting technique that fits an exponential curve to a data set and then uses that curve to extrapolate a future value.

Two-Sample F-Test

Like the ANOVA calculation for sample means, an F-test compares the variances for two samples to determine if they come from the same population. Unlike the mean or avarage of a population, the variance is a measure of the spread of data around a mean. F-tests are discussed in Chapter 6.

Fourier Analysis

Fourier analysis is a method of curve fitting, where a data set is fit with the sum of a series of sine and cosine curves. Fourier analysis calculates the coefficients that are multiplied times the sine and cosine curves before they are summed. Thus, the Fourier coefficients are a measure of how much of a particular frequency of oscillation is contained in a data set. Fourier analysis is most useful for examining data that contains periodic changes, to determine what frequencies make up the data. For example, a measure of outside light levels would have large coefficients for sines and cosines with 24-hour and 12-month periods.

Histogram Coefficients

The Histogram tool calculates the data for a histogram chart. A histogram chart displays the number of data values found in different ranges (bins). The histogram tool examines a list of data values and ranges, counts and returns the number of values found in each range. For example, optical spectra is almost always presented as a histogram of number of photons counted per energy bin.

Moving Average

The moving average is a method of smoothing a data set by averaging a small number of adjacent values. Each data point is replaced by the average of an equal number of data points above and below that data point.

Random Number Generator

The random number generator creates sets of random numbers taken from a given distribution. This is different from normal random numbers, that are drawn from a uniform distribution. Random numbers drawn from a distribution are used to model a process that emits values according to the selected distribution. For example, photons emitted from an excited gas have energies that form a normal (Gaussian) distribution about each of the spectral lines in the gas.

Rank and Percentile

The rank and percentile tool calculates the rank and percentile for each value in a data set. The ranking shows the relative standing of a particular data item with respect to all the other data items in a set.

Regression

The regression tool calculates a multiple linear-regression curve fit to a data set. Regression methods are described in Chapter 6.

Sampling

The sampling tool extracts random samples from a data set.

T-Test

There are three t-tests included in the Analysis Toolpak. T-tests are statistical methods for determining if two values are statistically equal. When comparing statistical data, two numbers that are not identically the same may be statistically the same. For example, if you calculate the means for two samples, they are unlikely to be identical, even if the samples are chosen from the same population. The difference is caused by the variations of the data about the means. If the difference in the means can be completely accounted for by the random variance of the data, you can say that, with some level of confidence, the means are the same. For the t-test, a student's t value is calculated and compared to a table of student's t values. A table of student's t values can be calculated using the TINV() function. Student's t-tests are discussed in Chapter 6.

Paired Two-Sample for Means

A two-sample test, where each item in one sample is paired with an item in the second sample. The test determines if the means are different.

Two-Sample with Equal Variances

A two-sample test, where the variances of the two samples are assumed to be equal. The test determines if the means are the same.

Two-Sample with Unequal Variances

A two-sample test, where the variances of the two samples are assumed to be unequal. The test determines if the means are the same.

Z-Test, Two-Sample for Means

A Z-test is used to test differences between the means of two populations. While the t-tests are primarily used to see if two means are the same, the Z-test is used when you expect that they are different and want to test that difference.

Special Functions

Special functions are solutions to differential and integral equations that have a special significance in science and engineering; that is, they show up a lot in the solutions to science and engineering problems.

Bessel Functions

There are four variations of Bessel functions available. Bessel functions are solutions of Bessel's equation, which is often found in problems involving the wave equation. The four solutions calculated by these functions are for four variations of Bessel's equation.

BESSELJ()

Calculates $J_n(x)$, the solution to Bessel's equation.

$$x^2 \frac{d^2 y}{dx^2} + x \frac{dy}{dx} + \left(x^2 - n^2\right)y = 0$$

BESSELI()

Calculates $I_n(x)$, the solution to the Bessel equation for imaginary arguments.

$$I_n(x) = (i)^{-n} J_n(ix)$$

BESSELK()

Calculates $K_n(x)$, a solution of the modified Bessel equation for imaginary arguments.

$$K_n(x) = \frac{\pi}{2} i^{n+1} \left(J_n(x) + i Y_n(ix) \right)$$

BESSELY()

Calculates $Y_n(x)$, the solution to Weber's Bessel equation, also called a Neumann function $(N_n(x))$.

$$Y_n(x) = \lim_{v \to n} \left[\frac{J_v(x)\cos(v\pi) - J_{-v}(x)}{\sin(v\pi)} \right]$$

ERF()

Returns the value of the error function integral. Error functions often occur in the solution of diffusion problems.

$$\mathrm{ERF}(z) = \frac{2}{\sqrt{\pi}} \int_0^z e^{-t^2} \, dt$$

ERFC()

Returns the value of the complementary error function. Like the error function, the complementary error function often shows up in diffusion problems.

$$\text{ERFC}(z) = 1 - \text{ERF}(z)$$

Distribution Functions

Distribution functions are used to model the spread or occurrence of measured data. For example, random data forms a normal distribution about the mean of that data, and the failure rate over time of newly manufactured items generally follows a Weibull distribution. Distribution functions are in Excel's Statistical Functions category.

BETADIST( )	Cumulative beta probability density function
BETAINV( )	Inverse of the cumulative beta probability density function
BINOMDIST( )	Binomial distribution probability
CHIDIST( )	Chi-squared distribution
CHIINV( )	Inverse of the chi-squared distribution
EXPONDIST( )	Exponential distribution
FDIST( )	F probability distribution
FINV( )	F distribution (used to calculate a table of F values)
GAMMADIST( )	Gamma distribution
GAMMAINV( )	Inverse of the gamma distribution
HYPGEOMDIST( )	Hypergeometric distribution
LOGNORMDIST( )	Cumulative lognormal distribution
NEGBINOMDIST( )	Negative binomial distribution
NORMDIST( )	Normal cumulative distribution
NORMINV( )	Inverse of the normal cumulative distribution

NORMSDIST( )	Standard normal cumulative distribution
NORMSINV( )	Inverse of the standard normal cumulative distribution
POISSON( )	Poisson distribution
TDIST( )	Student's t probability distribution
TINV( )	Student's t distribution (creates a table of t values)
WEIBULL( )	Weibull distribution

APPENDIX
D

Using External Libraries with Excel

D

In addition to all the built-in functions and functions created with Visual Basic for Applications, you can create functions using a compiled language and use them in an Excel worksheet. To do this, you need a compiler for your language that creates dynamic link libraries (.DLL) for the Windows version of Excel, or numbered CODE resources for the Macintosh version of Excel. Most modern compilers that produce fully executable programs can create DLL or CODE library files.

> **WARNING** Not all compilers can produce a .DLL file, so be sure to check the compiler documents to be sure it has the capability. The Visual Basic compiler cannot produce .DLL files, while Microsoft C and C++ can.

To create Excel add-in functions in Windows, create a normal function using the language of your compiler. This function should have the same structure as a normal function in your chosen language, with the exception that it must not depend on global variables or common blocks of data. All data passed to the function must be through the function's interface. Next, compile the function into a .DLL file. In most cases, your compiler will have a switch for selecting a type .DLL output file. In addition, create a declaration that describes the interface to the function for Excel. The declaration contains the name of the function, and the number and type of arguments it needs.

> **WARNING** Be sure to create a version of your DLL that matches the version of Excel that you are going to use it with. If you are using Excel version 5, you need a 16-bit DLL, while if you are using Excel version 7 (there is no version 6) you will need a 32-bit version of your DLL.

For example, the following C program in the file MYLIB.C was created and compiled into the library file MYLIB.DLL. The program itself simply takes two arguments, calculates and returns the sum. The __export flag in the function declaration causes this function to be made available to procedures outside the .DLL file. Without it, the function would only be available to procedures within the library. The __pascal flag forces the arguments to be passed using the Pascal conventions and the __far flag tells the compiler that the calling program will be in a different segment of memory.

```
double __export __pascal __far addem(double, double);

double __export __pascal __far addem(double one, double two)
{
double aValue;
aValue = one + two;
return(aValue);
}
```

In addition to the program, you need a declaration file, MYLIB.DEF, to declare the functions as external. The declarations also includes WEP, which is the windows exit procedure. An exit procedure is needed to remove the library from memory when you are done with it. You must either write your own exit procedure, or use the default procedure.

```
LIBRARY        MYLIB
DESCRIPTION    "MyLib example .DLL"
EXETYPE        WINDOWS
CODE           PRELOAD MOVEABLE DISCARDABLE
DATA           PRELOAD MOVEABLE SINGLE
HEAPSIZE       1024
EXPORTS
  WEP          @1          RESIDENTNAME
  addem        @2
```

NOTE Not all compilers have a default exit procedure you can reference. If they don't have one, you must include it in your code, even if it does not have to do anything.

On the Macintosh, you do substantially the same thing, but you must compile the function into a separate CODE resource by setting compiler directives. You can have only one external function per CODE resource, and it must be the first function in that code resource.

In Excel, declare the new function using an Excel Declare statement. The Declare statement is placed in a Visual Basic for Applications module sheet. The Declare statement tells Excel how many and what kind of arguments the procedure needs. The Declare statement has one of the following syntaxes depending on if it is a subroutine or a function. Subroutines do not return a value, while functions do. Note that not all the options are listed in the following syntax statements. See the online manual for the complete syntax of the Declare statement.

Subroutine Declaration

```
Declare Sub name [CDecl] Lib "libname" [Alias "aliasname"]
        [([arglist])]
```

Function Declaration

```
Declare Function name [CDecl] Lib "libname" [Alias "aliasname"]
        [([arglist])][As type]
```

name	A procedure name to use in the worksheet
CDecl	A keyword for the Macintosh platform that indicates that the procedure uses C language calling conventions.
libname	The name of the library file that contains the procedure being declared.
aliasname	The name of the procedure stored in the DLL if it is different from the name already declared. Use this to rename a function if it conflicts with an existing function.
arglist	The list of arguments and their types that are to be passed to the procedure. The structure is the same as a Visual Basic for Applications argument list.
type	The type of value returned by a function.

Once declared in a Visual Basic for Applications module, the function can be used in a worksheet like any other function.

For example, to declare the addem function in MYLIB.DLL, created above, use the following declaration, in a Visual Basic for Applications module sheet.

```
Declare Function addem Lib "MYLIB.DLL" (ByVal aVal As Double,
   ➥ ByVal anotherVal As Double) As Double
```

The ByVal identifiers are needed in the argument declaration, because you are passing values to the function and not the addresses of the locations where the values are stored. This is usually a good idea, as it does not give the function an address in the middle of Excel to play with. Otherwise, an error in the declaration of the size of the arguments would let the function overwrite some memory locations within Excel. On the other hand, if you are passing a large amount of

FIGURE D.1:

Using an attached function in a worksheet. The text in column D shows the contents of the cells in column C

	A	B	C	D
1	Arg 1	Arg 2	addem	
2	18	34	52	=addem(A2,B2)
3				
4			52	=CALL("d:\xlsebook\examples\mylib.dll", "addem", "BBBI", A2,B2)
5				
6				
7			2E+09	=REGISTER.ID("mylib.dll","addem","BBB")
8			52	=CALL(C7,A2,B2)
9				
10				
11				
12				
13				
14				
15				
16				
17				

data, such as an array, to a function you generally must pass it by address to save memory.

Once declared, you can use the function in the worksheet or in a Visual Basic for Applications program. For example, if you type **18** in A2, **34** in B2 and **=addem(A2,B2)** in C2, the result is shown in Figure D.1.

Another way to access a function in a .DLL file is to use the Call and Register statements. For example, if you enter **=CALL("mylib.dll", "addem", "BBB", A2,B2)** in cell C4, you get the same result as cell C2. The Call function both registers or declares the function and executes it. The third argument tells Excel what type of variables the function uses and what type it returns.

The Register.ID function is also used to declare and load an external function, but does not execute it. The Register.ID function returns the registration number for the external function. The registered function can then be executed with the Call function by referring to its registration number. For example, enter **=REGISTER.ID("mylib.dll","addem","BBB")** in cell C7, and it returns the registration ID number. In cell C8, enter **=CALL(C7,A2,B2)**, which refers to the registration number with the first argument and the arguments of the function with the others, and it again returns the sum of the contents of cells A2 and B2.

INDEX

Note to the Reader: Throughout this index **boldface** page numbers indicate major discussions of a topic. *Italic* page numbers indicate illustrations.

SQL statement, viewing, 262
SQRT() function, 20, 23, 310
SQRTP() function, 20, 23
square of VDT operator, 479
stability criteria, **489**
standard deviation, 38–39
standard error of y estimate, **287–288**
  function for, 309
standard errors of coefficients, **289–290**
Standard toolbar, 56, *57, 58, 59*
  Function Wizard button, 18, *58*
STANDARDIZE() function, 37
star, absolute magnitude of, **88–91**
Static statement, 205
statistical functions, **35–41**
  for database, 267
Status bar, 57
STDEV() function, 36, 38
STDEVP() function, 36, 39
steady-state electrostatic potential, 478
steam tables, *319–324, 320*
Step Into tool (Visual Basic toolbar), 191
Step Macro tool (Visual Basic toolbar), 191
Step mode, for debugging, 238
Step Over tool (Visual Basic toolbar), 191
STEYX() function, 37
Stop Macro tool (Visual Basic toolbar), 191, 196
Stop Recording toolbar, *59*
stopping criteria, for iteration, 391–392
stress and deflection in cantilever beam, **98–102**
string creation functions, 32
String data type, in Visual Basic, 204
Structured Query Language (SQL), 259
Student's t test, 287, 290
Sub procedures, 212
  vs. Function procedures, 216
subroutines
  declaration, 534
  storage in Dynamic Link Libraries, 48
SUBSTITUTE() function, 32
SUBTOTAL() function, 20
subtraction operator, 16
successive approximations method, **386–393,** *392*
  convergence in, **388**
  iterative method as, 456
sum of squares of regression and residuals, **291–292**
SUM() function, 20, 23, 313
  for integration formulas in Visual Basic, 374
SUMIF() function, 20
summing series, **334–347**
  iterating series in worksheet, **339–341**
  using Visual Basic function, **342–346,** *346*
  in worksheets, **334–338**
SUMPRODUCT() function, 20, 23
SUMSQ() function, 20, 23
SUMX2MY2() function, 20, 23

SUMX2PY2() function, 20, 23
superheated steam data points, 319
superscripts, 81
Sybase, 259
SYD() function, 43

T

T() function, 31
Tab Order dialog box, *221,* 221
tab-delimited files, 247
  importing, 250–251, *251*
Table dialog box, *105,* 105
table lookup functions, **44–47,** 318
tables. *See also* engineering tables
  creating with copied formulas, **70–96**
  creating with Data ➤ Table command, **96–106**
  creating for silicon resistivity calculation, **140–142,** *142*
  manually recalculating, 106
  multiple-input, multiple-column, **91–96**
  for 3D chart, 163–164, *164*
  two-input, **85–91**
tabular data, importing, **251–253**
TAN() function, 21, 24
TANH() function, 21, 25
Taskbar (Windows 95), *57*
Taylor series method, for initial-value problems, **438–442,** *442*
TBILLEQ() function, 43
TBILLPRICE() function, 43
TBILLYIELD() function, 43
TDIST() function, 38, 40, 529
Teach Text (Macintosh), 247
temperature dependence of intrinsic carrier density, **79–82**
temperature profile in overstressed silicon diode, **160–162**
terminal-emulation program, text file from, 246
Text Box button (Standard toolbar), 56, *58*
Text Box tool (Drawing toolbar), *172,* 177
text in cells, 5
Text Import Wizard, 248–250, 254–255
  dialog box, 246
  Fixed Width option, 253
text operator, 16
text strings
  comparing, 15, 32
  joining, 14
TEXT() function, 31
thermal conductivity, 112
  of gallium arsenide, **293–300,** *296, 300*
  of silicon, analytical equation for, **60–69**
thermal-runaway state, 139
thermoelectric cooler, **111–120,** *120*
time functions, 34, **35**
TIME() function, 34, 35
TIMEVALUE() function, 34, 35, 109
TINV() function, 38, 290, 529

TipWizard button (Standard toolbar), *58*
TipWizard toolbar, *59*
titles, 65–67
  adding to charts, **135,** *135*
  freezing, 96
TODAY() function, 33, 34
Toggle Breakpoint tool (Visual Basic toolbar), 191, 238
Toggle Grid tool (Visual Basic Forms toolbar), *192,* 214
toolbars
  built-in, *59*
  buttons, xxvi
  displaying, 58
Tools menu
  ➤ Add-Ins, 48
  Query, 259
  ➤ Assign Macro, 191, 197, 215, 233
  assigning procedure to, 195
  ➤ Data Analysis, ➤ Regression tool, 296–298
  ➤ Macro, 198
  ➤ MS Query, 260
  ➤ Options,
    Calculation tab, 389, *390, 418*
    Calculation tab, 1904 checkbox, 5
    Calculation tab, Automatic Except Tables button, 96–97
    Calculation tab, Iteration, 396
    Calculation tab, Maximum Iterations, 392, 396
    Calculation tab, Precision As Displayed, 3
    Chart tab, 146
    Edit tab, Enable AutoComplete For Cell Values check box, 66
    General tab, Reference Style, 7
    View tab, Formulas checkbox, 69
    View tab, Gridlines, 68, 76
  ➤ Protect Document, 100
  ➤ Protection, ➤ Protect Sheet, 109
  ➤ Record Macro,
    ➤ Mark Position for Recording, 196
    ➤ Record at Mark, 196
    ➤ Record New Macro, 195, 198
    ➤ Stop Recording, 196
    ➤ Use Relative References, 197, 199
  ➤ Solver, 313, 403
  ➤ Tab Order, 221
transient heat flow in copper bar, continuity equation for, **487–491,** *491*
transport, hyperbolic partial differential equations for, 494
TRANSPOSE() function, 26, 27, 46
trapezoid rule
  to calculate gamma function, **374–376,** *376*
  for integration formula, **364,** 373
TREND() function, 37, 39, 292, 293
Trendline dialog box, *305*
trendlines, **304–306**
  regression formula using, *306*

What's on the Disk?

The disk included with this book contains over 150 worked examples of science and engineering calculations performed on an Excel spreadsheet. The disk contains all the examples developed in each chapter of this book, as well as solutions to all of the review problems found at the end of each chapter. All of the topics listed inside the front cover of this book are included in these examples.

The disk contains three files: README.TXT, EXAMPLES.EXE and REVPROB.EXE. README.TXT contains instructions for using the disk. The two .EXE files are self-extracting LZH archives, created with LHA version 2.13 (©Haruyasu Yoshizaki, 1988-91). EXAMPLES.EXE expands into a series of workbooks that contain all of the examples developed in the chapters. REVPROB.EXE expands into the solutions to all of the review problems. The files in EXAMPLES.EXE require about 1.2 MB of disk space in their expanded form and the files in REVPROB.EXE require 2.8 MB.

To expand the files, create a new directory on your hard drive, copy one of the archive files to that directory, and double-click the file to execute it. The archive automatically expands all of the files it contains. The two archives can be expanded into separate directories, or they can be expanded into a single directory.

The extracted workbook files are readable by Excel (versions 5 and later, on a Windows, Windows 95, Windows NT, or Macintosh-based computer). Note to Excel 4 users: to read these worksheets, you must open them in Excel version 5 or later, and then save them in Excel 4 file format. You will lose all the Visual Basic modules during that conversion.

Macintosh users have three options: expand the archives on an MS-DOS or Windows computer and transfer them to the Macintosh, use SoftPC or SortWindows to expand the files directly on your Macintosh, or download them from the Sybex Forum on CompuServe (within CompuServe type GO SYBEX). To transfer the workbooks to a Macintosh, put them on a floppy disk and insert the disk into your Macintosh. If you have PC Exchange, DOS Mounter or similar software installed on your Macintosh, the disk will mount and you can copy the files to your hard drive. If your Macintosh displays the "This is not a Macintosh disk, Do you want to initialize it?" alert box, eject the disk and use Apple File Exchange to transfer the files from the DOS-format disk onto the Macintosh hard drive.